BARRIE:
THE STORY OF A GENIUS

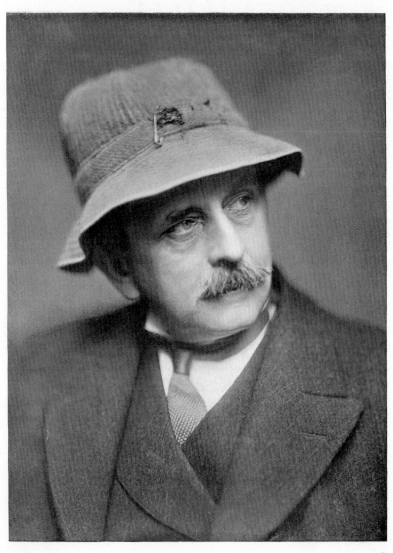

SIR JAMES BARRIE IN 1921
From a photograph by Lizzie Caswall Smith.

BARRIE

THE STORY OF A GENIUS

BY

J. A. HAMMERTON

LONDON
SAMPSON LOW, MARSTON & CO., LTD.

FIRST
Edition
September
1 9 2 9

MADE AND PRINTED IN GREAT BRITAIN BY PURNELL AND SONS
PAULTON (SOMERSET) AND LONDON

CONTENTS

v

ACKNOWLEDGEMENT

A STONE'S throw away lives the celebrated novelist and dramatist whose life and work form the subject of my book: I can see his windows from here. For reasons which I offer in my first chapter I have carried through a task of some difficulty without seeking the approval or the assistance of him whose romantic career and genius it is my aim faithfully to chronicle and appreciate. But, where so much original research and verification of detail are involved, I have been glad to avail myself of the good offices of those in a position and of a mind to assist, and to the many who have in one way or another given me their help I return grateful thanks. Especially am I indebted to Mr. Joseph Alexander, of Burnbank, Kirriemuir, to whose enthusiasm and energetic inquiries I owe a great deal. To Mr. David Elder Anderson, of Sandbach, Cheshire, I am also indebted for valuable assistance, while to Mr. John F. Mills, editor and proprietor of The Kirriemuir Observer, my obligations are many. Throughout the text of the book other acknowledgments are made that need not be repeated here; but I must add the names of my friends Mr. Francis Aitken and Mr. Cranstoun Metcalfe who have given me valued assistance, especially with the proofs of both the American and the English editions.

The Savage Club,
Adelphi Terrace,
London.

ILLUSTRATIONS

vii

ILLUSTRATIONS

CHAPTER I

THIRTY YEARS AFTER: CERTAIN PERSONAL MATTERS

Why do we have to wait until after the funeral service for reliable summaries of knowledge about our leading men? Impartial biographies of the living would do genuine service to the public. Some are published, but too few. The trouble is that biographies of the living are generally conceived in a sentimental and highly misleading spirit of adulation. They need not be. Honesty, while difficult, is by no means impossible.—ARNOLD BENNETT in The Evening Standard, December 22nd, 1927.

JUST on thirty years ago I wrote some magazine articles on the books and personality of J. M. Barrie. Three pleas might be offered in extenuation: (1) a heady enthusiasm that could be described only as Barriolatry, (2) something over two years spent at Nottingham in (as it pleased the vanity of a young editor to fancy) the journalistic succession of the Wizard of Thrums, and (3) a ready market for these particular writings.

Thus bad begins, but there is worse to follow. For I gathered those articles together, and with sundry additions and emendations, lo, a volume entitled J. M. Barrie and His Books: Biographical and Critical Studies. This early book of mine was so kindly received by the critics of 1900, as I have been surprised to find on a recent perusal of the many and lengthy reviews; it was so generally praised that to-day I am not ungrateful to two unpleasant persons who each gave me a 'slating.' For the book had many crudities that now reveal themselves to an eye grown keener in criticism after a generation of experience.

The comment of The Literary World, a popular weekly review of those days, puzzled me at the time. Its critic wrote:

Twenty or thirty years hence Mr. Hammerton may have to re-write his biographical and critical studies of Mr. Barrie, and then, perhaps, he will—without having to feel ashamed of his earlier work—repent having published this volume.

1

BARRIE: THE STORY OF A GENIUS

That seemed to me at the time an odd thing to say about a book which the gentle critic—a kindly soul, who, happily, still flourishes —had already described in terms of praise that I should now blush to reprint. Yet, here I am, just on thirty years after, essaying the task which he, with a foresight rare in criticism, had appointed for me; but still unrepentant. Why should we repent our early ineptitudes? To recognise them is a sign of growth. It is given only to genius to produce finished work without trial and failure.

In my young enthusiasm for the work of J. M. Barrie I was indifferent to the fact that he himself was only *nel mezzo del cammin;* what he was going to do interested me far less than what he had done: that seemed sufficient. The critic of The Literary World felt that Barrie (thirty years ago) had merely 'conducted a series of brilliant experiments,' that A Window in Thrums might be no more than 'the promise of something vastly superior.' If that was why he thought I should repent of my premature appreciation and re-write it when three decades had gone, I do not agree with him even now. For Barrie the novelist stands no higher to-day than he did in 1900, and I was then concerned only with the story-writer: it is Barrie the dramatist who has added immense and rich territories to the empire of his fame. An apposite question for the literary critic would be whether or not Barrie's books, with all their charm, were merely experiments preliminary to his plays, which fulfil 'the promise of something vastly superior.' Some suggestions for an answer may be found in the following pages, though my present intention is more biographical than critical. Meanwhile I must offer my reasons for helping a critic to appear a prophet, while rejecting the grounds of his prophecy.

Nothing could better illustrate the change that has come over public taste since the end of last century than the fact that I was then strongly urged by my publishers not to deal with any of Barrie's adventures in the theatre, as the great Nonconformist reading public that loved him as a story-writer had grave misgivings about him as a dramatist—and it was that audience to whom my publishers looked for the sale of the book. To-day all his plays are issued in book form by the erstwhile 'religious' house that so wisely published his Auld Licht Idylls when others had spurned it, and it is Barrie's work for the theatre, rather than his books, that has made the age to come his own—a judgement that differs from the opinion I gave, perhaps somewhat hastily, in 1900. But I erred in good company, for the critic of The Times delivered himself thus about Barrie's efforts on the stage in September, 1900: 'The more we see of Mr. Barrie's talent on the stage, the more we sigh for his talent in the novel. There he can give us touches of genius—but only there. Mr. Barrie has no genuine dramatic faculty.'

Matthew Arnold was right: 'the theatre is irresistible,' and for all these thirty years it has not only taken the best of Barrie's art, but—thanks to him more than to any one dramatist—it has so overcome the ancient prejudice of the 'unco guid' that an Auld Licht or, indeed, any sort of Presbyterian, can now go as openly to the theatre or music-hall as he used to go to prayer meeting.

The Barrie that confronts the critic of to-day is a Barrie that differs from him of 1900, not only in the degree of his fame, but in the kind of his achievement, and his ambient is that of a world set free as against that of a world chafing in its bondage to outworn ideals of faith and conduct. No writer of genius could be less didactic than the author of Peter Pan—and I am not unmindful of The Admirable Crichton, Dear Brutus, and other plays of his that have a moral to enforce—yet, more than most of his contemporaries, has he helped his generation to move into the spiritual freedom of to-day without loss of regard for the sterling qualities of the generation that so recently went down to its grave. This we owe to his unfailing humanism—using the word in its larger and not the strictly classical sense—which enables him to look at all mankind with the amused and pitying eye of humour.

For the moment I need not elaborate the proposition implicit in that last sentence; but I must make the observation that this unfailing humanism is not a quality that has given distinction to his plays alone; it inheres in all his other writings early and mature. Indeed his best qualities of art and emotion are common to both his books and his plays.

What are the books he has written since 1900? Two only: The Little White Bird in 1902; Peter and Wendy in 1911. The first named, wherein the immortal Peter makes his earliest appearance, ranks among the author's finest adventures in that realm of fantasy and faëry which he was soon to enter as conqueror by way of the stage. But it did not appreciably advance his standing in the world of letters. Peter and Wendy, with all its moonbeam beauty, is still a 'book of the play,' a restatement in story form of a thing that had already come to wondrous life upon the stage: a thing upon which, in the long run, its author's reputation may chiefly rest: his surest grip on fame.

Thus it is not very wide of the mark to say that Barrie had laid aside the pen of the novelist with the passing of the romantic 'nineties, in which his literary star had risen; that he was ranging far from Thrums for inspiration, and finding his true *métier* in writing for the stage. Certainly he had done with Thrums and the Kailyard by 1900, and yet even my friendliest reviewers in 1900 assured me that many a literary work of genius was still to come from the Wizard of Thrums, and so speedily put my little book out of date. 'The time,' wrote Robertson Nicoll in his too lenient review, 'has not come for a complete estimate of Mr. Barrie, who is emphatically one of those writers from whom surprises may be looked for.' Well, we have had them; but not even that gifted critic could then have guessed what they were to be.

These surprises are my reasons for seeking to discover in myself if the ashes of an early enthusiasm, which had once blazed up and then slowly sunk to smouldering state through long years of widely divergent interests, could be fanned into flame again. I have been attracted by the experiment, and am not without hope that many readers of this later day may share my curiosity.

But this is to be no case of 'cauld kail het again,' no touching up of old stuff for a new market. In writing this entirely new review of the life and work of James Matthew Barrie my hope has been to achieve something less unworthy of its subject than I have long considered my earlier effort to have been. Several invitations to reprint that forgotten book with some added matter that would bring it 'up-to-date' have been resisted, and nothing of it will find its way into the pages of the present volume.

The time has long since passed when it was necessary to apologise for writing a book about a living person. In this connexion I feel that I was something of a pioneer, as you could have numbered on your fingers all such books existing in the late 'nineties, and the reviewers were inclined to accept them with a grudging spirit, as if compounding a felony, so long had it been supposed that you must not write a book about a man who had not attained the hallowed distinction of the tomb, though you might write columns of journalistic praise or abuse of him. Nowadays critics even write books about other critics, and every living author of creative genius has had one or several books written about his work and personality. On that score, therefore, and perhaps, alas, because there cannot be another three decades of Barrie 'surprises,' the critics are less likely to look askance at this new book of mine.

A Glasgow critic of my earlier effort, while acknowledging the interest and value of the biographical matter I had then brought together—matter, by the way, available to anyone who knew where to look for it—said that when I came to speak of Barrie's

4

literary achievement I indulged in mere eulogy. A most reasonable charge, as I now perceive, but one that will not be laid against me on the present occasion. For although I have recaptured an old enthusiasm—a delightful experience let me tell you— I am persuaded that it is not the less worth having even if maturer judgement discloses in its object certain flaws that once passed undetected. Thus, some warts may show in the portrait of a genius that disengages itself from these pages.

For I am so cordially in agreement with Arnold Bennett's dictum on biographies of the living, which I have set at the head of this chapter, that I deliberately offer this new work of mine as an unauthorised biography, to indicate that in the long and arduous task of its documentation and writing I have in no least detail applied to its living hero for information, nor in any way sought his approval of my labours. It is published without his knowledge or consent.

When a biographer places himself in the hands of a living person about whom he proposes to write, that moment he raises the chief barrier to the honesty which Arnold Bennett rightly demands of anyone essaying such a task as I have here set myself. I well remember a critical biography of an eminent man of letters, now dead, being written in his lifetime by a distinguished journalist who still survives, and the eminent one was so greedily interested in the chapters as they were submitted for his approval that he himself extended them immensely beyond the dimensions which the biographer had thought proper. When the ponderous work appeared it contained, to its writer's helpless displeasure, about as much matter in the interpolations as the total of his own writing! That would have been the last thing that could have happened with the present work if the co-operation of the celebrated man whose life it records had been asked and given; but one need not stress the point that to expect impartiality in a biography which has been compiled under the approving eye of its subject is to expect too much.

I have endeavoured throughout this book to look upon the subject of it less as a living celebrity whom I might see in the Strand any afternoon than as a literary phenomenon of the greatest interest to all lovers of literature, and to write about him with as much detachment as if he had lived a century ago. At the same time it is idle to pretend that any biography can be quite impartial. The simple fact of choosing a subject to write about indicates a certain partiality towards it, and an account of the life of any sort of hero from which all enthusiasm was excluded would result in something bloodless and unattractive.

5

BARRIE: THE STORY OF A GENIUS

There is so rare a constancy of success in each step of the romantic career of Sir James Matthew Barrie, Bart., O.M., LL.D., that the onlooker is engaged with a peculiar interest in the man himself, quite apart from the many manifestations of his genius. Barrie's Career would make as good a novel as Beauchamp's, were there another Meredith to write it. For it has been spun from the true stuff of romance, if that may be defined as the happening of events as we wish them to happen. And the one exception but proves the rule and adds the requisite touch of sentiment and pathos.

'Scotsmen worship Success.' How often as we walked along the Strand has this jibe been thrown at me in his sly way by one whose passing hence has left the storied pavements between Adelphi and Ludgate a bleaker stretch for me! It was a fixed idea with Clement Shorter, and always, as I now recall, associated with his intimate friend of old years, Sir William Robertson Nicoll. And once or twice the familiar tag was quoted in our exchanges of gossip that followed the passing-by of a person so ordinary in his appearance that never an unknowing eye would look at him twice: the Wizard of Thrums, the creator of immortal Peter Pan, no less. He to his Adelphi eyrie, Shorter and I to our editorial desks in the heart of Newspaperland.

Always I resented Shorter's notion of the Scot as a worshipper of mere success. Shorter admired the successful no less than Nicoll, and possibly his admiration was not so free from envy. If the success achieved is the reward of merit and industry, or the material increment of genius, surely it is no greater discredit to succeed than it is for the impractical genius to fail? Were it otherwise, the even tenor of Barrie's wonderful career would be a reproach he would find hard to bear.

In this chronicle of the events that mark his progress from conditions of humble life to those of national honour, world-wide fame, and great wealth, we may detect some of the factors contributory to his unexampled prosperity as a man of letters, but it is no part of my task to go routing after these ingredients of a success with which I am less concerned than with the things that happened by the way. Indeed, I would have my reader engage with me here in a sort of journey to Serendip, being less anxious to arrive than to travel, and ready at any moment to strike off on a bye-path, but never wandering too far from our highway: the life and genius of that 'queer little deevil' (*vide* Corp Shiach) who has bewitched the whole English-speaking world with the inventions of his imagination.

6

There was once a noisy lampoonist who wrote in a book: 'Dr. Hammerton is quite amusing. His notion of the tremendousness of Dr. Barrie and of the vast superiority of the Scotch does him credit. One day, perhaps, he will wake up to the fact that Dr. Barrie is not among the persons who write literature. And even though Dr. Hammerton should never realise it, the fact remains.' It is more than a quarter-of-a-century since that was written, and to-day I have better grounds than I had then for my certitude that Barrie is an enduring ornament of our literature. But I would 'place' him very differently: not with the great novelists, to whose company he once aspired, not with the Hardys, the Stevensons, nor even the Conrads, but, by virtue of A Window in Thrums, with such rarer spirits as Goldsmith, Charles Lamb and Dr. John Brown, and on an exalted though somewhat lonely pedestal as the most original genius that has written for the modern theatre. In his early book just mentioned and again in several of his later plays, notably Dear Brutus and Mary Rose, he makes his nearest approaches to that perfection which is attained only when form and content seem to fuse in one piece of enduring beauty.

CHAPTER II

A LADDIE IN THRUMS

1860–1868: Kirriemuir

> O, the braw, braw toon o' Kirrie! What a years that I hae
> lo'ed it
> And I winna seek to leave it tho' I'm spared anither score;
> I'd be greetin, like a laddie for the auld reid hooses croodit
> Lookin' down upon the steadin's and the fields o' Strath-
> more.
> —VIOLET JACOB.

ON a day of furtive sunshine as I walked along the Brechin
Road, in Kirriemuir, near the Tenements, a bright-faced lassie,
daringly dressed in summer things—for the too familiar rain-
clouds were threatening—went by in company with another who
had evidently been paying her a visit. 'Oh, an' another thing:
I forgot to tell you that Sir James Barrie was born in our house,'
I heard her say. I was on my way to have a look at that very
house, now a few yards distant, and it was odd to overhear this
casual remark; more odd to reflect that she had forgotten to mention earlier the one thing that could make the house different from
all the other undistinguished little houses in the row.

Among the birthplaces of Scotland's literary celebrities, Barrie's,
though roomier than the world-famous cot at Alloway, like that
of Burns may be described as humble. I suspect on the part of
a local writer a kindly desire to apologise for its lowliness when
he reminds us that the Tenements in the days of Barrie's boyhood
were considered 'very desirable' residences; their tenants rather
to be envied. By comparison with the common but-and-ben,
when they were newly built they must have seemed a great
improvement, each house boasting just double the accommoda-
tion of the familiar weaver's cot. But we need make no pretence
that it was at any time other than a very modest home, where a
family that threatened to grow too large for its constricted walls
had come into being.

> The auld hoose, the auld hoose,
> What though the rooms were wee!

8

J. M. BARRIE IN HIS EIGHTH YEAR
Photographed at Glasgow.

Face page 8

KIRRIEMUIR FROM THE 'COMMONTY'
The Gairie Linen Works in foreground, the Cemetery on the Hill in right background.

THE TENEMENTS, KIRRIEMUIR.   [*Mitchell Laing*
The Birthplace of J. M. Barrie is the white building on the right; small building in foreground is the wash-house.

must have sounded peculiarly appropriate to the Barries when remembering their old home in later years.

As it stands to-day it contains two small rooms downstairs, and two more above reached by a steep and narrow stair. The ceilings are so low that a tall man would feel inclined to stoop as he moved about the rooms. The upstairs apartment on the left had been originally Margaret Ogilvy's kitchen; the position of the boxed-in bed that stood in it then can still be traced. The other was the parents' bedroom. On the ground floor were a parlour of sorts and the father's 'wob' room. As the family grew David Barrie had to shift his loom to an adjoining house, and both kitchen and parlour were then downstairs. The four apartments of the tiny house stand to-day without further alteration, saving only the extra window in the back wall of the quondam upstairs kitchen giving upon the Brechin Road. This was put in when James was a little boy. He told Mrs. Thomson, who has occupied the house for more than twenty years, that he remembered playing about on the scaffolding when the builders were at work on the window. There may have been a little 'rafter room' in the roof, indicated by the small skylight in the slates, but Miss Addison, Bell Lunan's daughter, who was a young girl when James was an infant in arms, and was allowed to carry him round the parlour on the day of his christening, tells me that the loft was never used, Margaret Ogilvy being afraid of the children coming to grief in going up or down the ladder to the trap-door that opened perilously over the steep little stair. The trapdoor must have been papered over for scores of years. So we may take it that the garret where James 'first tasted blood' was not in his birthplace, and I can state with equal certainty that it was not in the next house to which the family removed at Forfar.

It was in his parents' bedroom on the upper floor of the house at Lilybank in the Tenements on May 9th, 1860, that James Matthew Barrie was born. On the following Sabbath he was baptized ' at the poopit fit ' of the South Free Church.

The father, honest David Barrie, was then in his forty-sixth year and such small prosperity as he was ever to enjoy had yet to come. On the day of James's birth their first set of hairbottomed chairs, for which the mother had long been saving up her sixpences, came to grace the parlour downstairs on the left of the doorway. The chairs marked visibly an epoch in the family fortunes; the new infant in the bed upstairs was as it might be.

Now this is a matter of more biographic importance than may

at first appear. The littleness of that little house conditioned not only the early years of J. M. Barrie's life, but also the bent of his mind. Had he been born in a house of lofty ceilings and spacious, finely-furnished rooms, where all material comforts were at hand, the world had never heard of the humour and pathos of an Auld Licht community. It would surely have heard of James Matthew Barrie, but the vivid intimacy of his early work could hardly have been possible. His star was a lucky one and here was his first gleam of fortune. ' In God's providence,' says his eminent townsman, Dr. Alexander Whyte, ' I was born in a poor rank of life.' That will pass as another way of stating that honest poverty has merits which may not be perceived by those whose early portion it is. The weekly rent paid for his father's home in the boyhood of J. M. Barrie was less than the genius who was born there could have earned at any time these forty years for a dozen words from his pen; he might have bought the freehold of all the Tenements with the fee he could command for an afternoon's composition.

'Wee Jamie'—like so many who have made a stir in the world, Barrie is short of stature, though in early boyhood he was of average height, his slightness of frame and eerie fineness of feature suggesting the 'wee'—was the ninth of Mrs. Barrie's ten children. When James was born, Alexander Ogilvy, the oldest of the family, was already in his nineteenth year, and had gone to Aberdeen University in company with his life-long friend, Alexander Whyte. The fourth of the children, Elizabeth How, of whom we shall hear again, had died, a child of two, nine years earlier, the fifth, Agnes Matthew, born December 23rd, 1850, having been the first for whom the hillside grave was opened in January, 1851. Mary Edward, the eldest daughter (who became Mrs. Galloway), had her fifteenth birthday three months before, while Jane Ann Adamson, the novelist's favourite sister ('already a tragic figure to those who know the end,' he says in Margaret Ogilvy) and the original of 'Leeby,' was a girl of thirteen at the time. David Ogilvy, sixth of Margaret's bairns, whose tragic death seven years later was to have so profound an effect on his mother's health ('How my Mother got her Soft Face'), had reached the middle of his brief span of fourteen years. Two more sisters, Sara Mitchell in her sixth year, and Isabella Ogilvy (afterwards Mrs. Murray) 'going in three,' as they say up there, completed the group of youngsters that crowded the little house of David Barrie when his son of genius first saw the light in that upstairs room: a total of six to which in another two years one more was to be added when Margaret (afterwards Mrs. Winter) the tenth child and last of the family arrived, July 9th, 1863. Of all the group only James Matthew and Margaret survive.

The Scottish laddie of poor circumstances, when he is not sullen and gauche, is often self-conscious and sensitive. There is no acceptance of honest poverty in Scotland as a station to which the Lord has called us. The ways of God may command respect, but the humblest Scot believes that he can improve the divine dispensation, so far as it touches him personally, by exerting himself to the betterment of his position. Even Dr. Whyte while in that poor rank to which the providence of God had called him had one commanding impulse: to escape from it. Hence the national passion for 'getting on.' Hence also the initial self-consciousness.

If the sensitiveness of little James Barrie was somewhat out of the common, an impish liveliness of spirit saved it from taciturnity. Whence that trait of character came we need not inquire; but it was not inherited either from Margaret Ogilvy or David Barrie. There will be much to say of the mother in a later chapter; of the father we do not know enough. The mother-worship of the sensitive boy is a natural and a beautiful thing, but it has left the figure of the father shadowy. Those who knew David Barrie best believed that his character might have inspired an idealised biography worthy to stand with that of his well-beloved wife. 'One who proved a most loving as he was always a well-loved husband, a man I am very proud to be able to call my father,' was the fine tribute of his son written while his father was alive to read and to rejoice in it.

There is no mention anywhere that David Barrie, the father, was ever else than a man of the most genial and friendly disposition. No stories are told of him that suggest a man of moods; rather he would appear to have been, like his wife, of an even temper, gentle, sympathetic, and a general favourite among his neighbours. Clean-shaven in his later years, he was at the time of which I write a typical Forfarshire figure of a man; a fine, open, intelligent countenance, the mouth mobile and humorsome, the brows broad and full, and a fringe of whisker framing the face, of which both lip and chin were shaven. His eldest son, Alexander, was the only one of his family who inherited his fine physique. When David Barrie came to his end in his eightyeighth year a carriage accident was the cause. He began life at the loom, but he had an appetite for learning, more common in his time than in ours, and, by dint of self-education, he had acquired considerable literary culture by the time that James was born. In his youth he had ventured as far afield as

Manchester in search of employment, but had returned to Kirriemuir and the hand-loom before his marriage, which took place in 1841, when he was in his twenty-seventh year.

A devoted member of the Free Church, his religious horizon was probably wider than that of most Auld Lichts, though his wife, who was brought up in that communion, was not less liberal in mind than he, and her father, the stone-mason, who was a 'stoop' (support) of the Auld Licht Kirk, was a man of vision, true piety and tolerance. David Barrie's respect for book-lore gave him a veneration for all men of intellectual gifts. Education had become a fetish with him. No father was ever more resolved that his sons should have the best schooling, at no matter what sacrifice to himself. The parental thriftiness that enabled the oldest boy, who was both brilliant and companionable, to go to Aberdeen University must have bordered on the heroic. A weaver's weekly earnings amounted then barely to one pound, worked he never so hard. David Barrie, though known as a 'small manufacturer,' made not much more than a common weaver, and there were many mouths to feed in the Barrie home by the time Alexander was ready for Aberdeen. Eighteen years later, when James went to Edinburgh, matters were very different; the days of scraping and vigilant economy were past, though those of plenty had still to come.

It is astonishing to think how much David Barrie achieved in the way of self-culture during those years when his day must have been so fully occupied with the dire task of earning the daily bread: he had need of a cheerful disposition, and that saintliness of character to which Dr. Whyte bore witness was doubtless tried and tempered then. But he strove to some purpose, as he was able, when the day of steam power came, to adapt himself to the changed time and to step from the hand-loom to the counting house—a step that involved the temporary removal of his family to Forfar, and prepared the way for the new and more leisured period of life in his native town that was to begin two years later.

In these earlier years of the laddie there is no reason for supposing that his parents or his brothers and sisters were hopeful that a child of genius had come among them. His mother would have her dreams, but the boy who played about the Marywell Brae, or adventured up the Den to the Reekie Broth Pot and the Coffin Brig, or looked with awe upon the Stannin' Stane when he went as far afield as the whin-covered Hill, was just 'ane o' Margaret Ogilvy's bairns.' He was no freakish child. As he grew he entered into all the concerns of the boys in his neighbourhood, and he had his own playmates, like the rest of them. No Corp

Shiach has put it on record that Jamie was a wonder. There is reason to believe that he did earn a reputation as a story-teller among his school friends at the Hanky School, and at the Free Church School which he attended in succession; but whenever he had the chance he was to be found on that spacious playground on the Hill that lies beyond the Cemetery walls, taking his part in games with his playmates, perhaps a little timorously, though not shyly: his bashfulness being first noted after his Kirriemuir boyhood had ended, and when he came back to his native place at times as a promising young scholar.

As a little chap he was full of pranks and healthy mischief. Often his mother would be after him for some childish naughtiness, and he would dart out of his own home into that of Bell Lunan next door, and, jumping into her kitchen bed, claim sanctuary there when his mother arrived in pursuit. His interest in Bell Lunan was remarkable; the stout little staff which she needed in all her movements about the house or as far as the garden patch outdoors, seemed to fascinate him. He would slyly take it away when she was seated a step or two from her cottage door and dare her to walk these few steps without it, and she would make the painful effort 'juist to please the laddie.' Little did he guess the importance of the part Bell and her stick were destined to play in his life; but many years after her death, and long after he had made himself famous with his stories of the Auld Lichts and the creation of Jess, whose portrait, as we know, was in outward essentials limned from Bell Lunan, his sentimental interest in her stick led him to beg it of her daughter as a souvenir, and to give it a place among the treasures of his London home.

Cricket, his interest in which has been one of his pre-occupations, he must first have taken up, in the casual fashion of village lads, with his playmates from the Brechin Road neighbourhood. The game has always been in high favour at Kirriemuir, and even now is not outdone by football, which, in Barrie's boyhood, was hardly known there, the first football that was seen in Kirriemuir having been a present from Alexander to his young brother.

His love of fishing dates from this early period of his boyhood. His instructor in the art of angling, who still survives, was Robert Volume, a pupil teacher at the South Free Church school, and his companion on many an expedition was James Robb, nearly two years his junior, with whom he has kept life-long friendship. Mr. Robb was a guest at Sir James's Adelphi retreat in the summer of 1928; what 'cracks' the two must have had of their lang syne adventures by Prosen Water! When Barrie would go round to Robb's home to ask him to go fishing, Robb's mother would stipulate that before he went he should carry enough water from a distant well to enable her to do her Monday's washing, and Barrie as a loyal playmate would take his share of this task. How enduring is Barrie's love of fishing may be gathered from a letter he sent to Dr. Whyte on July 8th, 1920, quoted by Whyte's biographer: 'I hope all is well with you and the household,' he wrote, 'despite the rain. To-day I had to mend my umbrella with tin-tacks—a masterly performance. The fishing will be good in the Prosen this week-end.'

Even in such persistent survivals as children's games there has been change since Barrie's boyhood in Kirriemuir; the very names of some of them are unknown to the school children of to-day, although their traditional rules may still exist under other guises. Caipey-Dykie and Dumps, the latter a game that was played with a marble larger than the ordinary 'bool' familiar to Kirrie lads as a 'taw'—do any of the boys and girls at play in the spacious school-yard within a stone's throw of the Tenements know anything of these? I doubt if they do.

But there was a game, highly popular when Barrie went to school at Kirriemuir, that is still played by children in all parts of rural Scotland under a variety of names. In the west we knew it as Smugglers or Smuggle; in the east country it is usually Smuggle the Geeg or Smuggleerie, there being a marked preference among dialect speakers in Forfarshire and the east to add 'ie' to numerous words to which no one in the west would ever think of giving the diminutive: a 'close' in Lanarkshire is always so described, but in Forfarshire it is more often a 'closie.' In this game of Smuggleerie the players form two sides, one of which, the smugglers, takes possession of the geeg, which may be any small object, a pocket knife, a watch key, a marble. Retiring a distance from the 'den' where the other group of players for the moment remains, the geeg is passed to one of the smugglers, who quickly separate, running off in all directions. This is the signal for the pursuers to start after them. A wild chase through the lanes and wynds and closes of the town, over walls and through backyards, then takes place, the object of the smugglers being to get back to the starting place without being caught by one of the pursuers. In this game Barrie, being slight of body and fleet of foot, was usually entrusted with the geeg, and his nimbleness very often enabled him to get it home to the satisfaction of his side.

Another diversion of a less sporting character in which, according to Mr. Robb, Barrie was as open as any of the other 'wild sackets' to take his part, was known locally as Chickie Mailie, a name that would mean nothing to a Lanarkshire lad who may have played the trick often enough. A bobbin of thread was required for the operation, the end of the thread being fastened to a pin which was pushed into the outside woodwork of a cottage window and about a foot from the pin a button was fastened on the thread. The young rascal who was working the trick (which had to be done in the dark) retired some ten or twenty yards from the window, paying out the thread as he went; he could then make the button tap with monotonous irritation against the window, and enjoy with his fellow-conspirators the satisfaction of knowing that he was disturbing the peace of the inmates of the room. The climax was usually reached by means of an empty bottle, placed in such a position on the window sill or elsewhere that it could be easily upset by pulling a thread, and so crashed on the ground, or sometimes it was thrown against the wall of the house, bringing the inmates in haste to the door to find out the cause of the mysterious tapping and the breaking glass. At this juncture the boys pulled in their lines and bolted.

There was yet another favourite trick which brought much pleasure to those who performed it, and it was said in Kirriemuir that little Jamie Barrie invented it, but it is really 'old as the hills' and used to be a most acceptable feature of Harlequinade. You made up neatly in brown paper a little parcel of any rubbish, carefully tying it with string and attaching to it a long piece of thin cord. When no one was looking, and the hour being about the gloaming so that the trail of the cord would not be too readily noticeable, you laid your parcel in the middle of the Brechin Road, and, with the end of the string in your hand, hid in some obscure corner. There you patiently waited until a passer-by saw the parcel and picked it up. On one occasion a somewhat self-important bailie of the borough spied the bait, and, after tapping it with his foot, concluded that it might be worth taking home, whereupon he lifted it, and, tucking it under his arm, continued on his way. Picture his amazement, after he had taken a few steps, when the parcel was roughly jerked from underneath his arm and went speedily, and apparently of its own volition, towards a stack of timber in Jamie Eassie's wood-yard. Barrie and Robb were the two little niggers in this wood pile.

It will be noticed that these rascally amusements of the young Barrie partook, in some measure, of the nature of fishing, involving as they did the use of lines. His partiality for them may have been due to his keenness as an angler. Many a Saturday was spent by these two playmates at 'the fishin,' trout streams in the neighbourhood being numerous, and the Melgam and the Crombie their favoured waters. These expeditions involved a good deal of tramping to and from the scene of their sport, and a 'jeelie piece' from Margaret Ogilvy would be all they had to sustain them for hours on end. Often they had the satisfaction of securing a lift from a farmer's cart when returning footsore towards Kirriemuir.

Mr. Robb recalls an occasion when he and Barrie were sent on an errand to Milnacraig, about eight miles distant from their home, a penny to each of them being the reward, paid in advance. On their return journey, when they had completed more than twelve miles of tramping and were parched with thirst, Barrie had the bright idea of pooling their joint resources and purchasing a two-penny bottle of lemonade at a wayside 'shoppie,' and, having equally shared this refreshment, they continued their journey home. Another of these Saturday adventures recalled by Mr. Robb is especially interesting for a detail which links it with the doings of Sentimental Tommy. On this occasion the two companions were accompanied by some other playfellows from Kirriemuir on a ramble as far as Tannadice, some seven miles away, and, on approaching this village, for some freakish reason the boys all turned their jackets inside out, a sartorial eccentricity which was so little approved by the boys of Tannadice that the Kirrie lads were subjected to a volley of stones, before which they ignominiously fled. There was a convention of children's play in those days that the reversing of the jacket constituted a complete disguise, but this would seem to have been unknown to the Tannadice lads. Tommy, as his admirers will remember, was familiar with it.

The Hanky School which James attended for a season, when he was not yet seven years old, was the little seminary kept by the Misses Adam in Bank Street, a few minutes' walk from the Barrie home. It was of little account educationally, and appealed chiefly to the mothers of large families as an economical way of getting the younger bairns off their hands for a few hours daily, and starting them in the preliminaries of school life. But, like every experience of his life, this brief period at the Hanky School was to be turned to fine literary effect in later years as all Barrie readers know. The Misses Adam were the daughters of the Rev. Thomas Adam, who on his retirement from the ministry in the south of Scotland had come to live in Kirriemuir. The ladies were gentle souls, and shrank from the use of the tawse, which used to be so effectively wielded by schoolmasters;

but the inattentive scholar at the Hanky School was apt to receive a smart 'dirl' on the knuckles administered by one of the Misses Adam with a ruler, while other misdemeanours were punished by the pupil being locked in the coalhole under the stair that led to the teachers' private residence above. Occasionally some fault was expiated by the pupil having to leave the schoolroom and sit in solitude at the foot of the stair in the lobby. This was an experience that James did not entirely dislike, as on one occasion when seated there old Mr. Adam, coming down, gave the little culprit a peppermint sweet. The prospect of a repetition made him partial to this particular form of punishment.

The Education Act was not to come into effect for another six or seven years, and the scholastic world of the day was in a chaotic state. An idea of what country schooling meant at that time in rural Scotland is given in Barbour's Life of Alexander Whyte. Whyte 'kept school' for a time after quitting the shoemaker's bench in Kirriemuir—'Ay, and a gey puir shoemaker he was; but he's been a fine preacher to many folk in Edinburgh who were sair needing it,' said old David Barrie forty years later —to earn a living while preparing for his university career. It was at a little roadside hamlet boasting the Biblical name of Padanaram, on the road from Forfar to Kirriemuir, that Whyte, at eighteen years of age, acted as dominie, his salary seven shillings a week. The schoolhouse was an addition built on to one of the cottages, and it is now used as a store by the owner of the village shop. Whyte's biographer gives these details:

The inside measurement is about 18 by 14 feet, and the floor is of beaten earth. The 'dominie's desk' stood in one corner, and on either side of a narrow passage were the benches, which are said to have accommodated nearly fifty scholars, the most advanced of whom paid $3\frac{1}{2}$d. a week in fees. The number seems incredible, but is hardly greater than that accommodated in those days in other Scottish rural schools but little larger. . . .

The young dominie's life was a strenuous one. Daily he had to walk four miles each day between the Southmuir and Padanaram. Often he was obliged to learn overnight the lesson which he had to teach the senior scholars next day. And the salary was less than he might have been earning at the loom or the shoemaker's bench.

It was thus that other Kirrie lads, intent themselves upon a university education, had to win their way to it. Both Alexander Barrie and Alexander Whyte graduated M.A. at Aberdeen in April, 1862, the one receiving first class honours in Classics, the other second class in Mental Philosophy. The event was

17

marked by Alexander Barrie presenting Whyte with the four
volume edition of Alford's Greek Testament, thus inscribed:

ALEXANDRO WHYTE, A. M.
Amico Dilecto et Magnopere Æstimato
Hoc Signum Caritatis Parvum
Donavit
A. O. Barrie
April 7, 1862.

When we remember that Barrie and Whyte, 'his dear and very
greatly esteemed friend,' were then occupying lodgings in Aberdeen
which cost 3s. 6d. a week, the best they could afford, we can
the better appreciate the self-sacrifice of the young student who
had to scrape together so large a sum as £3 12s. in order to provide that Greek Testament.

Alexander Barrie had the true genius of friendship, and no
cloud ever came between him and Whyte while life endured.
When, in 1867, Whyte took up his first pastoral post at Free
St. John's, Glasgow, he had the felicity of finding Alexander
Barrie there as classical master at Glasgow Academy, a post he
had entered upon in September of that year. A pleasant reference to the friendship of the two 'Alecs' occurs in a letter written
by Whyte to his sister in May of that year:

On the 17th June Mr. Barrie and I start for a holiday tour on the
continent of Europe, and I would like to hear from you before we
start. We will be away six weeks. . . . We start from Glasgow on
Monday, the 17th June, pass through London, spend a day or two in
Paris, and spend our first Sabbath in Geneva. Walk through Switzerland and spend the next Sabbath in Milan, the next in Venice; then
set our faces homeward by the Rhine. Won't that be a splendid tour?

We can guess somewhat of the excitement such news would
bring to little James; it may have supplied a background for
his story-telling to his companions of the South Free School
to which both he and his chum James Robb were now transferred.

But I now perceive that my excursion to Padanaram might
leave a false impression of Kirriemuir's educational resources in
the 'sixties of last century did I not hasten to avert that. There
is really no sort of comparison between the roadside hamlet and
the busy town of weavers. Nay, Kirriemuir was already famed
for its schools; as early as 1831 there were no fewer than sixteen
in the town and neighbourhood. Our authority for that is
Dr. Easton's Statistical Account of the parish, which adds: 'The
number of persons upwards of fifteen years of age who cannot

18

read or write is not one to a thousand.' From the early years
of the century Kirrie men who had flourished in business in
other towns took a delight in enriching the educational endow-
ments of their native place, and the splendid Webster's Seminary
had been a beacon light in the world of education for nearly two
score years before little James Barrie was trudging, not unwil-
lingly, to the dame school in Bank Street. The presence of so
fine a school in the town tended to key up the lesser establish-
ments, and no compulsory act was needed to make the Kirriemarians respect the schoolmaster.

Indeed, it can be said that Barrie was born into an educational
atmosphere; he could not well have avoided becoming a scholar.
By the time he went to the Free Church School at Southmuir
he had the knowledge that his big brother was going to be classical
master at the Academy in the great city of Glasgow, while both
his parents had their hearts set on making James also a scholar
worthy of such a brother. His sister Mary was already a teacher,
and in due time his other sisters also took up some form of
educational work.

If we hear nothing of James being noted as a prize-winner
at the Free Church School, and the few stories that are preserved
of him there tend rather to suggest a casual attitude towards
the serious business of that seminary, that may be due to the
fact that it is always the light side of our school days which
memory presents to us. Ask his old companion, James Robb,
what he most readily recalls and it will be the story of a mad
cow! The animal was seen cavorting along the Glamis Road
just when the scholars were going into school again after an
interval, and instead of returning to their tasks off went the two
Jamies and one or two others, fired by the adventurous possibilities of the pursuit. So far did they carry the chase that it
was an hour or more before they realised that they had clean
forgotten about school, and then, in all good faith, they hurried
back to their lessons at a quarter to four, just a quarter of an
hour before the class dismissed. A frank explanation of their
lapse from duty resulted in the teacher sentencing the culprits
to stay late for twenty minutes every day for a week and write
so many lines apiece. Jamie Barrie was the leader in this and
many another 'ploy.' It was seldom that this involved neglect
of his class work, for his diligence at school was never in question;
he was not less anxious to learn than his parents were to encourage him; and of his play, we need no better chronicle than
may be found in Sentimental Tommy and Margaret Ogilvy. In
all the delightful episodes of the Jacobites in the Den and in

the first three chapters of Margaret Ogilvy we have the essence of autobiography: remembrance touched with imagination. I suspect even the wagging of the head to have been a boyish trick of James as well as of Tommy when particularly pleased with a juvenile achievement of the pen.

Apart from his school tasks he was often busy with pencil and crayons, having a taste for lettering and design, and there exists at least one example of his boyish work in the form of an illuminated text in which a small Guido head of Christ with the crown of thorns is neatly inset, the whole being very tastefully designed.

A novelty of those days was the zoëtrope, a simple invention which was the forerunner of the cinematograph. It consisted of an open drum-shaped box, the upper part of its circular side pierced with slits, and, inserted inside, a strip of paper with printed figures in progressive stages of movement, so that when the drum was rotated on a spindle the eye saw through the upper slits the printed figures as an animated procession. At W. B. Mills's newspaper shop in Bank Street the strips of figures were sold for use in the zoëtrope, and as a son of W. B. Mills was one of Barrie's playfellows James was an occasional visitor to be amused with the zoëtrope. There was also, and far more important, the attraction of a toy theatre. Young Mills owned one of these playthings which so fascinated R. L. Stevenson, and which would seem to have been no less fascinating to J. M. Barrie, whose boyish enthusiasm for the puppet show is not forgotten among the few who linger in Kirriemuir from those distant days. He was full of energy, resource and invention with this toy theatre, and in W. B. Mills's house we can picture the future wizard of the British stage curled up behind the curtains of the big 'concealed bed' working the tiny puppets in the toy theatre placed at the front of the bed the better to be seen by the juvenile audience.

To the jubilee number of The Kirriemuir Observer, October 3rd, 1919, Sir James sent a felicitous little note touching this matter of the toy theatre and it ought to have its place in this record. It is as follows:

Dear Mr. Mills,

May The Kirriemuir Observer continue to prosper exceedingly. There was a time when it was not merely my favourite but my only newspaper, just as the old shop in Bank Street was my introduction to literature, and in a room above it (the stage being a bed and the actors puppets) I saw my first play. Always thro' those memories I

A LADDIE IN THRUMS

see the kindly face of W. B. Mills, whom we will remember with affection on the Jubilee of his paper.

Yours sincerely,

J. M. BARRIE.

While this does not confirm my suggestion that he who, some forty years later, was to stand an acknowledged master of theatrical technique, began his stage craft with the puppet show in Bank Street, it proves, at least, that here was his first peep into a new realm of fancy.

Immediately opposite the door of the birthplace stands a tiny wash-house—I found Mrs. Thomson, the present occupier of the birthplace, busy 'wringing out' in it—and in one of the latest of his confessions Barrie has suddenly invested with a peculiar glamour this old and decrepit structure. Here at the age of seven he made his first appearance as an actor on any stage! His 'fellow conspirator' was James Robb, and both wore Glengarry bonnets. The nature of the play he does not describe beyond its thrilling finale, which was a struggle between the two performers as to which could put the other into the boiler, 'though some say I addressed the spell-bound audience.' The charge for admission to the show was so many pins, a marble, or a top ('preens, a bool, or a peerie'). When, nearly forty years on, he came to write Peter Pan, it was to this same wash-house that his mind went back for the original of the little house the Lost Boys built for Wendy in the Never Land, 'the chief difference being that it never wore John's hat as a chimney.' On news of this getting about some enterprising American tried to buy the wash-house and have it transhipped to alien soil, but to a country, be it said, where the admirers of Peter Pan are numbered by the hundreds of thousands, for the little folk of America took Peter and Wendy and the Lost Boys and all the other fairy folk of that wonderful play as instantly to their hearts as did those of the old country. Major R. D. Lauder, in November, 1928, purchased the birthplace and the old wash-house that they might be preserved for the nation, but, I for one, hope that he may not be allowed to carry out his alleged threat to remove the structure to Kensington Gardens. That sentimental landmark belongs to Kirriemuir alone.

A memorable and tragic year in the story of Barrie's Kirriemuir boyhood was 1867. Alexander Barrie was then nearing the end of his period as a teacher in the distant town of Bothwell, Lanarkshire, where, with his sister, Mary, as assistant, he had opened a private school; in September he was to take up his first

21

important post as classical master at Glasgow Academy. His brother, David, was now a bright and promising lad of fourteen years, for whom Margaret Ogilvy was picturing a career at college not less brilliant than Alec's had been; on whom indeed the mother's love seemed more centred than on any other of her children. David, too, was at Bothwell, under the care of his elder brother, who had made himself responsible for his education. On a day in January he had gone skating with a companion there. They had but one pair of skates between them, and these were David's; a present, no doubt, from Alexander, of whose kindness to all his brothers and sisters there are so many instances. David, after having enjoyed a few spins on the ice, took off his skates and lent them to the other, who, in starting away, accidentally collided with him and upset him so heavily upon the ice that his head was badly injured in the fall. For a few hours only did he survive the removal to his brother's lodging.

The 29th of January, 1867, was a terrible day for Margaret Ogilvy. First came the telegram to say that her darling boy was seriously injured, and urging that she and her husband should come at once to Bothwell. Gravely the two set out from their little home down hill to the station, where David Barrie, with that caution he always showed, made further inquiry at the telegraph office before going to the train, and learned that another message had just been received to say that his name-son was dead. He had no need to tell Margaret that their journey would be in vain, she read the dread news in his face, and fell in a faint at his feet. This was her tragedy (told in these matter-of-fact words), which forms the subject of one of the most delicate and moving chapters her son of genius has written. She never saw her beloved boy again. So great had been the shock to her that when the little coffin which enclosed his body was brought to her home and laid upon the table in the parlour to await its burial in the hillside grave the doctor would not allow her to have it opened, fearing that the further shock would be more than her sorrow-racked mind could stand. And Margaret could but clasp her mothering arms for the last time around the coffin in which her dead boy lay.

Little imagination is needed to conceive the change that came upon the Barrie home with this tragic break in its happy family circle. It was young James's first stark encounter with grief. His sisters who had died in infancy were but names to him. It was to be long before Margaret recovered her old bright interest in the daily round of life, and we know how eager James was to

bring the smiles back to her face again; how pathetic his efforts
to make her laugh when sorrow was brooding:

I suppose I was an odd little figure. I have been told that my
anxiety to brighten her gave my face a strained look and put a tremor
into the joke (I would stand on my head in the bed, my feet against
the wall, and then cry, excitedly: 'Are you laughing, mother?'), and
perhaps what made her laugh was something I was unconscious of,
but she did laugh suddenly now and then, whereupon I screamed
exultantly to that dear sister who was ever in waiting to come and see
the sight, but by the time she came the soft face was wet again.

He kept count of the times he contrived to make her laugh, and
it was the doctor's suggestion that if he told her this the very
telling of it would win him another laugh. 'Not only did she
laugh then, but again when I put the laugh down, so that, though
it was really one laugh with a tear in the middle, I counted it as
two.'

Thus, in the brief time that little James spent in Kirriemuir
after that tragedy, he had crept 'far ben' into his mother's heart,
as we know from his own avowals in Margaret Ogilvy. While
Margaret was winning back her health and happiness in the
devotion of her children and her husband that good man was so
occupied with his loom and the studies that were soon to free
him from its thraldom that, like so many of the toiling fathers,
he was robbed of much of the most abiding joy of parenthood:
the pleasure of sharing in the childish anxieties and excitements
of his little ones.

One who knew both Mr. and Mrs. Barrie well tells me that
his recollection of David Barrie is of a very kindly and human
personality, less 'ta'en up' than his wife about their young son,
who has left us in no doubt that it was his mother who most encouraged him in his earliest literary adventures. She entered
into his boyish enthusiasms with a brave assumption of delight,
for her heart was still heavy with the loss of her darling Davie.

The juvenile taste of James was early set upon the romantic.
It may be doubted if David Barrie would have been so ready to
applaud this taste as Margaret Ogilvy proved; not from any
narrow prejudice, but from the essential seriousness of his attitude to life and religion. I have spoken of the father as a man
of considerable literary culture, and we have ample testimony
to both his saintliness and his geniality, but it would be wrong
to picture him as a man in any sense touched with genius: there
is no evidence that intellectually he stood high above the average,
for we must remember that in the Kirriemuir of his day the

intellectual mean was very high, and he had need to be something 'by ordinar' who stood above it. We shall probably be guilty of no injustice to the literary taste and mental powers of David Barrie if we think of him as an earnest soul, striving always after ideals of good, notable rather for qualities of character than for exceptional gifts of intellect.

Now if we were to take Barrie at his own word we should be in the thick of the most vital chapter of our story. He is only turned seven, and the days of the laddie in Thrums are passing swiftly; a month or two and they are over. Indeed, save for a year or so at Forfar, ending in the spring of 1872, and a spell at their new home in Kirriemuir that year, after his eighth year he was to be only a visitor at his parents' home; the young scholar on holiday from Glasgow or Dumfries, the undergrad from Edinburgh, but already a chiel who was 'takin' notes.' For the days of his early boyhood, with which we are concerned at the moment, we have to turn chiefly to his own printed pages to discover from his later attitude to boyhood in general something of what his own may have been: a risky proceeding, and with none riskier than Barrie. These self-revealing pages, if helpful to the biographer are also his snare. Barrie the romancist has the playful habit of inventing so much of his own youth that to disentangle the hard facts from the airy fancies is a delicate task. We must not be too ready to accept as autobiographic all that he offers in that vein. 'The author's pet animal is the whale,' is quite as truthful a confession as many anecdotes of his early life in Kirriemuir that have passed current for authentic personalia in the books and newspapers of the last forty years.

We should deal warily then with what he has himself written of the laddie in Thrums, but nevertheless here is the place to consider it and to catch some glimpse of the boy in the man. The boyhood of the commonest mortal must present some features identical with those of the genius. There is the uniqueness of true individuality in the anxious little lad of seven trying to cheer his sorrowing mother by standing on his head in bed, but a point on which he dwells more than once concerns a trait of boyhood which I believe to be very common—the delusion of having participated in events that happened long before one's birth. Things of our childhood told to us by our parents or others, statements of fact, fantastic or even silly stories, stick in our memories and grow up with us, so that in later years we seem to have lived them instead of having heard them only, the occasions of their telling completely forgotten.

THE BARRIE HOME AT FORFAR
Showing the house and kailyard in the Limepots,
now Canmore Street, as they were in 1872.

BURNBANK TERRACE, GLASGOW
Where J. M. Barrie lived with his brother Alexander,
1868-1870, while attending Glasgow Academy.

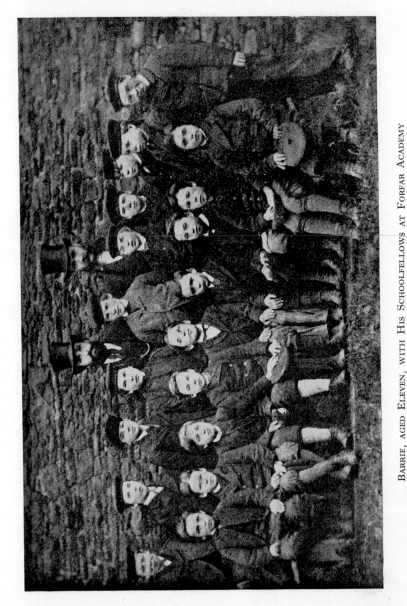

BARRIE, AGED ELEVEN, WITH HIS SCHOOLFELLOWS AT FORFAR ACADEMY

He is the first figure seated on left. Fourth from right is David Elder Anderson who kindly lent this photograph.

A LADDIE IN THRUMS

There were stories that Barrie heard as he sat by his mother's knee in Margaret Ogilvy's kitchen, and the essentials of these tales were so implanted in his memory that as he grew he seemed to recollect their happening more clearly than events that had really taken place in his own boyhood. 'I have seen many weary on-dings of snow,' he writes, 'but the one I seem to recollect best occurred nearly twenty years before I was born.'

So strong a hold did his mother's stories take on his budding imagination that the lives of the Auld Lichts, who fought their little battles and sank into their quiet graves before he was born, and whose ongoings were the chief subject of his mother's talk, her limited world of experience, became more real to her eerie, pale-faced little boy, and far more interesting, than the lives of his contemporaries. That is why, as he tells us, his books deal mainly with the days of his mother's youth and not with his own.

His fond remembrance of his own boyhood which he indulges so often is our best assurance that it must have been a time of deep happiness and splendid dreams. We may be permitted to doubt, however, whether his recollection of its 'horror' is the man remembering the boy or the artist imagining:

The horror of my boyhood was that I knew a time would come when I also must give up the games, and how it was to be done I saw not (this agony still returns to me in dreams, when I catch myself playing marbles, and look on with cold displeasure). I felt that I must continue playing in secret, and I took this shadow to her [his mother] when she told me her own experience, which convinced us both that we were very like each other inside.

Perhaps that may have been so, and if so, here indeed the boyhood of genius differed from that of all the other laddies in Thrums. The true attitude of boyhood to itself is to be done with it and on to manhood. But here was Barrie already re-hearsing the rôle of Peter Pan. Indeed, if we regard him as the protagonist of his own immortal play we shall be nearer the truth than many a critic has supposed. There is much of his own boyhood and his own self in Sentimental Tommy, and this I re-assert despite Robertson Nicoll's disapproval: it is there for the seeing. This wee Jamie Barrie as a laddie in Kirriemuir was just such a 'queer little deevil' as the early Tommy, though much of the make-believe which Tommy is made to enact amidst the realities of the Den may have been performed on the far more wonderful stage of a little boy's imagination. After all, it is there that the real things happen, and whether or not a group of Kirrie bairns were playing at Jacobites in the Den, with James Matthew Barrie, aged nine or ten, as their leader, is of no consequence; the certainty is that those scenes of Sentimental Tommy are projected from an imaginative boyhood, and not the pure invention of later artistry.

Tommy Sandys became famous through writing a book which was entirely in harmony with his dominating characteristic—the capacity for vicarious feeling and suffering. He was not married, he was a perfect 'sumph' in the presence of a woman, when he made a great reputation with his Letters to a Young Man about to be Married. (Here I suspect the author of acquaintance with P. G. Hamerton's The Intellectual Life.) This was in line with one of Barrie's pranks six or seven years after his Kirriemuir days, when living with his brother at Dumfries. He is said to have written letters to the local papers signed 'Paterfamilias,' urging the desirability of schoolboys having longer holidays.

But we have only to turn again to the memoir of his mother for the keynote of Tommy's character. Of his boyish companionship with his mother, he writes:

We read many books together when I was a boy, Robinson Crusoe being the first (and the second), and the Arabian Nights should have been the next, for we got it out of the library (a penny for three days); but on discovering that they were Nights when we had paid for Knights, we sent that volume packing, and I have curled my lips at it ever since. The Pilgrim's Progress we had in the house (it was as common a possession as a dresser-head), and so enamoured of it was I that I turned our garden into Sloughs of Despond, with pea-sticks to represent Christian on his travels, and a buffet-stool for his burden; but when I dragged my mother out to see my handiwork she was scared, and I felt for days, with a certain elation, that I had been a dark character. Besides reading every book we could hire or borrow, I also bought one now and again, and while buying (it was the occupation of weeks) I read, standing at the counter, most of the other books in the shop, which is perhaps the most exquisite way of reading.

This, I apprehend, should not be taken as applying to that period of his Kirriemuir boyhood which ends when he is but eight years and four months old; it contains an echo of his later Forfar period, or of his subsequent stays at Strathview. The garden best adapted for illustrating Christian's travels would be that at Forfar; those at the Tenements and at Strathview, even to the enlarging eye of romantic boyhood, must have seemed too small. The stories which he read with fascination in a certain periodical of that time suggested to him an idea that was to help his mother in her task of making a clouty (rag) rug:

A LADDIE IN THRUMS

The notion was nothing short of this, why should I not write the tales myself? I did write them—in the garret—but they by no means helped her to get on with her work, for when I finished a chapter I bounded downstairs to read it to her, and so short were the chapters, so ready was the pen, that I was back with a new manuscript before another clout had been added to the rug. Authorship seemed, like her bannock-baking, to consist of running between two points. They were all tales of adventure (happiest is he who writes of adventure), no characters were allowed within if I knew their like in the flesh, the scene lay in unknown parts—desert islands, enchanted gardens, with Knights (none of your Nights) on black chargers, and round the first corner a lady selling water-cress.

But harking back to the chronicle of the laddie in Thrums, all too soon a day has come when the need to forward James's education without overstraining the family purse brings the longest period of his Kirriemuir boyhood to an end. This day falls in the month of August, as it is recorded on the school roll of Glasgow Academy that on the 19th of August, 1868, 'Barrie, James,' aged '7,' (an error) of 5 Burnbank Terrace, enters as a scholar in the '2 E' or Second English Class. This fact was first published in the Glasgow Academy Chronicle of December, 1924, but its significance has not yet been duly appreciated. So wedded are we to the idea that all the intimacies of Barrie's boyhood must be referred to Kirriemuir that we are unwilling to associate his early years with any other town; least of all with Glasgow. Very few readers in that city will receive without some surprise the information that for the greater part of three years the future author of A Window in Thrums lived with his big brother in what was then a quiet and fashionable street off the Great Western Road.

If his actual boyhood in Kirriemuir was ended thus early, his imaginative boyhood in Thrums was just beginning. For his early removal from his birthplace and his parents' home to the educational and fraternal care of his brother, first in a great commercial city, and later, after another spell of home life with his parents at Forfar and Kirriemuir, in a still more distant provincial town, with his brother again, were circumstances that gave a vividness to his Kirriemuir experiences which these would not have possessed had they been maintained without interruption throughout his youth. The more he was cut off from Kirriemuir the more fondly his mind would dwell upon it; the farther he was away the truer the imaginative perspective in which he saw it. In his return visits from Glasgow and Dumfries was born his real love of his native place and its Auld Licht community.

27

CHAPTER III

THE YOUNG SCHOLAR

1868–1878: Glasgow—Forfar—Kirriemuir—Dumfries

Taking up his Glasgow abode in 1867, Alexander Barrie would fix upon Burnbank Terrace because of its nearness to the Academy, which occupies a commanding site on the high western banks of the River Kelvin, Burnbank Terrace being distant a matter of only ten minutes' walk. To the present writer, who in later years lived hard by Kelvin Bridge, there is a peculiar interest in picturing little James Barrie footing it beside his big bearded brother along the Great Western Road and over the bridge to the old Academy. Those were impressionable days for the laddie from Thrums, yet nowhere in any of his writings do we find anything reminiscent of Kelvinside, although there is a faint trace of it in his speech, or at least of what has been described as 'Keelvinside.' Indeed this period of Barrie's boyhood is almost a blank in all published records or reminiscences of his life. An intimate friend of his Kirriemuir days who still enjoys his friendship admitted to me that he was not aware Barrie had ever been to school in Glasgow. Such a quiet little fellow he would seem to have been at Glasgow that nobody noticed his presence in the Academy. He slipped in and out of his corner of the classroom without exciting remark, known vaguely to 'Cocky' Alexander, 'Mousey' Walker, and the more adventurous lads of his time just as 'wee Jimmie Barrie' and regarded perhaps with a little diffidence as brother of the classical master whom the boys admired for his manly bearing, but whose injunction to the scholars, 'continue,' thus oddly emphasised, was often a point for their impish mimicry.

Sixty years ago Hillhead, as the district lying immediately west of the Kelvin is known, was an outward suburb of Glasgow: its most aristocratic residential part, with the green countryside at its doors. Alexander Barrie, like his friend Whyte, was a great walker, and many a tramp they had together through Hillhead to the pleasant lands of Kelvinside, Temple, and Jordan

28

Hill; all long since built out of recognition with stone and mortar. At times, we may be sure, Alexander would take his little brother as far afield as his legs could carry him into these country places. But never a hint have we had that Barrie knows aught of Glasgow, though his stay in its west end coincided with the building and opening of its splendid University at Gilmorehill, on the heights that overlook Kelvingrove Park. It is clear that in Glasgow he felt he had no continuing city; he was just a laddie from Kirriemuir, who let the stream of Glasgow life flow past him unheeded, his thoughts still with his ain folk some eighty miles to the north. It is probable, too, that Alexander Whyte, whose sister Elizabeth, the 'little Yankee girl,' had come from America to keep house for her brother, and whose home at 14 Shaftesbury Terrace was a pleasant twenty minutes' walk from Burnbank Terrace, would have the little Kirrie lad there on some of the many visits of his elder brother. The scene of Whyte's first ministry (1866–1870) as colleague of the celebrated Dr. Roxburgh at Free St. John's, in George Street, will soon have passed away, the old church, which stood two streets east of the Municipal Buildings, having been bought by the Corporation to be pulled down, and some new municipal offices erected on its site.

One would have expected to find some reflection of these years in Barrie's earlier writings, but I have nowhere detected it, and can only conclude that in the strange surroundings of Hillhead and the overpowering largeness of the city he was driven back imaginatively to the Hill of Kirriemuir and the Marywell Brae, his school days at Hillhead passing in a continual state of longing for the end of the term which would take him back to his more familiar places, to his mother and his sisters.

No events of outstanding importance marked these Glasgow schooldays, or we had surely heard of them from a participant whose readiness to draw upon his own immediate experience is so pronounced a feature of all that he has written. All that we know 'officially' is to be found in the school roll of the Academy. When he came back to Glasgow after the summer vacation of 1869 he was enrolled again, on August 21st, in the Second English Class, his age being erroneously given as eight, and, perhaps because of his repetition of this class, he carried off the first prize in its Third division and he also won a prize for religious knowledge. In the succeeding year he would seem to have prolonged his stay at Kirriemuir for two months beyond the usual vacation (or it may have been illness that kept him away from school) as he was not enrolled again after the 1869–70 session until October 25th, 1870, and this session he did not complete, leaving the Academy at the end of June, 1871, when his brother resigned his mastership, or at an earlier date in the same year. The Academy Chronicle has it that 'he left in that session for Dumfries Academy with his brother, who after leaving Glasgow became an Inspector of Schools'; a statement which I believe to be at variance with the facts.

An event of outstanding importance had really happened, however, but not in Glasgow. In the early summer of 1870 a great day arrives in Kirriemuir, and James happens to be at home at the time: a day of high excitement. The Barrie family is removing to Forfar, and all of them born in the Brechin Road house are to experience their first 'flitting.' Margaret Ogilvy was not well enough to take any part in the removal, and did not even go to Forfar with the others. She stayed for three weeks with her great friend and neighbour, Bell Lunan, in her house next door to the old home, and when she was well enough to travel to Forfar the house that had been taken by David Barrie there was ready, with the old friendly things awaiting her. Its four rooms were slightly larger, its ceilings higher, its entrance and stairway ampler than those she had left in the Tenements, but the furniture would all 'fit in' just as at Kirriemuir.

David Barrie has reached the turning-point of his life. He is not only saying good-bye to the Tenements, where he has so long lived and laboured; he is moving into a new state. The hand-loom has been abandoned, and henceforth he will sit in an office with day-books and ledgers on his desk, and be concerned with the doings of other workers who are serving that great new monster of industry, steam power, as embodied in the Forfar Linen works of Messrs. Laird. No small matter this for a man of fifty-six, whose whole working life has been spent, so far, at the treadle of a hand-loom; and we may be sure that it has been the subject of much prayerful consideration.

With the last of the pots and pans safely bestowed in the cart, little Jamie perches himself on top and sets off on this adventure by road, the others of the family going by gig. His way would lie through Tillyloss, I fancy, to save the horse from the heavy pull up the Brae in the more direct route to the Forfar road through Southmuir. In either case the main road goes through an open country of rich farm lands, still as rural as when the Barrie flitting went past the door of Dr. Whyte's old 'schulie' at Padanaram, and came at length within sight of Forfar at that other hamlet of Biblical name, Zoar—strangely unlike the scene which the Lord showed Moses from Pisgah's height, 'the plain of the valley of Jericho, the city of palm trees, unto Zoar'—whose

30

identity has now been merged in that of the county town. The imagination of wee Jamie must have been richly occupied on that journey, and if there was sadness at leaving the Den, and the Hill and the Marywell Brae behind him, there was surely the eagerness of youth to enter an unexplored land.

Seated atop of that laden cart on a May day of 1870 the eager-eyed boy who was entering Forfar, thrilling like some old con-quistador advancing into a strange land, had actually started on his career of conquest. The romantic fancies, so soon to shape his course in life, were to be translated into dazzling realities in the after years. More romance: the arrival in Forfar of a laddie from Thrums was in a sense the coming of an enemy into the camp. For Kirriemuir and Forfar were old-time rivals, and in the first half of the seventeenth century the more bellicose inhabitants of the two towns met in combat—their weapons sticks and stones, and possibly some billhooks—at Muir Moss, about half-way between the two places, to settle a long-drawn wrangle about a piece of common land at Ballinshoe to which both towns laid claim. This 'battle' of Muir Moss was cele-brated in a doggerel stanza by Drummond of Hawthornden during a visit to the district in 1645:

> The Kirriemorians and the Forfarians met at Muirmoss,
> The Kirriemorians beat the Forfarians back to the Cross.
> Sutors ye are, and sutors ye'll be;
> Fie upon Forfar! Kirriemuir bears the gree.

To 'bear the gree' in Scots was to win the prize; but what the gain was to the weavers of Kirriemuir I am unable to dis-cover. That the encounter left a heritage of hate, like all battles great and small, is certain, and a hundred years later the For-farians were regarding with envy the prosperity of the hillside weaving town when the demand for osnaburghs had set so many shuttles agoing throughout Forfarshire. Even when the peaceful Barrie invasion took place the fires of old jealousy smouldered. On 'fast days' the lads of the two towns often met near Padanaram and fought boyish battles with stones and clods. This must have added piquancy to the event in the mind of our imaginative invader; the load of hair-bottomed chairs, mattresses, pots and pans, on which he was perched, would assume all manner of unfamiliar shapes more becoming to the romantic activity of the young adventurer's mind.

This event was of far more importance to James than any that had happened in Glasgow, and the course of things was to drift him away from Glasgow to Forfarshire again before Dumfries was to be ready for him. Alexander Barrie did not at once remove to Dumfries. The Education Act of 1872, under which he became an inspector of schools, did not come into force in Scotland until 1873, early in which year he was appointed to Dumfries and remained there as H.M. Inspector until he was transferred to the Edinburgh district in 1899. After resigning from Glasgow Academy he assisted Dr. Charles E. Wilson in the inspection of schools connected with the Free Church of Scotland. This would be in the year 1871–72, his field of work having Glasgow as its pivotal point. He was really now in training for the government post that he hoped to secure, or may have been promised, when the Education Act came into force, and in this period of change he felt, perhaps, that he could not so closely look after his young brother, who would be better with his parents until that government post had become a reality. Thus, barely a year after we find the Barries resident in Forfar, James comes north to join his parents, and is promptly entered as a scholar at Forfar Academy.

The new Barrie home in Forfar had amenities which the Tenements could not boast. It was almost a self-contained dwelling, with an exterior touch of character and a situation that was odd and unusual. The lane in which it stands was then known as the Limepots, but has since assumed the more imposing style of Canmore Street, a better name for it, since it skirts the base of the hill on which stood Forfar Castle, a stronghold of Malcolm Canmore. At a point where the narrow thoroughfare makes a bend there is a high stone wall that encloses a garden which it effectively hides, although the garden itself stands several feet above the road and is reached by a flight of steps to which a wooden door in the wall gives access. The wall extends to the lower part of the house upon whose gable end it abuts. In the Barries' time a projecting wing that marches with the street was a two-roomed house occupied by another tenant and reached by an outside stair from the street. The Barrie dwelling faced its secluded garden, or kailyard, but it had two windows in the gable end that looked along the Limepots to Castle Street; the lower was one of the parlour windows and a very pleasant room that is to-day, and was no doubt in the Barries' time. The six hair-bottomed chairs would be seen to greater advantage there than in their original setting in the Tenements. The kitchen, with its 'concealed bed,' stood on the right of an entrance hall several times larger than the tiny one at Kirriemuir, and a much wider flight of stairs led up to the two bedrooms, more spacious than those to which their new occupants had been accustomed. The present owner of

32

the house has added the two-roomed wing to it and abolished the outside stair, and what was Margaret Ogilvy's kitchen is now a bathroom, the bed recess being turned into a store cupboard; but the other rooms remain unchanged. A year or two back the once creeper-clad exterior was covered all over with a coating of cement, as the old stonework had ceased to be weather-proof.

This house I have described at some length because here was the actual scene of some incidents Barrie has left us to suppose as taking place at Kirriemuir. There is, indeed, a noticeable Forfar element in Thrums, for although he lived in it less than half the time he stayed in Glasgow, he was more at home here, more in harmony with the place. On rising ground above the house in Canmore Street there still stands a turret of the castle identified with Malcolm, the slayer of Macbeth, and this would be a fine romantic playground for the lad from Kirriemuir, though it figures in nothing that Barrie has written.

A precious document, fortunately preserved by Mr. David Elder Anderson of Manchester, is a faded old photograph, taken in the summer of 1871, showing nineteen of the scholars at Forfar Academy and two of the masters. A quaint group they look, the two bewhiskered masters in their 'lum' hats behind a standing row of lads in Balmoral bonnets, in front of whom is a second row of scholars, caps in hand, seated on a bench. At the left end of the front row is a boy, somewhat slighter than the rest, but of their average height; nothing distinguishes him from the others, unless it be a more intent look towards the photographer, a more obvious consciousness of the gravity of the occasion (whatever that may have been). The boy (need it be said?) is James Matthew Barrie.

Hardly anything is more futile than musing upon the promise of future greatness as revealed in the outward appearance of youth: after the greatness has been established.

There's no art
To find the mind's construction in the face,

or, as Barrie himself has said, 'there is unfortunately no science of reading other people's faces.' This schoolboy group is chiefly valuable as reminding us that genius in youth is not easily to be distinguished from dullness or ordinariness so far as face and form are concerned. One thing more the photograph shows: that Barrie, the man, preserves in a marked degree the features and expression of his boyhood. Knowing the mature appearance of the dramatist, there would be no difficulty in picking him out

33

as the boy of eleven among this group of nineteen lads. I suspect that the nine seated in the front row were those of smaller stature, and that is why James appears as tall as any of them. Mr. Anderson himself is there, and promises to be a man of similar build, so that I was surprised to find him of more than average height and burly of figure by comparison with the mature slightness of his illustrious schoolmate. Of the nineteen lads photographed together in the grounds of Forfar Academy fifty-eight years ago eleven or twelve are alive to-day, which speaks well for the vigour of the plain folk of Forfar. All these boys were the sons of poor parents, to whom even the modest school fee of seven shillings and sixpence per quarter was a consideration. Although there was but one genius among them, many of them rose to positions of importance in widely different walks of life, and James was not the only one who earned a title. The real 'show boy' of the Academy, the star mathematician, the one from whom most was expected, became a porter at a small station on the Highland Railway.

Our main concern with Forfar being the session that Barrie spent at its Academy, we cannot do better than straightway listen to Mr. Anderson as he recalls those distant days when he and Jamie 'ran thegither':

He was not in my class, although he was taken in the photograph which is now in my possession, but I got to know him and like him. He was a shy, sensitive lad, not over fond of athletics, but a keen lover of the country. I well remember happy afternoons spent round about Forfar chiefly because of the stories Barrie related, many of which must, even then, have evolved from his own vivid imagination. There were others, however, that were based on what he had read. Once he told me the gist of Ivanhoe in such a vivid and picturesque manner as to arouse in me a love for the works of Sir Walter Scott which I have retained ever since.

One episode in which Barrie and I were concerned is still fresh in my memory. It was a Saturday afternoon, and, free of all the school, Barrie and I set out for a ramble armed with a 'cookie' each and a penny to buy milk with. The Forest Muir was our objective. We were both fond of walking, but, like other boys, we did not do more than we could avoid. So, after crossing the brig at Zoar, we espied a ramshackle old pony cart going in our direction, and, with that bravado which is natural to all youngsters, we appealed for a lift. The only available seat was already fully occupied by two very stout old farmer bodies, who having pity on 'twa puir laddies with a long way to go,' stopped the cart.

Barrie and I clambered into the back of the cart and sat on the floor with legs stretched out under the seat heavily laden with the corpulent farmers. Thus we journeyed as far as they were going, and the while they carried on a conversation in a desultory manner, for the jolting cart with its extra load was not conducive to jointed speech. Their talk has long since escaped my memory, but I doubt if Barrie ever forgot it, and as it was the real 'Farfar,' I am sure he made use of it to enrich his vocabulary of local words and phrases.

Barrie possessed in those days that charm of wistfulness which I believe still characterizes him, and even then his aptitude for acquiring and storing knowledge was remarkable. The child has been father to the man.

That is a valuable and pleasing reminiscence of a brief but important period of Barrie's boyhood about which little has been told. It should be observed that if James was wistful then he could also be wilful. An authentic Forfar anecdote will illustrate his readiness to engage in pranks. Spring-Heeled Jack was a popular figure of juvenile 'bloods' in those days, sharing with Dick Turpin, Sweeney Todd and Sixteen-String Jack the admiration of young rascals who longed to emulate their fictitious exploits. Many attempted to play at Spring-Heeled Jack, for whom, I fancy, there was some basis of fact. On the road between Forfar and Zoar the presence of a Spring-Heeled Jack clothed in a white sheet, who leapt out of dark places and terrified servant maids and simple folk, was reported. One night when the carrier's cart was on its way to Forfar passing by Zoar the ghostly figure sprang towards it from a shady corner of the roadside. It chanced that a lame worthy was seated by the driver, his crutch in hand, and as the apparition came towards them he swung his crutch at it to such purpose that he felled its substantial framework to the ground. Within the sheet behold two young 'sackets,' James Barrie and Adam Harrison! The escapade was not too widely reported, as Adam's father was governor of Forfar Prison, but David Barrie would have something salutary to say to his son when he got home that night and owned up. To-day we like him the better for this boyish effort at frightfulness, and when, in later years, he wrote of villains jumping out at you from dark places in London he must have wagged his head at recollection of Spring-Heeled Jack and the Forfar Road at Zoar. Adam Harrison, who was two years Barrie's junior, died at the age of nineteen.

Mr. Charles Laing, of Falkirk, who was a schoolmate of Barrie's at the Academy, has sent me a reminiscence which shows the future romancer in his early rôle of story-teller:

I remember one summer afternoon when I left school in his company. Going out by the north gate we crossed the High Street, not without longing glances towards the window of 'Liz McLaren's' shop, where she dispensed 'black balls' and other toothsome eatables to the young gourmands of the Academy. Halfway down Green Street we turned into the Back Wynd, where we were greeted with the ring of hammer on anvil, and stopped for a minute, as all boys would, to watch Forsyth, the smith, sharpening chisels for 'Dargie,' the mason, plunging them when finished into a receptacle of water from which the steam rose as the heated iron sank.

After leaving the smith's door Jim began to tell me a story, and was fairly under way with it when we turned into the Limepots, or Canmore Street as it is now called, where presently we stopped before a high wall forming the boundary of the street to the southward. There was a green door in the wall, and Jim invited me to enter so that he could finish his story, in which I was as interested as the teller. Inside the door was a flight of steps flanked by walls of stone. We ascended the steps into the garden and I saw Barrie's home for the first and last time. It was situated on a little plateau about eight feet above the level of the street. The cottage and garden were surrounded with stone walls, and when the green door was closed there was a strange silence as of a cloister. No one was about, so we sat on the grass in front of the house while Jim continued his story. It was a 'strange eventful history' told with sparkling eye, full of the minutest detail and entrancing to the listener. The story is long since lost to my memory, but I recollect that on my way home I pondered over the incident and thought to myself 'He's a queer chap, Jim. Where can he have got that story? It's not like any a boy ever told.' And I have no doubt I concluded that he had heard it from the lips of some old body at Kirriemuir.

As I have already indicated, it is at this home in the Limepots that I would locate certain of the spiritual adventures of Barrie's early boyhood which in Margaret Ogilvy we are left to imagine as happening at Kirriemuir. Those brief Forfar days must on the whole have been an agreeable time to the young scholar, for it is a friendly town, perhaps a little too grey, with a quiet dignity about its main streets that reminds the visitor of some old Norman place; very foreign certainly, in its aspect, to any English provincial town. David Barrie would seem to have found his feet very soon in his new and unfamiliar sphere of work, and it is remembered by the few whose memories embrace that period that he was quickly an active and useful member of the East Free Church, which stands at a short distance from the house in Canmore Street, where his wife made many friends, although their sojourn in Forfar proved so brief. The Barries' sitting was on the minister's left, and I find that David and Margaret and also Jane Ann were regular subscribers to the Sustentation

Fund from May, 1870, until February, 1872, which may be taken as a record of their stay in Forfar.

At every turn where we might expect evidence of shyness, self-consciousness and retirement, we are met with the suggestion that David Barrie and Margaret Ogilvy were very self-possessed and sociable persons. Mr. David Anderson, for instance, was so drawn to the parents of his old schoolmate that for several years after young Barrie had gone out of his life he continued on terms of intimacy with them, frequently going over to enjoy their company when they had left Forfar and were finally settled at Kirriemuir. No better evidence of geniality and friendliness could be wished. The nature that can win the affection of other people's children is in tune with universal parenthood.

Things, on the whole, would appear to have prospered with the Barries in the county town. In spite of the ancient grudge the two towns bore each other, Forfar was friendly to the Kirriemuir family, yet when two years had barely run their course we find another move in contemplation. David Barrie has 'made good' as a factory clerk, he has been offered the responsible position of confidential clerk in the office of the Gairie Linen Works, which are to start operations at Kirriemuir at Whitsuntide, 1872, and thus has the satisfaction of returning to his native town in that 'genteel' capacity, and able to rent part of the new villa named Strathview, on the south side of the town at Southmuir. Half a century ago the office man stood relatively higher in the scale by contrast with the artisan than he does to-day. For many years after David Barrie had laid down his pen in the office of the Gairie Works his day-books and ledgers were shown to the young clerks as models which they were expected to follow.

As Strathview, next to the birthplace at Lilybank, will remain the most interesting of the Barrie landmarks a word or two of its history may here be set down. For some years the Barries' tenancy was restricted to the upper portion of the house, but when the ground floor rooms became vacant the Rev. David Ogilvy, perhaps with a long view to the inevitable retirement from his Motherwell charge, acquired the property, and his sister and brother-in-law continued to live in it, now occupying the whole, as his tenants. After he resigned the ministry in 1896, when he received the D.D. of Aberdeen University, Dr. Ogilvy resided for a time in Edinburgh, but made his home at Strathview with David Barrie, after the death of Mrs. Barrie, whose daughter, Sara, still acted as Dr. Ogilvy's housekeeper. The house, with all else that he possessed, was willed to Sara, but sixteen months after her father's death in 1902 she preceded her uncle in that last

37

journey to the cemetery on the Hill by some ten months, and not having altered his will Dr. Ogilvy thus died intestate. Alexander Barrie, as the eldest surviving nephew, had to take the necessary legal steps to gain possession of Strathview, and in this way the historic house became the property of Alexander Barrie's family. It is now in the possession of the youngest of his daughters, Miss Mary Cowan Barrie.

This new home-coming to Strathview, which was to be the last of Margaret Ogilvy's firesides, where great happiness and beautiful years were awaiting her, was also a home-returning for James, as a good many months were to pass before his next important move; indeed the rest of 1872, after the removal at the end of February, was spent between his Uncle Ogilvy's manse at Motherwell and Strathview; the longest spell of Kirriemuir that he ever had after his first leave-taking. And in this period, when free of the school and much in the company of his mother and sisters, we may place many of the episodes related in the quasi-biographic passages of his works. There was no garret, as we have seen, at the birthplace, nor at the Limepots, but there was one at Strathview, and as the kitchen and living-room were then on the first floor, here and now, if anywhere, we must stage that vital decision when he first tasted blood in the garret (a garret is an indispensable item in the *mise en scène* when the thoughts of imaginative youth turn to authorship) and determined that 'there could be no hum-dreadful-drum profession for me; literature was my game.' He was now twelve years old and 'nothing that happens after we are twelve matters very much.'

A quarter of a century later we have a glimpse of him from 'a dear little Scotswoman' who was blueing her doorstep in the Forfar Road as she chatted with an inquiring journalist (Miss Margaretta Byrde) in the summer of 1898. She said: 'Mony a time hae I seen him gae doon the Forfar Road, his mither wavin' an' he wavin' back tae her frae the window.'

Early in 1872 Alexander Barrie received his appointment as H.M. Inspector of Schools for the Dumfries district and set up house there at No. 6 Victoria Terrace, his sister Mary going thither to keep house for him. Once again the family circle at Strathview is contracted and James, who has been enjoying a long and happy interlude between two academical periods, finds himself withdrawn from the admiring companionship of mother and sisters to the purposeful task of education under his brother's guardianship. He becomes a scholar at Dumfries Academy in the autumn session of 1873. Now definitely a member of his

brother's household, James so continues through the most formative period of boyhood and youth.

When we say that Barrie, the romancer, won his early success
by writing of what lay nearest to his hand, we should remember
that all through the vital years of youth, until indeed he took his
M.A. at Edinburgh in 1882, Kirriemuir and its characters were not
the familiar objects of his daily contacts, but were studied by him
as a looker-on who had come back from a distance to observe
afresh, with an eye the keener from ranging elsewhere, the scenes
and persons so familiar in earlier boyhood that they might easily
have passed unregarded. His lucky star was in the ascendant
when he was first removed from home at the early age of eight
and again and finally, after sundry adventurings, in his thirteenth
year. Thus he could see Kirriemuir ever after in the tender light
of his own fresh boyhood and in the more magical light of his
mother's girlhood, through the stories she told him at the old house
where he was born, and at Forfar, and later at the ampler fireside
of Strathview when he came back from Dumfries or from
Edinburgh. The auld toon o' Kirrie never grew stale to him
from being too much with him late and soon. There is a point
here, I suggest, for the literary critic.

To piece together a picture of Barrie the young scholar at
Dumfries there is little need to forage beyond his own reminiscences, as openly given in recent years as in the earlier time of
his fame they were closely withheld. But before I draw upon
that rich and humorsome store there are one or two points of
fact and fiction to be noticed.

Exemplary of the fictitious Barrieana that used to bestrew the
personal columns of the press the following from a magazine of
1902 may be quoted:

It may be some consolation to the parents of the college boys who
know more of a flying wedge than of the *pons asinorum* to be told
that James Barrie, of A Window in Thrums, is only remembered at
school as a stupid boy who could play football well.

That gem was gravely headed 'From Athletics to Literature.'
Like so much of the inaccurate ana associated with his name, it
contains a half-truth, as Barrie in a speech at Dundee in May,
1922, said: 'I want to tell you for the last time, because I can get
no one to believe this, how extraordinarily good I was at football
as a boy. It is a solemn fact that I was seriously trained for a
Scottish fifteen.' If we accept this as the true half of the story
(though his Forfar playmate, it will be remembered, saw no sign

of athletic enthusiasm or prowess in him), we can assume the other half to be sheer invention. For witness the testimony of a classmate at Dumfries Academy, Mr. Alexander Dobie, Town Clerk of Maxwelltown, given to a London journalist in December, 1924, when the freedom of Dumfries was conferred upon the man of genius who was once a boy there:

Like young Barrie I was a wee bit shy lad myself in those days, coming from a country school to the Academy. But I could see then that he had a brilliant brain, and even his shyness could not hide that from his schoolfellows.

I remember well his splendid essays in English, his compositions, his fluent pen, his command of language. He was gifted with an extraordinary power of expressing his thoughts on paper. But if my memory serves me well young Barrie only worked when he felt inclined.

That, at any rate is not the invention of an irresponsible paragraphist, even allowing for the readiness with which a classmate might be expected to remember the splendid promise thirty years after the more splendid performance. Barrie was never a stupid scholar, we may be sure, though there is little evidence that he was ever a brilliant one. 'I did get two or three prizes at the Academy,' he says, ' and I always knew that I could get the second prize without working much, but that I could never get the first, however hard I worked.' The reason for this inability to achieve the first place was significant. There was another scholar at the Academy whose genius was already patent to all. The first place was always his; his brief life a tragedy of genius told in a few beautiful phrases fifty years after by his runner-up:

One day there was a timid knock at the door of the Rector's room, and a thin, frightened-looking boy, poorly clad and frail, came in. No doubt we all promptly summed him up as of small account, but I should not wonder though he was the greatest boy that ever sat on the forms of the old Dumfries Academy. I don't mean merely as a scholar, though in scholarship he was of another world from the rest of us; so he shone, pale star that he was, when he went to Glasgow University. and afterwards to Oxford, until—some one turned out that light. He was too poor, was that brave little adventurer. I think that explains it all.

The other boys felt that there was something winged about him, just as I did. He couldn't play games, and yet we all accepted him as our wonder one. What was it about James MacMillan that has stayed with me for so many years, and can still touch me to the quick?

WHERE PETER PAN WAS BORN
Moat Brae, Dumfries, and its garden by the River Nith, where Barrie played as
a schoolboy.

Face page 40

GROUP AT DUMFRIES ACADEMY IN 1874
Barrie is first on left in back row.

THE YOUNG SCHOLAR

I felt, when we were boys, that he was—a Presence, and I feel it still. Literature was to be his game, and what play he might have made with it! Your lost might-have-been.

> His spirit's bark is driven
> Far from the shore, far from the trembling throng,
> Whose sails were never to the tempest given.

I think the shade of Burns was restless on the night the caretaker's boy died.

We shall not be far wrong if we credit this long-forgotten James MacMillan with some share in influencing James Barrie to make literature his game also. MacMillan's grave, in St. Michael's Churchyard, Dumfries, is carefully tended, thanks to the kindly thought of his unsuccessful competitor for the first prize. In view of MacMillan's influence on young Barrie I am glad to be able to give the following excerpt from the Rector's report of the school year in which that ill-fated scholar passed away:

It was the sad duty of some of us a few days ago to follow to the grave the remains of another distinguished alumnus of this school, Mr. James MacMillan. He was one of the town bursars, and left in 1878, after obtaining the honourable position of dux of the school. His college career, both at Glasgow and Oxford, was very brilliant, but he was laid prostrate by an insidious disease, and for many a long year awaited the summons to depart. Very few young men have the ability to achieve equal success in the academical career, but all can imitate his untiring devotion to work and modesty in the midst of success. Had his health been equal to his industry and ability he would have made his name known in the world.

It was here that Barrie's mind was beginning to dwell upon authorship: Dumfries, with its landmarks of Burns and Edward Irving, the occasional visits of Carlyle, who had been Irving's rival, and the presence there of the philosopher's niece, Mary Carlyle Aitken, a friend of the Barries, still happily surviving at a great age: we can see why James's thoughts were being bent towards literature. Dumfries was really to be the making of him; his lucky star was beaming there. And yet the name of the place figures about as rarely in his works as that of Glasgow, so that had we not his own testimony to assure us we might suppose his days there to have been as colourless as those in the great city by the Clyde. Fortunately he has said so much of Dumfries in recent years that we are left in no doubt as to the zestful life he had there, or the value of those 'five happiest years' at its Academy in helping him along the road of scholarship. We can brush aside all the popular newspaper twaddle about his readiness to play truant, his excessive shyness towards his fellows, his poor achievements as a scholar, and see him as a very human lad, alive to all the high concerns of local boyhood, a bright and eager student, but outstanding from the ruck in his impish gift of humour. I like to think it may have been true that he wrote to the local papers over the signature of 'Paterfamilias' urging that pupils should have longer holidays, but I regard with suspicion the comment of him who first told the story: 'The pity is that the letter has not been preserved.' Barrie from the first has not only been a humorist, but the cause of humour in others.

Perhaps it was natural that at a Scottish school the most primitive form of humour should obtain. Still it is worth noticing that, by way of redressing the national deficiency first observed by Sydney Smith and since detected by every other Englishman, a manuscript magazine was started at Dumfries Academy with the promising title of The Clown. Its editor was Wellwood Anderson, whose uncle, Sir James Anderson, had commanded the 'Great Eastern' fifteen or sixteen years before at the laying of the first Atlantic cable. The amateur editor's father was the proprietor of a bookshop and library in the High Street, and noting the eager curiosity about all things literary displayed by our young scholar he gave him the run of the shop and the book-crowded attics, so that old bookshop soon became the portals of Paradise to the lad from Kirrie. To The Clown Barrie contributed in four parts: Reckolections of a Schoolmaster: Edited by James Barrie, M.A., A.S.S., LL.D. They were written in the style of misspelling originated by Josh Billings. He also wrote eight verses on The Seven Ages of man. In the editor's Answers to Correspondents appeared the first appreciation of the young humorist:

J. B.—Your 'Reckolections' are exceedingly well composed. Many thanks for No. 1 and No. 2. We will be very glad to hear from you again soon.

The reader will note the familiar Scottish misuse of 'will.' The unique four numbers of The Clown, totalling thirty-two closely written pages, fetched £510 at auction in London on June 21st, 1929. The significance of Barrie's contribution lies in its title; already you will perceive the selective ingenuity of its writer at work, for thus early he had begun to pose as a dominie, and in the assumed rôle of schoolmaster he was, within less than fifteen years from this date, to take the reading world by storm. 'Early this

morning I opened a window in my schoolhouse in the glen of
Quharity' are the first words of Auld Licht Idylls, and in 1892
the supposititious narrator of The Little Minister was still the
schoolmaster of the Glen.   The lad who was something of a
puzzle to his fellow-scholars at Dumfries Academy knew very
well what he was about, and having hit upon a good idea he cherished
it with a shrewd sense of its literary value.   'A stupid schoolboy
who was good at athletics'—how he must have chuckled when
he read that sort of stuff in the days of his success.   His enthusiasm for cricket, which gave rise to the legend, had more
to feed upon at Dumfries than at Kirriemuir or Forfar, and the
statement that his earliest printed lines were reports of his school
cricket matches for the local papers is probably true.

The end of his happy years in Dumfries was almost in sight
by the time his literary ambitions had advanced from school-
magazine sketches and brief cricket reports to the writing of a
three-volume novel.   At least it would have been a 'three decker,'
as they used to be called, had it ever got into type.   A Child of
Nature was the title; its background, naturally, Dumfries.   It
ran to 100,000 words and its author admits that 'it was a very
cynical work.'   This must have been the manuscript which the
eighteen-year-old author submitted to a publisher, who pronounced upon it favourably as 'the work of a clever young lady'
and offered to swing open the gates of literary fame to its writer
at the modest cost of one hundred pounds (he had a sixpence).
I say 'must have been,' but who knows that this publisher ever
existed outside the imagination of the author?   Ever since he
mingled the letters A.S.S. with others that were merely anticipatory after his name in the superscription of his Reckolections
of a Schoolmaster Barrie has shown a disarming readiness to
make fun of himself, and many of the comic legends that cluster
about his name have grown from commentators taking seriously
what he said in jest.   Hence my caution in accepting even so
likely a story as that about the clever young lady.   But there
need be no doubt about the novel itself, as its author has confessed
that forty-five years afterwards he came upon the manuscript
'and gently tore it up—just in case it should fall into the wrong
hands, you know.'   Bang went three or four thousand pounds
at that tearing.

It was at Dumfries that his taste for reading could be indulged
more freely than at Kirriemuir or at Forfar.   While neither father
nor mother was unduly narrow in the range of reading which they
permitted, there would still be a certain consciousness of restraint
at Kirriemuir and Forfar, which would press more lightly upon

the young scholar at Dumfries, where the married brother, *in loco parentis*, was evidently liberal-minded in the latitude he allowed. In consequence, the usual boyish tastes could be indulged with freedom: there was no priggish selectiveness in the subject matter of young Barrie's reading.

Here is the unashamed admission publicly put on record by him (Wallasey, February 27th, 1924):

In those tender days I used, when in funds, to devour secretly penny dreadfuls, magazines containing exclusively sanguinary matter. They were largely tales about heroic highwaymen and piracy on the high seas, but what most enamoured me were the stories of goings-on at English boarding schools. How different from the hum-dreadful-drum of my school. The masters were sneaks and the boys blew them up with gunpowder. I felt that those were the schools for me. My mind became so set on explosions that when a Sassenach sent me a box containing mysterious little red and blue tubes, I placed them one by one near the fire and then darted back, in confidence that they would go off. I daresay I wept when I discovered that they were only coloured chalks.

Soon came the awakening—and with it the moral, stalking toward me like two little policemen. In the pages of a very different sort of juvenile periodical called Chatterbox—a word that makes me quake and look behind me still—I read an article on the dire future in store for those who read penny dreadfuls. I tried to stand up to it—but no, no, not when black night fell. On such a night—the better for my fearful deed—I stole off to a distant field, my pockets stuffed with back numbers—a shovel concealed up my little waistcoat—and deep in the bowels of the earth I buried the evidence of guilt. If you would know how I felt for days afterwards I refer you to the similar story of Jonas Chuzzlewit.

Perhaps his introduction to Chatterbox suggests a friendly effort to wean him from Sweeney Todd and Spring-Heeled Jack; but the success of it, here so amusingly dramatised, was, I feel sure, only temporary. The fact that Barrie has subsequently located this episode of the burial of these 'penny bloods' at Kirriemuir in a field at Pathhead Farm (T'nowhead of the Idylls) need not diminish its authenticity. 'It was ages ago, but I could walk straight to that hole in the field now and delve for the remains.' Yet, I think it would be discreet not to put him to the test. It implies that he was a keen reader of romantic stuff before he was eight years old. Pathhead was 'a distant field' from the Tenements, but it was only a few yards away from Strathview. We must not hold him too closely to the actual spot of any adventure of his boyhood: he has the right to revise his stage settings as his fancy may dictate. But those boyhood days in Dumfries were the great days of Red Indian and pirate fiction. Mayne Reid with his Scalp Hunters and Rifle Rangers had long been a favourite; Butler's Wild North Land came out the year that Barrie went to Dumfries; W. H. G. Kingston, whose Peter the Whaler had had nearly a quarter of a century of popularity, was in the midst of his captivating series of 'Threes,' The Three Lieutenants appearing in 1874 and The Three Commanders brightening the following year for boyhood. Ascott R. Hope (A. R. H. Moncrieff, who died so recently as 1927) was also spinning his jolly yarns beloved of young Barrie, as one may judge from certain allusions in My Lady Nicotine. Above all, R. M. Ballantyne was good for at least two new books every twelvemonth, and his immortal Coral Island was our young scholar's prime favourite. When the Jubilee Edition of The Coral Island was published in 1907 it carried a charming tribute from Barrie in which his boyish enthusiasm for that delicious story was thus recalled:

Ballantyne was for long my man, and I used to study a column in The Spectator about 'forthcoming books,' waiting for his next as for the pit door to open. He wrote many (I think I looked upon him as the author of the Hundred Best Books, and wondered why that list ever needed to be a subject of controversy), but they all lagged behind The Coral Island. It egged me on, not merely to being wrecked every Saturday for many months in a long-suffering garden, but to my first work of fiction, a record of our adventures, The Log-Book.
We had a sufficiently mysterious cave, that had not been a cave until we named it, and here we grimly ate coconuts, stoned from the trees which not even Jack nor Ralph nor Peterkin would have recognized as likely to bear them. And more or less bravely we suffered for the same, the coconuts not being of the season that yielded Peterkin his lemonade. Here, too, we had a fire, lit as Jack contrived to light his, by rubbing two sticks together. So we said (even in The Log-Book, I daresay); but, of course, this fire came by more plebeian means, and never in our hearts did we believe in the efficacy of the sticks. No boy, so far as I knew, did believe in them. It seemed too beautiful a dream.

But forty years elapse, the scene changes to 'a solemn London club' (the Reform) and we are to picture the author of Peter Pan and an American friend meeting him there for the express purpose of demonstrating the making of fire as Jack had done it. 'In half a minute my friend and I had made a fire, at which we lit our cigars and smoked to the memory of Ballantyne and The Coral Island.' Here we have a glimpse of the self that went to the

making of the immortal Peter. For the veritable beginning
of Peter Pan was in that same Dumfries garden, a fact which we
have on the authority of the dramatist himself:

When the shades of night began to fall, certain young mathematicians
changed their skins, crept up walls and down trees and became pirates
in a sort of Odyssey that was long afterwards to become the play of
Peter Pan. For our escapades in a certain Dumfries garden, which
is enchanted land to me, were certainly the genesis of that nefarious
work. We lived in the tree-tops, on coconuts attached thereto, and
that were in bad condition; we were buccaneers and I kept the log-book
of our depredations, an eerie journal, without a triangle in it to mar the
beauty of its page.

'A certain Dumfries garden' was that attached to the residence
of the Sheriff Clerk of the time, Henry Gordon, whose two sons,
Hal and Stuart, were schoolfellows of Barrie. Its grounds sloped
to the waters of the Nith and it was called Moat Brae, a name that
endures in the Moat Brae Nursing Home which occupies the
residence and whose patients are sunned back to health amid
the sylvan scenes of those boyish adventures that were the remote
beginning of an immortal story. The house is an imposing one
of red sandstone with pleasing Tudor features, and the garden,
still crowded with massive trees, slopes very steeply to the waters
of the Nith below, where anglers are wont to be busy with rod and
line and where stately swans enliven a scene of peace and beauty.

We can see the germ of a famous scene in Peter Pan in the
following excerpt from the earliest of all Barrie's speeches, an
impromptu effort on the occasion of his distributing the prizes
at the Dumfries Academy at the end of June, 1893:

When I came to the Academy I meant to work hard—for a few days
at any rate—and I should have worked hard if it had not been for
another boy who led me astray. I do not mind telling you that his
name was Stuart Gordon. He came to me in my class and said 'What
is your name?' I told him. It did not seem to please him, and he
said he would call me 'Sixteen-String Jack.' I asked him his name,
and he said it was 'Dare Devil Dick.' Dare Devil Dick was a character
we used to take in weekly in penny numbers. He was not much believed in by our relatives, so we used to take him home under our waist-
coats. Dare Devil Dick's schooldays had been rather trying. One
of his masters had a difference with him about some matter of scholastic
discipline, and his master would not give way. You know what masters
are! So Dare Devil Dick retired from the school, and went away to
the Spanish Main and became a pirate. There was one picture I
shall never forget. It was Dare Devil Dick standing on the deck with

46

a number of pirates around him. A young lady was on each arm; one was fair and the other was dark—all is fair and dark in novels—and both young ladies had fainted; while Dare Devil Dick was saying: 'Advance another step, and I will blow up the powder magazine, and send you into eternity!' The Dumfries version of Dare Devil Dick asked me to join his pirate crew. I joined, and it was fatal to my prize-taking.

In that same speech he gave another amusing recollection of his Academy days which it would be a pity not to rescue from the oblivion of The Dumfries Courier and Herald of July 1st, 1893:

In my days in Dumfries Academy the girls of the school used to have books called 'Querist Albums' and the boys had a whole page on which to write their favourite authors or say whether they believed in love at first sight. In looking up one of those lately with my name in it I find my pet antipathy was the Academy bell. I have changed in that way now, but the Academy bell has not. My pet antipathy! I look back upon it with very pleasant feelings and very sad ones, too.

Clearly it is no exaggeration to say that Dumfries was to be the making of our author; Dumfries more than Kirriemuir. Those five years, whose freight of happiness is reflected in all his memories, definitely inclined him to romance and drama. His first editor, that Wellwood Anderson of The Clown, was also his first associate in theatricals that marked an immense advance on the days of the Bank Street toy theatre. He it was who induced young Barrie to become honorary secretary of the Dumfries Amateur Dramatic Club, of which he himself was the acting manager and moving spirit. Their first performances took place at the Assembly Rooms in the winter of 1876. The principal item was 'Le petit drame sensationel, en six tableaux, entitled Bandelero the Bandit.' The author of this piece was none other than J. M. Barrie, and the young dramatist himself appeared as Smike, the play being based upon some incidents in a Fenimore Cooper romance. The performance was not allowed to pass without a protest from a local minister who in the columns of The Dumfries Standard upbraided the Academy authorities for having allowed 'certain young men to befool themselves.' How pleased the author-actor would be to see himself already described as a young man!

In view of Barrie's later associations as a playwright with J. L. Toole and his historic theatre in King William Street, Strand, it is worth noting that Toole was the stage favourite of

47

both young Anderson and Barrie, which accounts for Clement
Scott's Off the Line, revised and condensed by Anderson,
preceding Bandelero, and an abridged version of Paul Pry completing the triple bill. Toole was, of course, the comic hero of
both these plays. The chronicler to whom I am indebted for the
information about the Dumfries theatricals adds:

In those days there were no girls in the Dumfries Academy available
as lady 'amatoors' and therefore the management had a serious difficulty
to face in filling the female parts. But this was solved by a com-
promise, Anderson consenting to appear in petticoats as Lizzie Coke
in Off the Line and Barrie impersonating Phoebe in Paul Pry.

If no girls were available that must have been because of the
low ebb of dramatic talent among them, for the Academy must
be identified with that 'mixed school of about 500 pupils' where
the girls were forward enough to take a plebiscite as to which
boy had the pleasantest smile. 'I won,' Barrie confesses, 'with
the result that I lost my smile. I suppose it is still jigging about
somewhere in the world, but it has never come back to me. A
tragedy in a nutshell. The moral, the old one—trustful little
boys, beware of girls.' Three elderly married ladies who attended
his burgess ceremony in 1924 had been girls at the Academy when
he was a scholar there.

From an article appearing in the old Westminster Gazette,
in February, 1904, I glean some further particulars of the last
season of the Dumfries theatricals with which Barrie was identified. The performances took place early in the year, first at the
Assembly Rooms and then at the Crichton Institution; he went
to Edinburgh University in the Autumn of that year (1878):

The second season of the Dumfries Amateur Dramatic Club opened
quite auspiciously with a formidable list of patrons. It was headed by
the Duke of Buccleuch, and included Henry Irving, W. H. Kendal,
Shiel Barry, Lionel Brough, and Charles Collette; and the public
performance took place in March, 1878. Again there was a triple bill,
opening with 'A new and original farcical absurdity in one confused act,
entitled Awkwardly Alike; or Which is Brown?' It was adapted by
Wellwood Anderson from something he had seen at an entertainment
given by the Wardroper Brothers. This was followed by The Weavers,
described on the programme as 'Mr. J. L. Toole's favourite comic drama
in one act,' in which Barrie played Adele and Anderson appeared as
Simmons; and finally we had The Shufflerig Party, with Barrie as
the Rev. Heavycloud Weatherdull. There are many Dumfriesians
scattered about who can look back over the past six-and-twenty years
and recall young Barrie's impersonation of a character somewhat

resembling that of Aminadab Sleek, in The Serious Family, the exquisite gravity of which sent the people into fits of laughter. The audience roared, too, over Barrie's deportment as Mrs. Brown (Adele) in The Weavers, especially when, with his characteristic burr, he cried out to Brown across the table, 'Har-r-ry, dear-r-r; you shouldn't eat peas with your-r-r knife!'

But we have Barrie himself to draw upon as a source of reminiscence of these distant and delectable days when his destiny was being shaped, and once more we have recourse to that wonderful Dumfries speech of his wherein sentiment and humour were so graciously united with the frankest statement of personal experience:

My first play was very properly written for the Dumfries Academy Dramatic Society, on whose boards I also made my only appearances as an actor. That was due to the histrionic enthusiasm of an Academy boy, certainly the best amateur actor I have ever seen, who I am glad to know is here to-day, and who blushes so easily—at least he blushed easily a century or two ago—that I shall cleverly conceal his identity under the name of Wedd. Never can there have been a more devoted follower of the Muse, or a stage manager with more ingratiating ways. During the winters of our existence his pockets were always bulging with stage directions, which fell on the floor as he was being caned, and all the time the masters were submitting him to drastic treatment he was considering how they would do for walking gentlemen. Our Wedd was truly great in low comedy, but not so convincing as a young lady with her hair attached to her hat, the sort of part for which he usually cast me. I may perhaps be allowed to tell you without unpardonable elation—so many years having elapsed—that at one of our performances a male member of the audience asked for an introduction. [Barrie does not mention that on this occasion the performance took place at the Crichton Mental Institution!] I think I did greatest credit to our admired Wedd on one occasion when the curtain rose on my husband and me about to partake of breakfast, and in his stage-fright my husband pulled the table cover and its contents to the floor. How would a superb actress have risen to that emergency? I have asked some of them—Sarah Bernhardt and others—and none of them conceived anything equal to what that Adele did—Adele was my name, I was taken from the French—but the unworthy youth who played my husband *would* call me Addle, to my annoyance—I went behind him, and, putting my arms round his neck—yet not forgetting even in that supreme moment to be wary about my hair and hat—I said, 'You clumsy darling!' The house rose—I don't mean they went out—several of them cheered, led on by Wedd who, when not actually on the stage himself, was always somewhere in hiding, leading the applause.

49

Thus was a great comedienne lost to the world. The next time I saw that play was in London, with Miss Irene Vanbrugh in my part. You may guess I was critical, and she was nervous. I told her I thought her good, but that she was lacking in some of my womanly touches.

The astute reader will find no great difficulty in piercing the disguise of Wedd, nor will he hesitate to agree with me about the constancy of Barrie's lucky star: every day of the young scholar's time in Dumfries was edging him famewards with just the kind of experience his peculiar genius required for its fulfilment. How ludicrous, too, all the stories of youthful taciturnity appear in face of these genial remembrances of old friendship, to which the future dramatist owed at least some slight measure of his success.

A genuine skill in sketching and caricature was another of the accomplishments for which the young scholar was noted at Dumfries. When Dr. Cranstoun, his old headmaster, died at Stroud, Gloucestershire, a good many years ago, it was stated that among his treasured possessions was a collection of caricatures drawn by his famous pupil. I am not aware that any example of Barrie's graphic art has ever been reproduced, so that we must rely on those who have seen them for the opinion of their merit: but in one of his Academy reminiscences there is good confirmation that they were something out of the run of ordinary amateur pencillings:

Once a learned professor came to the Academy to examine us, and after some days of it I decided to absent myself from the final proceedings. Other boys were sent in pursuit, and there was a hot chase until I discovered that if I went slowly they also went slowly: that, in short, they were as little desirous of returning to Lochaber as I was. Thus did they throw away those precious hours. I ought to have exposed them. I do so now. As it was, I remember going to the station and from a safe place watching the professor go off in his train, before I returned to the school to find, alas! that the exams were over. But Dr. Cranstoun had me that day, for he told me the professor had wanted me back only to commend me for a confiscated book of sketches.

These were, no doubt, the identical sketches I have mentioned, so that the headmaster would seem to have held on to them to the end. Even in his schoolmasters the young scholar was fortunate: this act of Dr. Cranstoun was clearly one of admiration and Barrie's reference to the mathematical master, John Neilson, has the true ring of affectionate remembrance. It was surely a unique experience for a famous author publicly to meet again after forty-six years his old schoolmaster, aged eighty-six, and to pay him this fine tribute:

THE YOUNG SCHOLAR

I have more pride in the presence of my old mathematical master here to-day than if you had produced any other man in Scotland. Those of you here who have sat under him, and many thousands outside, have reason, as I have, to roll that name (John Neilson) affectionately on the tongue, not necessarily because he was so determined to make us mathematicians whatever might be our own views on the subject—and I for one differed from him profoundly—but because in our most impressionable years he set us an example of conduct and character that kept a guiding hand on our shoulders when we went out into the world.

For many years he has been an ornament to what I think must now be called the most important of all professions. I have sought the company of schoolmasters in England because I find them often to be the pick of men, but if this were their prize-getting day and I had the distribution of the honours I know whom I should begin with—'First Prize, John Neilson.'

I wish I had said that to him long ago in my Academy days; it might have got a prize for me out of him. No, it wouldn't, no one could ever get around that man. The other masters one could work upon with some hope of a modest success—even Dr. Cranstoun, that fine scholar —but Mr. Neilson, the winds of our artifice beat upon him in vain. He was so dogged about his triangles that even I can still wave a hand of acquaintance to them if we meet in the market-place.

John Neilson died on September 24th, 1928, at his home in Catherine Terrace, Dumfries, in his ninety-first year, and among the floral tributes laid upon his grave was one that bore these words: 'With affectionate memories of Neilson, of whom Dumfries may well be proud, as I am of having been his pupil.—Barrie.'

Before we take leave of Dumfries and follow our young scholar to Edinburgh, whither his star next leads, there remain certain matters of interest to set down. First must be recorded his glimpses of Carlyle, who thus early had become chief of his literary enthusiasms, the main object of his hero-worship. Miss Lillian K. Barrie, eldest of the four daughters of Alexander Barrie, was an infant when her Uncle James, as an Edinburgh student, was back on a vacation visit at his brother's new home in Dumfries, Greenbank (now called Ben Reay), a fine villa in St. Michael's Street. In 1924 she was headmistress of Wallasey High School for Girls, and she persuaded Sir James to make one of his rare public appearances in distributing the prizes to the scholars on February 27th of that year. It was a proud day for Miss Barrie, and a happy one for her uncle, who indeed has never spoken in public without creating a desire in his listeners to hear him again at the earliest opportunity. For the moment we are concerned with his Dumfries reminiscences, which ran as follows:

BARRIE: THE STORY OF A GENIUS

I remember particularly one day when she (Miss Barrie) was about a year old. I think she was dressed—our heroine was dressed in one of those white things that were so fashionable that year, and she wore such a pretty bonnet. The scene was a pleasant Scottish town, and a very great man was passing at the end of our road. So I whipped up our heroine in my arms and ran with her to the gate, in order that she might be able to say in after-years that she had once seen Thomas Carlyle. In my school days I had often seen him myself, in his great shovel hat and cloak and thunderous staff—Jove come down for a stroll in his favourite country—and scores of times I had doffed my hat to him, but, alas, with no response. Someone, to boast of having been spoken to by Carlyle, once asked him on that road how far it was to Lockerbie, but he just pointed with his staff to a mile-stone and stalked on. I hoped he would bless your Miss Barrie that day, and perhaps he did, but it didn't sound like that. In any case it is interesting to us to know that those two once met.

Of Barrie himself a quaint story was recalled by Mr. Alexander Dobie, whom we have encountered earlier in this chapter. It concerns a trout stream near Dumfries that bears the queer name of 'Ae.' Young Barrie was travelling in a train between Lockerbie and Dumfries, and at a point where the line runs alongside the stream an old gentleman sitting opposite to Barrie inquired the name of the river. The incident, we are told, was recorded by Barrie himself in the school magazine somewhat in this manner (for I cannot suppose the original text has been followed):

I was meditating at the time, so only answered 'Ae.' Mistaking the monosyllable for the more familiar 'Eh?' the stranger repeated his query, and got the same answer. He tried the question a third time in a different form, and again the answer seemed to be the unattractive Scottish 'Eh?' Thereupon he lost his temper, and in explosive language said what he thought about the impoliteness of the impertinent young rascal.

The young rascal could have told the stranger many things about the Ae or the Cluden or any of the streams in the neighbourhood, for he was much given to rambling by their banks, and had a continual delight, not only in exploring the byways of the historic old town, but in tramping the surrounding countryside.

The country round Dumfries! [I quote once more the Burgess speech]. It is a lovely spot, God wot. Criffel, the Nith frozen, the Nith released, Torthorwold, Caerlaverock, Lincluden, the Solway, the very names of them are music to Scottish ears; when you and I were young they were our partners in the ball. We must always have something in common that others cannot share if we have sat out a

dance with the Cluden. She was my favourite partner of all, and sometimes she sang to me and sometimes I had a book with me to improve
her mind. Still I see

> . . . the river dimple by
> Holding its face up to the sky.

I wooed her in a canoe, but she was a capricious mistress and often
went off with the canoe, leaving me with the water. I daresay she is
carrying on the same diversions still—the Helens of Troy never mend
their ways. The next time one of you goes in pursuit of her—in a
canoe—I wish you would give her my love and say that I never think
of her without feeling wet.

Although the speech from which I have quoted so freely was
the raciest and most characteristic he has ever delivered, it was
not his first platform appearance in the town which was endeared
to him by such precious memories of youth. Thirty-one years
before (June, 1893), in the earlier period of his fame, the first
of all his speeches was made in the old Academy when he distributed the prizes at the end of the session. He had bargained
that he should not be asked to speak, but the occasion stirred
him to reminiscences, and I have often heard it said that on the
spur of the moment he delivered a speech brimful of his inimitable
fun and kindly memories. The full report of that maiden speech,
from which I have quoted on pages 46 and 47, is before me
now, but by comparison with the mellow richness of that of
1924 it reads thin and a little forced. It contains little that
the speaker did not say again to far better advantage—perhaps
not unnaturally—thirty years later.

And so to Edinburgh.

CHAPTER IV

HIS EDINBURGH DAYS

1878–1882

STEVENSON has observed that the happiest lot in life is to be born a Scotsman. I am far from being persuaded of the truth of this reflection, but I suggest that no happier lot can befall a young Scotsman than to be sent to Edinburgh University, though it ill becomes a Glasgow man to make this admission. No other town in the British Isles is so designed by nature and man for the inspiration of imaginative youth. Its winds may be 'snell, blae, nirly and scowthering' as R. L. S. records, but there is an ichor in its air that stirs the blood of youth, just as its romantic atmosphere stirs the imagination.

The Castle Rock of Edinburgh seems to give the city a place among the eternities: it creates in the beholder a sense of durable things. It is easy for the walker in Princes Street to feel that the glorious scene he looks upon will remain in its dominating features unchanged through the ages. And if he knows aught of its history every close and wynd is a scene in the human drama; a motley procession of great men and women, and great rascals, passes before the mind's eye. Comes first, no doubt, Queen Mary, with shades of the other three Marys; Darnley, Rizzio, John Knox, half a dozen Jameses that were kings, five of them shadowy, the sixth very distinct and assertive; Montrose goes by in a cart to his high gallows near the Mercat Cross, the Marquis of Argyll to be beheaded at the same fateful spot; dukes, earls, countesses galore, all with names magical of the past; queer characters such as Jenny Geddes and Lord Monboddo, picturesque villains like Deacon Brodie (not forgetting Burke and Hare), men of genius by the score: Dugald Stewart, Sir Walter Scott, Allan Ramsay, Fergusson, Christopher North, David Wilkie, Blackie, Lister, Young Simpson, Noel Paton, R. L. S. himself. A list of famous names associated with Edinburgh would be the framework for a history of Scottish genius. The bookish student will be the most likely to have a vision of that wonderful boy with

54

the lame leg scaling the giddy heights of the Castle Rock around which he was to weave his wizard spell when he had become 'Shirra' and the mysterious creator of the Waverleys. George Borrow, too, may appear to those who know his story, emulating the climbing feats of the great Sir Walter: an alien and intrusive figure his.

The spell of the place is as little to be evaded as its blustering winds; its appeal to the mind is as instant as its appeal to the eye. The acropolis-like Calton Hill suggested to N. P. Willis his epithet of 'Modern Athens,' but in the grand days of Scott that might even have been justified by its intellectual life. The intellectual atmosphere of Edinburgh has a fine invigoration for youth, and when Barrie turns up there, and on October 30th, 1878, has his name—'James M. Barrie, Kirriemuir'—entered in the Matriculation Album of its three-hundred-years-old university, that atmosphere is at its briskest. Certainly at no later time has eagerness after the things of the mind been more marked. The definite literary movement which we look back upon to-day as the peculiar manifestation of the 'nineties was then germinating. Stevenson had met Henley in the Edinburgh Infirmary five years earlier—R. L. S. had but recently quitted the university without a degree—and the famous friendship that began there was to prove most fruitful in the 'nineties when the one had gone to his grave on Mount Vaea and the other had fulfilled his great inspirational office as editor of The Scots (later National) Observer. An Inland Voyage had appeared in the May of 1878 and the lad who had come to Edinburgh University a few months later, in a speech which he made in Edinburgh eighteen years on at the Stevenson Memorial Meeting in the Music Hall, said of its author:

It has been said that he cared little about his old university in Edinburgh, but this is not true. The other day I heard of a letter Stevenson had written to one of his oldest friends. It was written from the South Seas. He said he was in a boat as he wrote, and while he had been lying there he had been thinking of his old days at Edinburgh University, the dreams he had dreamt in those days, and how little he had thought at that time that they would be realised now; and now they had been realised, and it had occurred to him that out of gratitude he might have put at the Corner of Lothian Street a tablet in which that little story might be inscribed, so that students who had grown downhearted might perchance look up and be cheered. I do not know whether that tablet will ever be put up, but I dare say many students will seem to see it there, and take comfort. I know another body of young men —younger men a little than Mr. Stevenson at all events—who took him as their model, who looked up to him as their example—I mean the younger writers of to-day of all classes, not merely the romancers, the realists as they are called, the idealists as they are called, the pessimists as they are called—they all see with different eyes, but they are all agreed that Stevenson, beyond all other writers of his time, was the man who showed them how to put their houses in order before they began to write, and in what spirit they should write, and with what aim, and with what clean tools, and with what honesty of toil. They know from him that however poor their books may be they are not disgraced if they have done their best, and, however popular, if they are not written with some of his aims they are only cumberers of the ground. They are only soldiers in the ranks, but they are proud to claim him as their leader, and when he calls his muster-roll he will hear them all answer their names, 'Here, here, here.' He is dead, but he still carries their flag, and because of him the most worthy of us are more worthy, and the meanest of us a little less mean.

Now I would not be thought to suggest that Barrie in 1878 was already a Stevensonian; nobody, other than Henley perhaps, so early had appreciated the genuis of R. L. S. It is probable that An Inland Voyage was unknown to our student, though The Sire de Maletroit's Door and some of the other stories and studies which had graced the fine magazines of that time (so strangely unlike the tasteless ephemeræ of to-day) would possibly be familiar to so omnivorous a reader as young Barrie, who had left the book-loving home of his brother Alexander for a ' crow's nest ' in Edinburgh. We have seen that at Dumfries his thoughts were definitely bent towards the literary life; already he was reading books not in the casual way of the common reader, but with that discriminating enjoyment which arises from observation of the author's style, ingenuity of construction and perception of character; he was reading as one who hoped some day that he, too, might be able to write ' a tale which holdeth children from play and old men from the chimney corner.' There might have been in the minds of his parents a thought of the pulpit or the law for their son James. That good brother who had been almost as a father to him since he was eight years old, and who was responsible for his maintenance at the University, would probably have thoughts of a scholastic career for him. Perhaps none of these careers would have been unattractive to the young student. I have a notion that in The Little Minister we may discern the romancer playing with the fancy of himself in the leading rôle; his literary attitude to lawyers is uncommonly sympathetic, and he has said that the teacher's is the noblest of the professions. But while the mind of the undergraduate may have dwelt with pleasant anticipation on all three callings, the ruling passion for everything literary brooked no denial.

THE OLD ACADEMY, DUMFRIES
A larger modern building with an imposing pillared front has taken its place.

VICTORIA TERRACE, DUMFRIES
At No. 6 J. M. Barrie lived 1873 to 1878 with his brother, Alexander.

Face page 56

TWO LANDMARKS OF BARRIE'S EDINBURGH DAYS

No. 14 Cumberland Street where the young student lodged on the top floor, and No. 20 Shandwick Place, a later lodging. The ground floor has been greatly altered for business premises in later years.

In his talks at home in Kirriemuir on his vacation visits there he may have been told the story of John R. Fyfe, the weaver who became a journalist. Fyfe's father had been a weaver and put his son to the loom in the common way of Kirrie folk, but the young lad was so set upon acquiring knowledge that he pursued it as keenly as others sought diversion, and having a natural gift for literary expression got some articles printed in The Perthshire Advertiser, whose staff he was invited to join, and so said good-bye to his loom. In 1832, at the age of twenty-two, he was a reporter on The Scotsman in Edinburgh and remained there some thirteen years, being at one time associated with Hugh Miller on the famous Witness. His next move took him to The Times, on which he speedily made a name as a brilliant journalist, but his life was cut short in 1854 when only forty-four years had gone. His son, however, named James Hamilton Fyfe (the mother was a Hamilton) also became a successful journalist and barrister-at-law, and with Frederick Greenwood founded The Pall Mall Gazette, a fact that may have had some connexion with Greenwood's early partiality to Barrie's Auld Licht sketches. Mr. H. Hamilton Fyfe, for many years the favourite special correspondent of The Daily Mail in world-wide travels, is the eldest son of the second Fyfe, so that the three generations now span just on a century of journalism.

Admiration and emulation are the true determinants in most careers. John R. Fyfe was the one hero of Kirriemuir who had left the loom to become a journalist; and the distance between a hand-loom in a Kirrie cottage and a position on The Times literary staff in its grandest days is hardly measurable. There were many eminent ministers and lawyers of whom Margaret Ogilvy had told her boy all that was likely to inspire him to go and do likewise, but here was a weaver who had done the big picturesque thing: the thing to fire the mind of a bookish youth, and above all the thing that he, with far better preparation, might also do. It is no mere fancy of mine when I suggest that in Rob Angus, the hero of When a Man's Single, we have a fictive figure whose origin might be traced to some Margaret Ogilvy story of the first Fyfe, although he had been dead long years before she was telling stories of her early days to her son James. It is at least highly probable that the young Edinburgh student of 1878 was already looking to a career of letters, and that journalism with its offer of immediate income (so essential to a youth of no estate) was the mark he aimed at. Old David Whyte, the Kirriemuir tailor, may have shown young Barrie the lure of the literary life, but the story of Fyfe would prove that journalism was an adventurous profession to which even a hand-loom weaver might aspire.

But why Edinburgh University for the laddie from Thrums? Aberdeen was the alma mater of Alexander Whyte and of Alexander Barrie, and it was for that University rather than the nearer one of St. Andrews that most Kirriemarians, bent on scholastic honours, commonly headed. The attraction of Aberdeen was doubtless the unusual number of bursaries there available, which provided just enough funds, eked out with supplies of oatmeal, smoked hams, herrings and the like from home, to enable a student to stay the four years Arts course. These bursaries were awarded on a test consisting chiefly of Latin prose composition, which made no excessive demand upon the capacity of an intelligent and eager scholar. But Barrie does not appear to have sought after bursaries, or, seeking, did not win. And the likelihood is that his brother Alexander, now in sight of the forties, who had in this year married the lady who was to prove his devoted companion through life and who outlived him by fourteen years, favoured Edinburgh for James: first because his own most intimate friend Alexander Whyte was established there at Free St. George's and fast making himself a power for good among the University students, and secondly, because of the inestimable advantage of studying English literature under Masson. There would be other considerations, no doubt, but these two were strong enough, and as Alexander was so nobly repaying the early sacrifices of his parents in the matter of his own education by bearing the cost of James's, his would be the determining voice in the choice of Edinburgh.

Barrie himself has told us that when he went up to Edinburgh it was Whyte who first guided him into the Old Quad and introduced him to the officials who controlled the matriculation. It happened also that one of the vital things which the student took from Dumfries to Edinburgh was a glowing enthusiasm for Carlyle, whose niece Mary Carlyle Aitken had been a friend of Mr. and Mrs. Alexander Barrie. Thus it was the happiest of fates that he at whose feet he had come to sit was an intimate friend of Carlyle and his intellectual peer—David Masson, Professor of Rhetoric and English Literature at Edinburgh from 1865 to 1895.

This splendid man was then at the height of his power (he was fifty-six in 1878), a well-spring of good from which innumerable young Scotsmen were deriving invigoration for the journey of life. For Masson was something immensely greater than a great critic of literature: a Gulliver in criticism, Barrie has called him,

Literature was to him not an end in itself but a means for the development of character. There was a serene largeness about the man that raised him high above the common level of the merely learned: he was of the company of the Hebrew prophets. Oddly enough it was to be one of Barrie's literary heroes that led what has been termed ' the revolt against Massonism,' and led it successfully. The young R. L. Stevenson was more concerned about literary expression than the thing expressed, while ' Massonism,' which was characterised by religious and moral earnestness, took small account of the elegancies of style, although one of his earliest works was a study of the styles of British novelists. Masson's own style was of the smooth-sluggish variety, lacking in lightness of touch and charm, but the profound piety and scholarship of the man made all that he wrote and all that he gave forth in his lectures of enduring value as criticism of life.

A university that could boast two such professors as David Masson and John Stuart Blackie, the one by his own life and teaching inculcating the abiding virtue of sincerity in all things, the other with his Celtic fire tirelessly attacking hypocrisy and humbug, was an intellectual El Dorado for earnest youth, and there were others, only slightly below the stature of these giants, to whom Barrie in one of his earliest pieces of literary journalism, An Edinburgh Eleven, paid generous tribute. But Masson exercised the greatest influence upon him. ' Though a man might, to my mind, be better employed than in going to College, it is his own fault if he does not strike on someone there who sends his life off at a new angle.' So he avers, and that someone in his case was Masson. ' I seem to remember everything Masson said, and the way he said it.' How deeply Masson's influence penetrated is seen in such a passage as this:

There are men who are good to think of, and as a rule we only know them by their books. Something of our pride in life would go with their fall. To have one such Professor at a time is the most a university can hope of human nature, so Edinburgh need not expect another just yet. . . . The test of a sensitive man is that he is careful of wounding the feelings of others. Once, I remember, a student was reading a passage aloud, assuming at the same time such an attitude that the Professor could not help remarking that he looked like a teapot. It was exactly what he did look like, and the class applauded. But next moment Masson had apologized for being personal. Such reminiscences are what make the old Literature classroom to thousands of graduates a delight to think of.

To the above I would add this whimsical illustration of Masson's popularity, as it is characteristic of Barrie's method of making fun of himself with a gravity of statement that often has resulted in his fancies being accepted as facts:

> The students in that class liked to see their Professor as well as hear him. I let my hair grow long because it only annoyed other people, and one day there was dropped into my hand a note containing sixpence and the words: 'The students sitting behind you present their compliments, and beg that you will get your hair cut with the enclosed, as it interferes with their view of the Professor.'

Literature and long hair were often in conjunction in those days. Stevenson was one who spared the barber, and there may be a tincture of truth in Barrie's story. Whether long or short in the hair, he was certainly a bright student of letters, and in Masson's class he took a high place, being *proxime accessit* for the Vans Dunlop Scholarship in English Literature. Masson must have taken more than common interest in his student, though no trace of that interest survives. Miss Rosaline Masson, who remembers Barrie as a student visiting her father, can recall nothing of his Edinburgh days.

On Masson's death in 1907 Dr. Hume Brown, the Scottish historian, wrote a singularly beautiful appreciation of the great professor who had sent Barrie's life off at a new angle, and no apology is needed for making a few extracts from that article here. It appeared in The Student, a magazine issued by the Students' Representative Council of Edinburgh University:

> If those who knew him most intimately were asked what was the characteristic that gave the tone to his whole nature, they could have no difficulty regarding the answer. It was the attitude of heart and mind suggested by the word *pietas* in its widest implication—an intense and enduring gratitude to all men and things to whom or which he could acknowledge any debt or obligation. . . . Of him it could be truly said that his days were 'bound each to each by natural piety.' When a student, he saw in Dr. Chalmers one who embodied for him the highest ideal of greatness and goodness in man, and to his latest day he could not speak of Chalmers without a welling up of the heart which was prompted by gratitude, not less than by reverent admiration. . . . 'Don't think of writing a popular book,' was his advice. . . . When it was said to him that this or that book was now little read, his comment was, 'But is it worth reading?'

Fortunate indeed were the students who came under the influence of this great teacher. But they were no less fortunate in having the rectifying humour of John Stuart Blackie, like, a refreshing breeze, to prevent them from taking life too seriously. Humour was not Masson's strong point. Barrie had his Greek

from Blackie, whose long occupancy of the Greek Chair ended
in the year that Barrie graduated. It was the comic side of the
Professor that mainly appealed to the student, if we may judge
by the character sketch in An Edinburgh Eleven. No wonder:
' " My occupation nowadays," he said to me recently, " is business,
blethers, bothers, beggars and backgammon." ' Again: ' I
think I remember the Professor saying that he had never made
five shillings by his verses. To my mind they are worth more
than that.' But allowing for the strained image of the weaver's
shuttle (so tempting to a lad from Kirrie) here is the finest impression of Blackie ever put into so little space:

Did you ever watch him marching along Princes Street on a warm
day, when every other person was broiling in the sun? His head is
well thrown back, the staff, grasped in the middle, jerks back and forward like a weaver's shuttle, and the plaid flies in the breeze. Other
people's clothes are hanging limp. Blackie carries his breeze with him.

Charming though these memory-sketches of his professors
are, and fresh as they remain after many re-readings, they are
chiefly interesting to us to-day because of their implicit autobiography. They might have been called ' My Happy Student
Days,' for it is the personality of the writer, his actual and imaginative experiences, that engage us even more tenaciously than the
personalities of his subjects.

When the Professor (Blackie) noticed any physical peculiarity about
a student, such as a lisp, or a glass eye, or one leg longer than the other,
or a broken nose, he was at once struck by it, and asked him to breakfast. They were very lively breakfasts, the eggs being served in tureens;
but sometimes it was a collection of the maimed and crooked, and one
person at the table—not the host himself—used to tremble lest, making
mirrors of each other, the guests should see why they were invited.

To say that the above is written from experience of one or
more of those breakfasts would imply that the Professor had
detected some peculiarity in his student Barrie, and Barrie says
that there have been times when he has been inclined to think
that he himself was the only person he knew who was not peculiar!
Blackie's method of selecting his breakfast guests was probably
no more than a fancy that came to the mind of one of them who
happened to be a humorist of genius. But there is the vividness
of actuality in this glimpse of a lively moment in the Greek class
when Blackie's mention of 'a distinguished politician' was the
signal for a 'rag':

BARRIE: THE STORY OF A GENIUS

'I will say Beaconsfield,' he would exclaim (cheers and hisses). 'Beaconsfield' (uproar). Then he would stride forward, and, seizing the railing, announce his intention of saying Beaconsfield until every goose in the room was tired of cackling. ('Question.') 'Beaconsfield.' ('No, no.') 'Beaconsfield.' ('Hear, hear,' and shouts of 'Gladstone.') 'Beaconsfield.' ('Three cheers for "Dizzie".') Eventually the class would be dismissed as—(1) idiots, (2) a bear garden, (3) a flock of sheep, (4) a pack of numskulls, (5) hissing serpents.

Again, 'he would knock a map down as if overcome with emotion, and at critical moments a student in the back benches would accompany him on a penny trumpet.' Here indeed was an atmosphere very different from that of the English class, but the Greek lessons did not suffer, and if their Professor helped to make keener his students' sense of humour that also was for their good. Not that Barrie's sense of humour needed any sharpening, for it is mainly the comic spirit that presides over his memories of those days, so that we may reasonably suppose he had an amusing time as a student.

Calderwood, the Professor of Moral Philosophy, is commended for his method of getting into touch with his students, but it is the comic side of his class that Barrie remembers best. One year there was in the class a youth with a squeaky voice and a stammer:

He sat on the back bench, and what he wanted to know was something about the infinite. Every discussion day he took advantage of a lull in the debate to squeak out, 'With regard to the infinite,' and then could never get any further. No one ever discovered what he wanted enlightenment on about the infinite. He grew despondent as the session wore on, but courageously stuck to his point. Probably he is a soured man now.

Calderwood was simple enough on one occasion to play into the hands of his students by expressing the opinion that there was a great deal of moral philosophy in 'The Dead March in Saul.' After this many a budding philosopher would absent himself from the class and send a letter to say he was away listening to 'The Dead March in Saul.' The same amiable Professor was also in the habit of asking his students to his house, and would have his ladies' class to meet them. He saw the ladies into the cabs himself. 'It is the only thing I ever heard against him,' says Barrie.

While all his teachers at Edinburgh are thus seen in retrospect through the kindly eye of humour, there is at the same time, ample evidence of the respect in which he held them and of his admiration for their skill and scholarship. Tait, who had the chair of Natural Philosophy, especially moved his old student to admiration. 'Never, I think can there be a more superb demonstrator.' Again: 'It comes as natural to his old students to say when they meet, "What a lecturer Tait was!" as to an Englishman to joke about the bagpipes.' But perhaps it was Tait, the superb lecturer, rather than Tait, the man, that impressed him most, as he soon leaves the Professor to pursue other memories. On the corner of one of his college books he would have us believe that he found a pencil note, which read, 'Walls got 2s. for T. & T. at Brown's, 16 Walker Street.' He goes on to explain:

I don't recall Walls, but T. & T. was short for Thomson & Tait's Elements of Natural Philosophy (Elements!), better known in my year as the 'Student's First Glimpse of Hades.' Evidently Walls sold his copy, but why did I take such note of the address? I fear T. & T. is one of the Books Which Helped Me. [The allusion here is to a series of contributions that had been appearing in The British Weekly with that title.]

We may be left in doubt as to whether our student was deeply engrossed in the study of natural philosophy, but it is obvious that he was busy studying human nature.

From Barrie's reference to the Debating Society, of which he was a member, it might not seem to have flourished in his time. His note on it is tucked away in the chapter on Tait:

We were the smallest society in the University, and the longest-winded, and I was once nearly expelled for not paying my subscription. Our grand debate was, 'Is the policy of the Government worthy the confidence of this Society?' and we also read about six essays yearly on 'The Genius of Robert Burns'; but it was on private business that we came out strongest. The question that agitated us most was whether the meetings should be opened with prayer, and the men who thought they should would not so much as look at the men who thought they should not.

But the University has usually possessed more than one debating society, and the smallness of this one is explained when we learn that its membership was limited to students from the region of Dumfries and Galloway. The society, which was instituted so long ago as 1847, is known as the Edinburgh University Dumfriesshire and Galloway Literary Society, and it is still alive and active. It was the only one to which Barrie belonged. The title of 'the grand debate' which always took place on the second last meeting of the session, and usually on the same topic, was really: 'Is the Present Government worthy of the Confidence of the Country?' Barrie gives it a comic twist by substituting 'this Society' for 'the Country.' The Society met at 5 p.m. on Saturdays each session from the second week of November till the third week of March.

Moreover, I have had the good luck to secure a welcome bit of Barrieana thanks to a former member having found among his old papers copies of the Debating Society's syllabuses for the sessions 1880–81, 1881–82, and 1882–83. Barrie's name figures in them all. On February 5th, 1881, the Society had under discussion the question: 'Should Women have Equal Rights with Men?' This was a set debate between two members: J. C. Thomson and J. M. Barrie. All who are familiar with the feminism of Barrie's work will be prepared to hear that he stood for the affirmative, whereas the syllabus reveals the unexpected fact that on this grave subject young J. M. Barrie opposed the proposition. What would Babbie, or Grizel of the crooked smile, have said to that? In the same syllabus I notice that the name of A. W. Williamson, M.A., occurs four times: this student became the Right Rev. Sir Andrew Wallace Williamson, K.C.V.O., Minister of St. Giles's Cathedral, Edinburgh, who died on July 10th, 1926.

In the following session the young debater in whom we are chiefly interested was almost as active as Williamson had been in the preceding. On November 26th, 1881, he read an essay on Tennyson's In Memoriam, and had to meet and answer the criticism of a fellow-student who is now the Rev. John Dinwiddie, minister of the parish of Ruthwell, Dumfriesshire. And the minute book of the period shows that Barrie also read another essay in December, 1881, on 'Faith and Reason, or the World in Chains.' This was cast in the form of a Socratic dialogue between two individuals who propounded and discussed in all seriousness the most odd and whimsical ideas. It ended in some such fashion as this: 'At that moment appeared two men who declared themselves to be the keepers of the disputants and removed them to the adjoining asylum.' Barrie must have been one of the more active members, as he joined the supper committee in 1881 and on an inclement night of February, 1882, he and his friend James Geddes were the only ones that turned up, 'there having been no quorum.' Barrie was the critic of an essay on Culture by R. Armstrong, M.A., at the meeting of January 28th, 1882; and a fortnight later he and another (W. Reive, M.A.) submitted the affirmative case in a debate on 'Is the Utilitarian Theory of Morals Correct?'

Having graduated at the end of his fourth session, when his name appears in the syllabus of the 1882-83 session as the critic of an essay on The Scottish Student by J. Bryden (now the Rev. James H. Bryden, minister of Markinch), it has the coveted M.A. tagged to it.

In these syllabuses of the D. & G. Debating Society it is noteworthy that the name of S. R. Crockett, who was a member, does not figure. Crockett was a Galloway man by birth, and might have been expected to give his active support to a society which represented his native county.

The subjects debated by the society were all, as befitted the youth of the debaters, deeply serious. ' Is Man the Creature of Circumstances?', 'Ought Extreme Measures to be Taken for the Suppression of Socialism?', 'Should Britain Adopt the Military System of Germany?', ' Is the Darwinian Theory of Evolution more Probable than that of Special Creation?' and such like topics engaged these Dumfries and Galloway lads who were training for 'the three professions,' Law, Divinity and Medicine, that of Letters being a by-pass into which any of them could turn off at his pleasure if he found that nature had given him what the University could not furnish. Probably at no time since he participated in these debates in the old Civil Law Class Room has Barrie been so occupied with the serious side of life, and one would like to know the line he took in supporting Utilitarianism; how Bentham, Mill and Spencer appealed to the young student, or what hard things he said about Mrs. Fawcett when he opposed Woman Suffrage.

' Its primary object (according to The Student's Handbook) is the development of the literary and dialectic faculties of its members by means of original essays and debates. In addition to this the Society provides an excellent training in the conduct of public business, and forms a centre of local patriotism for all exiles from the south-west corner of bonnie Scotland.' The annual subscription is now three shillings; it was probably less during Barrie's membership, as that approximates too nearly to the cost of a week's lodging in his student days.

It was put on record at the Jubilee Dinner of the Society that ' Barrie never took part in a debate, but read essays.' Mr. Geddes, on the other hand, recalls that Barrie occasionally spoke in the debates. These essays, however, earned Barrie something of a literary reputation as a student, and his first successes in journalism were watched by his alma mater with a sympathetic eye, for so early as 1886, one year before he had published a book, we find him being invited to contribute to The New Amphion, a collection of pieces issued on the occasion of the Edinburgh

University Union Fancy Fair. Among his fellow contributors were Robert Browning, Prof. Blackie, Andrew Lang, George MacDonald and R. L. Stevenson. William Hole, the artist, who was later on to be associated with the author of A Window in Thrums as the most noteworthy illustrator of his works, was one of the distinguished draughtsmen who embellished The New Amphion. Barrie's contribution was a slight but characteristic piece: 'The Scotch Student's Dream.'

At the students' suppers, which were held annually, at the end of the Winter Session, it was understood and insisted upon that everyone present should add to the enjoyment of the evening with a song, a recitation, or some sort of 'parlour trick'; the sword dance performed on the supper table by a nimble youth is among such items remembered by my informant. Barrie's contribution on these occasions was always an imitation of Henry Irving's Mathias in The Bells, and he is said to have done it extremely well, copying Irving's peculiarities of speech and gesture with the greatest fidelity, and adding just that touch of exaggeration which makes an 'imitation' the more effective.

Logic and Metaphysics our student had from the venerable Campbell Fraser. He admits that as a metaphysician he was a disappointment, although he began well, 'standing, if I recollect aright, in the three examinations, first, seventeenth, and seventy-seventh.' The reader will take this with the usual grain of salt; but Barrie's readiness to recollect the comic side of his classroom experiences is as strong in his Campbell Fraser chapter as in the rest, so that not even the dusty business of the logic class could daunt a student who attacked all subjects of study with a readiness to be amused. He seems to have gone through the University in a gay spirit of intellectual adventure, quite unlike the dour, determined attitude of the country lads who went to Aberdeen half-a-century ago resolved upon the acquirement of knowledge as their sole pursuit.

Fraser was the editor of the ponderous volumes in which Berkeley's philosophy of Idealism is enshrined or entombed. The abridged edition was all that Barrie attempted to master. 'There was one man in my year who really began the large Berkeley, but after a time he was missing, and it is believed that some day he will be found flattened between the pages of the first volume.' But our student claims one metaphysical triumph. He convinced (so he says) a medical that he had no existence 'strictly so called.' 'He got frightened, and I can still see his white face as he sat staring at me in the gloaming. This shows what metaphysics can do.'

66

It will be noted how time is on the wing: 'there was one man in my year.' The students now talked of themselves as men, but they were still very boyish when they tackled mathematics. Professor Chrystal succeeded to that chair when Barrie was at Edinburgh, and although we might surmise from a reading of the amusing chapter on Chrystal that Barrie was even less enamoured of mathematics than he had been of metaphysics, that, I think, would be a wrong conclusion. If he was not outstanding among the members of his class he was at least passably competent, thanks less to his professor than to his mathematical master at Dumfries, for whom, as we have seen, he had formed a sincere and lasting affection.

But none of his teachers meant to him anything comparable with the meaning of Masson, saving only Blackie. With Masson within the walls of the University and Whyte without, and a robust sense of humour to clarify his mind when life was threatening to become too serious an affair (the threshold of manhood is the time for that), the luck of our student still held good. There was also a colleague of Whyte's for whom Barrie had a very warm admiration both as a man and a writer; this was the Rev. Walter C. Smith, D.D., whose pulpit was at the Free High. Indeed, it would not be wrong to say that after Masson and Whyte, Blackie and Smith came next among the heroes of his Edinburgh days. Walter Chalmers Smith, D.D., who died in September, 1908, at the age of eighty-four, was one who seemed to be always on the point of achieving some large thing in literature but never quite succeeding. He is obscurely remembered to-day as the author of Olrig Grange, but the surviving few who 'sat under' him still retain memories of a very gracious and persuasive personality. He, too, had his extra-mural influence for good on Barrie, who devotes a chapter of appreciation to him in which this reminiscence is given:

During the four winters another and I were in Edinburgh we never entered any but Free Churches. This seems to have been less on account of a scorn for other denominations than because we never thought of them. We felt sorry for the 'men' who knew no better than to claim to be on the side of Dr. Macgregor. Even our Free kirks were limited to two, St. George's and the Free High. After all, we must have been liberally-minded beyond most of our fellows, for, as a rule, those who frequented one of these churches shook their heads at the other. It is said that Dr. Whyte and Dr. Smith have a great appreciation of each other. They, too, are liberally-minded.

Who 'another' may have been is a matter of some doubt. John Sandford was perhaps Barrie's most intimate friend, chiefly because of their literary sympathies, and the reference may be to him. He died in early manhood a few years after leaving the University. Or his own brother-in-law, Winter, also now dead, whose course at Edinburgh ran with Barrie's, might have been the fellow-student intended.

Dr. Smith held a Sunday afternoon Bible class for young men, and it would appear that Barrie, not content with attending Dr. Whyte's Sunday class in the evening after the second service, went also to Dr. Smith's. The desire for spiritual enlightenment which he had inherited from his Auld Licht and Free Kirk forebears was evidently not easily appeased. His pulpit allegiance, as we have seen, was also divided between Whyte and Smith, and when the student went to hear Smith he would usually see Blackie there, as that famous professor was a member of the congregation at the Free High. As helping us to recapture something of the atmosphere of Scottish college life that still endured in Barrie's time at Edinburgh (though Smith's own college had been Marischal at Aberdeen) these verses from Smith's poem 'Dill's Lodgings,' are worth quoting, and they may also be taken as illustrating the limitations of his poetic gift:

I see the little dingy street,
　　The little room three storeys high,
The little woman, clean and neat,
　　With kindly smile and kindling eye,
The paper chintz, the staring prints,
　　The bird whose carol would not cease,
And the cracked china ornaments
　　Ranged stiffly on the mantelpiece.

A dingy street among the poor,
　　Thronging with children day and night,
With sluttish women at every door
　　Gossiping in the waning light;
Yet O the nights I there have seen
　　The humour kindling every face,
The play of wit, the logic keen,
　　That glorified the homely place!

Simple our life, with little change,
　　And yet it was a bright romance,
Fresh with the wonderful and strange
　　Of youth's enchanted golden trance;
How fresh in powers, in faiths, in thoughts!
　　How full that fertile time appears!
We jotted down in pregnant notes
　　The sum of all the after years.

'The little room three storeys high' where Barrie lodged in Edinburgh and the sort of life that was lived there have never been directly described by him who alone could do so truthfully; but we have other means of picturing the conditions of his college days. In his first term this lodging was shared with a fellow student named Harrison, who died in the following year, and Barrie afterwards remained by himself in the same rooms. It was at 14 Cumberland Street, a featureless and unhistoric thoroughfare in the old part of the New Town. The street was probably better conditioned forty years ago than it is to-day, for it wears the rather dejected look of one that has seen more prosperous days. At Number 14 there is a common stair that serves four different dwellings on the upstair floors, the apartments on the street level having their doors in the 'close.' Needless to say, not a soul in Cumberland Street has the slightest suspicion that any person of note ever dwelt therein. At a later stage of his Edinburgh life the student removed to another lodging at 20 Shandwick Place, at the west end of Princes Street. I have also heard that he lodged in Frederick Street at one time. There or at Shandwick Place he would be staying at the time of his graduation, and he continued to lodge in Edinburgh during the post-graduate months he spent casting his line into the waters of journalism with the same patient confidence he had often displayed in fishing the Prosen.

A few steps from Frederick Street or a short walk from Shandwick Place, by Charlotte Square and Queen Street Gardens, brings one to 17 Heriot Row, one of the best known of Edinburgh's literary shrines, where R. L. S. lived from boyhood to early manhood. Stevenson was rarely in Edinburgh during Barrie's early days there, and by August 7th, 1879, he had shipped from the Clyde to New York, opening a new and strange chapter in his life; the longest and not the least happy chapter. But romantics command means of intercourse that defy time and space, and Barrie and R. L. S. being both romantics we need have no surprise at a remarkable encounter in Edinburgh between the two as related by one of them. I quote from the prosaic news columns of The Times which give to the record an air of authenticity that might else be lacking; Barrie himself is the informant, and the occasion the annual dinner of the Printers' Pension Corporation in 1926:

The only time I met Stevenson was in Edinburgh, and I had no idea who he was. It was in the winter of '79. I well remember the wind was 'blawin' snell' when I set off that afternoon with my notebooks to the Humanities class of the University of Edinburgh. As I was crossing Princes Street—a blasty corner—I ran against another wayfarer. Looking up, I saw that he was a young man of an exceeding tenuity of body, his eyes, his hair, already beginning to go black, and that he was wearing a velvet jacket. He passed on, but he had bumped against me, and I stood in the middle of the street, regardless of the traffic, and glared contemptuously after him. He must have grown conscious of this, because he turned around and looked at me. I continued to glare. He went on a little bit, and turned round again. I was still glaring, and he came back and said to me, quite nicely: 'After all, God made me.' I said: 'He is getting careless.' He lifted his cane, and then, instead, he said: 'Do I know you?' He said it with such extraordinary charm that I replied, wistfully: 'No, but I wish you did.' He said: 'Let's pretend I do,' and we went off to a tavern at the foot of Leith Street, where we drank what he said was the favourite wine of the Three Musketeers. Each of us wanted to pay, but it did not much matter, as neither of us had any money.

We had to leave that tavern without the velvet coat and without my class books. When we got out it was snowing hard, and we quarrelled—something about Mary Queen of Scots. I remember how he chased me for hours that snowy night through the streets of Edinburgh, calling for my blood. That is my only reminiscence of R. L. S., and I daresay that even that will get me into trouble.

The choice of 'the winter of 1879' for this charming recollection shows an unusually nice discrimination on the part of the narrator, who is ordinarily indifferent to such trifling details.

Barrie's resources were ampler than those of S. R. Crockett, whose name in a few years' time was so commonly to be linked with his when the flowering of the Kailyard was exciting the admiration and the derision of the critics in two continents. Crockett, who was born in the same year as Barrie, had gone to Edinburgh when only fifteen. The year after Barrie went up Crockett had already completed his Arts course, and, under pressure of financial need, he had become travelling tutor to a young American, returning afterward to study science under Tait and eventually theology at the New Theological College. He would not appear to have come in contact with Barrie in the year their terms overlapped, being two years ahead of him in class seniority, and when he came back to Edinburgh Barrie had taken his degree. Crockett had originally gone up from Castle Douglas School with a £20 bursary for four years, which represented his total resources from the outside. He has himself left this on record:

During my first three years I lived on about nine shillings a week. In the first year I added to my income by coaching, and it was imperatively necessary that I should do so, as, out of my revenue of £20, I had to pay £11 in fees. In the second and following years I did journalistic work, my first contributions, paragraphic reports, soon being printed in The Edinburgh Daily Review. But my earnings were not considerable, and I do not think that during my student life in Edinburgh I ever spent more than nine shillings a week. I shared a garret in an old house, which looked on the Park and Arthur's Seat, with my cousin, and afterwards with Macgregor, the artist, and we each paid three shillings and sixpence a week for rent, including coal and gas. For breakfast and supper we used to have oatmeal porridge; our dinner never exceeded sixpence each. When I was saving up to buy a book I would content myself with a penny roll and a glass of milk. I did not work very hard at my studies but read vastly, reading anything and everything; a constant visitor to the University Library.

As I have indicated that Barrie's resources at Edinburgh were not so meagre as those of Crockett, and they were certainly more substantial than Alexander Barrie's had been at Aberdeen, it would be wrong to read into the following reminiscence, which I quote from one of his early contributions to The Nottingham Journal, anything of an autobiographic nature:

I knew three undergraduates who lodged together in a dreary house at the top of a dreary street; two of them used to study until two in the morning, while the third slept. When they shut up their books they woke number three, who arose, dressed, and studied till breakfast-time. Among the many advantages of this arrangement the chief was that, as they were dreadfully poor, one bed did for the three. Two of them occupied it at the one time, and the third at another. Terrible privations? Frightful destitution? Not a bit of it. The Millennium was in those days. If life was at the top of a hundred steps, if students occasionally died of hunger and hard work combined, if the midnight oil only burned to show a ghastly face 'weary and worn,' if lodgings were cheap and dirty, and dinners few and far between, life was still real and earnest, in many cases it did not turn out an empty dream.

The foregoing is really an enlargement of an anecdote of which the two Alecs, Whyte and Barrie, were the heroes. Here I quote from Barbour's Life of Dr. Whyte:

He (Alexander Barrie) and Whyte only possessed one copy of a textbook which formed the chief subject of a forthcoming examination. They agreed each to use it for half the night, Whyte sleeping during the early part while Barrie studied. In the comfortless chill of the early morning watch Whyte awoke, rose and found the fire gone out and his friend sound asleep, his forehead resting on the table beside the open book.

BARRIE: THE STORY OF A GENIUS

Always bearing in mind that the conditions of student life in Aberdeen a score of years earlier were as much more rigorous than those prevailing during Barrie's time at Edinburgh as these, in turn, contrasted with the conditions of to-day, this further extract from the Life of Dr. Whyte may be thought appropriate:

Many of his fellow-students were engaged in the same double contest for learning and for daily bread; and not a few fell by the way. The work of a winter session in Aberdeen was often interrupted by the call to mourn for a classfellow who had succumbed to the threefold pressure of privation, overwork, and the rigorous climate; and a brilliant son of that austere alma mater, who himself died in middle life, once said that to read the prize lists of thirty years before was like listening to the roll-call of a regiment at the close of a severe campaign. It was afterwards said by Sir James Barrie that 'there were among Dr. Whyte's classfellows men who endured greater hardships to get an education than a traveller suffers in Central Africa.'

A story which Dr. Whyte used to tell with great relish, though its hero is the elder Barrie, is also worth remembering in the present connexion. He and Alexander Barrie had entered for a special examination and Whyte had prepared elaborately, making full notes.

The evening before, Barrie, who had not prepared at all, asked for his friend's careful note-book, threw himself down on the sofa and read it two or three times through. Dr. Whyte concluded, 'when the result was announced, Barrie was first, and I was nowhere.' Barrie afterwards admitted that this story rested on a substratum of truth, but hinted that, like the stories of their joint fishing exploits, Whyte's vivid imagination did not allow it to lose anything in the telling.

No similar story is told of James's achievement as an undergraduate. Indeed, the little that we do know tends to give the impression of an ordinary rather than a brilliant student. I have been told that at this time he was often subject to severe headaches, and used to pursue his studies with a damp towel wrapped round his head. On one occasion, at least, he put his head thus enveloped out of the window to show his sisters, who were standing on the pavement below, that their student brother was manfully sticking to his task despite his affliction! Some girl friends of these same sisters had christened James 'Peeweet' because of half-a-dozen recalcitrant hairs that stood erect on the top of his head defying all his efforts with brush and macassar to smooth them down with the rest. Apropos of this period of Barrie's life Sir Robert Blair, who was a fellow student at Edinburgh, wrote an article in The Teachers' World on 'My Schooldays' about the time of his retirement in 1927 from the post of Education Officer to the London County Council, and the following paragraphs which I select from it will be read with interest:

Such men as Robert Louis Stevenson, a few years my senior, S. R. Crockett, and Sir James Barrie, my contemporaries, were less conspicuous in the university lists than the modern world would expect. But Derby winners would not fit well into the cab shafts of a four-wheeler.

Crockett was not shy in admitting his capabilities, Barrie was quiet and unassuming; I think few of his fellow-students would have predicted for him the great place in literature which he has achieved.

Lord Haldane, Lord Salvesen, and J. Arthur Thomson were my contemporaries, and the 'show boy' of the university was J. W. Mackail, who had just won the Hertford and the Ireland scholarships at Oxford.

I am not able to add materially to the brief reminiscence just quoted; but from two correspondents I have notes that are worth printing. The first is from Mr. Charles Laing, to whom I am indebted for the interesting recollection of the story-telling episode at Forfar as related in my chapter on 'The Young Scholar.' He writes:

I might call this 'My Last Glimpse of Barrie'; it concerns the year 1881, when I was attending Masson's class of English Literature at Edinburgh University. I had lost sight of Barrie who had left Forfar for Dumfries about nine years previous to this event. The short winter day was coming to a close and the three o'clock bell for Masson's class was chiming as I entered the Old Quad accompanied by a fellow student belonging to Kirriemuir. As we passed along the terrace, following a small crowd making their way to the classroom, my friend said to me: 'Did you know Jim Barrie when he was in Forfar?' 'Yes,' I replied. 'Well, he attends this class,' said he, 'and there he is.' Following his pointed finger I saw a spare, short figure in a warm-looking Highland cloak a few yards in front. He was talking to his companion in an animated manner, and just at that instant the bell ceased and he passed through the open door, but not before I had seen his face. It was he, but little changed from the lad I had known at school. I passed in, took my accustomed bench and settled down to listen to the roll call, to which ordinarily I paid little attention. Soon the name 'James Barrie' was called and a quiet voice replied 'Adsum.' At the conclusion of the roll call Masson proceeded with his lecture on John Milton, little guessing, I am sure, that among the two hundred students listening to him, there was at least one who was planting his feet on the ladder of fame, and who was destined to become one of our foremost men of letters.

BARRIE: THE STORY OF A GENIUS

That 'warm-looking Highland cloak' was doubtless the handiwork of Margaret Ogilvy, as Scottish mothers were able to cut and sew a presentable Highland cloak when the complicated tailoring details of sleeve-making and collar-fitting were beyond their amateur skill. The knowledge that Highland cloaks were thus usually 'home made' induced many a lad to go coatless rather than appear at school in one of these cloaks, warm and picturesque though they were. It is evident that Barrie had none of this false pride.

The following I owe to Mr. Robert Galloway, of Birkenhead, another fellow student at Edinburgh, and if it adds little that is new it at least confirms the impression that there is little to add:

We were in some of the classes together—Latin, Greek, Junior Mathematics and English Literature, I think. We began the Arts course in the same year (1878), but as I was teaching some of the time I took one year longer to complete the curriculum, and did not take my degree till 1883; whereas he took his in 1882. But though we were together in many of the classes I was never actually in close contact with him. The classes contained on an average about 150 (or more) students, so that it was quite possible to go through the whole course with nothing more than a nodding acquaintance with some of one's classmates. He was, moreover, then as always, exceedingly shy and diffident, and I do not remember ever to have seen him either enter or leave a classroom with any companion. Some companions, of course, he doubtless had, but I was not one of the privileged ones, nor do I know of any who were. Nor did he, I think, connect himself with any of the debating societies of the College—at least I never saw him at any. Yet I remember him distinctly—a sallow-faced, round-shouldered, slight, somewhat delicate-looking figure, who quietly went in and out amongst us, attracting but little observation, but himself observing all and measuring up men and treasuring up impressions which were afterwards given to the world in his Edinburgh Eleven. He took a good place in several of his classes, but did not specially distinguish himself in any but the English Literature class, where he was fourth. In the examination, however, a little later in the same year (1882) for the Vans Dunlop scholarship in English Literature he was I think *proxime accessit* to the prize-winner.

It is worth noting, by the way, that the winner of the Vans Dunlop scholarship became principal of an Indian College, and beyond editing several literary class-books for Macmillans did not make his name an outstanding one in the world of letters. Fame is seldom to the prize-winners.

While confessedly chary of accepting as autobiographic any of the numerous references to his own youth that occur in Barrie's earlier writings, however much these may seem to be records or impressions of personal experience, I think that his amusing passage on 'the Library pound' in An Edinburgh Eleven may pass scrutiny in the main as a truthful tale. The students who used the library had to make a deposit of one pound as entrance fee, but the deposit could be withdrawn at any time if the use of the library became a matter less urgent than the use of the pound:

In the beginning of the session you join the library, and soon you forget about your pound: you reckon without it. As the winter closes in, and the coal-bunk empties; or you find that five shillings a week for lodgings is a dream that cannot be kept up; or your coat assumes more and more the colour identified with spring; or you would feast your friends for once right gloriously; or next Wednesday is your little sister's birthday; you cower, despairing, over a sulky fire. Suddenly you are on your feet all aglow once more. What is this thought that sends the blood to your head? That library pound! You had forgotten you had a bank. Next morning you are at the University in time to help the library door to open. You ask for your pound; you get it. Your hand mounts guard over the pocket in which it rustles. So they say. I took their advice and paid in my money; then waited exultingly to forget about it. In vain. I always allowed for that pound in my thoughts. I saw it as plainly, I knew its every feature as a schoolboy remembers his first trout. Not to be hasty, I gave my pound two months, and then brought it home again. I had a fellow-student who lives across the way from me. We railed at the library theory at open windows over the life of the street; a beautiful dream, but mad, mad.

There is a touch of poignant actuality in that passage, as I have been able to establish, for Barrie did, indeed, withdraw his pound on the 9th December, 1880, and there is no record of his having joined the library again during his course. The Borrowers' Register for the years 1878–79 does not appear to have been preserved, but as the only book that Barrie took out in the 1880 term was Dugald Stewart's Elements of the Philosophy of the Human Mind, which he had from 25th November until 9th December, it would seem that he made little use of the splendid library, which is one of the glories of the University. He evidently had more pressing need of the deposit than of the elements of philosophy, or his study of Dugald Stewart may have left him with enough philosophy to carry on without the aid of the library.

A pound meant a good deal to Barrie in those days, even though, as the reader will observe, he was able to exceed Crockett's lodging bill by eighteenpence a week. He had not yet that knack of earning occasional pounds which Crockett had so early acquired in his eagerness to have money to spend. But his tastes were simple, and he had no itch to spend what he had not yet earned. His lodgings were certainly of the plainest. When he particularizes 'the dusty little lodging, with its battered sofa, its slippery table cloth, the prim array of books, the picture of the Death of Nelson, the peeling walls, the broken cloth' he is very likely cataloguing its actual contents. But it is probable that there is no more than fancy in the story about his once meeting in Fleet Street his room-mate of those distant years, who asked him if he remembered the landlady with whom they quarrelled because she wore Barrie's socks to church. 'We found her out one wet afternoon.'

If that landlady ever existed (which we may take leave to doubt) she could hardly have been identical with the one who is the subject of a Barrie story related by a Glasgow journalist some thirty years ago. The paragraph deserves to be read again for the pleasing side-light it throws upon the sympathetic nature of her lodger:

This landlady, according to the story, was so much respected and beloved by those students under her care that after her death one of them wrote to Mr. Barrie suggesting that a memorial be placed over her grave. He received a letter enclosing a cheque for £15, and warmly praising the old lady. Mr. Barrie's interest did not stop here; he enquired if anyone was looking after her cat, as the last time he had seen her the thought that she might pass away first had troubled her not a little. This is worthy of the author of A Window in Thrums.

One of the objects of his hero worship came into his life about this time—Joseph Thomson. Although Barrie was making little use of the library, he had formed an acquaintance with Alexander Anderson ('Surfaceman'), a poet of some distinction, whose literary worth had been recognised by his appointment as assistant librarian to the University in 1880. Anderson hailed from Kirkconnel, Dumfriesshire, and had been employed as a railway platelayer, hence the pseudonym under which his verse had attracted attention, and a friend of his was another and younger Dumfriesshire man, Joseph Thomson the explorer. Thomson was only two years older than Barrie and yet in 1880 (at the age of twenty-two) he had the unique experience of having headed an expedition into Central Africa on the death of its organizer, Keith Johnston, the geographer, with whom he had gone out as lieutenant. At twenty-three he was the author of To The Central African Lakes and Back, and it is easy to see why Barrie, who had the thrill of meeting him on various occasions in the company of 'Surfaceman,' conceived so great an admiration for him. He has never lost this sense of homage to the strong men who can go out into the wild places of the earth and look into the bright eyes of danger. The Edinburgh acquaintance with Thomson was renewed later in London and, as we know, one of the chapters of An Edinburgh Eleven is devoted to this engagingly modest hero. An actual happening is humorously described in it. Thomson had been invited to address an important gathering in London on his return from one of his later expeditions. The meeting was in a room of 'the most over-grown hotel in London,' but no Thomson had appeared by the time it was due to start. Two or three of his expectant audience, Barrie among them, went in search of the explorer, and it fell to Barrie to discover him shyly waiting in an ante-room off one of the endless corridors. Gently leading him to the reception room, Barrie was there hailed as 'the man who found Thomson!' In An Edinburgh Eleven the incident is dressed up thus: 'The leader of the party, restraining his emotion, lifted his hat, and said "Mr. Thomson, I presume?" This is how I found Thomson.' A sly dig at the bumptious Stanley and his 'How I Found Livingstone,' which was still a popular travel-book. Thomson died in 1895 at the age of thirty-seven.

During the later terms of his university course Barrie was able to enjoy the society of his sisters, Sara and Margaret, who for a year or two were also resident in Edinburgh. The resources of the Barries allowed for none of the daughters being able, had she been wishful, to lead a 'lady's life.' They all had to earn their livelihoods as soon as opportunity offered, and Sara and Margaret had the good luck to find, both at the same time, agreeable employment as governesses at Miss Oliver's School in Rutland Street, Edinburgh. I know of one lady who was a boarder there at the time mentioned, and she can remember how the Barrie girls endeared themselves to all associated with them by their goodness of heart and sympathetic interest in the scholars. Their brother used to call regularly at the school to see his sisters, but the lady in question would not appear to have been impressed with the future Wizard of Thrums, as she was unable to contribute any recollection of him. Sara and her sister Isabella had first started school-teaching in a small way at their uncle's manse at Motherwell, Isabella specialising in music and the elder sister teaching the elementary course of that time. So successful were they that their school quickly outgrew the limited room which could be spared for it in the manse, and special premises had to be rented. Most of the family seem to have possessed the flair for teaching, but there is no trace of anything pedagogic in the writings of Barrie, though schools and scholars are so frequently the subject of his characterisation.

So far we have had only the slightest character touches on Barrie the student: Sir Robert Blair's 'quiet and unassuming' is as much as can be said apart from the inferences that may be drawn from the student's attitude to his teachers and the highly-coloured anecdotes he himself has chosen to introduce into his Pencil Portraits from College Life. Those schoolboy intimacies which at Dumfries resulted in his many friendships and his amateur dramatic activities have no counterpart at College. Here is sterner business than the old Academy stood for. The school-boy could afford to have his adventures when the serious days of the University were still in the distance, but the undergraduate had a duty to him who was bearing the cost of his education. He had to concentrate upon his studies in the four academic years that were to bring him to the successful conclusion of his Arts course. His amusements had to be not something foreign to these studies, but inherent in them. He had to find his fun in his work, and we cannot read An Edinburgh Eleven without feeling that in this he succeeded greatly. But it was an amuse-ment that at the time was not shared with many of his fellow students. His friendships were few and unimportant, though I know of at least one that had not grown stale in forty years. Whereas we saw him at Dumfries Academy a lad of many chums, entering heartily into their boyish interests with no particular shyness, at Edinburgh he was drawing more into himself, shyness was growing with the habits of study; no more amateur theatricals, no more athletic exploits, but work, the serious work of one with examinations to pass and a degree to earn. It was now that his shyness, which became proverbial and the accounts of which have often been greatly exaggerated, was first noted. This is well illustrated by an unpublished anecdote communicated to me by one of the latter-day worthies of Kirriemuir, Mr. Joseph Alexander, who was a boy of six at the time of Barrie's birth.

On December 23rd, 1880, James's sister, Isabella, was married to Dr. Murray, and the student was then at home on vacation from Edinburgh, staying at his father's house, Strathview, where a wedding party was given. Concerning this Mr. Alexander supplied me with the following:

Barrie is six years younger than myself, consequently I hardly knew him when at school here although my sisters and I were intimate with other members of the family. When Isabella was married to Dr.

Murray we were invited over to a party in the evening. James had left Kirrie by that time, but was present at the wedding. It was a young people's party and I don't think that either David Barrie or Margaret Ogilvy made their appearance. James was so bashful that he also could not be induced to join, except that under great pressure he consented to come in to recite The Dream of Eugene Aram. I remember being surprised at the dramatic intensity of the reciter, and at the time I thought he exaggerated the intended effect of the poet, but later understood it to be quite an orthodox rendering. After the recital he immediately left without speaking to one of the company! From a perusal of his Margaret Ogilvy I have no doubt he was in close confab with her, and very likely with his father also during that evening.

An odd picture, that of the twenty-year-old student so retiring and already so withdrawn from the life of his native town that he evades a meeting with his sister's friends on the one occasion when it would have been easy and natural to make their acquaintance. The long silent hours of study and the relative indifference to college friendships which we must attribute to him were having their effect in producing actual shyness, and starting the legend of his taciturnity. But the probability is that those few fellow students with whom he did venture upon friendship had the richer offering when this reticence had been overcome.

There is, again, the clear note of personal experience in Barrie's description of the capping ceremony. The student here whose gait is springy, whose little jacket lacked the tails it should have had, is none other than that 'James M. Barrie, Kirriemuir,' who had matriculated on October 30th, 1878, and now, within a week or two of completing his twenty-second year, is restless to be about the business of a journalist, and probably considers half the battle won when he can write himself down M.A. It is a charmingly human passage:

Who has thrilled as the student that with bumping heart strolls into Middlemass's to order his graduate's gown? He hires it—five shillings —but the photograph to follow makes it as good as his for life. Look at him, young ladies, as he struts to the Synod Hall to have M.A. tacked to his name. Dogs do not dare bark at him. His gait is springy; in Princes Street he is as one who walks upstairs. Gone to me are those student days for ever, but I can still put a photograph before me of a ghost in gown and cap, the hair straggling under the cap as tobacco may straggle over the side of a tin when there is difficulty in squeezing down the lid. How well the little black jacket looks, how vividly the wearer remembers putting it on. He should have worn a dress-coat, but he had none. The little jacket resembled one with the tails off, and, as he artfully donned his gown, he backed against the wall so that no one might know.

I have seen the 'photograph that followed' and a very pleasing portrait it is, the 'mortar board' and gown being worn with an easy grace. The face is particularly handsome, the countenance open and calm, the eyes alert under wide brows, the nose sensitive and shapely, the lips surmounted by a neatly-trimmed moustache. The copy I have examined was that given by Barrie himself to Bell Lunan, who was so soon to be his model for a literary portrait that securely founded the fame of the limner.

'Happy the passengers,' says R. L. S. as he pictures the trains going south through Princes Street tunnel, 'who shake off the dust of Edinburgh, and have heard for the last time the cry of the east wind among her chimney-tops.' But An Edinburgh Eleven leaves on the reader so strong an impression of the writer's happiness in his college days that we may be sure the grown man who was going away from it as 'J. M. Barrie, M.A.' said *au revoir* to his lodging, to the Old Quad, and to the grey antique city with genuine regret, and a pleasant mingling of sentiment with his youthful cynicism.

And it was a proper occasion for sentiment. The train that took him home to Kirriemuir, though it was transporting him to old familiar scenes, was really taking him away on the grave business of finding a career. His long period of preparation was at an end. From the days of the Hanky School to the close of his university life he had passed some sixteen years in pursuit of education, and the time had now arrived when his parents and his elder brother were to be more than repaid in witnessing the quiet confidence and quick success with which he set about the task of finding an opening.

Already, before the end of his college days was in sight, he had been busy with pen and paper in his spare hours at that table with the slippery cloth writing 'essays on deeply uninteresting subjects' which he sent off to editors who promptly sent them back.

He had become a writer for the press though his rewards were of the slenderest. Towards the end of his course he had contrived to get himself appointed as a dramatic critic on the staff of The Evening Courant, and week after week he had the thrill of seeing himself in print with a paragraph or two about one of the plays put on by the touring companies that opened in Edinburgh every Monday. There is an amusing story told by one who knew him slightly as a student, about noticing by chance on the table of a Princes Street florist a card attached to a lovely bunch of roses intended for presentation to a charming actress visiting Edinburgh: the card bore the name of the young critic. The stage door had the same allurement for him in those days that it had for most of us when we were in the romantic age. He asserts that his great delight was to behold the players 'not when dressed for their parts but as they emerge by the stage door. . . . The stage-door keeper is still to me the most romantic figure in any theatre, and I hope he is the best paid!' The student Barrie even undertook to criticise grand opera, despite his innocence of all technical knowledge.

Thus early he had found the theatre irresistible, and his free press tickets were enabling him to study stage technique with a view to trying his hand at a play some day. His ambition was to be something far more important than a mere critic of plays, but the practical side of him was glad to be a critic for the sake of the free pass to the stalls. And his college friends, such as Mr. James Geddes, who has long been well known in the south of Scotland as a solicitor at Dumfries, and a poetic pair named Young and Sandford, were often his 'dead head' companions at the play. Poems by Two was the title of a slender volume which Young and Sandford offered to an unsympathetic public at that time, and Barrie and Geddes used to go into bookshops to enquire if there was a copy of this new work on sale, thus hoping to stir up a demand for it, yet dreading that some bookseller might have a copy and wondering how they could avoid buying it. No doubt Barrie would have been as resourceful as his own Tommy in that event, but his ingenuity was never put to the test.

Although he received his degree on April 21st, 1882, and with the end of the term would probably go to Kirriemuir on a visit to his parents before he went back to his brother's home at Dumfries to spend a part of the summer and to discuss his plans and ambitions with the good genius of his college life, he returned to Edinburgh in the autumn with the hope of getting some employment on the press and with the intention of working hard upon an exhaustive study of The Satirists of the Restoration, with which he proposed to take the literary world by storm. It was during this winter in Edinburgh that he was busy 'wooing literature with contributions that were all misfits.' Mary Queen of Scots he had marked down as the central figure of his first romance, which he was to get on with as soon as he had disposed of the Restoration satirists. As he has never got through with the study of Skelton, Nash and the rest of them, he has never been able to take up Queen Mary; the programme of youth is subject to frequent 'alteration without notice.' He must have repaid his library pound for the session of 1882-83 as he spent many an hour in the University Library that winter surrounded with books that were to yield him material for his projected literary study. He was now launched on his career as a man of letters. All that he awaited was the clamour of editors for his writings. Their voices must have sounded singularly faint and far away. But he was not daunted, and he tells us that the malignancy of publishers could not turn him back:

> Literature was my game. It was not highly thought of by those who wished me well. I remember being asked by two maiden ladies, about the time I left the University, what I was to be, and when I replied brazenly, ' an author,' they flung up their hands, and one exclaimed reproachfully, ' and you an M.A.?'

The way in which he was to achieve his ambition of becoming an author was by no means so clear to him on quitting the University as it was soon to be made when he contrived to enter through the door of journalism.

His pen was never busier than at this time, though the main products of the winter of 1882-83 never attained to the glory of print. He was still writing dramatic criticism for The Courant, and possibly did some paragraphing as well. He still haunted the theatres of Auld Reekie, and even Moss's old Music Hall in Chambers Street was not unfamiliar to him. What would they have said about that at the South Free in Kirriemuir, not to mention the Auld Licht Kirk? He also continued as a member of the Debating Society in this post-graduate session, as we have seen, acting as critic of one of the essays in November. His zeal for the literary life led him to take the initiative with his poetical friend Sandford and young Geddes, then a law student in founding a literary club that was to have for its model nothing less than Dr. Johnson's. Who were to play the rôles of Reynolds, Burke, Goldsmith and the rest we cannot guess, nor can we picture young James Barrie as the grand cham of Edinburgh letters; but it is a charming revelation of his literary enthusiasm, and it is to be regretted that the scheme barely survived its birth, else John's Coffee House, opposite St. Giles's, chosen after much deliberation as the home of the club, which was named the Touchstone, might have taken its place among the literary taverns.

As we shall presently see, his luck still held, even allowing for his exceptional natural gifts, his scholarly equipment, and his practical method of approach. It was no fondly foolish swain that went a-wooing the Grisette of Journalism, but a very shrewd, hard-headed admirer, who knew that the object of his young love well deserved his attentions. This love story will engage us in the succeeding chapter.

But before finishing with the subject of his Edinburgh days it will be worth peeping at the pages of Home Chimes a matter of four years ahead (February, 1887, to be precise), and gleaning a verse or two from a poem of seven stanzas printed therein. It is entitled The Old Lecture Room: Edinburgh University Revisited and its writer is J. M. Barrie. The poem is undistinguished and without merit, even though its author thought well enough of it to introduce it into When a Man's Single. It is of great interest, however, as illustrating its author's life-long fondness for make-believe. He is imagining himself an old man of almost fifty, which he no doubt thought a venerable age at that time:

> ' Take off the stranger's hat! ' the shout
>   We raised in 'fifty-nine
> Assails my ears with careless flout;
>   And now the hat is mine!

Thus he begins and passes on to recall his imaginary college friends of thirty years before:

> And Rae of all our men the one
>   We most admired in ' Quad '
> (I had this years ago), has gone
>   Completely to the bad.

> In our debates the moral Mill
>   Had infinite address;
> Alas! since then he's robbed a till,
>   And now he's on the Press.

There is truth and observation and the accustomed touch of sly exaggeration in the foregoing lines, and after several other cunning contrasts he concludes effectively on a sober note:

> There's none here now who knows my name,
>   My place is far away;
> And yet the college is the same,
>   Not older by a day.

> But curious looks are cast at me:
>   Ah, herein lies the change—
> All else is as it used to be,
>   And I alone am strange.

CHAPTER V

1883–1886: Nottingham and London

WHEN James M. Barrie, M.A., returned to Kirriemuir in 1882 on a summer visit to his father's home preparatory to addressing himself to the task of finding an opening for his literary talents he had come back to a household very different from that he had known at Strathview ten years earlier. Of all Margaret Ogilvy's family there were but two remaining there: that devoted second daughter, Jane Ann, who was never to leave it, and Margaret, the youngest. The eldest daughter, Mary, had become Mrs. Galloway in the autumn of 1879, and Isabella had married Dr. Murray in the winter of the following year, while Sara was now at Motherwell, keeping house for her uncle, the Rev. David Ogilvy, who had adopted her as his daughter.

The joy with which the mother welcomed her son back from college was tinged with the fear that she would soon have to reconcile herself to even longer periods of separation than during his years at Dumfries and Edinburgh, as the sooner he could find employment and begin in earnest his life's work the better it would be for him. Kirriemuir was no place for a man to make his base of operations in an assault upon the strongholds of Fleet Street. If one could write well enough and was clever in choosing attractive subjects, the life of a freelance might be lived in Kirriemuir as well as in Bloomsbury, thanks to the post. But it was clear to him that Edinburgh was a better base for his literary operations, and that is why we find him back at his old lodging there after he had spent the remainder of the summer recess at his brother's villa in Dumfries, now bright with three or four little Barries of the new generation.

Though the post is indispensable to the freelance, it can also be the terror of those who have not found the formula wherewith editors may be induced to accept their offerings. Many a foolscap envelope would be pushed through the letter-box in the autumn and early winter of 1882 addressed to ' Mr. J. M. Barrie,

84

M.A.,' in his own hand-writing and containing a manuscript of his with a printed slip attached expressing the unfelt regret of this or that editor. What subjects were dealt with in these rejected manuscripts and what the lucky ones that were printed and brought magical guineas through the post to their young writer are dark secrets which have never been disclosed. We know, however, that there were flutterings of delight at Strathview in the bosoms of Margaret Ogilvy and her daughters when they heard that something of Jamie's had got into print, and the old Kirrie woman who said ,' Weel, it's a guid thing the laddie can make something at his writin'; he could never hae made his livin' at the mills ' must have been informed of these very early and obscure appearances in type which not even the showiest of later successes can eclipse in an author's enjoyment.

The lot of a freelance in the 'eighties of last century, and even into the first decade of the present century, was no enviable one, in spite of what we shall find our hero saying later on when he looks back upon it from the security of an established favourite's income. An article when accepted might not get into print for many months, a year or more, and the cheque that paid for it might be delayed until publishing day. Meanwhile its writer had to live, and unless he had other resources or had made a lucky start with an unusual number of acceptances he would know the meaning of ' hand to mouth.' To get ' something regular ' was therefore the ambition of every journalist in those days. Now, when a hundred writing men can find a living where one used to subsist leanly, ' something regular ' is still the thing desired. Barrie had not long to wait: that lucky star of his still shone.

His sister Jane Ann saw an advertisement in a newspaper—possibly a copy of The Daily News that had strayed up North, as it was then the recognized medium for journalistic jobs, just as The Morning Post was for butlers—and got her brother to reply to it. Masson, himself an old journalist and editor, gave him a fine testimonial. An answer came in the form of an offer of the post of leader-writer on The Nottingham Journal at the salary of three pounds a week. Though less than a dustman earns in our post-war days, the salary was not to be despised in 1883 when, at the beginning of January, having been 'rashly engaged' (as he puts it), our future Crœsus of Letters, after a farewell visit to Kirriemuir, set out from Dumfries for the pleasant town of Nottingham to begin his wonderful career. Shorn of its frills, there remains in this passage from Margaret Ogilvy a truthful impression of the domestic commotion caused by the great event:

BARRIE: THE STORY OF A GENIUS

At the moment I was as uplifted as the others, for the chance had come at last, with what we all regarded as a prodigious salary, but I was wanted in the beginning of the week, and it suddenly struck me that the leaders were the one thing I had always skipped. Leaders! How were they written? What were they about? My mother was already sitting triumphant among my socks, and I durst not let her see me quaking. I retired to ponder, and presently she came to me with the daily paper. Which were the leaders? she wanted to know, so evidently I could get no help from her. Had she any more newspapers? I asked, and after rummaging, she produced a few with which her boxes had been lined. Others, very dusty, came from beneath carpets, and lastly a sooty bundle was dragged down the chimney. Surrounded by these I sat down and studied how to become a journalist.

Concerning the rapidity with which he mastered the art of leader-writing and every other branch of journalism there will be abundant evidence presently to submit. What the young journalist may not have realised at that critical moment of his life was the good fortune that had taken him to the staff of a third-rate provincial newspaper. Genius will out; but, like all sensitive plants, it flourishes best in a favourable exposure. It would have been a misfortune for our young journalist had he been appointed to the editorial staff of The Scotsman (which was naturally his immediate ambition) or The Glasgow Herald. These papers were prosperous enough to employ large staffs of adequately paid writers and sub-editors, and the inclination to settle down obscurely but comfortably as a 'member of the staff' was a snare which ambitious youth had to guard against. On the Aberdeen papers wages were low and work was heavy, so that one quickly gained varied experience, and had never a wish to linger beyond the time needed to find a more attractive job in London. That is why in the old days you couldn't throw a stone in Fleet Street without striking a journalist from Aberdeen. The Nottingham papers were of no higher standing than those of Aberdeen; not so well edited indeed, and less individual. No editor so original as Dr. William Alexander, of The Aberdeen Free Press, author of Johnny Gibb of Gushetneuk, had been associated with any of them; though the Guardian had G. A. Henty, the boys' favourite of a past day as a leader-writer, and Mortimer Collins, the poet-novelist, brother of the more famous Wilkie, had also been on its editorial staff at one time. Among Barrie's colleagues on the Journal there were three of some note who came to London: —H. J. Hibbert, well known in his day as a writer on the theatre, 'Dicky' Mann, who became chief of the Central News Agency's parliamentary staff, and T. Lennox Gilmour, for years an able leader writer on The Morning Post, who at one time was private secretary to Lord Rosebery. Of the three, only Mr. Gilmour survives to enjoy the intimate friendship of his famous colleague of the old Journal.

There were three morning dailies in the town: the Guardian, the Express and the Journal, the last-named being the oldest and the weakest of the three. A weekly of some distinction, The Mercury, which had ceased to exist before Barrie's coming to the town, was owned and edited by the father of Philip James Bailey, author of Festus. Of the three morning papers the old Journal, moribund though it was in 1883 (the Express absorbed it in 1887), was the only one that had an 'atmosphere.' The other two were efficiently conducted political newspapers. There was about the Journal a pleasant old-world air that reflected perfectly the antique atmosphere of the town itself.

Up to the close of last century none of the larger towns of England was so charming. In the 'eighties it was in some ways an ideal place for a literary man, presenting as it did so many interesting phases of life that a student of character could not fail to profit by a stay in it. Neither a great city nor yet a sleepy town, it was something of both. The bustle of commerce was seen in its thronging streets and its many factories; yet it retained much of the old-fashioned village life. Old Nottingham was really a congeries of large villages that had put their arms around each other's necks and made a great thriving town. The new and the gaudy mingled with the old and the historic, the rude rustic lingered beside the smart 'city' man, the factory and the warehouse fought an unequal battle with the orchard and the garden, even to the very heart of the town. Its Market Place was one of the largest in England, and the Goose Fair held there for generations was famed throughout the land like that of Beaucaire in France. There was some show of intellectual activity, although the moral tone of the place was distinctly lower than that of any town in which the young man from Kirriemuir had sojourned. All is now changed: gone is the *rus in urbe*; great buildings with cinemas on their ground floors flaunt themselves where quaint old hostelries stood; big railway stations have taken the places of small ones where infrequent trains used to puff leisurely in and out.

My own memories of Nottingham date ten years after Barrie's, and are still full of fragrance; the delicious scent of the hawthorn in Maytime wafted down the leafy groves about the Forest through the city streets is with me as I write. There is no marked enthusiasm for Nottingham in anything that Barrie has written.

BARRIE: THE STORY OF A GENIUS

Thirty-two years ago a Nottingham clergyman was lecturing on the Thrums books, and drew from their author this avowal:

I thank you for your letter, and wish you had a better subject for your lecture. I don't know of any personal article about myself that is not imaginary and largely erroneous. But there is really nothing to tell that would interest anyone. Yes, I was in Nottingham for a year, and liked it well, though I was known to scarce anyone. If you ever met an uncouth stranger wandering in the dark round the castle, ten or twelve years ago, his appearance unimpressive, a book in each pocket, and his thoughts three hundred miles due north, it might have been the subject of your lecture.

'I liked it well enough' is faint praise, and yet Nottingham might be placed second only to Kirriemuir, and Margaret Ogilvy's stories of her youth as a formative force in the early literary career of the novelist, who, by the way, was never strong on dates and periods of time, as he was nearer two years than one in Nottingham, going there in January 1883 and leaving in the late autumn of 1884. His Tinker Bell was ringing her loudest when he came to Nottingham. Had he been called to Birmingham, or Leeds, or Manchester, Tinker Bell would have been heard but faintly. Old-world Nottingham was the place for him at that time, and the old Journal the best of all papers in England for him to write in. Luck you may call it, but they would have given it a different name in the Auld Licht Kirk.

The Journal had no editor in the proper sense; it came together in the early hours of each morning without any directing hand other than that of the foreman compositor. Barrie had almost a free hand in his own department, that of the editorial and literary columns. There were sub-editors and reporters who each did his work in a communal spirit which enabled the foreman to have enough type-matter set to fill the columns of the paper in order to go to press about two or three in the morning. It was Barrie's good fortune to be allowed to write as much as he liked and whatever he liked so long as the compositors were asking for 'copy.' To the end the Journal was set by hand, its dying days witnessing the rise of the linotype throughout the newspaper world.

The opportunity to fill columns of space with one's writings is one that any earnest young journalist should welcome. Practice is the great thing, and the knowledge that what he is writing will in an hour or two be set in type and printed is at once an encouragement and a restraint, since it imposes a sense of responsibility. But few journalists have ever rivalled Barrie either in capacity for work or in early ripeness of style. In addition to writing his daily editorials, which at times would run to more than two columns of twelve hundred words in length, he also contributed every Monday a special article signed Hippomenes, and every Thursday the same signature was appended to a column of gaily written notes headed A Modern Peripatetic. There is no journalist on any daily paper in the British Isles to-day whose weekly tale of work would equal that. We live in softer times.

Like a true journalist, there was no subject about which Barrie was not prepared to write a column. George Augustus Sala boasted that he would write a column on anything, even a blade of grass. Hippomenes wrote on Etc.; cameos of character such as Prigs, Parasites and The Third Sex ('They are youthful clergy-men as a rule'); literary studies on Lear's Fool, Prefaces, The Novel of the Year, and An Old Morality Play; light philosophical discursions on abstractions like Ridicule, Modesty, and Satis-faction; moralisings on Mothers-in-law, Waiters or Mrs. Grundy: all furnished attractive subjects for the pen of this ready writer. Many of them would be suggested by some happening of the moment, some recent experience of the writer. Provincial London, appearing in August, 1884, may have betokened his first visit to the Metropolis, and Railway Travelling, a month later, would be based upon a personal experience either going home or follow-ing his London trip; while his article on Hogmanay, appearing on December 29th, 1883, we may attribute to an exiled Scot growing sentimental on the approach on his first New Year's Day away from home. Printers' Errors and More Compositors' Freaks are obvious in their inspiration, but I cannot now guess what Potato Gospel stood for.

In all, he wrote about eighty 'specials' over the signature of Hippomenes, and a glance at the list which I compiled from the columns of The Journal many years ago is sufficient to prove their writer a born journalist: the quality of human interest inheres in their very titles. Though we shall hear of Stevenson years later writing to Meredith that Barrie had a journalist at his elbow, it was a journalist whose mark was literature—not merely journalism and never journalese—from the day he put pen to paper. There is a pleasant literary flavour about those early and long forgotten efforts of his journalistic days, a con-stant play of humour, and an inquisitiveness about things theat-rical that indicates the bent of his mind so long before he appeared as a playwright. One of his longer contributions was The Com-plete Playgoer. It was cast in dramatic form, and was given in three parts, each averaging two columns. This was quite the crudest and most amateurish thing he printed, and as it appeared a few weeks after his joining the Journal staff it was probably one of his unaccepted pieces written either at Edinburgh or at Kirriemuir after his graduation.

A still lengthier piece of work, amounting indeed to the respectable dimensions of a serial story, ran through the weekly Supplement of the Journal from June 1st until August 10th, being eleven instalments in all. This was announced in a somewhat wordy advertisement in the daily issue as an attractive feature of the weekly, and its writer was described as 'The Author of The Complete Playgoer,' a doubtful distinction, but good enough to serve where the actual name of the author was completely unknown. The announcement of the serial bears traces of having come from the same pen as the story itself, and as Vagabond Students must rank as the first published fiction by J. M. Barrie and is therefore of great bibliographical interest, I here transcribe some extracts from the advertisement, which was frequently repeated in the Journal as it filled a good bit of space economically:

VAGABOND STUDENTS

By the Author of ' The Complete Playgoer '
(Hippomenes of The Nottingham Journal)

Original sketches of life at a Northern University.

Tells how four Academic Cads and one Academic gentleman spent the Long Vacation.

Relates how five undergraduates conducted a Punch and Judy Show round Scotland.

What the Scholastic Vagrants did; how they did it; whom they did; and who did them.

CHAPTER HEADINGS

1—The End of the Session.
2—A Students' Supper Party.
3—The Puppet Show.
4—Jennie's Diggings at Cockcrow.
5—Gentleman Chimley is left behind.
6—The Début.
7—The Student and the Maiden.
8—At the Sign of the Golden Key.
9—Opportune Reappearance of Gentleman Chimley.
10—A monstrous fine woman.

11—The Detective.
12—A tidy little bit of goods.
13—En route to the North.
14—Miss Sally Dulcimar.
15—Life preserving on a new principle.
16—Was it an Elopement?
17—We are engaged.
18—Breach of Promise!
19—Oh, woman, woman!
20—Exeunt omnes.

QUOTATIONS FROM THE STORY

'Man,' said the Law Student nervously, 'was not meant to live alone.' 'Go to bed,' rejoined Sandilands sternly, 'and sleep it off, or I'll punch your head.'

Grind, grind, grind
With eyelids heavy and red;
A student sat in his lonely digs
With a wet towel round his head.

I'm plucked, I do admit it, I'm spun, my mother dear,
Yet do not grieve at that which happens every year;
I've waited very patiently, I may have long to wait,
But you've another son, mother, and he will graduate.

If you're a cynic, Jennie, it's your duty to hang yourself.

Two points are to be noted concerning Vagabond Students. First, in this, his earliest effort (apart from the merest juvenilia) at a long piece of sustained writing, he wisely chooses to write of what he knows, of a phase of life he has himself been experiencing, and secondly he most probably wrote the story when he was still a student at Edinburgh or during his post-graduate days there. As its author has chosen not to disinter Vagabond Students (a good and intriguing title), nor indeed to recover a single one of his numerous contributions to the Journal, we can restrain our curiosity concerning these with the thought that anything in them worth preserving he would subsequently utilise in some later sketch or story, as he does the quatrain beginning 'I'm plucked,' which reappears in An Edinburgh Eleven. There never was artist less prodigal of his material, or readier to reshape to perfection something he had first hewn indifferently. A third point may be noted. The Comic Muse inspires Vagabond Students in common with all its author's earliest literary efforts. It is a humorist that is courting the Grisette. Vagabond Students was a rollicking yarn of real and imaginary adventures, introducing a number of his college friends and acquaintances, among whom I think I can spot Mr. James Geddes as ' Jennie,' so-called by reason of his famous ancestress who threw the stool at Dean Hanna in St. Giles's.

The notes of A Modern Peripatetic—the column had a couplet under the heading:

> They talked as they walked
> They read as they ran—

were of unequal merit, but for a young and inexperienced journalist they were distinctly good, little reflective passages such as this being above the common standard of the provincial press forty to fifty years ago:

The glue that keeps the world together is self-esteem. It is terrible to think of what might happen did Smith sometime take it into his head that it was not worth his while to try to out-do Robinson, or Brown that life would still be worth living though his income was fifty pounds per annum short of Jones's. Self-esteem takes the form of a vehement desire to rise superior to our neighbours, and in all Great Britain there is not in all probability a single street which does not contain at least one superior family. A superior family is one that esteems itself so very much that it cannot avoid looking down on its surroundings, and it is perfectly happy in the knowledge that its drawing-room is one foot by one and a half larger than any other in the vicinity.

The young cynic is at work here and beginning already to develop his own particular vein of humour:

The candid critic is a gentleman of whom all authors approve when he praises their last volume. ' What I wanted,' they explain, ' is no gush of praise, as from a friend, but simply a calm, just review, slating my work if it deserves slating, commending it if it deserves commendation.' Noble fellows! Then when the critic, who is very young in this case, observes that the work bears distinct traces of genius, is Shakespearian without Shakespeare's coarseness, reminds one of Milton in his best moments, and suggests Tennyson before the Poet Laureate's hand lost its cunning, the author smiles gently to himself and repeats that what he wanted was an honest criticism, and he thinks he has got it.

There is the ' Barrie touch' in the following paragraph, where his gentle art of exaggeration makes a good beginning:

I remember being invited, with a batch of other undergraduates, once to assist at a banquet given by a college professor to his private lady students. When I know that I am expected to talk to young ladies I prepare some half-dozen suitable remarks to fire off at intervals, and I was on the point of commencing number one, which was no doubt of a frivolous nature, to the genius who was placed by my side, when she raised her saucer eyes, and asked me eagerly whether I did not think that Berkeley's Immaterialism was founded on an ontological misconception. I contrived to whisper that such had always been my secret impression, then quietly fainted, and was sent home to be bled.

These are fair samples of Barrie's early journalistic manner, and it will be seen that he came to his first (and only) editorial post fully equipped for his task; even leading articles (which his mother began to read for the first time when he started to write them and gave up the day he stopped) presented no sort of difficulty to this young man from the North, who seemed to have been born with a pen in his hand.

It has often been said that the Journal took on a literary air the day that Barrie joined it and lost it the day he left. This is not true, as the Journal always had 'literary' leanings, the other dailies being more concerned with their proper business of finding and circulating news. But Barrie's fresh and unconventional style immensely enlivened its somewhat stodgy columns and (I am differing herein from Robertson Nicoll) even in the leaders his hand was traceable. The young leader-writer had two pet subjects when he assumed the editorial 'we': Joseph Chamberlain and Henry George. Russel of The Scotsman told a lady once that when he was hard up for a topic he just had another 'dirl at Dr. Chalmers.' Barrie returned again and again to some new phase of Birmingham's idol and he never tired of denouncing George's Single Tax. These two were quite as useful to him as Dr. Chalmers was to Russel. The noteworthy thing about his leader-writing, from his first week onward, is its ripeness of judgement and its easy journalistic style, the 'we'-ing not overdone, as is so often the case with young editors. Remembering it was literally true that he had only a week's time in which to prepare himself for the particular job of leader-writer, the aplomb with which he carried it off means that he was in truth a born journalist. Perhaps the very facility that enabled him to fill his leader columns left him no great reverence for that once important, but now negligible, feature of our daily press.

A devout lady (he writes) to whom some friends had presented one of my books used to say, when asked how she was getting on with it, 'Sal, it's dreary, weary, uphill work, but I've wrastled through with tougher jobs in my time, and, please God, I'll wrastle through with this one.' It was in this spirit, I fear, though she never told me so, that my mother wrestled for the next year or more with my leaders, and indeed I was always genuinely sorry for the people I saw reading them.

No wonder he was 'known to scarce anyone' during his stay in Nottingham. His evenings would mostly be spent at his editorial desk in the Journal office, and he would not get back to his lodgings in one of the pleasant little groves of dwellings between Sherwood Street and Addison Street until two or three in the morning, which meant that he had to keep his bed till noon. His afternoons would often be taken up with his 'specials' or his notes, and after supper time the foreman compositor was clamouring once more for copy for these weary leaders. Thus he would rarely have time even for a constitutional in the Arboretum or the Forest. Saturday would be his only free day, for on Sunday evening he would have to go direct from the Presbyterian Church in Belgrave Square to the Journal office in Pelham Street to set about his editorial for the Monday morning issue. Nottingham's Sunday, with its general air of brightness, the many and busy taverns filled with folk from the surrounding countryside, and the crowds along Low Pavement and Derby Road, must have made Kirriemuir seem to him strangely remote both in place and time.

More than thirty years ago a well-informed writer in The Sketch, who had himself been on the Nottingham press, said that Barrie often sat writing at the window of his lodgings in the afternoon, and a young lady who felt some pity for the quiet, solitary Scotsman told the narrator that at times she did her best—'a most likeable best too'—to make him smile. 'It was useless.' There is an authentic ring about that story, but for a choice piece of base metal commend me to a mendacious article in M. A. P. for May 6th, 1905. I shall quote some paragraphs from this in order to illustrate 'the imaginary and largely erroneous' sort of personalia that has been appearing in the press about J. M. Barrie for more than thirty years:

I recently met a journalist who was employed on The Nottingham Daily Journal in the days when Mr. Barrie was a reporter on its staff, and he gave me some glimpses of the famous writer as a young man which may be of interest. Mr. Barrie, I was surprised to learn, was not popular with his colleagues. But his unpopularity was of a positive rather than of a negative order. If he made no friends, he sought to make none—at least, within the office. Reserved and silent to a degree, he kept his ambitions and himself to himself. Outside the office, however, he was intimate with two or three Scottish doctors settled in Nottingham, and one of them, who afterwards told the story to my friend, he surprised one evening by throwing aside the mask and declaring with flashing eye and uplifted fist his determination to get to the top at, to use Barrie's own words, ' whatever cost to myself or anyone else.'

While waiting for a ' call ' in the reporters' room, Barrie never joined in the jokes or horse-play of the others, but sat steadily writing, writing, writing. Both in and out of doors he had a dreamy, abstracted air; but, as a matter of fact, nothing escaped his observation, as his articles proved. Often at night he would be found standing at the corner of the main street watching, but without seeming to watch, the passers-by. And, although the most abstemious of men, he made no ' bones ' of going into ' gin-palaces ' and such places to study bibulous human nature over a glass of lemonade. Of Barrie's private life in lodgings little was known, but he was reputed to live for something less than sixpence a day.

As a reporter, Mr. Barrie's work lay mainly in the police courts, and he never failed to make the most of any humorous or pathetic incident that cropped up.

The paragraphs quoted represent about one half of this untruthful contribution, in which not one statement that is capable of proof will stand the test. Barrie was not a reporter, he probably never was inside a police station in Nottingham, and the picture of him, like poor George Formby, 'standin' at the corner o' the street' observing the pageant of Nottingham life for journalistic purposes is highly comic and purely imaginary. The exact nature of his work on the Journal (at no time did the word Daily appear in its title) admits of no doubt, and practically everything that he wrote while on its staff can be identified in its old files, including sundry feeble efforts at verse which it would be worse than body-snatching to disinter. Probably no author of our time has been the subject of more frequent misrepresentation of the kind above quoted, and certainly none has more laid himself open to it by a plentiful use of the personal pronoun in statements that are jestingly made. There are persons who believe that Barrie threw a clod at Lord Rosebery because he begins his sketch of that statesman in An Edinburgh Eleven with the words: 'The first time I ever saw Lord Rosebery was in Edinburgh when I was a student, and I flung a clod of earth at him. He was a peer: those were my politics.'

So recently as a morning in July 1928 an 'inspired' paragraph in a London daily about a strenuous young novelist, whose frequent illnesses and equally frequent periods of convalescence abroad have a curious knack of coinciding with the publication of his latest masterpiece or the impending production of 'the greatest story he has yet written,' contained the statement that when Barrie lived in Nottingham he shared a lodging with a poor young insurance clerk, now a well-known baronet, Sir Arthur Wheeler, who has prospered financially not less notably than his old room-mate, as he had just paid £100,000 for an island (geographical position unstated) in order that he might have a place where he could 'get away from things.' Barrie, as we know, is also fond of islands: there is one in Peter Pan, another in The Admirable Crichton, and the strangest of all in Mary Rose. Thinking that it might be one of these which Sir Arthur had acquired—though it did seem a long price for that isle of the Outer Hebrides, 'The Island that Likes to be Visited,' despite its reputed efficacy in getting one 'away from things'—I wrote to Sir Arthur, asking if there was perchance a word of truth in the statement that he had 'digged' with Barrie in the days of dreams and penury. I give below a passage from his reply:

I saw that paragraph in the paper the other day about my having shared an apartment with Mr. J. M. Barrie, and I was very much inclined to write and contradict it, but thought I would leave it alone. There was not a word of truth in the paragraph. I was born in Nottingham, and I lived there until 1899, and I have never seen Barrie. I do not know even what he looks like.

Quite seriously I suggest that if all the published 'anecdotes' in which Sir James Barrie figures were submitted to this test at least ninety per cent. would yield a like result. The careless way in which journalists have been apt to handle the truth when writing about Barrie is further illustrated in a newspaper clipping (source unidentified) that I find among my memoranda. It would seem to have appeared in March 1924, at the time of the death of H. G. Hibbert, and starts with these words: 'The late Mr. H. G. Hibbert and Sir James Barrie worked together on The Nottingham Daily Journal for twelve months in 1879–80.' Then follows a fairly accurate summary of some valuable personal recollections that appear in Hibbert's Fifty Years of a Londoner's Life, published in 1916.

But note the stupid mention of a date—1879–80. Barrie, as we have heard, was still a student at Edinburgh in 1882, and in 1879 he was only nineteen years of age. Hibbert was a subeditor on The Nottingham Guardian from 1879 to 1882, when he became assistant editor of the Journal and so continued until 1886. Hibbert himself is inclined to looseness of statement in his book, but it contains no mention of a date that would give the newspaper man warranty for 1879-80. I have to thank him, however, for putting me on the track of Hibbert's lively volume, with its acceptable additions to Barrie lore.

Two weeks before Barrie joined the Journal staff Hibbert had become its sub-editor. It appears that Barrie arrived in Nottingham and forthwith reported for duty on a Sunday night either at the end of 1882 or early in January 1883. Hibbert is perhaps a shade on the rhetorical side in describing the event:

On the dark landing, a-top of a broken staircase, stood a small, delicate youth unmistakably from Scotland. ' My name is Barrie. I am the new leader-writer! ' He proceeded to explain that he was ' a-awfully tired,' after the long journey from Edinburgh. He had taken the precaution of writing, in the train, a leading article which he hoped would satisfy the occasion. And he would like to go home to bed. The leading article was written in pencil, on both sides of the two fly-leaves, yellow glazed, of a pocket edition of Horace. The writing was minute and regular, and most legible—apparently. Actually, it was the tonic record of a Scottish drawl, softly extended and sweetly unintelligible.

What a 'tonic record of a Scottish drawl' may be I leave my readers to determine for themselves. It suggests nothing to me. Hibbert is fortunately clearer on matters of fact. The following sounds true, as I could match it with similar stories of niggling economies in the management of The Nottingham Express which I edited ten years later:

Barrie first asked three pounds a week in response to an advertisement. ' H'm ye-es,' said the senior proprietor. ' We pay monthly. That will be twelve pounds a month.' Barrie, I got to know, was a spendthrift in generosity of certain kinds. But the ingenious reduction of three pounds per week to two pounds seventeen and fourpence first perplexed and then eternally angered him. . . . The proprietors were two estimable and kindly men, very rich, who had inherited the paper from their father, an eccentric solicitor of great account in Midland counties politics in the 'fifties. They grimly watched the fine old paper die.

The statement about the proprietors and their attitude to the paper I accept without hesitation, and the strange state of affairs existing at the Journal office in Barrie's day is revealed in Hibbert's confession that the key for the very large building which housed thousands of pounds' worth of machinery was left for him under the doormat on Sundays so that he could gain admission and proceed with the preparation of copy while the mechanical workers

97

were free to attend evening service. The proprietors were mindful of the souls of the 'comps,' but recked little about those of the 'liter'y gents.' Hibbert adds some delectable details of 'Penny,' the foreman compositor, who was left 'to get the paper out' as best he could. He divided copy into two classes, (1) 'noos,' the importance of which he judged by the relative nearness of its place of origin; (2) 'tripe' which embraced all literary matter, such as leaders, reviews and special articles: indeed everything the new arrival from Scotland had contracted to supply. Hibbert goes on:

Barrie's work, acutely literary, was always in peril; and he suffered horribly. Our autocrat had a soft spot, but Barrie refused to negotiate it. For myself, I once procured the insertion of an historic speech on Protection by Henry Chaplin by marking it the introduction to Mansfield Flower Show. So it became 'preference copy.'

Barrie's contract, for, ' say, twelve pounds a month,' was to supply two columns of literary matter per day. One was to consist of a leading article, as to which general, but never particular, instructions were given, in an eight-page letter from the senior proprietor. . . . The Saturday ' leader ' was written for years by a local accountant of immense erudition, amazing views, and a literary style founded on Cobbett. His lucubration always filled two columns. I remember an article that began: ' God moves ('tis said) in a mysterious way. But the Nottingham waterworks company . . .' Barrie used to open the Saturday paper and fling it from him in a rage. Throughout his life in Nottingham he made no friends, was morbidly unhappy, and yet cherished the belief that he had a sacred trust in the editorial columns of The Journal. He had an immense sense of his importance. It was not vanity—just a natural contempt for all his surroundings, and a natural consciousness of his superiority. There was a corresponding constraint towards him on the part of the local newspaper men. And yet there were such good fellows among them!

I am not surprised to learn from Hibbert's pages that Barrie was 'frankly disgusted' with the low pot-house atmosphere of the Kettle Club, where the reporters foregathered at all hours of the day and night, and where much of their copy was written, as he describes in When a Man's Single. In another paragraph Hibbert lets his pen run away with him thus:

Barrie's first play was written in Nottingham, on approval, for Minnie Palmer. It ' discovered ' her, sitting on a mantelpiece. It was called, I think, Polly's Dilemma, and it was printed as a detail of the Christmas issue of The Nottingham Journal, so that he might borrow the type, economically make it into a booklet, and so try to sell the play. His first fiction was published in Bow Bells—twenty thousand words of succulent sentiment, for which he got three guineas. He bought some desired print, ' The Greek Slave ' I think, with the money, and pasted the story on the back as indicating its *fons et origo*.

The suggestion that Barrie pasted a twenty thousand word story from Bow Bells on the back of an old print is preposterous. At a fair estimate such a story would occupy say twenty pages, or ten leaves, measuring nine inches by twelve. Imagine pasting these on the back of a small picture! I doubt also the three guineas and the twenty thousand words; and above all, the reckless expenditure of a week's income on any old print. I have been unable to verify the publication of Polly's Dilemma, which was unknown to me thirty years ago, when the old files of the Journal used to stand alongside my editorial desk in the Express office. And mention of the Express reminds me that in more recent years, on April 8th, 1918, to be precise, that title gave way to the Journal again, possibly to make a better distinction between the local daily and a London daily that sells widely in the same area; so that after having been used as a sub-title to the Express for thirty years, Journal is again the actual name of a Nottingham morning paper.

The remainder of Hibbert's reminiscences of Barrie are gratefully transcribed below, though I cannot resist the reflection that the narrator's mother is made to assume a suspicious likeness to Margaret Ogilvy:

His lonely rooms in a suburban terrace backed on to the garden of my home. My sweet mother, in her expansive kindness, would go and signal to him that tea was a-going—Midland Counties tea, of many attributes. There was once an impossible interval, and he made amends for his absence with a still treasured copy of David Elginbrod, inscribed ' To the Face at the Window: He cometh not, she said.' Dear Soul! She specialized on forlorn journalists. There is a millionaire newspaper man of to-day to whom she had no more to say than: ' You poor, neglected thing! Just turn out all your socks.' And mended them.

Barrie of those days fancied himself as an actor. He would on the slightest provocation give an imitation of Irving as Romeo and Modjeska as Juliet. In his playlet, Rosalind, I think I recognize an encounter with a well-known actress of that day, Marie de Grey, who once startled the supper-room of a restaurant by impulsively reciting the epilogue to As You Like It. His rooms were curiously devoid of books. There was a Horace—that very Horace of the yellow, leader-written fly-leaves —and there was Bartlett's Familiar Quotations. If ever he were tempted to use a quotation he turned to Bartlett, and if it were among the Familiar, out it went.

He was the most shy, the most painfully sensitive creature, with an exquisite delicacy in regard to women. He drank nothing. And he used to assure me that after a most conscientious trial he found smoking detestable. Walking was a joy to him. I suppose we must have covered hundreds of miles of Nottinghamshire and Derbyshire together. He was years ahead of me in setting that first, rapturous, proprietorial foot on the pavement of Fleet Street in that proud ability to say, *Civis Romanus sum.*

All unknown to Barrie, and indeed to the world at large, there was living in Nottingham then a novelist of genuine power whose name will be looked for in vain in literary reference books: James Prior. What books he had written in 1884 I do not know, my first encounter with his work being the delightful one of reviewing his story, Ripple and Flood, in the Express some time, I think in 1896. Prior wrote chiefly on the green Midlands, and was in his later years called the 'Thomas Hardy of Nottinghamshire': a very proper description, as his rustics, though entirely original, resemble those of Hardy in their humorous way of looking at life:

' I'm not afeared o' th' future; but I'm like a woman an' a cow; she knows it's a cow but she's afeard it's a bull.'

' 'Ave you ever 'eard o' the Parson as thanked Providence for creating man to eat pig, when it might just as heasy have created pig to eat man? '

These passages are from his great novel A Walking Gentle-man, which, had it met with its due would have been reprinted scores of times since it appeared in 1907. When, some years after his death, which took place in 1922, a London publisher brought out a new edition of his Forest Folk Barrie declared that 'if, when I was in Nottingham, I had known that such a man as James Prior was living there, I would have rung every bell to get at him. He is a fine writer whose work I shall cherish.'

Amid all the myriad changes that have happened in Nottingham since Barrie's time, it is remarkable that the old Journal building has in large part survived. The author of When a Man's Single could have gone down to Pelham Street forty-five years after he had first set foot in it and walked again through the narrow passage and up the veritable stair that led to the Journal offices, though inside that door he would have found things strangely changed. Here is how the externals are described in When a Man's Single where the Journal becomes the Mirror, and Nottingham Silchester:

The Mirror's offices are nearly crushed out of sight in a block of buildings left in the middle of a street for town councils to pull down gradually. This island of houses, against which a sea of humanity

100

beats daily, is cut in two by a narrow passage, off which several doors open. One of these leads up a dirty stair to the editorial and composing rooms of The Daily Mirror, and down a dirty stair to its printing-rooms. It is the door at which you may hammer for an hour without anyone's paying the least attention.

Thirty years ago I remarked of this literary landmark: 'The block of buildings still remains, and there is no reason to suppose that the Corporation will seek to pull it down any time within the life of the present generation, as it is an exaggeration to say that it stands in the middle of a street, and the ocean bed which carries the "sea of humanity" on either side is wide enough for all practical purposes.' Nevertheless I was a little surprised when visiting the scene again, in the summer of 1928 to find it so little changed, and the stone-cut sign 'Journal Chambers' still there above the passage way to identify this first and most interesting of the Barrie landmarks in England. On the back elevation of the building to Victoria Street the words 'Nottingham Journal, Established 1710' still remain as a melancholy reminder of the transiency of all things journalistic, even the 'old establisheds.' Some day 'Journal Chambers' must come down, and the scene where Barrie began his masterful wooing of the Grisette will pass away, but happily it has attained to something like immortality in the pages of When a Man's Single, which in all that concerns the journalistic life of Rob Angus in Silchester bears a very close resemblance to the experiences of J. M. Barrie in Nottingham. We can suppose, for instance, that we have gone into that narrow passage above which the curious may still read 'Journal Chambers,' and that we have mounted a dark stair that is to take us back well-nigh half-a-century in time and to the more romantic town of Silchester:

The editor's room had a carpet, and was chiefly furnished with books sent in for review. It was more comfortable, but more gloomy-looking than the reporters' room, which had a long desk running along one side of it, and a bunk for holding coals and old newspapers on the other side. The floor was so littered with newspapers, many of them still in their wrappers, that, on his way between his seat and the door, the reporter generally kicked one or more into the bunk. It was in this way, unless an apprentice happened to be otherwise disengaged, that the floor was swept.

In this room were a reference library and an old coat. The library was within reach of the sub-editor's hand, and contained some fifty books, which the literary staff could consult, with the conviction that they would find the page they wanted missing. The coat had hung unbrushed on the nail for many years, and was so thick with dust that

John Milton (the junior reporter) could draw pictures on it with his finger. According to legend it was the coat of a distinguished novelist, who had once been a reporter on the Mirror, and had left Silchester unostentatiously by his window.

The slight touch of exaggeration in this description serves to heighten the truth of the whole. It is a readily recognisable picture of a second or third class provincial newspaper office forty or fifty years ago, when not a penny that could be saved was ever expended by the management on those little comforts that are now so commonplace they pass unconsidered. That coat, too, is a fine touch: it was probably common to every reporters' room in the country, and always a prolific source of legend. I have even seen it described in the press as having been found in the Journal office after Barrie's departure, and as having been worn by him during his editorial nights there.

The charm of the Mirror staff, who belong to a vanished age of Bohemianism, is intensified by the light touch of caricature with which the author secures them in our memory. Chief amongst them stands Penny, the foreman compositor. He was the most important man in the office, not excepting Mr. Licquorish, the editor (an entirely fictitious character), and Barrie depicts him as 'a lank, loosely-jointed man of forty, who shuffled about the office in slippers, ruled the compositors with a loud voice and a blustering manner, and was believed to be in Mr. Licquorish's confidence. His politics were respect for the House of Lords, because it rose early, enabling him to have it set before supper time.' Penny is wonderfully characteristic, he might serve for any foreman compositor of the old school; and his scenes with Protheroe, the sub-editor, are pictures of events that happened in hundreds of newspaper offices every day and every night up to the beginning of the present century. The foreman even to-day regards himself as the autocrat of the press-room, and will not on any pretext alter the time of getting his stereo plates ready for the machines. I know of one who refused to correct the proof of his editor's leader because it had not been returned in time—and that editor might have seemed a person of awesome importance, being the proprietor of the paper, a baronet and a member of Parliament.

Penny not only ruled the Mirror compositors, he domineered the editorial staff as well. There were occasions, however, when Penny's nature underwent a change. 'Sometimes about two o'clock in the morning Penny would get sociable, and the sub-editor was always glad to respond. On these occasions they talked with bated breath about the amount of copy that would come in should anything happen to Mr. Gladstone, and the sub-editor, if he was in a despondent mood, predicted it would occur at midnight. Thinking of this had made him a Conservative.'

The original of Penny, whom I met eight or nine years after When a Man's Single had appeared, was not in his person recognizable from the novelist's fancy portrait. He had given up the struggle with leader-writers, sub-editors, and reporters and was spending an age of ease as the proprietor of a trim little hotel in one of the suburbs of Nottingham. He was then the only one in Nottingham who remembered anything of Barrie, who, he said, gave him the impression that, behind a shyness of manner, he had the capacity for winning success. Others, who might have been expected to recognize the literary merit of which Barrie gave unmistakable evidence in his Journal contributions, were blind to his talent, or not sufficiently interested to appreciate its promise, but the original of Penny gravely assured me that he always felt Barrie would make his mark. Penny could even claim some slight share in Barrie's early literary efforts, as one of the first articles which the young leader-writer managed to 'place' in London was the description of a descent into a coal mine near Clifton Grove—a scene made famous in Kirke White's poem— and on this expedition Penny (so he told me) acted as his guide and counsellor. Penny's devotion to literature, however, had not, when I met him, extended so far as When a Man's Single, which he confessed he had not read. But he meant to read it some day—when he got time—'and I would like to see Barrie again before I peg out' he said. As the snows of many winters were upon the old compositor's head he must long since have pegged out, and I doubt if he ever saw Barrie again or read the pages that give himself a little hold on fame, even though his description there in no way tallied with his person, it being difficult to imagine him with 'a loud voice and a blustering manner.'

Billy Kirker, the chief reporter of the Mirror, represents a journalistic type that has disappeared. He was a thorough Bohemian, 'his ring, it was noticed, generally disappeared about the middle of the month, and his scarf-pin followed it by the twenty-first. With the beginning of the month they re-appeared together. The literary staff was paid monthly.' This was unusual, as few reporters of those days were able to wait so long for the modest reward of their labours, and weekly payment was more common. 'Enterprise without outlay is the motto of this office,' were among the first words of Billy's greeting to Rob Angus when he had summoned the courage to mount that dirty stair and face his fate inside The Mirror office. Here Barrie is possibly using an office joke in which the literary staff had pithily expressed a truthful criticism of the managerial policy. But Billy Kirker had no ill-will to his deadly rival on the opposition paper, as he explained with charming naïveté to Rob. 'Oh, no,' said Kirker, 'we help each other. For instance, if Daddy Walsh, the Argus chief, is drunk, I help him, and if I am drunk, he helps me. I am going down to the Frying Pan to see him now.' Before going he borrowed five shillings from the new recruit from Thrums. The Frying Pan is the fictitious name for a small public-house that, in my time, still stood near the Daily Express office, in Upper Parliament Street, but had ceased to be ' the press house.' Time was when the convivial crew known as the Kettle Club, whose chief delights were spinning yarns and hard drinking, had their headquarters there. Rumour had it that the shy Barrie was once induced to join this convivial circle; but we have seen in the M.A.P. mendacity quoted above to what absurdities rumour may attain.

A lively and realistic picture of the *milieu* in which the young leader-writer worked at the Journal office is to be found in an article which he wrote for Home Chimes while he was at Nottingham: the first appearance of the name 'J. M. Barrie' in a London publication (November 8th, 1884). The little sketch is informed with the true spirit of Barrieism: commonplace things are made vivid and memorable, being touched with picturesque exaggeration; there is the sparkle of humour in every paragraph; and the impersonal descriptive style of ordinary journalism is scrupulously avoided for a definitely personal statement of things seen. 'A Night in a Provincial Newspaper Office' is the title of this peculiarly interesting contribution:

The office clock points to five p.m.; a young man with grey hair rushes, key in hand, at the office door; the office mice and rats—who thrive intellectually and bodily on type—scamper to their holes; and the sub-editor is in possession. Pouncing upon the half-dozen telegrams that have preceded him, he tears them open, sees their drift, and heaves a great sigh of relief. Mr. Gladstone is still in good health. 'This morning the Right Hon. Gentleman, who was in unusual spirits, proceeded to the west corner of his Hawarden Estate, and there felled a tree.'

That is a brisk and arresting start, even if the joke about the mice is thin and strained, and there is the reality of fellow-feeling in his knowledge that the sub-editor's life is 'blighted by the presentiment that one of these days something will happen to the

A Barrie Landmark in Nottingham
Office of The Nottingham Journal which appears as The Silchester Mirror in
When A Man's Single.

133 Gloucester Road, London
Occupied by J. M. Barrie, 1894–1901.

Strathview
The Barrie House at Southmuir, Kirriemuir.

Prime Minister, which, in the form of "copy" will also finish him'
(the sub).

Seizing an evening newspaper, the sub-editor runs his scissors into
it, tears out the foreign intelligence and the markets, flings the gum-
brush at them, has them labelled on clean paper in less than no time,
and is in the case-room with his first 'copy' before the reader—noted
for his quickness—could say 'Jack Robinson.'

Very faithfully he describes the later arrival of the compositors,
the increasing frequency of the telegraph boys with their 'flimsies'
(he contrives to work in almost every bit of journalistic and typo-
graphic jargon, 'quads,' 'small caps,' 'fat,' and so forth, but
omits the sub-editor's word for his telegrams which slipped so
naturally from my pen), and the clamours of the foreman for
'more copy':

Wildly he manipulates his tools; he tries to write with a brush; he
recklessly dabs his pen into the gum-pot; he pauses in mid-air,
as it were, because he has no time to sit down. In vain. The 'devils'
are upon him. 'Copy!' shrieks one fiend. 'Five men standing!'
exultantly yells another. 'Copy, copy!' they cry in chorus, and wildly
more wildly—recklessly more recklessly—go the scissors of the lightning
sub-editor. If you were with him, he would have you slit up, labelled,
and in the case-room, you would be set, read, revised, stereotyped, and
published as a local, a general, a latest foreign, an advertisement, or a
fish market, before anyone had time to notice what had happened, or
the editor to see that the tragedy obtained prominence on the contents
bill.

There is a fine crescendo in the description of that thronging
office, reporters bustling in with their stories, written chiefly at
the Blue Pigeon, near by, the arrival of packets of news from
district correspondents, and finally the sudden start at a late hour
of a big 'news special' owing to the death of a world-famous man
of letters:

From the office boy to the editor, everyone takes the defunct sternly
to task for dying at such a preposterous time of night. It is not creditable; the staff feel hurt; a literary man might have been more considerate. The editor disappears into his private room to look up
'Death,' in Familiar Quotations, preparatory to angrily dashing off an
eloquent tribute to the memory of the deceased. The foreman bursts
into the sub-editorial room to announce that he is 'flooded' with
'copy,' to insist that the racing must be 'slaughtered,' if two columns
are coming from London, to state emphatically his low opinion of men
of letters, and generally to have it out with somebody. Back comes the

racing, to be cut down to a couple of ' sticks.' The reporter who puts his head in at the door to ask whether a clear, bell-like voice is called a mezzo-soprano or a mezzotint, is told that his concert notice is doomed; and the great ' dramatic critic,' with his four French words and seven adjectives, is ' held over until to-morrow in consequence of the unwonted pressure on our space.'

There is good fun in that paragraph, and the animated scene which it depicts was doubtless witnessed in all essentials by its writer on many a night at the old Journal office. The article winds up with a simple statement of facts so deftly phrased that it leaves an impression of sympathy and humour:

With two o'clock comes the adjournment of the House of Commons, and the sub-editor once more smiles—a wan smile. At three o'clock he is all but cracking jokes with the foreman, who almost responds; and at half-past he is only in the office because he is too tired to get out of it. Before four o'clock he is on his way home with a copy of the paper in his pocket—which he never thinks of reading—and the last thing he does before he goes to bed is to take in the morning's milk.

A typically sly Barrieism in A Night in a Provincial Newspaper Office occurs in his description of the editor, ' who always writes his leaders on the backs of rejected manuscripts—did you ever wonder why intending contributors are told to write on one side of the paper only?' The contribution has a special importance as disclosing a ripening style and a growing confidence of humorous phrase compared with some of his earlier Journal articles, but it is not entirely free from little crudities which a few months later could not find their way into any other article from the same pen.

As we lose trace of Barrie's hand in the pages of The Nottingham Journal after October 27th, 1884, and on November 17th of that year his first Thrums sketch, An Auld Licht Community, was printed in The St. James's Gazette, we may fix his farewell to Nottingham at the end of October. The story of his coming to London has often been told in his own words and these will be quoted by writers on Barrie many a score of times yet:

I wrote and asked the editor if I should come to London, and he said no, so I went, laden with charges from my mother to walk in the middle of the street (they jump out on you as you are turning a corner), never to venture forth after sunset, and always to lock up everything (I who could never lock up anything, except my heart in company).

But we need not assume that he merely sent in his resignation to the proprietor of the Journal, gave his landlady notice, packed his trunk and took the train to St. Pancras. More likely he first went home to talk matters over with his parents and to be with them at the year's end to ' bring in ' 1885. Then for the high adventure and the conquest of Fleet Street. In later years he was to look back upon it as the joy of 'being swallowed up in London,' but his true interest in London was to take possession of the place by means of his pen. The decision had not been hastily arrived at. Nottingham was never to be more to him than a stage on the road south; yet there was a day in Nottingham when he was in some danger of lingering in the provinces, for he applied to the editor of The Liverpool Daily Post (the late Lord Russell— then plain Mr. Edward) for an assistant editorship, and was happily passed over in favour of another candidate. This effort would betoken a readiness at that time to push his courting of the Grisette to the danger point of a proposal, and such an end to his wooing might have been disastrous; 'the other lady' (when the time came to make up to her) might have proved coy if she had heard how far things had gone with the 'darling jade.'

The young leader-writer was indeed doing a venturesome thing when he decided to cut adrift from his three pound job—ye fatly-paid journalist of to-day, just think of Barrie providing every week about fifteen or sixteen columns of twelve hundred words for sixty shillings! And this was no mere task work, as all that he wrote was informed with personality and a literary quality which would give it distinction among the journalism of to-day when three guineas for a thousand words is a common rate of pay.

It is wrong to suppose that Barrie had been able largely to augment his Journal salary by contributions to the London press. Any journalist who writes with his own right hand fifteen or sixteen thousand words every week has little leisure left for *hors d'œuvre* composition. Yet Barrie had contrived to place some articles of the 'turn-over' type, for which in those days The Evening Standard paid two guineas and The Globe one guinea. Though printed anonymously the journalists who wrote them had a peculiar satisfaction in their publication which could not be expressed in terms of mere money. Even An Auld Licht Community, which to that wise old editor Frederick Greenwood came as something dewy-fresh, unique, and revealed to him a new writer who had escaped the ruck, appeared without an author's name. The great thing, however, was that Greenwood did not merely print it promptly: he asked for more.

Greenwood did not at first print everything that Barrie sent him: he showed a perverse favour for his Auld Licht sketches and so encouraged the young writer to explore a vein that no other editor considered auriferous. For this he must always be remembered as Barrie's true literary god-father. Very soon, however, he was willing to print anything that his young genius of a contributor cared to send him. There was one other London editor who shared with Greenwood the honour of heartening the man from the North, and that was F. W. Robinson, himself the author of some fifty novels, long since forgotten, of which Grandmother's Money, written in 1860, was the only one that obtained more than ordinary success. In the first week of 1884 Robinson had founded a weekly magazine on the then familiar lines of Household Words, with the title of Home Chimes, to which he attracted a remarkable group of writers, some with reputations, but mostly young men who had yet to make their marks in literature. Of the company were Swinburne, Watts-Dunton, Westland Marston and his blind poet son Philip, Coulson Kernahan, William Sharp, Coventry Patmore, Bret Harte, Jerome K. Jerome, and J. M. Barrie. For two years Home Chimes lived a not too prosperous life as a weekly miscellany of fourteen closely printed pages, changing in 1886 to a monthly issue about the size of Chambers's, in which the convention of weekly numbers bound together was observed, and in 1887 it evolved into a proper monthly magazine of eighty octavo pages, so continuing for seven years more.

Our sole interest in it touches the items which Barrie contributed, and these I find, on investigation, were more in number than I had supposed. We can understand Barrie saying that when he came to London it was to him the place where Home Chimes was published when we know that it was the first metropolitan magazine to print an article bearing his name. His very first article published in the London press, however, appeared in The Pall Mall Gazette of August 9th, 1884. It was an amusing and highly imaginative description of The Manufacture of Penny Numbers, purporting to be written By a Manufacturer, which might give some colour to the Hibbert story about his having written a novelette for Bow Bells: experience enough to justify his enlarging on the methods of producing these penny numbers! But no evidence of the Bow Bells novelette is forthcoming. The two London editors that mattered to Barrie at this time were Robinson and Greenwood, and by a margin of nine days Robinson beat Greenwood in qualifying for precedence. The lively sketch of A Night in a Provincial Newspaper Office, from which I have already quoted, was printed in Home Chimes for November 8th, 1884, while An Auld Licht Community did not appear in The St. James's Gazette until the 17th of the same month, and his next, An Auld Licht Funeral, not until January 9th, 1885. His first contribution to Home Chimes was followed a fortnight later by Two Editors and a Pocket Edition of a Woman, a humorous tale of how the editor of The Middlecombe Courant (who wrote his leaders on the backs of old envelopes) contrives to outwit his rival of the Mirror (by the old trick of printing false news for the other to copy) and incidentally to marry that editor's cousin Molly Stewart. In all, Barrie had no fewer than nine contributions printed in Home Chimes during 1885: Gentleman Chimley's Affair of the Heart (Jan. 24th), With the Highland Smugglers (May 16th), Scottish University Life (May 30th), Davit Lunan, An Auld Licht Idyll (June 13th) later to find a permanent place in his Auld Licht Idylls, An Auld Licht Official (Sept. 5th), An Auld Licht Minister (Sept. 19th), John Hubbard's Husbands (Oct. 3rd), When the Snow Melts (Dec. 19th), and The Body in the Black Box (Dec. 16th). The last named was a 'thriller,' the taste for the gruesome being regarded in those days as peculiarly appropriate at the Christmas season. John Hubbard's Husbands both in conception and treatment was typical of Barrie's humorous vein. John had three sisters who were not 'getting off,' and by dint of writing for each of them love letters that cunningly disclosed to their respective swains precisely those qualities of head and heart which they most admired John had the satisfaction of seeing them happily married—hence *his* husbands!

Four more articles signed with Barrie's name appeared in Home Chimes during 1886, in this order: Vol. I, No. 2, A Journalist's Day; No. 5, Up Stream in a Canoe; No. 6, A Professional Wit who knew Shakespeare; Vol. II, No. 8, Hints to Persons who Propose Writing to The Times. In 1887 there were two pieces only: Vol. III, No. 17, The Haunted Hotel; No. 18, The Old Lecture Room (verse). These were probably his last contributions: he was now finding more profitable openings for his writings.

It will be remarked that as early as 1885 the idea of Auld Licht Idylls had already shaped itself in the young author's mind. It may have come 'as unlooked for as a telegram,' but with journalistic decision he dealt with that telegram, reading it as news of a new goldfield, in which he could stake out all the claims himself. I would also point out that of the fifteen contributions above mentioned eight were either fiction or imaginative sketches probably written with an eye to their later use in book form. 'You have no lurking desire to write a book, have you?' said the editor of The Daily Wire to Rob Angus. Barrie had this lurking desire, but managed to keep it a dark secret from the Grisette, whom he fobbed off brazenly with some admirable bits of journalistic work mixed with his more considered pieces of imaginative writing, so that she did not guess he was after the other lady all the time.

No matter how warmly Robinson admired the work of his new contributor, as the editor of a small weekly journal he could not offer him such hospitality as he found in the ampler columns of The St. James's Gazette, where many of his articles were quickly printed—they averaged one a fortnight throughout 1885–88—and in which the bulk of My Lady Nicotine and Auld Licht Idylls first appeared. Greenwood could print in one month as many of his contributions as Robinson could use in six. But Robinson, like Greenwood, was an editor who inspired his contributors with the most lively feelings of comradeship, and Barrie was ever grateful for the encouragement he received from these two kindly souls at the time when he most needed it.

Here it is interesting to note that when he had gone to Nottingham he was furnished by Dr. Whyte and Professor Masson with letters of introduction to the proprietor of the Journal, though these must have been of the formal type, as it is improbable that either of their writers was personally acquainted with the gentleman to whom they were addressed, and when Barrie made his bold descent upon London Dr. Whyte again sent him an introduction, this time of a personal nature, to a celebrated editor: W. T. Stead, then editing The Pall Mall Gazette, the deadly rival of the St. James's. Stead, as we have seen, had already printed a contribution of his sent from Nottingham, but nothing at all would appear to have followed Dr. Whyte's recommendation of the young writer to this brilliant but erratic editor.

No journalist ever stood less in need of introductions; the uniqueness of his writings was adequate commendation whereever he cared to offer them. Humour was their chief quality; humour which derived from a light-hearted view of life and a happy knack of giving personal experiences of the most trifling nature a comic twist that made them remarkable. There was also his insatiable interest in the wonder of the journalist's craft. No writer of eminence has ever maintained so steadfastly the illusion of the romance of journalism. To all young journalists there is a joy peculiar to the work. To be able to sit down with a pad of white paper and a pencil and to write page after page which will be printed to-morrow and read by thousands is a romantic sort of business that beats company-promoting or any of the mere money-making occupations. In time the romance usually rubs off, and the journalist feels that he might have done better at the law or managing a brewery (Barrie is said to have made about £300 by his miscellaneous journalism during his first year in London). But Barrie never lost his love for the romantic side of the craft. His first contribution to Home Chimes, as we have seen, was a slice (with trimmings) of the life in the Journal office, his last, written more than two years later, was an amusing article on A Journalist's Day. He was now a freelance in London, and the article gives a very vivid glimpse into the mind of one who is wooing the Grisette with ardour and understanding. He reads without a tremor about a shipwreck on a rocky coast as that gives him his chance for 'something about sea-washed cliffs.' 'Even if the cliffs were done by some other the day before yesterday, they may afford an opening for a few remarks on sea-gulls.' The days of My Lady Nicotine are in sight, though Barrie at this time was only playing with the fancy of being a heavy smoker; he was taking to the pipe by way of 'dressing the part' of a literary freelance. So the journalist of whom he was writing (who was in part his actual self and in larger part a creature of his fancy) 'glares into the fire over his pipe half the evening, and finds most of his topics there':

This journalist had thought back upon every event of his life and utilised everything in it of practical value. He is now thinking back upon the lives of his friends with the most encouraging results. Naturally reserved, he was until lately a man of very few companions; but he has discovered that there are few persons so uninteresting as not to have, at the very least, a leaderette in them, and he now makes it his duty to extract it. He is the most genial of men when on the scent of a good thing, but tends to get irritable when you wander from the point. He only hates one kind of creature. That is the traveller who is full of miscellaneous matter and refuses to communicate it. He would rip that man to get at the articles.

That there is at least an element of personal revelation in the above will not be denied, and the rapacity of the journalist athirst for topics for his pen is merely the comic expression of a feeling which every journalist will appreciate. As illustrating how the writer for the press can turn all sorts of personal experiences into saleable ' copy ' the following passage might enrich a Practical Guide to Journalism:

There are very few things that this journalist cannot turn to account. What would be a calamity to other men comes as a boon and a blessing to him. When his tailor misfitted him this spring he immediately made two guineas out of it; and thirteen shillings was his net gain last week for losing his luggage. The latter was in this wise. His traps were put into the wrong van at a northern station, and instead of coming on with him to St. Pancras, went to Euston. A few hours later they were delivered at his door, thus saving him a cab fare of three shillings. Having rested, he wrote a short article pointing out that it was an economical thing to let one's luggage go astray, and this he calculates at another ten and sixpence. Deducting the small coin with which he tipped a porter to inquire about his missing things, there remains a clear gain of thirteen shillings.

'There was fifteen shillings,' he adds, 'in a curiously-shaped staff which an unthinking friend lately took into his (the journalist's) chambers, and the lady who contrived to make him fall over her skirts was presenting him with another half guinea!' That staff we shall meet again in When a Man's Single. The reference to the trailing skirts is a reminder of fashion's changes.

For the unknown journalist making his way in London our best authority remains When a Man's Single. Just as that story helps us to picture the young leader-writer in his novitiate at Nottingham, so does it let in the light upon the life he led when early in 1885 he established himself in Bloomsbury as a writer for the press. Even though it is unfair in criticism to identify the romancist with his characters, especially in sentiment or action, it is legitimate to assume that such a passage as the following is coloured largely by personal experience and 'emotion recollected in tranquillity':

A certain awe came upon Rob as he went down Fleet Street on the one side, and up it on the other. He could not resist looking into the faces of the persons who passed him, and wondering if they edited The Times. . . . The mild-looking man whom Rob smiled at because, when he was half-way across the street, he lost his head and was chased out of sight by half-a-dozen hansom cabs, was a war correspondent who had been so long in Africa that the perils of a London crossing unmanned him. The youth who was on his way home with a pork chop in his pocket edited a society journal. Rob did not recognize a distinguished poet in a little stout man who was looking pensively at a barrowful of walnuts, and he was mistaken in thinking that the bearded gentleman who held his head so high must be somebody in particular. Rob observed a pale young man gazing wistfully at him, and wondered if he was a thief or a sub-editor. He was merely an aspirant who had come to London that morning to make his fortune, and he took Rob for a leader-writer at least. The offices, however, and even the public buildings, the shops, the narrowness of the streets, all disappointed Rob. The houses seemed squeezed together for economy of space, like a closed concertina. Nothing quite fulfilled his expectations but the big letter-holes in the district postal offices.

A first impression of London, differing not greatly from Rob Angus's, was no doubt retained for many years by J. M. Barrie: a London as different from that of to-day as the relative conditions of the unknown journalist in his obscure lodging in Great Windmill Street and the world-famous author who forty years after was looking out upon the most movingly beautiful and romantic scene in all the world from his memory-haunted rooms in Adelphi Terrace.

A peep at the Bloomsbury days was given on February 6th, 1922, at the Authors' Club, in a speech by Sir Robert Donald, formerly of The Daily Chronicle, who was himself engaged in London journalism when Barrie was freelancing.

Barrie, when he first came to London, lived in a little boarding-house in Bloomsbury, where he kept piles of newspapers in his room. He hardly ever went out, and he smoked all day. The newspapers were kept for suggestions for articles, but he could not be bothered cutting out the things he wanted. I asked him how he found anything among so many papers, and Barrie said, ' You turn them all over and go through them.'

What tricks the memory plays! Even Sir Robert Donald's Bloomsbury story does not stand examination, unless indeed we are to discredit Barrie himself, who in his introductory note to the Thistle Edition of My Lady Nicotine (1896) divulges the 'dark secret' that when he began to write the papers assembled in that book he was no smoker, and instead of having reluctantly given up the habit he was gingerly smoking his first pipe! 'How I drifted into writing a book on the subject,' he goes on, 'I cannot remember, but the desire to know both sides was doubtless the reason why I wrote as a slave to tobacco.' This is an important admission. Later on I shall have occasion to recall it when dealing with Sentimental Tommy, who might have made a similar confession. The St. James's contributions brought together in My Lady Nicotine were written in 1886-87, the period of Sir Robert Donald's anecdote, so his picture of the inveterate smoker may have derived colour from the later tradition started by the book itself.

Jerome K. Jerome was another who knew Barrie at this time, and in My Life and Times we shall find some reminiscences not less interesting but certainly more highly coloured. This, for example:

BARRIE: THE STORY OF A GENIUS

Writing letters to The Times, according to Barrie, is—or was in our young days—the legitimate ambition of every Englishman. Barrie was lodging in a turning out of Cavendish Square, and I was in Newman Street near by. I confided to him one evening that the idea had occurred to me to write a letter to The Times. It seemed to me a handy way of keeping one's name before the public.

'They won't insert it,' said Barrie.

'Why not?' I demanded.

'Because you're not a married man,' he answered. 'I've been studying this matter. I've noticed that The Times makes a speciality of parents. You are not a parent. You can't sign yourself "Paterfamilias," or "Father of Seven"—not yet. You're not even "An Anxious Mother." You're not fit to write to The Times. Go away. Go away and get married. Beget children. Then come and see me again, and I'll advise you.'

We argued the matter. Barrie, by the bye, sat down and wrote an article on the subject after I was gone.

As we have confirmation at at least part of this story in the article which appeared in Home Chimes in August, 1886, we shall let it pass; but for an unlikely yarn the cake would go to the following, which I quote as a curiosity although out of place in this chapter:

Barrie was an excellent after-dinner speaker on the rare occasions when he could be induced to overcome his shyness. His first attempt, according to his own account, was at a students' dinner given to Professor Blackie in Glasgow. Blackie had accepted on the express condition that there was to be no speech-making—a thing he could not abide. After the dinner, by way of a rag, Barrie, who was unaware of the stipulation, was half bullied, half flattered, into getting on his legs and proposing the Professor's health. For the first minute and a half the Professor stared at him, voiceless with amazement. When Barrie came to this being the proudest moment of his life and so forth, Blackie sprang from his chair and turned upon him like a roaring lion. Denouncing him as the offspring of Satan out of chaos, and the whole remainder of the company as fit only for the hangman's rope, he strode out of the room. Barrie, more dead than alive, sat down and tried to think of a prayer; but as the evening wore on, surrounded by hilarity, recovered his spirits. Toasts and speeches became the order of the evening, and somewhere near to midnight, Barrie—this time of his own volition—rose to add his contribution to the general happiness. Meanwhile the Professor, reflecting in the calm of his own study that perhaps he had been severe towards his youthful hosts, determined to return and make it up with them. He arrived at the moment when Barrie, warming to his work, was just beginning to be eloquent. The Professor gave one look around the room and then threw up his hands.

'Great God, if the chiel is na' at it still,' he exclaimed, and plunged back down the stairs.

THE COURTING OF THE GRISETTE

I find it as difficult to account for Barrie at a students' gathering in Glasgow, not to say Blackie's presence in a definitely hostile camp (although he was a native of Glasgow), as for the language put in the mouth of the professor. If Jerome had this on the protagonist's authority we must suspect Barrie's incurable habit of 'leg-pulling' when telling stories of himself.

But, to pick up once more the somewhat tangled thread of our narrative, it was soon after he came a-courting the darling jade in London that Barrie made the acquaintance of Alexander Riach, of The Daily Telegraph, then also London correspondent and later editor of the Edinburgh Evening Dispatch. Riach (whose surname he used for the hero of Better Dead) was a brilliant journalist and he made the Dispatch the brightest evening paper in the United Kingdom. Through him Barrie became a contributor in 1886, at first with occasional column articles, and when Riach went to Edinburgh, Barrie was a regular correspondent from London, not as a news paragraphist, but contributing for a time an average of two original articles every week on topics of the moment. These articles, noted for their lightness of touch and their vivacious style, fitted nicely into the policy of the Dispatch which, though the evening companion of the grave and reverend Scotsman, assumed a sprightliness that was new in daily journalism at that time. A guinea or two per column would be all that young journalist received for these contributions, and for most that he contrived to place with London editors at this time, though we may now regard him as having passed the stage which he thus describes in his rectorial address at St. Andrews thirty-five years later:

The greatest glory that has ever come to me was to be swallowed up in London, not knowing a soul, with no means of subsistence, and the fun of working till the stars went out. To have known anyone would have spoilt it. I didn't even quite know the language. I rang for my boots and they thought I said a glass of water, so I drank the water and worked on. There was no food in the cupboard, so I didn't need to waste time in eating. The pangs and agonies when no proof came. How courteously tolerant was I of the postman without a proof for us; how McConnachie, on the other hand, wanted to punch his head. The magic days when our article appeared in an evening paper. The promptitude with which I counted the lines to see how much we should get for it. Then McConnachie's superb air of dropping it into the gutter. Oh, to be a freelance of journalism again—that darling jade! Those were days. Too good to last. Let us be grave. Here comes a rector.

The name of J. M. Barrie was still little known, much of his writing at this time being anonymous, although he was glad to see his real name or his pseudonym Gavin Ogilvy printed whenever it pleased an editor to acknowledge his contributor. There was no obvious progress famewards. That Lord Rectorship was then remote as a star. One of the earliest signed articles he had printed in a magazine of note was a sketch entitled Gretna Green Revisited, in The English Illustrated for January, 1886. This was probably the outcome of an excursion from Dumfries when revisiting his brother there; for his freelance life in London had the great advantage that it now enabled him to spend about half of the year with his parents at Kirriemuir and to visit friends and relatives elsewhere in a leisurely way, though there are no records of jaunts abroad, or indeed of any desire to enlarge his experience by foreign travel.

Gretna Green Revisited makes a very modest show as an unillustrated item in a magazine whose purpose was to print pictorial articles, yet the subject was one that lent itself to illustration. This suggests that the editor may have found its brevity one of its merits in making up that particular number of his magazine. But here was J. M. Barrie rubbing shoulders with Wilkie Collins and David Christie Murray and there was joy that day in Bloomsbury and in Kirriemuir. The article, though only a piece of first-rate journalism, has many little passages that are 'pure Barrie,' with here and there a faint suggestion of authors who were then engaging him: Meredith and Stevenson. While the following extract will show its quality and the unmistakable hand of Barrie, I agree with Mr. Thomas Moult that 'the couples who dashed across the border with foaming fathers at their coaches' wheels' is Stevensonian, though I think R. L. S. might have substituted 'that' for 'who,' and I suggest that 'the stone bridge flashed fire to rushing hoofs' is Meredithian, but probably Meredith would have had it 'hooves':

Far-seeing Murray, the sometime priest of Gretna Hall informed me, succeeded Beattie at the toll-house in 1843, and mighty convenient friends in need they both proved for the couples who dashed across the border with foaming fathers at their coaches' wheels. The stone bridge flashed fire to rushing hoofs, the exulting pursuers, knowing that a half-mile brae still barred the way to Springfield, saw themselves tearing romantic maidens from adventurers' arms, when Beattie's lamp gleamed in the night, the horses stopped as if an invisible sword had cleft them in twain, the maid was whisked like a bundle of stolen goods into the toll-bar, and her father flung himself at the door in time to be introduced to his son-in-law. Oh, Beattie knew how to do his work expeditiously, and fat he waxed on the proceeds. In his later days marrying became the passion of his life, and he never saw a man and a maid together without creeping up behind them and beginning the marriage service. In Springfield there still are men and women who have fled from him for their celibacy, marriage in Scotland being such an easy matter that you never know when they may have you. The present landlord of this hostelry, a lightsome host, troubled with corns, who passes much of his time with a knife in one hand and his big toe in the other, is nephew of that Beattie who saw his way to bed by the gleam of postboys' lamps, and spent his days unsnibbing the Queen's Head door to let runaways in, and barring it to keep their pursuers out.

I am unable to share Mr. Moult's interest in this particular article to which he devotes so much space in his little monograph Barrie: A Critical Estimate:—'This successful article, printed in January, 1886, when Barrie was twenty-six years old, must be regarded as an epoch-making performance and examined accordingly.' If the facts were as Mr. Moult states, there might be some reason for critically examining this particular piece of Barrie's early journalism. The facts are not as he imagines them to be. He suggests that it was when Barrie was planning to 'repeat the small success' of this contribution 'with articles of a similar nature' that he had the sudden inspiration which sent his imagination Thrumsward by discovering that his native town had 'something quaint about it.' The reader who has followed me thus far in the present chapter is aware that several of the sketches afterwards re-shaped and grouped together as Auld Licht Idylls and others in the same vein that have never been printed had already appeared in The St. James's Gazette and in Home Chimes. In this connexion Barrie himself is less than just to F. W. Robinson, whom he curiously ignores in his preface to the American edition of Auld Licht Idylls, as a glance at the list of his 1885 contributions to Home Chimes will show that four of these—Davit Lunan, When the Snow Melts, An Auld Licht Official and An Auld Licht Minister—have Thrums as their background. Mr. Moult's ingenious examination of Gretna Green Revisited thus loses much, if not all, of its point. It was of less importance in Barrie's literary progress than any one of the earlier articles I have just mentioned. I suspect that this critic is not familiar with the Home Chimes items, else he would have found A Night in a Provincial Newspaper Office, dating fourteen months earlier than the Gretna sketch, quite as epoch-making. Much that his ingenuity discovered in that sketch he will find as readily in the other if he cares to examine it in the dusty pages of the old magazine which is likely to serve as its tomb. This, however, might be said for the apparently unsound superstructure Mr. Moult has reared upon the supposition that Gretna Green Revisited was one of Barrie's first magazine successes; it might have been written as early as any of the contributions to Home Chimes or the St. James's, and have lain in the editor's drawer for a year before publication. The English Illustrated being a more important and less accessible magazine than Robinson's little miscellany, a longer time would probably elapse between acceptance and publication of any manuscript in it, while the facilities of Greenwood's evening sheet for quickly printing an accepted contribution were normally as 313 to 12.

We shall not be far out in assuming that by the time his Gretna sketch appeared in The English Illustrated its writer had already made up his mind that he would chance his luck with a book as soon as he could find a sympathetic publisher. Newspaper articles and magazine contributions were all very well, but they did not help him in the glorious game of making the age to come his own, and he would not be happy till he saw his name on the back of a real book—the book was the cleverest instrument man had yet invented not only for the achievement of fame but for its endurance.

Already in 1886 it is clear that the idea of Auld Licht Idylls has taken definite shape in his mind, that he is playing a double game with the darling jade; his freelance journalism being now really experiments in literature intended, as soon as they suffice, with pruning, revision or re-writing, to furnish forth a noble octavo volume in blue buckram with gilt back as a love offering for the other lady. Being eminently practical, and having an excellent sense of direction in whatever he had set his desires upon, the young man who had first come a-courting the Grisette of Journalism was cautious enough not to be off with his old love before he was safely on with the new. For another three years or more, while journalism may still seem to claim him, let us make no mistake about it, he is hard at work to be rid of the jade for ever!

CHAPTER VI

THE MAKING OF A HUMORIST

1886–1888: London

THE affair with the Grisette could have been carried to any length: she never had a wooer more to her liking. 'Barrie is a beauty,' wrote R. L. Stevenson to Henry James in 1892. 'Stuff in that young man; but he must see and not be too funny. Genius in him, but there's a journalist at his elbow—there's the risk.' His reactions to the events of the moment were so instant and so uncommon that he seemed, to the few who knew him in 1886 and thereabouts, to be cut out for the highest honours of journalism, and even six years later, as we see, the journalist in him made so friendly a critic as R. L. S. apprehensive. But there never really was any risk. He could afford to be a journalist because he gave to all his journalism a literary leaven that leavened the whole lump; he could afford to be funny because his fun was original and distinctive. He is thus to be regarded as still a journalist when he is also our rising humorist: he is, with his accustomed adroitness, making the best of both worlds, journalism and literature, and his unique gift of humour is his mainstay in that achievement.

At this period of his career one is impressed with the absence of seriousness from his writings; his outlook on life between twenty-six and thirty is as joyous and irresponsible as it was when he wrote Bandelero the Bandit and played at Red Indians in Moat Brae garden at Dumfries. He was showing no sign of growing up, save that he could write better and get editors to pay for what he wrote; he was facing life with that gay curiosity which more than forty years afterwards we shall find him telling the young Rhodes scholars at Oxford is the only spirit wherewith they should go out to meet 'the mistress of the spindle.'

If we could imagine an admirer of Barrie so misguided as to attempt to do for him what Dr. John Kelman did for Stevenson— who, by the way, had just contributed Kidnapped as a serial to Young Folks, May–July, 1886—and to write a study of The

Faith of J. M. Barrie, he would find this period singularly barren
of material. Up to now Barrie shows no inkling of any philosophy
of life: he is enjoying its spectacle immensely, and is content to
state his experiences, and to recollect his emotions, with a comic
phraseology that tells his readers they are listening to a new and
individual voice. The note that he strikes at first most easily and
most frequently is one of flippant cynicism. Burlesque comes
natural to young men, and to 'get the laugh' is the too apparent
aim of much that Barrie is writing in his earlier days in Modern
Grub Street. 'Lightness of touch' is being demanded by editors
tired of the heavier handed Victorians (how dull are Sala, Suther-
land Edwards, Beatty Kingston, and the rest when re-read to-day!)
and this young journalist but recently come up from the provinces
with a most unusual capacity for saying quaint things in print
can 'deliver the goods.' He has no fad to foster, no deep sense of
social obligation as a publicist; he knows that 'to be interesting is
everything,' and that to be amusing in addition is to be irresistible.
He can be both, and I believe that, wagging his head like his own
Tommy of a later day, as he writes each new sketch for the St.
James's or the Edinburgh Dispatch, he says to himself, or it might
be to his invisible partner, not yet christened McConnachie.
'We're doing it again, I'm thinking!' Every day for two years
he had to be serious as a Nottingham leader-writer; but that is an
outlived phase; he finds that readers like more to be amused than
to be instructed, and he gets the greater fun out of amusing them.
Incidentally it also pays better. Were it otherwise he had been
equally ready to meet the demand, and would have met it not
less well.

His most productive years of freelancing were from the beginning of 1887 until the end of 1889. His contributions to
the St. James's were continued until June 1st, 1889, and in that
period amounted to about seventy, among them A Tale of a Glove,
A Home for Geniuses, and Preparing to Receive Company, afterwards reprinted in A Window in Thrums, and My Tobacco
Pouch, My Smoking Table, and The Perils of Not Smoking
which are included in My Lady Nicotine. In The Edinburgh
Evening Dispatch during the three years mentioned he wrote at
least two hundred articles on a great variety of topics, but mainly
inspired by the spirit of social satire and his abiding interest in the
journalistic life. I suspect the reflection of a trip to Paris in 1889
in the articles on How we Climbed the Eiffel Tower, Preparing
for the Continent: The Tourist's Purgatory, and The Open-Air
Café. By comparison with his work for he St. James's the bulk
of his contributions to the Dispatch were trivial, just the light

J. M. BARRIE AT THIRTY   [Fredk. Hollyer

BLACK LAKE COTTAGE, FARNHAM　　　[Rischgitz Studio
The country house formerly lived in by J. M. Barrie.

LEINSTER CORNER, LANCASTER GATE, LONDON　　　[McLeish
It was here that Barrie wrote Peter Pan.

reading for an idle hour which the editor asked of him. Even so, many of them were good enough to stand a second reading, such as A Holiday in Bed, The Theory of Carving, I Look So Young, On Running After One's Hat, and Shutting a Map, from which amusing paragraphs have been clipped times out of number by two generations of sub-editors searching for 'fill-up stuff.' His association with the Dispatch seems to have ended with 1890, Mr. Herbert Garland, in his Bibliography giving the last contribution as Mr. McCranky, on December 13th, but, as I am doubtful of some of the items in Mr. Garland's list, and aware of his numerous important omissions, I do no more than state the source of this information. It is clear, however, that of all that mass of three years' brilliant journalism the prevailing note was humour and a continuous amusement at the pageant of life which he had set himself the congenial task of describing.

Was ever writer for the press more happily situated? What pleased him most to produce was just what most pleased the public to read. These were indeed his golden days, and we can appreciate the wistful terms in which, when forty years have passed, we find him recalling them. In addition to his Wednesday and Saturday articles in the Edinburgh Dispatch he had one or two minor commissions of a regular sort for London journals, now difficult to trace, as they are lost in anonymity. His dramatic criticisms for Edmund Yates' old monthly Time (if my information is to be relied upon) should be mentioned. Strangely enough, Yates in his Recollections does not mention his own editorship of this publication, but as a lad who haunted the Mitchell Library at Glasgow, I remember it very well and recall my disapproval of its title. It was founded by Yates (then a Post Office clerk) in 1879 as 'a monthly miscellany of interesting and amusing literature,' and edited by him until 1884. Barrie would seem to have written for it under the editorship of E. M. A. Williams (1885–88), and I am told that he used to sit in the pit of the theatre, as William Archer did, that he might have the freedom of the critic who had accepted no favour from the management. His comments on the play were made with his characteristic humour and his fellow pitites furnished as much 'copy' for his pen as the traffic of the stage. The theatre was often the subject of the articles he sent to Edinburgh; so that we are witnessing at this period the future conqueror of the British stage stealthily spying out the Promised Land.

Call it luck, design, or what you will, there would seem to have been a happy turning of the wheels of chance in Barrie's continued attachment to the Comic Muse in his earlier work in London. If he was a literary genius with a journalist at his elbow, he was also a frivolous young cynic with a man of sentiment under the same skin, and presently we shall see that it was his ability to be funny that gave the other side of him a chance. It was the seed time of the New Humour, the formula for which might be expressed thus: Take eighty-five per cent of any comic stuff and fifteen of Dickensian sentimentalism, shake them lightly and let the sentimentalism precipitate itself at the bottom of the bottle; when the sediment is sufficiently treacly, deftly pour out the contents so that the sentimental sediment comes last and brings moisture to the eyes of the consumer.

Jerome K. Jerome used that prescription for so many years that it eventually ceased to be efficacious. Barrie never worked so crudely: he never was in any danger of being dubbed a 'new humorist,' for happening to be something of an artist as well as a genius, the cruder methods of the Jerome school were offensive to his taste. Yet he had been no less determined to make his readers laugh; if he was now making up to 'the other lady' he approached her in motley. It is as a humorist of rather a mocking disposition, inclined at first to make fun of serious things and displaying little reverence for anything, that Barrie makes his entry into the world of letters. And, as luck would have it, it was his determination to be funny that led him to his serious and enduring work.

The momentous thing happened quite unplanned. Though it came to him 'out of the blue,' it was no heaven-sent inspiration; merely an editor's need to enliven the columns of his new journal. This editor also happened to be a man of genius; his paper the adequate expression of his rare and complex personality. It had been founded in November, 1886, and from the first number had caught the affection of a public that was of the very salt of the country in its social and religious life and especially in matters of literary taste. That public was, relative to the general population, more numerous in Scotland and the north of England than in the south: it was largely Presbyterian in its religious attachment and Liberal in its political sympathies. It seemed to be peculiarly designed to receive and support a new writer who could tell it something fresh about the religio-literary life of the north, the enduring passion of the brilliant editor who had in one week made himself its expositor. This journal was The British Weekly: its editor was the Rev. William Robertson Nicoll, LL.D. The paper and the man were really one and indivisible. Barrie has written of him:

THE MAKING OF A HUMORIST

Seldom, I suppose, has there been an editor who was his paper so peculiarly as he was. He made The British Weekly ' off his own bat '— made it by himself out of himself; it was so full of his personality that he came stalking out of the pages, meeting every reader face to face, so that it can truly be said he paid a visit every week to every person who took in the paper.

Allowing for every favouring wind that blew upon the young humorist in London, his indebtedness to Robinson, to Greenwood, to Riach, here was the most fortunate of all his early associations: Robertson Nicoll. To his splendid enthusiasm Nicoll added the uniqueness of a driving power never before exerted by any one man of letters. When he 'took up' a new writer, the fortune of that writer was as good as made. Besides the unequalled value of The British Weekly as a literary force, it was associated with a publishing house into which Nicoll had breathed a new vitality, and though there were not wanting those who questioned the morality of the editor of The British Weekly lauding in his newspaper the books which he had chosen for his own firm to publish and which, as the writer of various 'literary letters' in other journals at home and in America, he did not hesitate to urge upon the reading public, he never praised anything that was unworthy; his instinct for all that was good in literature was unerring.

On a day in the summer of 1887—it would be about May Meeting time—Nicoll, knowing nothing of the young genius who had been toiling so assiduously for more than two years in his lodging at Great Windmill Street, happened to be in Edinburgh and in the Evening Dispatch one night he read with enjoyment an amusing burlesque of the Free Church Assembly, the writer of which was doubtless drawing exclusively on a fertile imagination. (This article, like so many others, has eluded the inadequately vigilant eye of Mr. Garland, the compiler of the Bibliography published in October, 1928.) Nicoll was in search of a contributor who could write for him in a breezy way about Scottish ecclesiastical affairs. Here was his man. A letter to the editor of the Dispatch disclosed his contributor as J. M. Barrie, and in The British Weekly of July 1st, 1887, a brilliant article entitled The Rev. Dr. Whyte, by an Outsider, and signed Gavin Ogilvy, was the immediate and historic result. For three or four years Gavin Ogilvy was the favourite contributor to The British Weekly, continuing to use that pseudonym in its columns even when the name of J. M. Barrie had become famous as the author of Auld Licht Idylls and A Window in Thrums.

BARRIE: THE STORY OF A GENIUS

Two wonderful years for J. M. Barrie are 1887 and 1888:
we see him harvesting in most favourable weather. All his literary
labours since the autumn of 1884 are now bearing fruit abundantly. In The British Weekly Gavin Ogilvy followed up his
initial character study of Dr. Whyte ('by an Outsider' was a
calculated mis-statement; no writer knew the great preacher
better or more intimately) with a great variety of sketches and
essays, including the series of character studies afterwards gathered
together as An Edinburgh Eleven, the first of which, Professor
Blackie, appeared in the issue of July 1st, 1887, and the last, the
Rev. W. C. Smith, on November 30th, 1888.

His dexterity as a humorous writer is well illustrated in his
article 'Ndintpile Pont (?)' which The British Weekly printed in
its issue of September 9th, 1887. He pretends that he has received
a request from 'a certain editor' to do a paper on that topic. He
has his misgivings about it, but he does not ask his editor if he
has read his scrawl correctly, as he would not like him to think
that he is not well up in the topics of the day. He shows the letter
to friends in a careless way, hoping for light. None of them help;
one only has the honesty to say he never heard of the subject, the
others say 'Oh!' or 'Ah' 'as if they understood thoroughly,
and a few had the hardihood to ask me how I mean to treat
it. I reply blandly, 'In the usual way,' and that seems to satisfy
them.' With excellent fooling he examines a variety of possible
readings:

The last man I showed it to must have thought that it was a lady's
name, for he said, 'Do you think she'll be pleased at your writing an
article on her?' Though this question took me aback, I replied, with
considerable presence of mind, that I was sure she would like it; and
then he asked if I knew her personally. I said I had known her intimately for years, and he said was she not a bit of an invalid, and I said
one of her lungs was completely gone. That evening I drew up a list
of all the celebrated women still alive that I could think of, and compared the names with Ndintpile Pont. The one that came nearest it
was Mrs. Oliphant. The last four letters of her name are not so
unlike Pont when you examine them with the hope that they are like
it. Tack the 'ile' of what seems to be the first word on to the 'Pont,'
and you get 'Ilepont.' Then look at Ilepont as the editor has written
it, and it might easily be Oliphant. That leaves 'Ndintp' unaccounted
for; but, after all, is it Ndintp? Is it not more like Margaret, which
is Mrs. Oliphant's Christian name? I sat down to write about Mrs.
Oliphant with a light heart, but before the first paragraph was finished
I became doubtful again.

THE MAKING OF A HUMORIST

After variously considering the possibility that 'Pont' might be 'pond' he finally favours 'punt' as a reading:

> It might certainly be Punt. I am living in a houseboat at present, and, of course, am frequently in punts. Is it Fishing off a Punt, or A Day in a Punt, or Our Houseboat Punt? Somehow it is difficult to feel certain that it is. . . . I have thought it over until the house-boat is going round and round, so my most honest course seems now to be to write to the editor saying that I won't be able to do an article this week, as I can't make out the subject.

Trifling though such an article might appear under the cold scrutiny of the critic, the easy grace of its writer is obvious, and the sort of talent required for such writing is rare. Reprinted in the two thousandth number of The British Weekly, nearly forty years after its first appearance, its humour had in no wise staled, and excepting only the reference to Mrs. Oliphant it was quite 'undated' The passage about the houseboat should be noted, as this indicates that the houseboat scenes of When a Man's Single and Walker, London were then being studied in actuality. It was this article by the way, that Robertson Nicoll chose to reprint in The Bookman of February, 1892, as illustrative of the unique quality of Barrie's journalism, remarking significantly that 'some of his best work is buried—not hopelessly—in newspaper files.'

Among the numerous Gavin Ogilvy papers was a series on The Literary Calling which appeared in April and May, 1889. These articles, which deal in the most practical way with all aspects of journalism, and include a paper on Books as Incomes, were just concluding when A Window in Thrums was winning the affections of the reading public. In a year or so the Gavin Ogilvy who was showing surprise that Charles Reade ten years earlier could have got so much as £100 from Greenwood for four articles in The Pall Mall Gazette would not be so impressed with such payment. They exhibit Barrie just at the moment when his own rewards and expectations are still moderate and his curiosity about journalistic life is still unappeased. Although the aim of the articles (probably suggested by Nicoll) is to furnish aspirants with useful hints and truthful information (and they do both extremely well) the humorist in their writing will not be denied:

> The other day a notoriously careless freelance was searching for a letter in his trouser pocket, and a cheque for twenty pounds fell out. The scene was a club, and a friend, lifting the cheque from the floor, handed it back to the owner, who again stuffed it into his pocket. Nothing unusual struck him in this action until he saw the other laughing, when he explained that he was really very careful about money.

BARRIE: THE STORY OF A GENIUS

He had a sheaf of cheques, he said, in a case in his inside pocket. Asked to what amount, he thought two or three hundred pounds; but was willing to make sure. The case was then overhauled. It proved to be one of the little leather cases that hold three letters with comfort, but now it bulged out like an alderman. It had burst at one end, and the owner took credit to himself for his forethought in having tied a bootlace round it. The contents were some fifty envelopes, nearly all of which contained cheques for sums averaging from two to fifty guineas. Some of them were a year old—their owner being surprised to see them—and in all they amounted to almost twice as much as he had thought. His way is to cash them one by one, as he needs them or comes across them, and he seemed rather perplexed to find that he was so wealthy.

The club referred to we may assume to be the Savage, which Barrie had joined on June 27th, 1888, when its rooms were in Lancaster House, Savoy Street, and of which he continued a member until 1895, after its removal to its present home in Adelphi Terrace, a stone's throw from his own residence of later years. He introduces the Savage as the Wigwam into When a Man's Single.

The temptation to quote from these significant papers on The Literary Calling is hard to resist, as there is scarcely a paragraph in them that does not contain something worth recalling, but I must content myself by reprinting only the concluding lines of his article on The Future of Journalism, allowing the reader to exclaim 'Is Gavin Ogilvy also among the prophets?'

I do not believe that journalism next century will be the power that it is to-day. We are a half-educated people, who ask our newspapers to think for us, and have not yet unveiled the mystery of the editorial we. Gradually, if we are to progress, we shall only ask for facts, and then make up our minds about them for ourselves. The editorial comments will not be given weight merely because they are printed, but because the writer is known to be a man whose views deserve attention. If this is correct, the only important function of coming journalism will be to give the news, and the best journalist will be he who knows what the news really is.

What is most noteworthy about all his miscellaneous work of these years is its consistently humorous flavour; its writer is seldom anxious to be taken seriously, though we have seen how wisely he can judge signs and portents when he cares. He is an amused observer of men and things, quite happy in this awareness of life and making no effort to probe deeply beneath its surface. Hence the instant success of his work as journalism, and if some of it remains journalism even when it appears in book form it is journalism that was far too good to be allowed to pass into limbo.

There is no better example of his journalism that is at least 'literary,' even if it is not literature, than his famous squib The Strange Case of Sir George Trevelyan and Mr. Otto. This was printed in the St. James's of July 29th, 1887, when Trevelyan (who died in 1928) was contesting the Bridgeton Division of Glasgow. Sir George Otto Trevelyan had shown some indecision in his Gladstonian allegiance, deserting the Liberal fold with Chamberlain in 1886, but returning to it in the following year as an avowed Home Ruler. Rarely has an electoral campaign been marked by so delicate a piece of satire as that which Barrie threw off to fill a column or so of the St. James's. No other journalist of his time could have written anything so keenly penetrating in its criticism, and yet we may doubt if Barrie greatly cared about the political issue which Trevelyan was contesting; probably if he had been a voter in Bridgeton he would have given his support to Sir George, as his political sympathies were inclined towards the Liberal party of that day. The satirist in him saw the opportunity for the journalist that inhabited the same skin, and the thing was done in a flash:

Some curious stories (he wrote) are afloat in Glasgow about Sir George Trevelyan. While he was speaking at a certain temperance institute on Monday an elderly lady, whose position near the platform gave her a good view of him, suddenly flung up her hands and fainted. At the hotel where Sir George is staying it is said that three of the servants have left already—one in convulsions. It is also stated that the Gladstone committee are in a very perturbed state of mind.

A reporter is said to have interviewed the lady who fainted, the three servants, Sir George's valet, and a Mr. Otto, and had gathered strange information. Tagg, the boots at the hotel, had seen Mr. Otto in the house, but was certain that he never arrived:

'Sir George and Mr. Otto are very like each other?' 'I suppose so; but you can easily distinguish them. Mr. Otto is smaller and meaner-looking, and his clothes are too large for him.'

'Will you tell me why you left the hotel so hurriedly?' 'I was frightened.'

'Why?' 'I don't know. Yes, it was Mr. Otto who frightened me.'

'Tell me how.' 'I don't like to. Sir George had told me to knock him at eight and bring him his letters. One morning I took them as usual. I gave them to him and retired. When I got downstairs I found that I had forgotten one, so I ran back and gave it to him—no, not to him, to Mr. Otto.'

' Then Mr. Otto was in the room? I thought you had never seen them together?' ' Mr. Otto was in the room, but Sir George had disappeared.'

Sir George's valet is interviewed. He is greatly perturbed, and threatens to leave on account of 'that Otto.' 'The doctors said it all came of drinking too much water,' he explains.

' Did Mr. Otto visit him at that time?' ' Visit him? I thought you knew all about it. How can a man visit himself?'
' But Sir George and Mr. Otto are not the same person?' ' I don't know about that. All I can say is that another week of this will drive me mad. . . .
' Stop a moment. You can tell me, perhaps, what Sir George's politics are?' ' He is a staunch Unionist.'
' And Mr. Otto?' ' He is an out-and-out Gladstonian.'

As these brief extracts will prove, there was a quality in Barrie's journalism that lifted it far above the ordinary level of newspaper writing, and while it may be true that Sir George was annoyed at the satire, he was too good a man of letters not to recognise and appreciate its uncommon merit. The cause of his annoyance may have been the fact that The Glasgow Herald, without comment, rather wickedly quoted the article on the day preceding the election, banking upon a lack of humorous perception among Bridgetonians to work to the disadvantage of the candidate, whose press champion The Glasgow Daily Mail gravely denounced the story next morning as a 'malicious fabrication,' and added that there was 'not an atom of fact in it.' Thirteen years later a writer in the same dull journal, reviewing a little book of mine about Barrie in which the episode of the political satire was restated, delivered his humourless soul in these terms:

Mr. J. M. Barrie will be greatly lowered in public esteem by a remarkable disclosure which is made by Mr. J. A. Hammerton. . . . The article not only implied that Sir George was double-faced but attributed to him the living of two lives, after the manner of Dr. Jekyll and Mr. Hyde. Sir George expressed great indignation at the gross libel, and even his Tory opponents were ashamed of it. Mr. Hammerton now states that the author of the outrage was Mr. J. M. Barrie. According to Mr. Hammerton, it was a ' squib,' and a ' very diverting sketch,' and a piece of ' delicate satire,' and a ' good specimen ' of Mr. Barrie's ' journalistic humour.' We have not seen anything much lower in journalism, and if it was ' delicate ' we wonder what could be indelicate.

As the Americans say, 'can you beat it?' Nevertheless the Scots as a whole are a humorous people. Those of them who are not are at least, like this Glasgow dullard, the cause of humour in others. The illusion of gravity which Barrie can achieve when giving off his most hilarious notions has more than once led to unexpected results with readers lacking the comic sense. An article of his in The Fortnightly Review for September, 1890, entitled Pro Bono Publico, and purporting to be a description of the work of a Society for Providing Materials for Volumes of Reminiscences, with sundry specimens of the anecdotes available, each marked in plain figures, brought a request from a German gentleman for some reminiscences to incorporate in a book upon which he was engaged.

His devotion to the Comic Muse at this period of his career was complete, his mind was assailed by no philosophic doubts, no dark problems of existence engaged his thoughts, the sheer joy of living and of writing about the folk he rubbed shoulders with in his daily pursuits is to be seen in all his work for the St. James's in London and The Dispatch in Edinburgh, and he had also imported humour into the columns of the religious British Weekly. His writings in the journals and magazines were steadily multiplying, and it is probable that as he wrote he would have a distant eye on the possibilities of working up some of them into books. He was too good a journalist to think first of his books and then try to make each new article a chapter of a book rather than an article for a newspaper. He was a great and unique journalist, quite aware that his future was to be remote from journalism, but by giving of his best to the periodical press he was soon to find that he had amassed so large a body of individual and distinguished writings that he could, with but little exertion, furnish forth from it the contents of half-a-dozen acceptable volumes if he cared. As the events will prove he chose (perhaps wisely) to use the merest fraction of this miscellaneous matter for reshaping into books. Robertson Nicoll used to say that the books of a good journalist could never be anything but the reprints of his worthiest journalism. Knowing this, Barrie had determined that his courting of the Grisette must, as soon as he could honourably contrive it, have an end, and we are witnessing him in these years 1886–1888 in the time of his transition. His earlier offerings to the other lady were really to be posies picked from the armfuls of pretty things he had originally fashioned for the darling jade.

And yet it happened that the first book which appeared with the name of J. M. Barrie on its title-page was written as a book and not intended for periodical publication. He was living in rooms in the Temple when this, his first book, was written and published. Better Dead came out in the day of the 'shilling shockers,' and it outwardly assumed their guise. It was published in November, 1887, but dated 1888 by Swan, Sonnenschein & Co., Paternoster Square, a house noted at that time for its list of somewhat heavy literature: studies in social science and works of technical interest were its staple. In addition it published a few 'commission books,' whose authors either bore a part of the cost or were glad to have their manuscripts issued in book form without receiving any initial payment, trusting to be rewarded by the royalties that would accrue. Better Dead was quite out of the run of this particular publishing house, and I doubt if its author fingered any 'advance.' He would be only too pleased to find a firm that would risk the printing and circulating of his first book. It was issued at the popular price of one shilling in a paper wrapper which bore a very striking design: good enough indeed to serve as a modern dust cover. As a matter of interest, I may mention that the draughtsman who supplied the design was an old fellow-academical from Dumfries, known to all his friends as 'Punch' Mitchell, and nephew of Donald Mitchell, sometime editor of The Dumfries Courier.

The title was boldly displayed, the initials 'B' and 'D' being ingeniously formed out of a drawn sword, its scabbard and buckle belt, together with a revolver and a twisting rope with a noose at the end of it, while below the sword, which dripped large gouts of blood, stood a white-bearded anarchist, dagger in hand, ready to strike at two shadowy figures of comic outline—Sir William Harcourt and Lord Randolph Churchill—jauntily occupying the lower foreground of the design. The name J. M. Barrie appeared in letters nearly half an inch high, and it is idle to suppose that the owner of that name was other than delighted to look upon this most appropriate pictorial introduction to his satirical shocker. I suspect that in the dull December days when it came out to brighten the bookstalls (where it would have the competition of the old-fashioned Christmas numbers) a slight figure might have been seen lurking about the Charing Cross Station bookstall watching eagerly for the stray passenger reckless enough to speculate a shilling on the little book which was to introduce his name to the reading public. Himself he comes near to disowning his first-born. 'Weighted with An Edinburgh Eleven, it would rest very comfortably in the mill dam'; but a tender moment of recollection supervenes:

THE MAKING OF A HUMORIST

And yet I have a sentimental interest in Better Dead, for it was my first—published when I had small hope of getting any one to accept the Scotch—and there was a week when I loved to carry it in my pocket and did not think it dead weight. Once I almost saw it find a purchaser. She was a pretty girl and it lay on a bookstall, and she read some pages and smiled, and then retired, and came back and began another chapter. Several times she did this, and I stood in the background trembling with hope and fear. At last she went away without the book, but I am still of opinion that, had it been just a little bit better, she would have bought it.

The truth is that not every author who has attained to fame can look back upon his first book with less reason to blush for its immaturity. The idea of Better Dead is first seen in a St. James's article bearing that title and signed 'By a Friend of His Species,' printed in April, 1885, and it advances a stage further in an Edinburgh Evening Dispatch contribution of January 13th, 1886, on The Society for Doing Without Some People, the writer of which is supposed to be A Humanitarian. Better Dead was, indeed it remains, an essentially Barriesque piece of satire. It is in essence of the same stuff as his later satire and differs only from the mass of his writings in lacking the softening relief of humour and sentiment. It is cold, hard, sophisticated: here is no hint of the naïve painter of *genre* subjects so soon to reveal himself. But it is undeniably clever and amusing. Its most obvious source of inspiration is The Suicide Club by Stevenson (a piece of writing half as long again as Better Dead), but probably the idea of trying his prentice hand with a shilling shocker came from the noteworthy success of The Strange Case of Dr. Jekyll and Mr. Hyde, which had been published in that form at the beginning of 1886.

Hugh Conway's Called Back (1884) and Fergus Hume's Mystery of a Hansom Cab (1887) were other outstanding examples of the shilling 'thrillers' which were then the main traffic of the bookstalls. The journalist in Barrie was quick to appreciate the value of appealing to the popular taste in outward form at least, though his inspiration was too strongly comic to allow him to compose a tale of mystery with a grave countenance. More, he had not in comparable degree the power of sustained story-telling which was Stevenson's, whose Jekyll and Hyde, a tale of thirty thousand words, written, destroyed and re-written in six days, was a veritable *tour de force*. The germ idea of Jekyll and Hyde came to Stevenson in a dream, and next morning he was all excitement exclaiming 'I've got my shilling shocker!' His feverish haste was to get the book out before Christmas,

131

1885, but by the time it was ready its publishers, Longmans, Green & Co., more cautious than Barrie's, withheld it on account of the bookstalls being flooded with Christmas numbers, and thus it appeared in January, 1886.

I learn with astonishment from Mr. Moult that 'Better Dead went into a second edition during the year of its publication.' That would indeed have meant an instant success, in view of my earlier information that it first appeared in November: but a second edition did appear in 1888 similar in all respects to the first save for the words 'Second Edition.' The blue buckram edition in my library is dated 1891, and it may be doubted if that would ever have been printed at all had not its author in the mean-time made his name famous with five other books. Despite all its cleverness, its wit, its sly criticism of certain features of social life, it made no sort of appeal to the great bookstall public, nor did it happen to be a work of genius like Stevenson's shocker. But it at least made its writer an author. Behold the vow he had taken in the garret fifteen years before fulfilled! That was some-thing. It was the Hogmanay to a Guid New Year; 1888 was to be a red letter year for J. M. Barrie.

While Better Dead was still lingering dustily on the bookstalls there appeared in April, 1888, with no blare of trumpets—no such bills as 'Another Book by the Author of Better Dead!'—a new volume entitled Auld Licht Idylls, price six shillings. Here is dignity, here comes a real pukka author! He dedicated his book to Frederick Greenwood for reasons already known to us; but it might as appropriately have been dedicated to the good fairy who made Robertson Nicoll read a certain sketch in the Edinburgh Evening Dispatch less than a year before. Never was there a happier concatenation of circumstances: a young author with the pen of genius, a sympathetic editor with a widely circulated weekly journal for bookish readers, and a publishing house pre-pared to 'push' the books which he recommended. Instant to appreciate the rare quality of Barrie's homely sketches of Scot-tish character, Nicoll had become forthwith his devoted admirer; in the good sense of the word, his exploiter. Barrie bought his first tall hat 'to impress editors' and has recalled how he climbed the stairs of an office in Paternoster Row wearing that shiny topper to meet for the first time this great journalist, who was so little impressed by anyone's attire.

Auld Licht Idylls had a friendly and appreciative press. Mr. Moult has alleged that 'while no English-speaking writer is held in such affectionate regard by readers and playgoers alike, his genius has consistently been deined serious appreciation.' To this statement I must demur; the facts are against it. There used to be a legend that George Meredith struggled for many years against lack of appreciation, that he could not get a hearing for his work, but the legend was a mere newspaper *cliché* brought out afresh by each paragraphist, as I sought (and I think success-fully) to show in a study of his life and work. There is no legend that Barrie's genius has been denied serious appreciation; it is a statement which I encounter for the first time in Mr. Moult's monograph, and this is the place to question it. Rather is there an impression that he has been made too much of; that he i Fortune's white-headed boy.

What is serious appreciation? An eminent novelist has argued that sales are the criterion, and certain dramatists have maintained that the box-office is the touchstone of merit. Well, Barrie's admirers could appeal with the serenest confidence to his sales and to his box-office receipts if they cared, but they know that neither means 'serious appreciation.' though they are the lure of every man that writes a book or a play. The hope of a novelist or a writer of any sort is that his contemporary critics will speak well of his work. What, then, happened to Barrie's Auld Licht Idylls? There was a veritable chorus of praise from all the im-portant journals and reviews in Great Britain. Hardly a querulous note. Even Scottish journals were ungrudging in their approval, The Glasgow Herald finding it difficult to speak of the book in adequate terms 'without laying oneself open to exaggeration.' And let me tell the English reader that when Scottish critics praise a fellow countryman who has gone to London they have to suppress a strong impulse to belittle him; the Englishman enter-tains no greater delusion about the Scots than the notion that they are clannish. So hearty was the commendation which Auld Licht Idylls received from the critical press in the spring of 1888, that its author was already a made man.

Reconsidering the book forty years afterwards, one feels that the latter-day critic might be forgiven if he expressed surprise at the enthusiasm it evoked when it came fresh from the press. He might also wonder how all the pother about its Scotch dialect arose. In the copy of Auld Licht Idylls lying on my desk out of a total of 187 pages not more than thirty are in Scotch, and of these no fewer than nineteen occur in one chapter, The Courting of T'nowhead's Bell. That was the only chapter which the author had been unable to get any editor to print before it ap-peared in the book. The chief fault of the book is the miscel-laneous nature of its contents, most of which are in no sense 'idylls.' Its abiding value in Barrie's literary development is that it provides a sort of undress rehearsal for most of the characters that were later to play their parts, 'word perfect,' in A Window in Thrums, The Little Minister, and the two Tommy books. A few of these were to suffer radical change when they reappeared: notably Mr. Dishart. 'Before he was in his teens he was practising the art of gesticulation in his father's gallery pew. . . . He was never more than comparatively young.' This cannot be the Gavin Dishart we are to meet at close quarters later on.

The great merit of the Idylls is the success with which its author assumes and maintains the rôle of schoolmaster in the glen of Quharity. The illusion of a middle-aged chronicler is complete from the unforgettable opening of the first chapter (the chaptering is an artifice to give an appearance of cohesion where the reality is absent) to the concluding sentence of the last. 'Early this morning I opened a window in my schoolhouse in the glen of Quharity, awakened by the shivering of a starving sparrow against the frosted glass.' A fine opening to that wonderful little piece The Schoolhouse, which keys the tone of the whole book. Then follows the long sketch of Thrums: a sort of roll call of the Auld Lichts. Here the author is preparing the background for the play of characters comic and pathetic that is to engage him for years to come. Next comes The Auld Licht Kirk, in which, as in Thrums, the point of view is still that of a humorous mind laughing at the foibles of his folk and as ready to expose their weaknesses as their better qualities. 'You could generally tell an Auld Licht in Thrums when you passed him, his dull vacant face wrinkled over a heavy wob.' 'The only really tender thing I ever heard an Auld Licht lover say to his sweetheart was when Gowrie's brother looked softly into Easie Tamson's eyes and whispered, "Do you swite (sweat)?"'

It is Gavin Ogilvy, the schoolmaster, who is supposed to register these unpleasant things, but the author could hardly hope to escape ill will for being so bluntly truthful, and he did not escape it. He was not out to give an entirely flattering portrait of the Auld Lichts, or he could never have written such a chapter as Cree Querry and Mysy Drolly, which I never read without a rising indignation at the Thrums laddies who used to run after Cree and Mysy taunting these poor souls with the suggestion that they would have to wind up in the 'poorhouse,' 'at which the grey old man would wince, as if "joukin" from a blow.' Cree, when tormented by the boys as he neared the workhouse with his cruel load of yarn, 'sat down on his barrow shafts terrified to approach, and I see them now pointing to the workhouse till he left his barrow on the road and hobbled away, his legs cracking as he ran.' There is nothing of the idyll here; only stark realism, relieved by a piece of proper sentiment at the close, which finely proves that Cree's life was not a failure. And then I reflect that boys everywhere are naturally cruel animals, a tag from Jump-to-Glory Jane coming to mind:

Those flies of boys disturbed them sore.

But in the main the Idylls is the work of a humorist and it is essentially a work of imagination. Critics unfamiliar with the facts of the author's youth suppose him to be describing things seen, and relating events within his own experience: a marvellous reporter. My readers are aware that his boyhood in Kirriemuir was limited to a few fleeting years, and that there are few actual episodes in his Thrums stories with which he had first-hand acquaintance. In every detail Auld Licht Idylls is a work of creative art, and such of its characters as had originals in Kirriemuir had passed from the scene long before its author thought of writing about his native place. His descriptive power is so extraordinary that every feature he seeks to illumine, every scene he would illustrate, stands out with almost startling vividness.

Seventy years before Barrie wrote his Idylls John Galt had had to meet the discouragers who told him, when he first offered his Annals of the Parish to the publishers, that nobody wanted to read Scotch stories, and for some years that manuscript lay neglected until Blackwoods plucked up the necessary courage to print it. The famous house of Macmillan (also of Scottish origin) might have been Barrie's publishers to-day (and they must surely regret a missed opportunity) if they had not turned down Auld Licht Idylls when its author submitted the book to them.

Up to the appearance of the Idylls and its being acclaimed by press and public as a new work of genius, Barrie must still be considered as a journalist with a unique gift of humour, and the fact that he was then seriously contemplating a biography of Russel of The Scotsman suggests that he had not quite settled with himself (or agreed with McConnachie) upon the sort of magic that was to make the age to come his own. There is something of it in the Idylls, hardly any of it in Better Dead; most of it was still up that wizard sleeve of his. We may have lost a master-piece of biography in the projected life of Russel, but we can well afford the loss in view of the energy it released for the creating of more enduring and more beautiful things

The success of the Idylls left no doubt in the minds of his publishers and their sagacious editor that this new author must continue. When it appeared he had been running a serial in The British Weekly, and in six months more that serial invaded the bookshops, brave in the navy-blue livery that was the garb of a Barrie book for many a year afterward. A new impression of the Idylls was also selling steadily. The author of When A Man's Single: A Tale of Literary Life was given as Gavin Ogilvy in the serial issue; in book form the open secret of his identity was avowed. Again the success of his book was assured by its opening chapters and if the truth must be told the high promise of those first three chapters is barely maintained throughout the remaining eighteen of the story. It is in them that we get the first clear hint of the coming Barrie: the master of simple pathos, the acute observer of the larger and more serious things of life. There is a finely cumulative effect in the narrative beginning with those arresting lines: 'One still Saturday afternoon some years ago a child pulled herself through a small window into a kitchen in the kirk-wynd of Thrums. She came from the old graveyard. . . .' That effect is most impressive at the end of the third chapter where Rob winds up his big watch, goes down on his knees to say his prayers, 'and then, remembering that he had said them already, rose up and went to bed.'

When a Man's Single may not appear a masterpiece under the critical microscope. From a lesser writer than its author it would have been accepted as a brilliant performance. Apart from its permanent autobiographical value, and the fact that out of it was carved the author's first stage success which sent his career off at a new angle, it is to be classed with those works that are more note-worthy in their promise than memorable in achievement. In its weekly instalments it would read better; as a book to be read straight through it becomes too fore-shortened, the events are seen to be imposed from outside in the arbitrary manner of melo-drama. Indeed, all the old Adelphi machinery is here; complete with false baronet and those improbable encounters between the personages which we used to associate with the penny novelette. If the mark which the J. M. Barrie of 1888 aimed to 'wed' (in his admired Meredith's phrase) was that of novelist in the grand manner, his arrow went somewhat wide of the target. Himself, he entertains no illusions about his first novel as a work of art, and in his introduction to the collected edition of 1896 he gives a frank explanation of its disjointed nature, which he rightly attri-butes to the fact that it began its serial publication when no more than those splendid opening chapters had been written; 'soon I was only one chapter ahead, and after that, I think I never increased the distance between us though I could feel its breath on my

THE HOUSE ON THE BRAE
Showing ' The Window ' in the gable end.

THE SCHOOLHOUSE IN GLEN CLOVA
Immortalised in Auld Licht Idylls and The Little Minister.

Face page 136

A Latter-day Tammas Haggart   [*Clifton Johnson*

In ' Jimsy Duthies ' Cot   [*Clifton Johnson*
An old time weaver's living room in Kirriemuir.

neck.' And he frankly admits that 'it is a method of publication I hope never to adopt again.'

Withal, it is a book rich in entertainment, infinitely more delightful in its disjointed chapters than many a novel of flawless construction, and as it is the work of an unrivalled humorist (who was to prove capable of writing even an obituary in the comic vein with perfect taste and delicacy), the reading world was thankful for it, and remains grateful. Journalists especially find it endlessly fascinating as the truest picture of journalistic life ever drawn in fiction. The gusto of youth exhales from its pages. How exhilarating the scene where Colonel Abinger comes upon Rob poaching in his stream! There are so many other passages told with equal verve that one feels we have here a book which defies Euclid and proves that the part may be greater than the whole. It is when we encounter instances like the following that we feel the novelist has not quite arrived:

' No, Sir Clement Dowton, I bear you no ill-will, but I do not love you. Years ago I made an idol and worshipped it, because I knew no better, but I am a foolish girl no longer, and I know now that it was a thing of clay.'

But I confess that I am less interested in the story as a story than in its details as implicit autobiography, and I will suggest that in such a passage as I transcribe below it is not unfair to read J. M. Barrie for Rob Angus:

Rob never found any difficulty afterwards in picking out the shabby eating-house in which he had his first meal in London. Gray's Inn Road remained to him always its most romantic street because he went down it first. He walked into the roar of London in Holborn, and never forgot the alley into which he retreated to discover if he had suddenly become deaf. He wondered when the crowd would pass. Years afterwards he turned into Fetter Lane, and suddenly there came back to his mind the thoughts that had held him as he went down it the day he arrived in London.

The conception of Noble Simms, the Bohemian freelance, is masterly in its truth and humour, and the members of the Savage Club for two score years have rejoiced in the glamour their Saturday nights derived from Barrie's chapter on The Wigwam, into which, by the way, he worked the set of verses on Edinburgh University which he contributed to Home Chimes of July, 1887.

By December, 1888, when An Edinburgh Eleven by Gavin Ogilvy was published as a British Weekly Extra at one shilling,

the name of J. M. Barrie was already better known than his pseudonym. It appears on the title-pages of all subsequent editions.
The sale of this sparkling brochure was not remarkable; it took
eight years to go into a third edition—and not a line of 'Scotch'
in it! I have no record of how it was received by the reviewers
—it would not appear to have attracted any great attention—
but in the 1891 summer issue of The Student, the Edinburgh
University magazine, there is a reference to it in a general review
of Barrie's literary deeds up to that time. What the Edinburgh
students may be supposed to have thought about the little book
is worth enquiring. While it would be foolish to assume that
the opinion of one student-reviewer is the voice of his university,
it is not improbable that his point of view is common to many
of his fellow students. Here at least is what The Student would
have us think of An Edinburgh Eleven:

Mr. Barrie's Edinburgh Eleven is bright and clever, charmingly
inaccurate, and romantically overdrawn, but it is scarcely what we
expect from so powerful a pen, nor, if the truth must be told, does it
do much justice to his old University and its students. We scarcely
think that the already all too grotesque humanity we northern students
really are will be much improved or corrected by Mr. Barrie's witty
descriptions. His style in this sort of book becomes forced and stiff,
the humour at times grows stale or smacks of resurrection.

There speaks the voice of prejudice. We can understand the
students being sensitive to criticism or comic description of themselves and their professors: the younger the more sensitive. But
it is nonsense to say that the book presents his alma mater in
anything but an attractive light, or with any feeling other than
that of genuine sympathy and admiration. To describe its style
—written as it was about the same time as his best prose—as
'forced and stiff' is merely some smart youth's desire to be
critical at the expense of his betters. The penetrating and courageous study of Stevenson alone would redeem the little book
from so foolish a charge. The truth is that each of its eleven
sketches is charmingly written, and the whole informed with
cunning humour and fresh observation.

Within a few months of its appearance its author came before
the reading public again with another work so vastly more important that by comparison An Edinburgh Eleven shrank greatly
in significance, and speedily shared the fate of those books which
are reprinted journalism. His biographers, however, will always
be grateful for that unique record of Barrie's college days.

THE MAKING OF A HUMORIST

His literary career, which was to prove a long succession of surprises, has thus far been a steady progression towards fame and fortune: his main objective the entertainment of his readers in the development of that gift of humour which characterises Auld Licht Idylls and redeems When A Man's Single, a humour that comprises

A deal of Ariel, just a streak of Puck,

if I may so apply a line from Henley's sonnet on R. L. S., written in 1888. We have seen him at work as the thoroughly competent journalist, taking over fresh from college his first office job as to the manner born; next as the brilliant freelance, writing on a multiplicity of topics with a rare charm of style that made him a marked man in many an editorial office, then entering the world of books with a buoyant confidence in his own powers, and though missing the mark as novelist still bringing so many other attractive qualities to the pursuit of story-telling that his lack of constructive technique was held to be a slight matter. By the end of 1888, when he is not yet thirty, his name is mentioned in literary circles as that of the coming man.

There is another and a younger writer whose name is also attracting attention now and for whom this is likewise a red-letter year: no fewer than five slim shilling books with blue-grey wrappers bearing amateurish designs were conspicuous in the bookshops of 1888: Soldiers Three, In Black and White, The Story of the Gadsbys, Under the Deodars, and The Phantom Rickshaw had been exported to the homeland from India to introduce a new genius to his own countrymen. Kipling, five years Barrie's junior, resembles him in hardly any literary feature, save in being intensely himself. What a year that was for modern English letters!—especially when we remember that W. E. Henley had in 1888 assumed the editorship of The Scots Observer after Nicol Dunn had launched it none too brilliantly. Both Barrie and Kipling, like many another who attained to varying measures of fame—G. W. Steevens, H. D. Lowry, Barry Pain, H. G. Wells, Gilbert Parker, Marriott Watson, Arthur Morrison, and G. S. Street may be named—were presently to be numbered among 'Henley's Young Men,' who, under his temerarious leadership, were to take so large a part in the literary conquest of the 'nineties.

CHAPTER VII

SUCCESS: THE AUTHOR ARRIVES

1889–1890

THE reader whose memory goes back to the year 1889 may recall the thrilling interest which the world of book-lovers was then taking in the performances of two young competitors for literary fame: Kipling, with his sudden spate of shilling story-books that had first been 'tried out' on his Anglo-Indian audience and his virile Barrack-Room Ballads, starting with the immortal Danny Deever, in the Scots Observer (I have most of them cut out and pasted in an old common-place-book), seemed to shoot ahead of Barrie for the moment. Nothing quite like Kipling had happened before. English to the core of him, he appealed to his own countrymen with an exotic newness of style and a mastery of story-telling that had no parallel in his native literature. Instantly he had the English-speaking world at his feet. Not so Barrie. Where the lusty young singer of Empire and teller of strange tales seemed to proffer his literary wares almost truculently, the gentle humorist made a shy and diffident gesture for the affection of those who could be moved by the sympathetic presentation of scenes from lowly life.

Actually the humour and pathos of the Auld Lichts were qualities as strange to the mass of English readers as the doings of Mulvaney, Ortheris and Learoyd. Both writers, however, 'had a way with them,' and from now on they became a constant source of journalistic curiosity and public interest. Kipling at twenty-four was a sophisticated and travelled man; Barrie at twenty-nine was a home-keeping, chimney-corner man, who had travelled chiefly in 'the realms of gold.' Indeed, not until this year (1889) do we find any mention of his having even crossed the Channel; he does not seem to have shared his brother's wander-lust. It was really fortunate that no traveller's itch sent Barrie abroad in those days. In that event he would not have found his native countryside so absorbing.

SUCCESS: THE AUTHOR ARRIVES

Kipling and Barrie were admittedly the two foremost names among the bright band of new writers who seemed to arrive at the critical moment to breathe a hopeful and purposeful spirit into a literature which, with the decadent trend of the waning century, was threatening to become morbid and joyless. It is true that Stevenson had already brought into contemporary fiction a new sensitiveness to form and that Meredith, Hardy and many another good, if lesser, Victorian was still in his vigour, while such competent craftsmen as Robert Buchanan and Christie Murray were busy serving their generation; but withal it was a time of feminine stirrings; woman rights were being shrilly argued by aggressive females (Mrs. Lynn Linton intervening), Mrs. Mona Caird was asking Is Life Worth Living, and a callous press was daily reminding its women readers that their sex outnumbered the other by a million, 'the superfluous million,' by appealing to whose tastes the twentieth century was to witness a number of adventurous journalists become millionaires.

It was also the day of Adelphi drama and melodramatic fiction. East Lynne was a standard of success not only at the libraries but on the stage. The virility of Kipling and the winning charm of Barrie came, therefore, with singular freshness, and were factors of importance in counteracting the decadent movement, seen at its bleakest moment of introspection in the lines of one of its poets:

> God gives me grace to look upon
> This dung, my heart, without disgust.

We find a reflection of those restless times in some happy lines from Punch which I am glad to quote in support of what is no more than a personal and uncorrected impression:

> In dull days of sensational horrors, and wild, would-be humorous hums,
> What delight to fly darkness, and watch the Auld Licht from a Window
> in Thrums!
> Let pessimists potter and pule, and let savages slaughter and harry:
> Give me Hendry and Tammas and Jess, and a smile and a tear born
> of Barrie.

With his accustomed readiness to seize upon some episode or folly of the moment as a theme, or to use it merely as a tag, we find Barrie adapting the superfluous women topic of the daily press for the title of a short serial story he had written in 1888, the publication of which began in the January number of The Young Man, a minor monthly of the time, and was continued through the twelve issues of 1889. As the periodical in question was more noted for the promptness of its payments than for their munificence, it is improbable that the author of A Superfluous Man, as the story was called, received more than a very modest fee for it. The success of Auld Licht Idylls had not yet produced a soaring market in Barrie rates, and the magical methods of A. P. Watt in 'boosting' authors' prices were only beginning to be tried. Not that A Superfluous Man was worth any remarkable rate of payment, or indeed that it was not adequately rewarded; for it is scarcely up to the average of much of its author's earlier work. Most likely it was written to redeem a promise to the editor (F. A. Atkins, an early Barrie enthusiast) to send him 'something about thirty thousand words in length' suitable for printing in twelve short instalments.

Like the heroes of Better Dead and When A Man's Single, like their author and many thousand others, the hero, Dan Moor, comes from the country to try his fortune in London. But it is not from Scotland, far less from Thrums, that he sets out. He comes all the way from Ballyhewan, in Ireland, and has the advantage over most in setting out with a presentation purse of sovereigns and the good wishes of his friends. As a story A Superfluous Man is of no account, and would have gone down into the grave from which the literary offspring of the undistinguished have no resurrection had not its only begetter meanwhile happened to turn out a man of genius and of fame. Still, should Barrie be made to endure a gaol delivery of all his juvenilia and the uncollected writings of his earlier maturity, his reputation would lose nothing by A Superfluous Man, which is not without numerous little touches essentially characteristic; his reputation is capable of sustaining even the self-scarification of his earliest indiscretions in print.

In the event of A Superfluous Man ever appearing in a final collection of Barrie's writings it should be noted by those critics of a future day who will be called upon to discuss it that it was written at the same time as a book of his which must ever rank as his first masterpiece. The year was half-spent when A Window in Thrums made its appearance. July is accounted an unseasonable month for book-publishing, but it has this advantage for young authors: they get more attention from the reviewers if they publish in the 'off season.' Barrie had not yet reached the stage where he could afford to ignore all such adventitious aids to publicity, and possibly the shrewd mind of Nicoll suggested this midsummer venture. But the book in question was shaped for success let it appear when it might. It immediately attracted wide attention. Its name, intriguing and original, was heard wherever bookish gossips met. This young writer had arrived, and America was pricking up its ears, the house of Harpers having just issued When A Man's Single.

From this time the Kailyard school may be dated, though it was a year or two later that Dr. J. H. Millar, its severest native critic, so dubbed it. Whereas Auld Licht Idylls, as I have pointed out, contained a negligible amount of Scotch, in A Window in Thrums the first eight pages stand almost alone in being free from the Forfarshire idiom. And the Window sold for a while at the rate of two to one compared with Idylls, the latter making up most of the leeway eventually thanks largely to the demand for Barrie's works in general awakened by the Window. The reading public seemed to find no difficulty in understanding the local dialect so boldly reproduced by the author; perhaps it experienced a flattering pleasure in finding itself able to read an unfamiliar tongue. His cleverness in securing this result has seldom been acknowledged. His Scotch is vastly easier to the southerner than that of Scott or of Stevenson. It tinctures the speech of his characters with a raciness of the soil, but rarely obscures the meaning that is intended to be conveyed.

A curiously wrong-headed criticism of Barrie's use of dialect occurs in Mr. Thomas Moult's otherwise very intelligent appreciation of his work. I have read the following with hearty disagreement in his examination of A Window in Thrums:

Not yet, moreover, was the author aware that if the dialect speech of a 'regional' story is to be artistically introduced it must not be literally reported, but idiomatically suggested. 'Ou, she's naething by the ord'nar': but ye see she was mairit to a Tilliedrum man no lang syne, an' they're said to have a michty grand establishment. Ay, they've a wardrobe spleet new; an' what think ye Tibbie wears ilka day?' So runs an utterance, selected at random, by one of the characters of A Window in Thrums. And it will be noticed that the author endeavours to achieve his effect mainly by mis-spellings:—
'I fair forgot,' Hendry answered, 'but what's a' yer steer?'
Jess looked at me (she often did this) in a way that meant, 'What a man is this I'm tied to!'
'Steer!' she exclaimed. 'Is't no time we was makkin' a steer? They'll be in for tea ony meenute, an' the room no sae muckle as sweepit. Ay, an' me lookin' like a sweep; an' Tibbie Mealmaker 'at's sae partikler genteel seein' you sic a sicht as ye are!'

The critic then goes on to compare Barrie's use of dialect with the presumably superior skill of J. M. Synge, who can suggest the colour of the Irish brogue in a speech by Pegan Mike from The Playboy wherein not a single word contains 'a wrongly placed letter.' By contrast, he asserts that Barrie's methods are crude and inartistic. The critic here is surely following a false scent. The idiom that is spoken by even the common people of Ireland is not rooted in an archaic speech like that of the Scots (the Gaelic is not in question), and to turn any page of the purest English into Irish little more is needed than to read it aloud with the brogue. The genius of J. M. Synge would seem to be the ability to write his Irish speech in common English words, leaving the reader to supply that intonation, which more than the words themselves, make them 'Irish.' By the same reasoning Kipling's 'mis-spelt' rendering of Mulvaney's talk makes Soldiers Three inartistic! If we were to take the examples (not too happily chosen) which Mr. Moult offers in support of his case and turn them into English, how would they appear? Something like this:

'Oh, she is nothing beyond the ordinary; but you see she was married to a Tilliedrum man not long ago, and they are said to have a mighty grand establishment. Yes, they have a wardrobe split new; and what think you Tibbie wears each day?'

'What is all your excitement?' Hendry would have to ask, and Jess would answer:

'Excitement! Is it not time to be excited? They'll be in for their tea in a minute and the room not so much as swept. Yes, and me looking like a sweep; and Tibbie Mealmaker that's so particular genteel seeing you such a sight as you are!'

The critic will probably retort that I have here done nothing more than transliterate from the Scots to the English, and I do not pretend that I have attempted to suggest how the true tang of Scots speech might be retained without writing the words as they would be spoken, but I will defy the author of A Window in Thrums, and every other who has sought to interpret Scottish life, to convey any true impression of his characters without approximating in his written words to the actuality of their utterance. One might suspect from Mr. Moult's study of Barrie that he has never penetrated so far north as the actual scene of the stories on which he delivers judgement. If he had he would have found considerable difficulty in making his English speech understood by the peasantry, and a greater difficulty in understanding their replies. The Scottish tongue is not entirely, as he supposes, a mispronunciation of modern English, but in large part derives, like Anglo-Saxon itself, from the ancient Gothic. In common with the speech of all the inhabitants north of the Humber, but excluding the Highlands (Mr. Moult makes the cardinal error of confusing Lowlanders and Highlanders), it has retained through the ages many thousands of words that are purer Anglo-Saxon than most that are common to modern English. When we remember that Jamieson's Dictionary of the Scottish Tongue, a work by no means complete, comprises close upon three thousand large quarto pages, we can realise that what the Englishman knows as Scotch is something that must have a genius of its own and is no mere patois of English.

I reaffirm that it is one of the many merits of Barrie's Scottish stories that, by an entirely artistic use of his native tongue, he has contrived to present to the world a community of people as foreign in many respects to the town-dwelling Englishman as the Finns or the Norwegians, without undue sacrifice of their characteristic speech. Their manner of expression is often inseparable from the thought or emotion to be conveyed. How else, indeed, would it be possible to suggest to any reader the true atmosphere of the grim Scottish humour that informs The Statement of Tibbie Birse? In Scottish rural life burials are events of the highest social importance, and to ignore a relative in sending out the invitations is no less than a public insult to the person passed over; not to be included among those entitled to hold the cords whereby the coffin is lowered into the grave may lead to a fatal breach of friendship among the living. Pete Lownie had been buried and his brother-in-law Davit Lunan had not been asked to the funeral. Listen to Davit's wife, Tibbie Birse, whose sister's husband has been laid in the graveyard at Thrums without Davit's assistance:

'Though I should be struck deid this nicht,' Tibbie whispered, and the sibilants hissed between her few remaining teeth, 'I wasna sae muckle as speired to the layin' oot. There was Mysy Cruickshanks there, an' Kitty Wobster 'at was nae friends to the corpse to speak o', but Marget passed by me, me 'at is her ain flesh an' blood, though it mayna be for the like o' me to say it. It's gospel truth, Jess, I tell ye, when I say 'at, for all I ken officially, as ye micht say, Pete Lownie may be weel and hearty this day. If I was to meet Marget in the face I couldna say he was deid, though I ken 'at the wricht coffined him; na, an' what's mair, I wouldna gie Marget the satisfaction o' hearin' me say it. No, Jess, I tell ye, I dinna pertend to be on an equalty wi' Marget, but equalty or no equalty, a body has her feelings, an' lat on 'at I ken Pete's gone I will not. Eh? Ou, weel. . . .'

Conceive, I ask you, that absolutely perfect glimpse into a Scottish rural mind turned into English phrases, or equally the abiding human comedy that is contained within this further passage from Tibbie's statement:

' Mind ye, Jess, I hae no desire to be friends wi' Marget. Naething could be farer frae my wish than to hae helpit in the layin' oot o' Pete Lownie, an', I assure ye, Davit wasna keen to gang to the bural. " If they dinna want me to their burals," Davit says, " they hae nae mair to do than to say sae. But I warn ye, Tibbie," he says, " if there's a bural frae this hoose, be it your bural, or be it my bural, not one o' the family o' Lownies casts their shadows upon the corp." Thae was the very words Davit said to me as we watched the hearse frae the sky-licht. Ay, he bore up wonderfu', but he felt it, Jess—he felt it, as I could tell by his takkin' to drink again that very nicht.'

Is there any phrase in either of these two examples that obscures the essential feeling which Tibbie was so naïvely expressing? I do not think there is, simply because the author has been careful in his use of the vernacular so to phrase it that nothing of the original is lost and yet the whole remains intelligible to the English reader. He might have justified the epithet of ' inartistic ' by introducing half-a-dozen words that might have been used but which would have left the English reader completely guessing.

More, his critic quarrels with him for writing ' ben the house.' Says Mr. Moult:

Again and again the non-Scot, who cannot be expected to know that ' a but and ben ' is a house of only two rooms, and that ' ben the house ' means the other room or other side of the house, seeks instinctively at the end of the book for a glossary that is not there.

Scottish readers will smile at this Sassenach criticism. It certainly does seem to suggest that a brief glossary at the end of A Window in Thrums would have been useful to Mr. Moult. The ' ben ' room can never be the ' but.' When the housewife in a Scottish cottage tells you that ' the guidman is but the house ' you will look for him in the kitchen and not in the parlour. I have heard it suggested that ' ben ' might be derived from the Old French, in common with the Scottish ' bein,' meaning well-to-do or comfortable ('a bein house to bide in '), as contrasting the better room with the common kitchen apartment which might equally have derived its ' but ' from *bout*, the Scottish vernacular containing, as students are aware, many hundreds of words from the sixteenth-century French. This facile etymology cannot be accepted, however, as both words are immensely older than any Scoto-Gallicisms. Anglo-Saxon has its *binnan*, and ancient

Belgic its *binnen*, signifying ' within,' and *bute* or *buta* in Anglo-Saxon means ' outer.' Such a phrase as ' the ben end of one's dinner,' meaning the main portion of it, shows how the ancient meaning of ' inner ' has become enlarged.

In view of the oft-quoted " No Scotch dialect, please ' as an editorial injunction to Barrie in his early sallies into Fleet Street, I have read with some surprise in a contemporary Scottish review of the Idylls that it stood out from the ruck of studies of local life ' so numerous at the present time.' This would suggest that there was already some pre-Barrie demand for chronicles of humble Scottish life, however indifferently native writers were meeting it. It is a phenomenon of literary history with which I cannot pretend to be familiar. Indeed I shall register a doubt that the reviewer's phrase was more than an ill-considered piece of rhetoric. Were it else, we should have to regard the author of the Idylls as deliberately catering for this demand by exploiting the humours of his native town, whereas we know that he came to the great work of his literary life in the most casual fashion. It is true that there were many writers of humorous character sketches in Scotland and in the north of England: ' Jeames Kay,' ' George Roy,' ' James Strathesk,' ' Archie McNab,' are names that occur to me at the moment, but none had more than a restricted local vogue: none of these could have hoped to do more than attain a purely regional success. Nearly seventy years earlier, the novel of Scottish life and character had been founded by a man of genius, when John Galt published his Annals of the Parish and followed it in 1822 with Sir Andrew Wylie, and in 1824 with The Entail. Even his less successful novels are brilliantly written, patently true to Scottish character and charged with hearty humour. David Moir's richly humorous Mansie Wauch, directly inspired by Galt, also takes us back to the second decade of the nineteenth century. In these, if we like, we can discern the beginning of the Kailyard school. They are certainly as deserving of that epithet (meant to be contemptuous, like Cockney to the works of Dickens) as any of the later and quite unrelated group that sprang up in the early 'nineties with the success of Barrie's stories of Thrums.

A Window in Thrums displays a great advance upon Idylls in almost every direction. Here was no need to make a miscellaneous bundle of sketches appear a homogeneous work: the Window is the real thing. There is but one chapter that might be held out of place: Tammas Haggart's comic reflections on A Home for Geniuses, and as it is characteristic of the real Barrie, it is better to have it here an intruder than, like so many others, buried in the files of forgotten magazines and reviews.

BARRIE: THE STORY OF A GENIUS

According to Robertson Nicoll's biographer, to The British Weekly fell the honour of first publishing most of the chapters of the Window, and its editor used to be fond of telling that when he received the MS. of the concluding episode, ' Jamie's Homecoming,' he telegraphed to Barrie ' the one word " Immortal " and by that word I stand.' Barrie was yet to write a better book, a more perfect whole, but Nicoll's judgement, hasty though it may have been, did not err when he sent that telegram, and his later reassertion was no mere case of ' what I have written I have written.' Garland's Bibliography (as notable for its omissions as its inclusions) traces but eight of the twenty-two chapters in the Window to The British Weekly, and does not indicate that ' Jamie's Homecoming ' ever appeared there or anywhere else before it was printed in the book.

A Window in Thrums is marked by a fine serenity of style, a largeness of sympathy, a truthfulness that compels our acceptance. It is a curious mixture of realism and romanticism, of humour and sentiment. For the first time its young author has rid himself of his cynicism: he is at last in earnest. There is a nice balance of emotion between the chapters, whose very titles indicate something of this: ' Preparing to Receive Company ' precedes ' Waiting for the Doctor,' which is followed by ' A Humorist on his Calling,' succeeded in turn by ' Dead this Twenty Years '—perhaps the best short story of sentiment Barrie has written—and so on, the effect being steadily cumulative. Regarded as a complete work it is really a triumph of the episodic manner. Each chapter—again excepting the seventeenth—is an articulated part of a whole, and is yet complete in itself. The story is of the slightest, but at no point are we conscious of its meagreness, because of the rich revelation of character in every paragraph. From the studied leisureliness of the opening chapter, ' The House on the Brae,' we are won afresh to the sympathetic schoolmaster, that admirable projection of Barrie's self, who is again the narrator as in the Idylls, and we submit ourselves willingly to his avowed intention of illustrating the beauty and heroism of lowly life. Hardly can we conceive any other means whereby the character of Jess could have been portrayed for us with equal conviction of its realness. Through those friendly eyes of the schoolmaster we seem to look into her very soul. It is a triumph of method as well as of understanding. Here we feel that, for the first time, the author is fully alive to the universal significance of the humble household: his comprehension of character is now three dimensional where before it was concerned with surfaces.

SUCCESS: THE AUTHOR ARRIVES

While I am not prepared to defend Barrie at every turn from the critics who accuse him of pushing sentiment to the point of sentimentality, I do assert that nowhere in A Window in Thrums does he cross the debatable line: not even in A Tale of a Glove.' If we must withhold our approval from Jess in her excess of motherly jealousy after she finds the glove in Jamie's pocket, and if the narrator seems to give his approval to an action which we cannot but stigmatise as mean, we need not identify the narrator with the author. More, the action of Jess is of a piece with the Scots mother of her day, whose attitude to her children was not commonly so free and self-sacrificing as that of the English mother or of the latter-day Scottish mother. Personally, I do not question the truth of this episode, which has importance in advancing the climax of the story, now quickly approaching.

I think it worth while interpolating here an extract from a letter written to Barrie in December, 1892, by Robert Louis Stevenson, who some little time before had read A Window in Thrums for the first time. I may have read this letter at the time of its publication (1899), but it had certainly gone from my mind when penning the preceding paragraph, and only by chance have I come upon it to-day in the revising of this chapter. It is the letter in which R. L. S. confesses that Barrie 'is the man for my money,' and it is satisfactory to find so great a critic writing with enthusiasm about the episode of the glove:

The Glove is a great page; it is startlingly original, and as true as death and judgement. Tibbie Birse in the Burial is great, but I think it was the journalist that got in the word ' official.' The same character plainly had a word to say to Thomas Haggard (*sic*). Thomas affects me as a lie—I beg your pardon; doubtless he was somebody you know, that leads people so far astray. The actual is not the true.

When quoting from this particular letter I might as well include in this place the succeeding paragraph, since it also touches the book now under discussion. Though it is three years after the publishing of the Window that Stevenson writes his famous phrase about there being two of them whom Sir Walter would have welcomed, he might have been as epigrammatically inspired had Barrie's book reached him two or three years earlier:

I am proud to think you are a Scotchman—though to be sure I know nothing of that country, being only an English tourist, quo' Gavin Ogilvy. I commend the hard case of Mr. Gavin Ogilvy to J. M. Barrie, whose work is to me a source of living pleasure and heart-felt national pride. There are two of us now that the Shirra might

have patted on the head. And please do not think when I thus seem
to bracket myself with you, that I am wholly blinded with vanity. Jess
is beyond my frontier line; I could not touch her skirt; I have no such
glamour of twilight on my pen. I am a capable artist; but it begins
to look to me as if you were a man of genius. Take care of yourself
for my sake. It's a devilish hard thing for a man who writes so many
novels as I do, that I should get so few to read. And I can read yours,
and I love them.

Not again in any of his writings is Barrie more consistently
honest with himself. He is concerned only to state the truth
as he has seen it, or received it, of certain aspects of lowly Scottish
life, and in doing so without false sentiment or jarring humour
he achieves genuine pathos. In his introduction to the collected
American edition of his works (1896) he makes this admission:

When the English publishers read A Window in Thrums in manuscript they thought it unbearably sad, and begged me to alter the end.
They warned me that the public do not like sad books. Well, the older
I grow and the sadder the things I see, the more do I wish my books
to be bright and hopeful, but an author may not always interfere with
his story, and if I had altered the end of A Window in Thrums I think
I should never have had any more respect for myself. It is a sadder
book to me than it can ever be to anyone else. I see Jess at her window
looking for the son who never came back as no other can see her, and
I knew that unless I brought him back in time the book would be a
pain to me all my days, but the thing had to be done.

Especially when we compare the Window with the Idylls do
we perceive the greater depth of feeling and the higher artistry
which it exhibits. The story of Nanny Coutts who ' died with
a lie on her lips,'—' Ay,' she said, ' Sanders has been a guid man
to me '—is the story of thousands of wronged women in every
land, and it is told with rare economy of words.

Perhaps the best appreciation of the Window expressed in a
few words is contained in the subjoined excerpt from an article
in an early issue of The Speaker, a weekly Liberal review which
was founded by Wemyss Reid in January, 1890, and numbered
Barrie among the many distingushed authors who contributed
to its first volume. The writer was A. T. Quiller-Couch:

What is the tale about? A little cottage, not specially picturesque;
an invalid mother; the commonplace death of her first-born son, and
the commonplace ruin of her second-born. No character is extraordinary, of plot there is nothing at all; the catastrophe might befall
any young man, whatever his nationality or station of life. . . . But
search about in English literature, and where will you find a story of
like quality of pathos written by an Anglo-Saxon?

SUCCESS: THE AUTHOR ARRIVES

For The Scots Observer Barrie was now writing occasionally, his articles being chiefly political satire, and anonymous, though his name appears in the list of Signing Contributors. He was very far from sharing the uncompromising Toryism of his editor, but, as his friend Marriott Watson put it, 'he found it impossible to resist the humorous attractions of certain features of the Liberal party.' From the biographer's point of view the most interesting of his contributions in 1889 was one on The Coming Dramatist. He had already written much about the stage, but not yet had he tried his hand as a playwright, so that the closing paragraph of the article in question is significant in the light of after events and of the new direction his creative genius was soon to take.

One would think (he writes) that there are novelists with us who could write plays that would be literary as well as effective. Some of them have tried and failed, but obviously because they did not set about it in the proper way. Plays and novels require quite different construction; but the story-writer who is dramatic could become sufficiently theatrical by serving a short apprenticeship to the stage. There are such prizes to pluck for those that can stand on tiptoe, that the absence of an outstanding dramatist is as surprising as it is disappointing.

Before 1889 had run its course the name of J. M. Barrie was known across the Empire, and had roused attention in the United States as that of a new British author who, in less than eighteen months, had taken front rank in contemporary letters by virtue of three books which he had published within that space of time; especially A Window in Thrums. There was general agreement as to the worth of his achievement; there was confidence that he had great things and possibly many surprises in store for all lovers of good literature. That he was a writer of genius seemed to be taken for granted. The few who were inclined to curl the lip at certain of his characteristics, which they did not hesitate to describe as literary tricks, were seldom prepared to question the originality, the uniqueness of his talent.

Nothing spectacular, however, marked his entry into his kingdom. Scores of others, long forgotten, before and since this year of 1889, have been heralded by the critics with loud fanfares of tin trumpets, whose echoes have scarcely died away before the authors themselves have ceased to attract. A steady, ever increasing popularity has been Barrie's happier lot, and although in this notable year we are witnessing him at the true outset of his fame, when forty years have passed we shall find no record of its diminution or eclipse, but that it has weathered all the gales of criticism, honest or jealous; above all, that it has outlived the most perilous of its vicissitudes in surviving, first the excesses,

151

and finally the extinction of the school of imitators which in a year or two was flooding the bookshops with sketches of Scottish life and character.

His interest in contemporary letters, which from his student days has known no abatement, is seen in the illuminating study of George Meredith's Novels printed in The Contemporary Review, October 1888, and in his appreciative examination of Thomas Hardy: the Historian of Wessex, in that review for July 1889—the same month in which A Window in Thrums came out. Mr. Baring-Gould's Novels formed the next of his critical studies in The Contemporary (February, 1890): a penetrating criticism, wherein the lack of 'heart' in Baring-Gould's otherwise brilliant fiction is effectively exhibited as a reason why it is unlikely to secure the lasting affection of readers. After the conclusion of A Superfluous Man the same little magazine that had the honour of publishing it had also the distinction of giving another Barrie series to its readers, Young Men I have Met appearing in The Young Man from January to June, 1890. The subjects of these slight but sparkling sketches were The Sentimentalist, The Supernumerary, The Prig, The Student, The Comic Man and The Dreamer.

More interesting than any of these essays and sketches in literary appreciation, however, was the Thrums story in two parts contributed to Good Words for January and February, 1890. A Tillyloss Scandal was its title, and the popularity of A Window in Thrums induced an American 'pirate' to circulate an unauthorised book containing this story and other Auld Licht sketches that had not appeared in Idylls. The volume, which attained considerable success in America, being exploited by more than one unscrupulous publisher, was in after years formally disowned by its putative parent and probably commands a high price among American collectors to-day.

One of the wittiest pieces of criticism Barrie has written took the form of a charming satirical fantasy entitled Brought Back from Elysium, printed in The Contemporary of June, 1890. It is in dialogue, the scene being 'the Library of a Piccadilly Club for high thinking and bad dinners,' and the time midnight. The author's intention is delicately to satirise the literary follies of the day, when the wordy discussion of style and form was completely obscuring the greater question of the novel's content. Four typical novelists are assembled: A Realist, a Romancist, an Elsmerian and a Stylist. The third in the list will convey little to my younger readers, for Robert Elsmere is probably as dead a novel as any that fluttered Victorian dovecots and ceased to be. The literary type implied still persists, in common with

J. M. BARRIE IN 1895   [*Downey*

Face page 152

MARGARET OGILVY WITH HER DAUGHTER JANE ANN
Mother and sister of J. M. Barrie, they died within three days of each
other and were buried together on the same day.

the others, and many later types which the obscure coteries have produced without in the least exciting the interest of the great body of modern book readers. 'The clock strikes thirteen and they all start.' They are met together to be introduced to a select company of ghosts whom Stanley, so recently successful in his quest of Emin Pasha, has undertaken to bring back from the Grove of Bay-trees in the Elysian Fields. A fifth novelist joins the group. He is an American and has a suspicious resemblance to Henry James. When the American learns the purpose of the meeting he protests that the expected visitors from Elysium are 'antiquated and played out,' and says they will not come:

Romancist. You don't understand. Stanley has gone for them.
American. Stanley!
Elsmerian. It was a chance not to be missed. (*Looks at his watch.*) They should have been here by this time; but on these occasions he is sometimes a little late.
(*Their mouths open as a voice rings through the club crying 'I cannot stop and argue with you; I'll find the way myself.'*)
Realist. It is he, but he may be alone. Perhaps they declined to accompany him.
Elsmerian (*with conviction*). He would bring them whether they wanted to come or not.
(*Enter Mr. Stanley with five ghosts.*)
Mr. Stanley. Here they are. I hope the row below did not alarm you. The hall-porter wanted to know if I was a member, so I shot him. Waken me when you are ready to send them back. (*Sits down and sleeps immediately.*)

The ghosts introduce themselves in turn as Scott, Fielding, Smollett, Dickens and Thackeray. 'They used to call me Thack,' says the last named. The vanities of the modernists are neatly hit off as they address themselves in turn to the visitors, seeking to show their superiority to the great novelists of the past. 'May I ask what was your first step toward becoming novelists,' the Elsmerian enquires:

Smollett (*with foolish promptitude*). We wrote a novel.
Thackeray (*humbly*). I am afraid I began by wanting to write a good story, and then wrote it to the best of my ability. Is there any other way?
Stylist. But how did you laboriously acquire your style?
Thackeray. I thought little about style. I suppose, such as it was, it came naturally.
Stylist. Pooh! Then there is no art in it.
Elsmerian. And what was your aim?
Thackeray. Well, I had reason to believe that I would get something for it.

BARRIE: THE STORY OF A GENIUS

Elsmerian. Alas! to you the world was not a sea of drowning souls, nor the novel a stone to fling to them, that they might float on it to a quiet haven. You had no aims, no methods, no religious doubts, and you neither analysed your characters nor classified yourselves.

A whole essay on the futility of style is contained within this scrap of dialogue between the Stylist and Thackeray:

Stylist. Style is everything. The true novelist does nothing but think, think, think about style, and then write, write, write about it. I daresay I am one of the most perfect stylists living. Oh, but the hours, the days, the years of introspection I have spent in acquiring my style!

Thackeray (sadly). If I had only thought more of style! May I ask how many books you have written?

Stylist. Only one—and that I have withdrawn from circulation. Ah, sir, I am such a stylist that I dare not write anything. Yet I meditate a work.

' Give me a chair and a man with doubts,' says the Elsmerian, ' and I will give you a novel,' and the American later intervenes to assure the ghost of Dickens that in Boston, where they 'place' everybody, he is 'ticketed a Caricaturist.' The ghost of Boz retorts by saying that he likes best the old way of writing novels, that ' of being simply a novelist,' at which the American sneers ' You could not have written a novel about a lady's reason for passing the cruet.'

The dramatic skill of Barrie is exhibited in the cleverness with which the whole fantastic scene is brought to an appropriate end with Stanley marching off his ghosts in military formation after Thackeray has responded to the Elsmerian's good-natured request for a last word of advice:

Thackeray. As old-fashioned novelists of some repute at one time, we might say this: that perhaps if you thought and wrote less about your styles and methods and the aim of fiction, and, in short, forget yourselves now and again in your stories, you might get on better with your work. Think it over.

Mr. Stanley. Quick march.

(*The novelists are left looking at each other self-consciously.*)

Brought Back from Elysium is one of Barrie's many miscellaneous pieces that are worth reprinting. Dramatic students especially will be interested in observing the ease with which its writer uses the dialogue form, and the happy phrasing of the stage directions which convey in a word or two a wealth of meaning.

The last of his literary studies for the Contemporary, a friendly criticism of Mr. Kipling's Stories, which appeared in the number for March 1891, was probably written in this year, and in The

Fortnightly for September 1890 there had been printed Pro Bono
Publico, that fine example of his gravely comic manner.

His contributions to The Speaker, already mentioned, were
still more important, and most of them might well have been
—indeed should have been—reprinted in book form long ere this.
There was a series of eight Thrums Gossips, all conceived and
written in the best Barrie manner. They possessed an added
interest in being confessedly written from London, their writer
dropping for the nonce his character of schoolmaster at Glen
Quharity. The first of The Speaker sketches, The Little Nursery
Governess, which appeared on March 29th, 1890, before the
Thrums series started, was twelve years later to form the second
chapter of The Little White Bird. A much admired feature of The
Speaker was its Literary Causerie, usually contributed by Augustine
Birrell—the gentle art of Birrelling was here seen at its best—
though occasionally another writer filled that page, and at least
twice in 1890 Barrie did so, his first causerie being another amusing
discussion of illegible handwriting, and the second a criticism of
Herman Merivale's dramatisation of The Bride of Lammermoor
and the acting of Irving and Ellen Terry in the principal parts.

To The British Weekly during 1890 he contributed near a
dozen articles and reviews, among them a vivacious study of
' Q,' in which Gavin Ogilvy was very frank in his literary opinions.
' Mr. Quiller-Couch is so unlike Mr. Kipling,' he asserted, ' that
one immediately wants to compare them. They are both young,
and they have both shown such promise that it will be almost
sad if neither can write a book to live—as, of course, neither has
done as yet.' Kipling had then published eight of his volumes
of short stories wherein were several he has never bettered, though
the days of Kim, The Jungle Book and Puck of Pook's Hill were
still distant; ' Q ' had written Troy Town and The Splendid
Spur, and one would like to know what Gavin Ogilvy thinks of
his later achievement.

The name of J. M. Barrie had not before been so prominent
in the magazines and reviews as in 1890. Its possessor seemed
in danger of approximating to the condition so abhorrent to G. A.
Sala, that of a ' prolific writer,' but not again shall we find him
so readily responding to the wiles of editors desirous of printing
his work. He added but one book in this year to his growing
list, and that was another harvesting of papers from the St. James's.
My Lady Nicotine was published by Messrs. Hodder & Stoughton
late in the spring season and had a very satisfactory reception
in the press. At no time have the sales of this book attained to
anything like fifty per cent of those of the Window, which would

indicate that delightful and original as it is in conception and execution, and in its humour equal to the best that Barrie has given us in book or play, the entire absence of the serious element little commended it to the great body of readers who had been moved by the pathos and tender beauty of the Window. It is essentially a book of laughter. Its author is here at his merriest, but contriving, even before he had been so admonished by R.L.S., not to be too funny.

Sir Arthur Quiller-Couch has confessed that Meade Primus to his Proud Parent, an unsigned Barrie article which he read in the St. James's some time in the winter of 1887–88, was 'my introduction to the most romantic of all my literary loves,' and I should suppose that all who are fond of the natural 'human boy' will declare that the twentieth chapter of My Lady Nicotine entitled Primus to his Uncle is their favourite in that book. This is the article which had first won Q's affection in the St. James's, but slightly re-cast, and a more humorous or more truthful interpretation of a boy's thoughts on the grave question of his uncle's recurring Christmas present, or indeed on any subject that might move the boyish mind, has never been written.

The uncanny insight into the mind of youth which is one of the outstanding characteristics of Barrie's fiction was used with true comic effect in a series of sketches contributed about this time to the St. James's giving the views of a school boy on many topics. It is to be regretted that his intention to reprint in volume form these delightfully entertaining papers has never been carried out. Indeed, we might have missed My Lady Nicotine had it not been that Barrie was constrained to give permanent shape to the newspaper sketches which comprise the body of that work in order to secure his copyright therein, the attentions of the American 'pirate' (a type of literary highwayman now almost extinct) having become embarrassing to the young British author for whom Fame was wreathing her laurels.

Attached to My Lady Nicotine is a curious history which has no concern with its literary merits, but may be held to be more humanly interesting than any question of art or beauty. As we know, on the admission of the author himself, when he was writing the newspaper sketches which eventually furnished forth the book, and which there is hardly any doubt were meant for gathering into an individual work, he was the most diffident of worshippers at the shrine of My Lady Nicotine; his oblations were truly sacrificial. A fascination of make-believe has affected him at all stages of his literary life. He has stood as the poles asunder from his admired Meredith in all his fiction. He is never a manipulator of puppets; no matter what he may have said to the contrary, he is always a fellow-actor with the creatures of his imagination. The pleasures of smoking so amusingly extolled in My Lady Nicotine were derived more from imagination than from actual experience. If we can imagine 'Gae bring to me a pint of wine!' as the outpouring of some teetotal bard, we should have a situation not greatly different from that of Barrie at the time o' writing My Lady Nicotine. But, as Max Nordau has observed, the outward assumption of an emotion often repeated may in the end produce its inward realisation and bring something of reality into the acting. Perhaps it was to justify his assumed rôle that Barrie took to the pipe, and he must have smoked, however diffidently, a good few ounces of the particular mixture which he celebrated as 'Arcadia,' by the time My Lady Nicotine appeared.

This mixture was the special product of a Wardour Street tobacconist in a small way of business. Many a reader, in common with the present writer, will remember the shop in question and the Spanish name of him who traded his fragrant wares within it: Carreras. Shortly before My Lady Nicotine appeared the original blender of the mixture which Barrie was immortalising sold his business to a Mr. Yapp for £3,000. It is related that one afternoon when the author had gone to Wardour Street to purchase his usual supply of Craven Mixture (for that was the name of the blend) Mr. Yapp, who would appear to have taken some interest in literature as well as tobacco, thought that he recognised the features of the quiet little man being served at the counter and, after he had gone, learned from the assistant that the customer was a certain Mr. Barrie. With commendable shrewdness (so the story goes) he instructed the assistant that when Mr. Barrie came again he was to contrive that he did not leave without Mr. Yapp having the chance of speaking to him.

And so it fell out that the tobacconist in a few minutes on a day in the succeeding week laid the foundation of a fortune that is almost fabulous, although he himself did not enjoy its fullest measure. Mr. Yapp is alleged to have addressed himself to Barrie thus: 'Am I correct in thinking that the Craven Mixture for which you come to my shop is the original of the Arcadia Mixture in your book?' On Barrie's answering in the affirmative the tobacconist went on: 'Then would you bestow on me a great favour and make the same answer in writing?' The author's assent was readily given and there is probably no devotee of the weed who has not long been familiar with the facsimile of Barrie's certificate which henceforth appeared on all the tins and packets of Craven Mixture and was widely used for press advertising. Mr. Yapp offered to supply the author who was to make his fortune and the still greater fortunes of those who came after him with free Craven Mixture for the rest of his life; an offer that was naturally declined.

That is the story as stated by Mr. Thomas Moult. It reads well, and I tell it again—knowing it to be another addition to the interminable list of 'yarns about Barrie'—merely because it has the usual residuum of truth in it. Mr. Moult assures us that in a matter of three years after the appearance of the book the enterprising tobacconist had the good fortune to be able to re-sell the business to Mr. Bernhard Baron for a sum approximating to £100,000. Even this considerable fortune, I would add, shrivels into insignificance when compared with the present financial state of the business that has grown out of Arcadia Mixture, the Carreras Company of to-day having a subscribed capital of £1,425,000 which is valued by the market on the current share prices at no less than £17,061,250. Mr. Bernhard Baron was famous for his philanthropy, millions of his profits being distributed in charity. A week or two before these lines are being written his latest public gift, amounting to half-a-million of money, was announced. Surely never before from a little acorn of literary humour anything so tremendously substantial has grown.

Now, had Mr. Moult ever smoked an ounce of Craven and taken the elementary precaution of verifying his facts—his bright little book has too many errors of fact—he would have known that the mixture is called 'Arcadia' and not 'Arcadian' as he calls it more than once, that Barrie's letter addressed to 'Mr. J. J. Carreras' was written seven years after the publication of My Lady Nicotine and therefore many details of the story he relates are instantly vitiated. As the certificate, which undoubtedly was worth untold gold to Mr. Baron, is a document of some interest, I copy it below, remarking that it is written in reply to a letter, which throws further suspicion upon the Yapp yarn:

18th Jan. 1897

Dear Sir,

In answer to your letter, it is your Craven Mixture—and no other—that I call Arcadia in ' My Lady Nicotine.' I see no objection to your announcing this if you want to do so.

Yours truly,
J. M. BARRIE.

Mr. J. J. Carreras,
7 Wardour Street.

When W. E. Henley reviewed My Lady Nicotine in The Scots Observer he suggested that Barrie had still 'a long way to go' before he gave us the truly great book we were all so eagerly awaiting. Not so long a way as Henley thought. For although 1890 was allowed to pass with the publication of only My Lady Nicotine, there was good reason. For most of that year the author had been engaged upon his first work of fiction which was to follow the grand manner: The Little Minister, the serial publication of which had been arranged as the great attraction of Good Words for 1891. That is why the book-loving public which was taking to its bosom the young Scottish author had to be content with My Lady Nicotine as his only book between July, 1889, and October, 1891. It was also the last volume consisting in large measure of re-cast newspaper contributions to which he put his name. His mind was now set upon worthier things, upon the highest creative work of which he was capable. So My Lady Nicotine was in some sort his good-bye to literary journalism, and also a farewell to the purely comic manner.

In all he had now published half-a-dozen books, all comparatively short, two of them so slight indeed that together they did not total as many words as a very short novel, and were obtainable by the somewhat limited public that bought them at the modest price of one shilling each. The other four were issued each at six shillings, a price that was soon to become the standard of all novels until the economic upheaval of the Great War made strange changes in book values. But their writer had something far more precious to offer his generation than the mere spinning of words, and brief though his four successful books appear when regarded from this material point of view their essence was potent enough to prove to an already immense circle of admirers at home and overseas that Barrie was, as R. L. S. later phrased it, the man for their money.

One may fairly say that Barrie was now established as a public favourite. Yet there would appear to have been some measure of uncertainty as to whether his hold on fame was secure, for under the date April 25th, 1891, I find Robertson Nicoll writing to Marcus Dods in this strain:

Barrie will succeed and that soon. He is one of the men—more numerous, I fancy, than we think—who are every way improved by success—softened, humbled, and redeemed from cynicism, and I do not know any man of letters with such a future. My admiration for him constantly rises.

Whatever lingering doubt there may have been as to the security of his position in the front rank of contemporary authors at the end of 1890, before another twelve months had passed there was none.

CHAPTER VIII

THRUMS OR THEATRE?—YEARS OF ACHIEVEMENT
AND EXPERIMENT

1891–1896

THE year of The Little Minister must be rubricated in the chronicle of J. M. Barrie. Already we have witnessed two vital years: 1888, with no fewer than three Barrie books to engage the critics, and 1889, with A Window in Thrums as its one and sufficient masterpiece. Now comes 1891 and the 'big thing' which Barrie's numerous admirers were so eagerly awaiting. Good Words, a magazine that deservedly enjoyed great popularity in its day (edited for many years by the famous Scottish divine, Dr. Norman Macleod, whose brother Dr. Donald had succeeded him in the editorial chair), was the favoured magazine of 1891 by virtue of the serial publication of The Little Minister in its pages. But already its sun was setting and the wide interest which the Barrie serial awakened served only to add a touch of splendour to its decline.

The writing of his first long story had, of course, been the preoccupation of the preceding year: he had resolved never again, after his experience with When A Man's Single, to compose a serial instalment by instalment while the printers waited for his copy. Even the Contemporary essay on Kipling was probably penned in 1890, though it did not come out until March of 1891. The editor of The British Weekly was evidently as little satisfied as Oliver Twist, and to meet his requests Barrie permitted the reprinting of a dozen or so of his old Dispatch articles, such as A Powerful Drug and Shutting a Map, but a group of five sketches of Life in a Country Manse may have been specially written this year. He had little or no time now to spare for the miscellaneous work of literary journalism. Two contributions to The National Observer, five to The Illustrated London News, and a sonnet in Good Words represent the total of his periodical appearances in this the last year that his name was appended to any miscellaneous writing, saving half-a-dozen reprinted items in The British Weekly during 1892, and a particularly interesting 'middle' in The National Observer of February 17th, 1894. Barrie the journalist has definitely given place to Barrie the novelist by 1891.

A glance at one or two of the pieces above mentioned will be instructive. The subject of the sonnet in Good Words for April was John Nicol, who had been sub-editor of that magazine for a quarter of a century, and had acted in similar capacity on The Sunday Magazine and The Contemporary Review. A friend and countryman of Barrie's, his recent death had drawn a letter of condolence from Gladstone, who esteemed him highly as a man and a journalist. Nicol's place was taken by another literary journalist of greater distinction, William Canton, author of The Invisible Playmate. Barrie's 'In Memoriam' verses I have always remembered for their opening line—

They never have been men who falsely say;

but the sonnet is more to be commended for its sentiment than for its poetic beauty. It serves to remind me, however, that its writer must be numbered with those who, being conscious masters of prose, have been loath to admit themselves not equally gifted in poetry. There are scores of journalists who could write poetry as good as these verses to the memory of John Nicol, or indeed any verses that Barrie ever wrote; but few are they who could match the prose of even his lesser works.

Among its very brilliant list of Signing Contributors which The National Observer was regularly advertising at this time Barrie's name appears, but I suspect him of writing several articles that bear no signature. The earlier of his two signed contributions in 1891 appeared in the issue of May 9th. It is a story in the Defoe manner, entitled The Family Honour, and I should not be surprised to learn that it was inspired by some local legend he had heard in his boyhood of the secret of Glamis Castle, which stands less than five miles south along the road from the House on the Brae. Glendowie is the name he gives to the ancient Scottish castle that harboured the indescribable monster, the Thing that had obstinately endured for many centuries. A strange monster indeed, for while no grown person could look upon it without the direst results, to little children it was the gentlest monster imaginable, and played with them tenderly, yet when these children grew up they could recall the Thing only with horror unspeakable. The story tells how the terror and shame of many centuries was at last destroyed by

one of the Glendowie family and taken away to Africa for burial!
By no means a great story—it does not achieve the 'grue' with
anything like the devilish ingenuity of R. L. S.—to come from
the master-hand that gave us the enduring beauties of The
Little Minister in this same year, but a piece of great interest
to the Barrie bibliographers, and therefore to be noted in this
place. The second, appearing November 21st, was entitled
The Minister's Gown, a sketch in his familiar manner. The
gown was subscribed for by the ladies of the congregation,
mainly on the initiative of one who commanded their respect
because she herself owned a seal-skin coat, and the source of
trouble it proved to the earnest young minister is delightfully
described, the little piece ending with a 'snap.'

Clement Shorter began in 1891 his brilliant tenure of the
editorship of The Illustrated London News, and in a week or
two had transformed that journal from a rather antiquated budget
of pictures accompanied by perfunctory letterpress into a beautifully illustrated weekly in which the literary features were as
attractive as the pictorial. He always considered it one of his
editorial successes that he was able to induce Barrie to collaborate,
in 1891, with the very brilliant group of contributors he secured
for his new and entirely successful enterprise. The five papers
that Barrie managed to write for him were all in the humorous
vein. The Wicked Cigar, appearing February 21st, is a typical
bit of Barrie fun. Count Tolstoy had been writing in The
Contemporary on the evil of smoking. 'He maintains that
tobacco makes fiends of men, and cites several well-known cases
in which murderers could not do the deed until they had smoked
a cigarette.' The writer then goes on to admit that tobacco
fires us to villainy, and confesses that is why he smokes. 'All
the villains I know smoke. It is notorious that publishers take
a few whiffs before drawing up the agreement which they send
to authors to sign.' His job as a novelist demands that he shall
feel villainous at times. 'For my own part, I should give up
smoking gladly if I could discover any easier way of feeling
villainous.' Everett's Beard, in the issue of March 14th, gets some
good fun out of the need to shave twice a day. The Playwright
and the Fowl, a fortnight later, is alleged to be 'an odd story'
told him by a dramatist in the smoking-room of the Garrick
Theatre on the first night of Lady Bountiful. It concerns that
dramatist's agitation at a bantam that used to look scornfully
and crow at him just when he had thought out a particularly
good bit of dialogue at the farmhouse where he was writing his
play. 'How can I sit composedly through the first night of

my plays when it seems to me that at the end of every dramatic speech and in the middle of every situation I hear cock-a-doodle-doo?' I wonder if this dramatist may not have been the same that introduced 'Cock-a-doodle-doo' into a play called Peter Pan thirteen years later! The Mystery of Timetables, April 11th, followed the more conventional lines of newspaper humour. More noteworthy than any of these was The Inconsiderate Waiter, in the Christmas number. No Barrie student need be told that this gem of wistful humour became the eighth chapter of The Little White Bird eleven years later.

The Little Minister did not conclude its magazine run until the end of the year, but in October it was published in book form by Cassell & Co., who probably had outbidden Isbister & Co., the owners of Good Words, for the book rights. It was among the last novels of note that came out in three-volume form. The day of the 'three-decker' was well-nigh over in 1891. Throughout most of the Victorian era, novels, properly so called, had been published in three volumes and were notorious for their wordiness. In that age of ampler leisure, when readers were few by comparison with the masses of to-day, both novels and works of travel were given a ponderosity of form too often reflected in their contents. Quite probably the method of publication, which was largely dictated by the demands of the lending libraries, encouraged writers to pad out their works so that their material value might seem not overpriced at 31/6 for three massy tomes. The modern movement to break away from this antiquated and cumbrous style of publication was one of the changes brought about by the increased literary activities of the early 'nineties. It may seem strange to the younger readers of to-day that when so lively and so fresh a contemporary author as Sir James Barrie made his first appearance with a full-length novel it came out in three large volumes, but The Little Minister, though in its title suggestive of 'first, secondly, and thirdly,' had nothing in common with any of the lengthier fiction of its day. The one-volume edition was published in February, 1892.

How much nearer Barrie had been to achieving a really big thing in fiction than even Henley had suspected a year before may be judged by the enthusiasm with which the appearance of the novel was hailed by that brilliant editor and merciless critic in The National Observer for October 31st. His review was headed A Book of Genius, and he wrote in this strain:

Here is another book of genius. 'Tis a big word, and one not often used in this place. But we use it now with a full sense of the weight of it, and a clear perception of our own responsibility. Mr. Barrie has played many parts in his time—brief as that time has been—and has played them all well. But he had not given his true measure heretofore. That he had wit, gaiety, charm, an admirable gift of observation, humour the quaintest and oddest, a singular command of certain sorts of character—all this we knew. But it is a great and delightful surprise to find him writing what cannot fail to prove the novel of the year: a year, be it remarked, that has witnessed the production of work by such men as George Meredith, Thomas Hardy, and Rudyard Kipling.

It cannot be said that the reception of The Little Minister was sensational; its immediate success in the bookshops could not be compared with that of Ian Maclaren's Beside the Bonnie Brier Bush three years later, the cumbrous form of publication being partly the reason; but on every hand one heard the new novel discussed with evident admiration. The critics accepted it as a book of genius rather than a perfect work of art, which indeed no one can hold it to be. Whatever it lacks in form and design it more than makes good in the sympathetic presentation of its characters, and the vivacity with which their emotions and their actions are described. Robertson Nicoll, to whom the autographed MS. of the novel was presented by its author and who treasured that for the rest of his life as a very precious possession, says in a letter written to one of his correspondents within a week or two of the publication of the book: 'I agree with you that The Little Minister is wildly improbable, but is it not a rich book, with many pretty little things about it? There is much heart in it too.' These three or four lines might be held to express the opinion of the general body of readers, who were not greatly concerned about the technique of the novel so long as they had good entertainment.

After all, literary reputations are made by the common body of readers who, while being conscious of having received full measure of enjoyment from an author, are content to leave to the coteries the endless and aimless discussions of style and form which Barrie himself had so caustically criticised in Brought Back from Elysium. Like that company of ghosts who had converse with the moderns, he set himself to tell a good story as well as he could, and if it falls short, as we may frankly admit it does, of certain qualities demanded by the canon of the novel, it remains a good story nevertheless.

The critic who takes up The Little Minister with the intention to criticise will derive almost as much satisfaction from the openings which its author offers him as the reader who is willing to surrender himself to the entertainment of the story. If we are prepared to agree with H. G. Wells that the novel as a literary form may take any shape its author cares to give it and still retain its right to be classified as a novel, then before the The Little Minister even the critic must be dumb. But this Wellsian dictum is altogether too sweeping, and we cannot blind ourselves to the fact, however much we may admire the genius of Barrie, that The Little Minister is not developed along the lines which, quite obviously, its author had set himself to follow at the beginning of his task.

As a novel it begins to break up in the third chapter, when Jean announces to Gavin that 'there's a curran folk at the back door, and their respects to you, and would you gie them some water out o' the well?' The author had started with the clear intention of holding his characters in leash, which is essential to the grand manner of the novel, but so early as this chapter they begin to tell him that they will do pretty much as they like, and so they continue throughout the forty odd remaining chapters of the story. The story is stopped at any moment for the telling of an anecdote which need neither be new nor always worth the telling save as illustrating the Auld Licht mentality.

The method of telling the story, moreover, occasionally gives to it an air of unreality, for at one moment the narrator in his assumed character of Dominie may be up the Glen, as in the very amusing eleventh chapter, and in a twinkling he is relating a most intimate conversation that is taking place in the Manse down at Thrums. This whole chapter, with all its precious humour and rich entertainment, I regard as in no wise necessary to the progress of the story. The method of telling, however, has its compensations. In Chapter XXI, where the narrator's tragic love story and Margaret's part therein are most delicately described by implication, like an etching that derives its form and density from shadows rather than from line, and again in that lovely twenty-second chapter, where the crisis of Gavin and Babbie's romance is reached, the method of narration entirely justifies itself.

There is, by the way, an interesting account of the Dominie's literary ambitions and his sense of frustration which I would suggest is less an objective description by the author than a revelation of self at that particular time. I think I have already described Barrie as a chimney-corner man, and when my eye lighted upon this passage the other day I found it difficult to decide whether my description had originated spontaneously or had come down to me through some previous mental association of the author with the narrator. Here is the passage:

BARRIE: THE STORY OF A GENIUS

Up here in the glen school-house after my pupils have straggled home, there comes to me at times, and so sudden that it may be while I am infusing my tea, a hot desire to write great books. Perhaps an hour afterwards I rise, beaten, from my desk, flinging all I have written into the fire (yet rescuing some of it on second thoughts), and curse myself as an ingle-nook man, for I see that one can only paint what he himself has felt, and in my passion I wish to have all the vices, even to being an impious man, that I may describe them better. For this may I be pardoned. It comes to nothing in the end, save that my tea is brackish.

Personally, after many readings of The Little Minister I confess to the difficulty of meeting the adverse critic on his own ground, and to renewed enjoyment of the story at each re-reading. Not only are most of the incidents highly improbable, but they are too often imposed upon the story by the urgent need to give it movement, and the result in these cases is essentially melodramatic. An example of this is seen at the end of the chapter on The Continued Misbehaviour of the Egyptian Woman, when after a perfectly charming scene between Gavin and Babbie (in which by the way Babbie thus early anticipates one of her numerous atavisms by telling Gavin she lived up a tree, a jest that Wendy turns to earnest in Peter Pan), we are suddenly informed:

When the little minister had gone, a man came from behind a tree and shook his fist in the direction taken by the gypsy. It was Rob Dow, black with passion.
'It's the Egyptian!' he cried. 'You limmer, wha are you that hae got haud o' the minister?'
He pursued her, but she vanished as from Gavin in Windyghoul.

It would, however, be singularly unprofitable to go through a work of so much inherent beauty to multiply instances such as these and yet in one way it might be instructive, for the incident just mentioned and many another I could give—especially that of Babbie's interview with Micah Dow when the latter is seated on the Standing Stone—all have, when translated to the stage, a real dramatic value. Nay, the plot of The Little Minister is more convincing as that of a stage play, whereas its abiding value in the revelation of character is diminished by translation to the stage where some of its characters come perilously near to caricatures. I like to think of it best as 'the Fairy Book of Thrums,' which is the author's own fanciful description of the Standing Stone and its legends. The Little Minister is the most truly Thrumsian of all Barrie's books and whatever its demerits as a novel may amount

166

to is a matter of small consequence. Most of us will be willing
to endorse the opinion of Sir Arthur Quiller-Couch, who in The
Bookman for February, 1892, wrote of it thus:

Now that The Little Minister has been before the world for a month
or two, and we are getting over the first flush of our admiration, certain
voices are already to be heard whispering that Mr. Barrie is not quite
a novelist, and perhaps never will be. I see what these critics mean:
though the answer is that as long as Mr. Barrie continues to give us
books of genius, it does not concern us, and can hardly matter a pin's
fee to him under what petty title he is classed. I can see, with these
critics, that Mr. Barrie is not yet able to rely upon construction. . . .
And in what essential point should the writing of a good novel differ
from that of a good biography, as Mr. Barrie's countrymen Boswell
and Lockhart understood it? If A Window in Thrums be literature,
and The Little Minister a beautiful story, then nothing is gained or lost
by giving or denying their author the name of novelist.

Barrie's success as a novelist was patent to all in 1891, even
before The Little Minister attained to book form in the autumn
of the year. The British Weekly of July 2nd had given away a
sixteen-page supplement devoted entirely to extolling the qualities
of the author of A Window in Thrums and offering many happily
selected examples of his journalistic humour. Robertson Nicoll
himself compiled this very effective pamphlet, which also contained
several illustrations of Thrums scenes and a finely engraved wood-
cut portrait of Barrie from a Hollyer photograph that soon became as familiar as the portrait of Carlyle with hand to head
(which it somewhat resembled in pose) that used to be seen in
every bookshop of the land. This British Weekly supplement
was important as being the first presentation of the author's
personality to an audience already singularly sympathetic through
his numerous contributions to the pages of that journal, and it
did a good deal to popularise his name at that time. Secure in the
affections of the reading public he was now bent upon carrying
his flag into another field, where success might be harder to win,
but the rewards more alluring, and where, indeed, his heart had
been from the first
His initial effort in the theatre was made in collaboration with
his friend H. B. Marriott Watson, an Australian journalist and
novelist who was one of the most active of Henley's young men
and with whom Barrie had first become acquainted when writing
for the St. James's, to which Watson was editorially attached.
Younger than Barrie by three years and about twice his size, it
is pleasant to remember him, a tall, burly, genial figure of a man,
who died October 30th, 1921. Watson had a fine, vigorous

style and wrote numerous novels, not one of which made a hit, though none of them was an unworthy piece of work. He excelled in the short story, and A Poppy Show contains some of his best. He had designs on the stage and his was the idea of doing a play on Richard Savage, the picturesque poet who shared bohemian days with Dr. Johnson. He propounded the plot to Barrie, who willingly collaborated in the writing of a four-act play, and on April 16th, 1891, it was put on at a matinée at the Criterion.

The occasion was honoured by W. E. Henley writing a rhymed prologue, which was printed in the programme. The play derived no more than a few incidents from the life of Savage, and the poet as presented in it was a purely idealised personage. The acting was good. Bernard Gould (the stage name of Sir Bernard Partridge, the famous Punch cartoonist) discharged the title-rôle, and that he was 'an unconscionable time dying' was attributed to the authors rather than to the actor. On the whole, the critics' verdict was adverse, and the trial trip of the matinée ended the career of the play. Its production was the one occasion that Barrie responded to the half-ironical call of 'Authors.' Lewis Hind was present, and in his reminiscences said: 'Barrie was the size of a lead pencil, Marriott Watson a fir tree.' The authors thought well enough of their play to have it printed as a foolscap octavo booklet of 42 pages, which is now worth many times its weight in gold. Henley's prologue is not included in the pamphlet.

Years later an anonymous writer in M.A.P. who had also been present at the matinée told a good story apropos of Richard Savage, in which one of the characters was a 'highly melodramatic villain' whose favourite oath was *maledita!* He stated that about a fortnight after the performance he was present in the Rhetoric class of Edinburgh University at Masson's opening lecture of the winter session. It is news to me that the winter session starts at the beginning of May in Edinburgh, but we will let that pass, as the other details seem to be credible:

The classroom was packed with medicals and divinity men in addition to its proper occupants, while that grizzled old giant of Scottish literature held luminously forth on the subject of Keats and Gifford. Beside him, on the dais, looking supremely uncomfortable at being thus exalted, was the author of Richard Savage, which had already passed into the limbo of still-born plays. But when a whisper passed around that this was Barrie, the novelist of A Window in Thrums fame (a book which everybody then was reading), what an ovation he received, what a storm of cheering! The whole classroom rose at him!

At the close of the lecture the place resounded with cries of 'Speech, Barrie, speech!' while he glared at the door with the eyes of a hunted creature. The Professor took him encouragingly by the arm; but Mr. Barrie, with rapid and decisive shakings of his head, slipped off the dais, and literally rushed away among the throng of hurrying undergraduates. I happened to be just behind him, and the spirit of mischief, latent in every medical student, impelled me to groan out *maledita !* with as close an imitation of the melodramatic Captain as I could command. He swung round at once, looking for the perpetrator, and his face was lit up with infinite humour. We were the only two in the crowd who understood the allusion, which he seemed thoroughly to enjoy.

'The sacred lamp of burlesque' burned brightly in the 'nineties; the days of musical comedy were still happily distant. As a comic criticism of the times burlesque had a value to which its spectacular successor in public favour has never pretended. And it would have been strange if Barrie, whose early writings disclose so marked a partiality for satire and burlesque, had not followed his bent in his first effort as a playwright. Richard Savage we need not regard as his first attempt: the blame being shared with another. In Ibsen's Ghost we have the real start of his career as a dramatist, and it is conceived in the true spirit of burlesque.

The student who cares to look into the dusty pages of The National Observer for 1890—none are more worth having the dust blown off them, as they are crammed with excellent reading— will find an anonymous contribution in the issue of October 18th. It is entitled The Ghost of Ghosts and purports to be an extract from Every Man His Own Ibsen. It is a dialogue between Ibsen characters in which the much discussed features of that great innovator's dramatic methods are brilliantly satirised. This may have been the germ of the comic curtain-raiser Ibsen's Ghost, or Toole Up-to-date—there had been a succession of 'up-to-dates,' Faust and others at the Gaiety—which was first played by Toole, at his own theatre, at a Saturday matinée on May 30th, 1891. The author's name was not printed in the programme at the first performance, an odd fact taken in conjunction with the anonymity of The National Observer skit.

The author of Bandelero the Bandit had been true to his schoolboy admiration for J. L. Toole in fitting that comic actor with a slight but cleverly conceived part. Although the piece occupied only half-an-hour in performance, we have the testimony of Mr. H. M. Wallbrook, an acceptable authority, that it was the wittiest burlesque he ever saw and that it 'raised more laughter in Toole's Theatre than many a three-act farce had evoked.' In that exquisite chapter of reminiscences with which he dedicates 'To the Five' the text of Peter Pan, published in October, 1928, the author describes Ibsen as 'the mightiest craftsman that ever wrote for our kind friends in front,' and he tells us that 'on the first night a man in the pit found Ibsen's Ghost so diverting that he had to be removed in hysterics. After that no one seems to have thought of it at all. But what a man to carry about with one!' Ibsen's Ghost was, within its well-defined limits, a success, which was proved by the fact that many playgoers came expressly to enjoy this dainty *hors d'œuvre*, whereas it was a common thing in those days for one-act curtain raisers to be played to half-filled houses. Mr. Wallbrook states that the text was never printed in English, but that a German version was published in Germany, where Ibsen was then more sympathetically regarded than in England, and where presumably the criticism implicit in Ibsen's Ghost would be more readily appreciated.

At the close of 1891, therefore, Barrie's outstanding achievement remains The Little Minister; nobody could prophesy any future for him as a dramatist; but his own mind was made up, having first tasted blood at Toole's, that the theatre was his game, just as firmly as it had once been set upon the writing of books. And with good reason. He was already busy developing the houseboat episodes of When A Man's Single into a play which was to be called The Houseboat, a title that had to be changed when it was found to have been used before. Walker, London, in every way a happier title, supplied his admired comic hero J. L. Toole with one of the finest parts he ever played. Jasper Phipps, the hairdresser who went off alone on his honeymoon a week before his marriage, was conceived in the terms of Toole's own unctuous humour, and his success was never for a moment in doubt. Walker, London, a farcical comedy in three acts, was produced at Toole's Theatre, King William Street, Strand (long ago pulled down), on February 25th, 1892, with a brilliant cast. The play was warmly received; almost rapturously. Not that it provided anything surprisingly novel, or brought a new technique to the stage,—which might have been said about Lady Windermere's Fan produced five nights before it—but it offered a freshness of humour, an oddness of fancy, and a charmingly unconventional setting. The stagecraft of the author was shown in the ease with which he carried his story through three acts of continuous movement without change of setting.

His fellow-Scot, J. F. Nisbet, then dramatic critic of The Times, was one of the very few who had doubts about the play:

The most undeniable quality of Walker, London, is its originality. There is nothing for the plagiarist to lay hold of; its gossamer-like structure, if too rudely grasped, even for the purpose of analysis, would crumble to dust. To the dilettante playgoer this ' comic play ' may be welcome for its freshness and unsubstantiality; but whether the general public will care for Mr. Barrie's thin extract of humour, which they may find more piquant than satisfying, is a question.

Clement Scott in The Daily Telegraph said, in my judgement, the right thing so far as any critic could say it, of Barrie's achievement at this time, when he compared him with Robertson, though the dramatist was to travel to realms beyond the ken of him who wrote Caste:

Mr. Toole has made a discovery. He has found a new Robertson. Mr. Barrie, the brilliant author, reminds one of Robertson far more than a score of Robertson's feeble imitators. There is no flaccidity about Mr. Barrie. He is a Robertson of to-day, a Robertson up-to-date—not so sentimental, but quite as human, as observant, as pungent, as laconic, and a Robertson who has that strange dramatic mastery over the simplest and apparently the most trivial details of life. Mr. Barrie is a remarkably dramatic craftsman. The delicacy of his humour is already well known; but no dramatist since Robertson has so conquered, as if by intuition, the supreme difficulty of his art. It is a most fascinating play, and Robertson himself could not have painted a purer, a healthier, or a more truly English scene. It is comedy—true, observant comedy of the most exhilarating kind.

Of the company playing Walker, London, at its original production one was fated to have a long and distinguished association with the works of its author—George Shelton, who has appeared annually for twenty-two years as Smee, the pirate, in Peter Pan. In the autumn of 1928 he wrote a pleasant little book of reminiscence, It's Smee, in which he says that Walker, London, was the greatest success Toole ever had; 'it ran for over a year and made a very considerable contribution to the estate which Toole left at his death.' He also makes this interesting statement concerning the production of the play:

During such a long run as this play had it was inevitable that gags should creep in. However, after a time they were objected to by the author, and a rehearsal was called for cuts. We went right through the play on that occasion, and as the gags came along Barrie, in his quiet way, said ' Out,' and so it went on until every gag was banished. I may mention that Toole was not among the culprits.

With Walker, London, a great advance has been made towards ascendancy in the theatre. A writer in The Players of June 10th, 1892, made a very happy allusion to this. He said of Barrie:

BARRIE: THE STORY OF A GENIUS

He rapidly acquires the mastery of a new branch of literature. When he was rehearsing Ibsen's Ghost, he had no idea what he wanted; dress and business he left alike despairingly to the company. But when he rehearsed Walker, London, he had precise views about every detail. The Little Minister teaches us that it is quite possible that Mr. Barrie may one day give the stage a great romantic drama, full of passion and colour.

That is as near prophecy as a critic can hope to get, and the reference to Barrie's new skill at rehearsing is confirmed by Joseph Harker, the scenic artist, who painted the set for Walker, London, as charming a stage picture as any I can remember. In his Studio and Stage (1924) he writes:

Sir J. M. Barrie I first met at the time of his production of Walker, London. He was a very quiet and undemonstrative onlooker at the rehearsals, entirely self-effacing save in the few instances in which his dictum was made. On these occasions he would assert himself with a sudden access of vigour, impressing on you his wishes in a way that quite plainly indicated that he knew exactly what was wanted and that he was capable of seeing that he got it.

There was still a very long way to travel before it became evident that the playwright in Barrie was one day to get the better of the novelist, just as the latter had got the better of the journalist. Nearly six years more are to be notched up by old Father Time before the dramatist 'arrives.' While he is experimenting, failing and also making a success of sorts on the stage, his literary fame is spreading everywhere, and he can now afford to be as discriminating in his rare appearances in print as he was formerly unrestrained. A new book by Barrie has become an event of long expectation and anticipatory interest. For four years he seems content to rest on his literary laurels; four years during which he is quietly at work on two books and a play that will in their due time set free a spate of literary discussion and heighten public interest in their author. These are things that will occupy our attention in the two ensuing chapters. There remain, however, many matters vital in the life and work of the novelist that must be chronicled here.

There befell in May of 1892 an event that made a deep impression on Barrie at the time, and drew from him an unforgotten expression of his emotion. His youngest sister, Margaret, was engaged to be married to a promising young minister of the Scottish Free Church who six months earlier had been appointed to the pastorate of Bower in Caithness. Three weeks before the time appointed for their wedding this young minister while out

visiting was thrown from his horse and killed. A second tragedy
thus projected its shadow for a time across the declining years
of Margaret Ogilvy, who at Strathview, in the companionship
of her husband, long since retired from the linen mills, and in
the company of her devoted daughter, Jane Ann, and her name-
sake, the youngest, had been enjoying a lovely eventide, serene in
the knowledge that her little Jamie of the Tenements had made
himself for ever famous and that, in great part, owing to her own
cherished memories of the days of her girlhood.

Barrie had hastened to Kirriemuir at news of the tragedy,
as the dead man had not only been the betrothed of his sister,
but his own close friend. To the congregation at Bower he wrote
on his sister's behalf a letter that was read out from the pulpit
during the funeral service; a letter that, for solemn beauty and
understanding, it would be hard to match from any of the great
letter-writers. In a way it might stand as a confession of Barrie's
faith. It was printed in The British Weekly, May 19th, 1892,
and in The Pall Mall Gazette of the same date; but the text
which I give below is from a copy of the letter that was in the
possession of the late James MacArthur, founder of The Bookman
(New York), in whose issue of February, 1897, he printed it:

Kirriemuir, May 11, 1892.

To the Session and Congregation of the Free Church of Bower:

To you, at the grave of him who was in three weeks' time to become
her husband, my sister sends her love. She has not physical strength
to be with you just now in body, but she is with you in spirit, and God
is near her, and she is not afraid. You are her loved ones, for it was
you who, under God, called him to Bower, and gave him the manse
to which he was about to bring her, and, as he loved you, she loves
you. God, who gave his Son for the redemption of the world, has
told her that He had need of the disciple's life also, and that he died to
bring his people of Bower to God's knees. So God chose His own
way, and took her Jim, her dear young minister, and she says, God's
will be done; and she thanks Him for taking away so suddenly only
one who was ready to face his Maker without a moment's warning.
His great goodness, she says to you, in not taking some one who was
unprepared, is her comfort, and should be yours. And she prays
that Mr. Winter's six months' ministry among you, and his death
among you while doing his duty, has borne and will continue to bear
good fruit. And always she will so pray, and she asks you to pray
for her. And she says that you are not to grieve for her over-much,
for she is in God's keeping.

This is a word from her brother, who cannot leave her to come to
the funeral of his dearest friend, the purest soul I have ever known.
It is a word about her. You have never seen her, but you knew him,

and they have always been so alike in the depths of their religious feelings, in their humility, and in many other things you knew about him, and loved him for, that you may always think of them as one. There were four years and a half of their love-story, and it began the hour they first met. It never had a moment's break; there was always something pathetic about it, for they never parted, and they never wrote but solemnly and tenderly, as if it might be for the last time. The wistfulness of his face, which you must all have noticed, meant early death. They both felt that the one would soon be taken from the other, though he thought that he would be the survivor. Theirs was so pure a love that God was ever part of it. Let all the youth of Bower remember that there is no other love between man and woman save that.

J. M. BARRIE.

The edition de luxe of A Window in Thrums, printed on large paper and containing a set of seventeen vigorous etchings of Thrums characters by William Hole, R.S.A., was one of the publishing events of the autumn on both sides of the Atlantic. This edition was dedicated 'To the Flower of Manhood, one in a lovely and mournful story, the late Rev. James Winter, M.A., Free Church Minister of Bower, Caithness, whom two will always see upon the Brae till they also cross it for the last time.'

If 1892 had been allowed to pass without another dramatic effort, not so 1893, which saw two attempts. After the sureness of touch that one seemed to detect in Walker, London, it is astonishing to find the same clever hand fumbling so maladroitly in Jane Annie and Becky Sharp. The first-named was described as 'a new and original English comic opera,' and had for alternative title The Good Conduct Prize. It was a two-act piece produced at the Savoy Theatre under the management of D'Oyly Carte, on Saturday, May 13th, 1893, with a distinguished cast which included Rutland Barrington, Rosina Brandram and Decima Moore. As there was no Gilbert and Sullivan opera between The Gondoliers (1889) and Utopia Limited (1893) it may have been one of the periods of estrangement between those two fiery geniuses when D'Oyly Carte was at his wits' end to find substitutes to keep the Savoy going. In Jane Annie he drew a blank where he had hoped for a prize.

It would appear that Barrie originally undertook to write the book of the opera single handed, but, falling ill after he had completed the first act and part of the second, he invited his friend, Conan Doyle, who in the preceding year had become famous with his Adventures of Sherlock Holmes, to complete the writing of Act 2, the plot of which was already fixed. Most of the lyrics in that act are chargeable to Conan Doyle. Barrie alone bears responsibility for those of the first act. He had none of Gilbert's genius for verse at once comic and tuneful nor for the construction of an opera that advances with its lyrics instead of standing still while these are sung. In ten years' time he was to know most that could be learned about stagecraft, and by then, with a plausible theme for comic opera in The Admirable Crichton, he wisely kept to prose comedy.

The career of Jane Annie was a brief one: failure was acknowledged in the withdrawal of the opera after a few performances. This was Barrie's second and last experience in collaboration, and had there been a call of authors again it would have been the case of a fir tree and a pencil once more, as Doyle is, if anything, more generously proportioned than Marriott Watson was. The main reason for the failure of Jane Annie—named, by the way, after Barrie's favourite sister—was the fact that it lacked the crispness of both plot and verse to which Gilbert had accustomed Savoy patrons, and the music of Ernest Ford was disappointing to ears attuned to Sullivan. The piece was much superior to many that have since registered hundreds of performances, and the lyrics, though quite unworthy of two such brilliant men of letters, were vastly better than such atrocious stuff as

> Rose Marie I love you,
> I'm always dreaming *uv* you

which filled Drury Lane many hundreds of times not long ago.

Although Sir Arthur Conan Doyle in his Memories and Adventures admits that the complete failure of Jane Annie 'was a bitter thought for both of us,' it is evident that it did not damp the spirits of one of them, for a few days after the failure Barrie sent to Doyle a joyous parody of Sherlock Holmes entitled The Adventure of the Two Collaborators. This, we are told, was written on the fly-leaves of one of his books, and as it runs to something like a thousand words I would suggest that the book had either a superfluity of fly-leaves or the writing must have been microscopic. In any case there is no doubt about the effectiveness of the parody, which the author of Sherlock Holmes describes as 'the best of all the numerous parodies,' and very happily calls 'a gay gesture of resignation over the failure which we had encountered.' Watson and Holmes are together in their familiar room over-looking Baker Street when they see 'two gentlemen advancing rapidly':

'They are two collaborators in comic opera, and their play has not been a triumph.'

175

BARRIE: THE STORY OF A GENIUS

I sprang from my chair to the ceiling in amazement, and he then explained:

' My dear Watson, they are obviously men who follow some calling. That much even you should be able to read in their faces. Those little pieces of blue paper which they fling angrily from them are Durrant's Press Notices. Of these they have obviously hundreds about their person (see how their pockets bulge). They would not dance on them if they were pleasant reading.'

Asked by Watson if there is anything else he can tell him about them from their demeanour in the street, he replies:

' A great deal. From the mud on the boots of the tall one I perceive that he comes from South Norwood. The other is as obviously a Scotch author.'
' How can you tell that? '
' He is carrying in his pocket a book called (I clearly see) Auld Licht Something. Would anyone but the author be likely to carry about a book with such a title? '

In such occasional trifles as that, thrown lightly from his pen, the richness of his gift of humour is hardly less evident than in some of his longer and more studied pieces of writing. There is about all his comic writings an ease, an apparent lack of effort, which, more than anything else, makes them inimitable. But the writing of really good comic verse was not among his many fairy gifts, and that should have been clear to him after his futile effort to compete with W. S. Gilbert.

Three weeks had scarcely passed when, the bitter taste of failure lingering still, he made another attempt to justify himself with those who expected something even better than Walker, London. Disappointment awaited both him and them. Becky Sharp, staged at Terry's Theatre in the Strand, June 3rd, 1893, was from all accounts an ill-judged effort. Fortunately, it was ' only a little one,' forming part of a ' quintuple bill,' but it had an excellent cast and lacked nothing in the acting. He had gone to Thackeray for both plot and characters. According to Edward Morton (author of San Toy and a competent critic, who died in 1922) the play 'reproduced, word for word, the language of Thackeray without reviving the spirit of Vanity Fair,' and 'gave no more sign of a great talent for the theatre than one may find in Mr. Pinero's first pieces.' When the curtain came down upon Becky Sharp Barrie's anxious admirers, who in their zeal for his Auld Licht stories feared that the stage might snatch him away from what they considered his predestined task, could breathe more freely at this further failure in the theatre.

THRUMS OR THEATRE?

Regarded from the vantage ground of our later knowledge, there is a sense in which these five quickly following bids for stage success are seen to be not less significant in the chronicle of Barrie's achievement than the novel of The Little Minister itself. Readers who have no personal recollection of the national prejudices that endured up to the close of last century cannot realise the audacity of this young writer who, not content with having captured an immense reading public, in large part composed of a class to whom the theatre was the busiest mart of Satan in his capacity of soul-snatcher, was prepared to put his gifts of genius at the service of this evil institution. Of the inhabitants of Kirriemuir there would be a handful at most who in 1891 had ever set foot in a theatre or witnessed a stage play. Even in the great cities there were many thousands to whom the theatre was a house of sin.

That an author whose appeal had been mainly to the religiously minded should be so little heedful of this prejudice showed a resolution and an independence of action for which he has not always been given credit. His friend, Robertson Nicoll, and the religious publishers with whom he was connected, must have had their moments of heart-searching when the name of the best-selling author on their list was being flaunted on theatre bills. There was still so much to be done with Thrums. The vogue of the Kailyard was just gathering way at this time, and its originator's experiments in the theatre may have seemed a little remote to admirers of his books. His books in turn persuaded readers who were curious about his other activities that if he was experimenting with stage plays he could only be doing something for the good of the theatre. Nor will it be long before we shall see that they were right.

Until it became evident in the progress of my chronicle that the importance of this period in Barrie's history greatly exceeded any question of Auld Lichts or Thrums, I had headed it The Kailyard in Full Bloom, and had I been content to let that inadequate heading stand, I do not think that the reader would have suspected on the part of the writer the slightest gesture of depreciation. In its day, the term Kailyard was applied to a school of Scots writers whose activities were due to the success that had attended the discovery of Thrums. It was meant as a sneer for work that was meretricious. At first Barrie stood alone, and there was no whisper of Kailyard; but by the time S. R. Crockett had made a hit with The Stickit Minister (1893) and Ian Maclaren with Beside the Bonnie Brier Bush (1894), whose reception in all English-speaking lands was more unrestrained than any that Barrie had so far experienced, it was clear that the demand for sketches of Scottish life had assumed the dimensions of a 'boom.'

A phenomenon common to all things human seems to be that when they are approaching their most glorious hour the forces of reaction have already started. Those of my readers who can recall the circumstances of the Kailyard vogue will remember that some corrective was necessary. Book readers on both sides of the Atlantic seemed temporarily to have lost all sense of literary values, and more than a score of writers whose names are now long forgotten had no difficulty in sailing their frail barks upon this favouring tide. The subject would hardly repay the pains of detailed investigation, but, trusting to memory alone, I can recall the names of Fergus Mackenzie, author of The Humours of Glenbruar; Gabriel Setoun (T. N. Hepburn), author of Barncraig, and Sunshine and Haar; Halliday Rogers (also a pseudonym), author of Meggotsbrae; David Lyall (the pen-name under which that talented Scottish novelist Annie S. Swan ingeniously assumed a new Kailyard manner); W. D. Latto (Tammas Bodkin), and Jane Findlater who, though later famous as a novelist chiefly in collaboration with her sister Mary, began with The Green Graves of Balgowrie. A number of English authors also set about delving in English cabbage patches. Harry Lindsay (H. L. Hudson), with his Methodist Idylls; J. Marshall Mather, who wrote Lancashire Idylls; and John Ackworth (Rev. F. R. Smith), author of Clog-shop Chronicles, are three whose work I remember. Superior to most of the writers named were two Irish Kailyarders, Frank Mathew, whose At the Rising of the Moon is a book of lovely sketches in which the quality of wistfulness inheres, and Jane Barlow, whose Irish Idylls, Bogland Studies and a long series of charmingly written stories in the same vein signified a successful career of letters. What Americans are fond of terming 'the saturation point' was very speedily reached, and in the course of a few years, after this orgy of Scotch, provincial English and Irish, editors and publishers were again as little inclined to accept dialect stories as Barrie at first had found them.

The most uncompromising critic of the Kailyarders was Dr. J. H. Millar, then a brilliant university lecturer and later Professor of Constitutional Law and History at Edinburgh. In his Literary History of Scotland, a very able work, published some ten years after the blooming of the Kailyard, he had in no way softened in his feelings towards these objects of his early dislike. His antipathy to Barrie and all his works remained undiminished.

THRUMS OR THEATRE?

For the moment I need not stay to examine his verdict on Barrie, but his observations upon the detested school and two of its chief exponents may be put in as evidence for the plaintiff:

The vogue of Mr. Barrie's weaver-bodies and elders of the Original Secession was not long in bringing into the field a host of rivals; and the 'Kailyard' School of Literature, as it has been termed, presently burst into existence. The circulating libraries became charged to overflowing with a crowd of ministers, precentors, and beadles, whose dry and 'pithy' wit had plainly been recruited at the fountainhead of Dean Ramsay; while the land was plangent with the sobs of grown men, vainly endeavouring to stifle their emotion by an elaborate affectation of 'peching' and 'hoasting.' Two writers of the class referred to stand out with especial prominence, one the *Jean qui rit*, the other the *Jean qui pleure*, of the movement. Samuel Rutherford Crockett abandoned the ministry of the Free Kirk for the wider sphere of usefulness which the career of letters affords. . . .

The vulgarity of the works of 'Ian Maclaren' (the Rev. John Watson) is less robust than that of Mr. Crockett's; but it is none the less offensive that it is more subtle and insidious. . . . Without professing to decide so nice a question of taste, we may allow that there is a perfectly distinct flavour in the work of the two authors. In Mr. Crockett we have the boisterous horse-play of the bothie; in Mr. Maclaren we have the slobbering sentiment of the Sabbath school, with a dash of 'gentility'. . . .

What the Scottish public really thought of the Kailyard writers is naturally a little difficult to decide. Of genuine and wholehearted admirers there may have been a select circle. I should conjecture that amusement at the 'facility' of the English and American public was at least as widely spread as admiration. If the English and American public chose to pay for what they took to be the accurate presentations of the Caledonian on his native heath, why, it was no business of any 'brither Scot' of the author's to dispel the illusion. A few, no doubt, there were who resented this holding up of their fellow-countrymen to the ridicule and contempt of all sane and judicious human beings.

Severe though these strictures of Dr. Millar's may appear, and exaggerated as I hold them to be in certain of their implications concerning individual writers, it is undeniable that if he had been content to apply them in more general terms to the school as a whole they would have lost nothing of their force and gained something in truth, being freed from the very obvious personal prejudices of their writer. There are few critics to-day who will be prepared to find much of enduring value in Beside the Bonnie Brier Bush or The Stickit Minister, but both books had merits of truth and observation which commended them at the time to the sympathy of a reading public that had been

179

first caught by the incomparably finer qualities of Auld Licht Idylls, A Window in Thrums and The Little Minister.

The main sufferer from the excess of public enthusiasm during the Scottish vogue was he who had been, as Millar truly states, 'the chief agent in the resuscitation of the tale of Scottish life and manners': Barrie himself. And yet at no time in competent literary opinion was Barrie seriously bracketed with the numerous imitators who crowded into print after he had pioneered the way. There is no accounting for a 'best seller.' Why Beside the Bonnie Brier Bush, a work so inferior by comparison with A Window in Thrums, should have been so clamorously received, especially in America, who can say? Perhaps the fact that Maclaren offers sentimentality where Barrie offers sentiment and that the exiled Scot readily responds to sentimentality may have accounted in some measure for its extraordinary success in America, where it was actually turned into a play that held the stage for a time. Possibly the emotion evoked in the very title of the book had something to do with its popularity. For this Lady Nairne and an old Scottish air were something responsible :

> There grows a bonnie briar bush in our Kailyard,
> There grows a bonnie briar bush in our Kailyard;
> And below the bonnie briar bush there's a lassie and a lad,
> And they're busy, busy courting in our Kailyard.
>
> In days o' mair simplicity, true love was thus declared,
> And many a maid's been woo'd and won in our Kailyard;
> But now we're a' sae carefu' grown, we maun be on our guard,
> And boddies screw their mou's at love in our Kailyard.

Let all this be as it may, and let the critics, if they will, use Kailyard in contempt, the fact remains that Barrie had rediscovered an eternal truth when he found that the drama of life can be better seen and understood upon the small stage of the little town or the cotter's home than upon the larger stages planned for the spectacular. The kailyard was as worthy of the attention of the artist as the manor house or even the palace of kings, and presently there may be occasion to suggest that even Barrie himself was not yet fully conscious of his own literary function as its interpreter.

A possibly disturbing factor to both work and ambition at this stage of Barrie's career was ill health. The fact that he was unable to complete Jane Annie off his own bat was due, as we have heard, to an attack of illness. For two or three years he seems to have been subject to recurring periods of indifferent health, during which his plans for theatrical ventures would suffer more acutely than the current of his literary work, although that also must have been slowed. In a serious attack of pleuro-pneumonia he was nursed back to health by the talented actress who had made a notable hit as Nannie O'Brien in Walker, London. For Mary Ansell, a lady of great personal charm joined with high qualities of mind, the playwright had conceived the warmest admiration during the happy days at Toole's, and a romantic attachment between the two culminated soon after his convalescence in their marriage. The ceremony took place privately at Strathview, Kirriemuir, on July 9th, 1894, the bridegroom not being well enough to face the ordeal of a public service, and for many a summer thereafter the graceful figure of Mrs. J. M. Barrie was a familiar one about the braes of Kirriemuir, the holidays being usually spent at Strathview. When the novelist and his wife used to take their walks abroad they had a devoted companion in a massive St. Bernard dog which, as we shall learn in due course, was fated, after certain transformations, to have a prominent niche in the gallery of his master's immortal characters.

There is in My Life and Times by Jerome K. Jerome a paragraph of particular interest at this point of my narrative. He is writing of his own play—and a very pleasant play it was—Woodbarrow Farm:

I introduced J. M. Barrie to Mary Ansell. That also was a by-product of Woodbarrow Farm. I had a travelling company of my own playing the piece in the provinces, and had engaged Mary Ansell for the ingénue. Barrie was producing Walker, London, with Toole at the old Folly in King William Street; and asked me if I could recommend him a leading lady. He didn't want much. She was to be young, beautiful, quite charming, a genius for preference, and able to flirt. The combination was not so common in those days. I could think of no one except Miss Ansell. It seemed unkind not to give her the chance. I cancelled the contract and sent for her; and next time it was Barrie who introduced her to me, as his wife.

At the beginning of the year Barrie had been in good enough health and spirits to do what he did not attempt for another thirty-four years: take the chair at a Burns dinner. On this occasion he had accepted the invitation to preside at the annual meeting of the Greenock Club, and we may be sure that both before and after the event acute suffering attended his nervous reactions. Many years later he confessed to a friend of the writer's, who approached him with a request from a famous Burns society to preside at its annual festival, that he would have done so but that the anxiety with which he anticipated such an event and the nervous exhaustion that followed meant his existing for three days before and as many after in a state of misery. In more recent years much of this old-time nervousness would appear to have been outlived.

After the Greenock dinner of January 25th, 1894, he evidently recovered his cheerfulness of spirits very quickly, for there is an historic account of it in the pages of The National Observer for February 3rd, where the curious will find it headed Mr. Barrie in the Chair. A peculiar interest attaches to this article. There never was any doubt that its writer was Barrie himself. I had been to the trouble of looking it up again in the old files at the London Library and making some extracts. Two days later I received from Glasgow a copy of The Evening Times of that city containing a complete reprint of the article in question together with a facsimile of the opening page of the manuscript, which is in the possession of a Glasgow admirer. It is in Barrie's best script, being written with his right hand long before that 'gave out' and forced him to take to his left. Every Barrie student has long known of the existence and the authorship of this article, and it is incorrect to say that it 'roused the ire of his admirers'; it amused them and the more astute soon guessed its authorship, and scored one up to Barrie for having played so good a joke on his readers, a joke which, on being taxed with it, he did not repudiate. I append some passages from this diverting contribution, since it so happily illustrates the readiness which its author has often shown to poke fun at himself and, in so doing, occasionally to provide a bit of truthful self-criticism:

I was introduced to him, and we both held out our hands. Having shaken his, I let go. His remained in the air, as if the ceremony was new to him. Several others were introduced, and he gave to all his hand to do what they liked with it. This being over, he placed it by his side. We then adjourned with unwonted solemnity to the hall where dinner was to be served.

On the way I had time to sum up my impressions. He was evidently anxious to please. The way in which the arm shot out, like a pirate lugger from its hiding-place, was proof of this. The natural solemnity of his face is a little startling to one who has come out to dine, but there is no doubt that he made several gallant efforts to be jolly. I noticed this, not only in the ante-room, but throughout the evening. When a joke was made you could see him struggling, not with his face alone, to laugh heartily. It was as if he tugged the strings that work the organs of risibility, but either the strings were broken or he had forgotten to bring the organs. Only once did he manage a genuine smile, but some of us forgot ourselves and cheered, and it fled. So far as I could see he got it beneath the table. . . .

On his table was a large épergne full of flowers. I saw him move his chair stealthily, inch by inch, until he was fairly behind this épergne.

On the left and right he shut himself in as far as possible with bottles and cruets. He then settled down for a jolly evening. I was too far away to hear what he said when he engaged in conversation. . . . The man who got most out of him was the head waiter, to whom (this should go into the minute-book of the club) he said, ' Clear,' ' Cod,' ' Mutton,' 'Haggis,' ' Roedeer,' ' No, thank you.' His favourite remark is ' H'm,' with which he expresses surprise, thankfulness, indignation, delight, grief. He also asks questions with it, and he has a ' H'm ' that is final.

There is, I would add, little doubt that to Mr. Barrie in the Chair more than to anything else that has been written about him must be attributed that immense body of newspaper myth and legend with which his personality has been surrounded and in a measure obscured. That he has often been described in terms that would suggest a boor, or at least a person of uncouth manners, shy and awkward as a yokel, is hardly surprising. The hasty paragraphist is not always responsive to the kindly caressing touch that is to be found in all Barrie's satire and is not absent from Mr. Barrie in the Chair. If he deals his victims some resounding thwacks, that is all for their good, and before he has finished with them he is patting them on the back, as all good satirists do.

To The National Observer a fortnight later he sent a charming article entitled Wrecked on an Island, which, so far as I can ascertain, was the last of his contributions to miscellaneous journalism. For that reason alone it should be noted, and still more on account of its subject and the great affection he was to show for islands in works of his later years. Up to 1894 the island had not been too conspicuous in his scenic efforts, although he asserts in this article that 'some low person' would probably count up the number of times he had mentioned islands in his writings and thus disclose his weakness. Might this have been written in anticipation of the parts that islands were to play in his later fancies? Already in 1894 it is possible that the island of Peter Pan and those of Mary Rose and The Admirable Crichton were all looming up on the horizon of his mind. This love of his for an island is boyhood's common heritage from Defoe and more particularly the bond of all who have read Coral Island.

Among the advantages of having an island to get away to, he suggested that of avoiding compilers of symposia who used to be continually asking popular authors all sorts of embarrassing questions for publication in the mazagines. 'The editor of a popular weekly, whose 650,000 readers will receive intellectual stimulus if you tell them whether you work on beef or bacon,' was one of these nuisances which he specifies, and he plays delightfully with the idea of possessing an island all to himself.

BARRIE: THE STORY OF A GENIUS

What sort of an island? A mysterious island like Jules Verne's is not easy to beat, but though we gaze entranced at the wonders worked by that magician's magicians, we feel sadly that such an island is not for us. We lack the science. At the best we should have been told off to cook the dinner or carry bricks. No, we want an easier island, one in which, when Fritz says the butter is done, you go out and look up and behold this is the cow tree whose juice, when solidified in the shadow of a rock, is an excellent substitute for butter. (The Swiss Family were, perhaps, only wrecked in Whiteley's, but nobody need let on.)

He winds up by remembering that all islands of adventure must possess savages. 'Shall (*sic*) you have them fierce or tame?' he asks. He is forced to conclude on a note of melancholy:

But, alackaday, these joys are only for the imagination. Put on your silk hat, and off you go for your two shilling lunch. I must return sorrowfully to my last. There is no island for you and me.

So far as one may reckon, lacking a date, it was some time this year that Barrie, in one of his then rare appearances as an after-dinner speaker, made a speech that has become historic. When his first editor and friend, F. W. Robinson, was contemplating retirement from his editorial chair a number of his old contributors organized a dinner in his honour, at which Jerome K. Jerome presided and Barrie occupied the vice-chair. If I am correct in assuming that the approaching demise of Home Chimes was the real occasion of the dinner, it was in some sort a funeral feast, but with such a gathering of wits the occasion would none the less be a merry one. Among those present was Theodore Watts (before he added Dunton) who had been a frequent contributor of verse to Robinson's magazine. He was then identified with The Athenæum as its leading reviewer, and he wrote a report of the dinner for that staid and solemn weekly, which rarely condescended to print such items. Coulson Kernahan, in his genial volume of recollections, Celebrities, quotes some lines from this report which I have borrowed for inclusion here:

Mr. Jerome K. Jerome occupied the chair, and Mr. J. M. Barrie the vice-chair, and both made speeches full of wit and humour. A special interest was lent to the occasion by the fact that several writers, some in the land of fame, and some already on its borders, made speeches in which they affirmed that their introduction to literature was in the pages of this unpretentious magazine. The brilliant author of Auld Licht Idylls said that when he first set out for London in search of literary success London was, in his mind, mainly ' a city in which the office of Home Chimes was situated.'

A Favourite Barrie Photo of the Late 'Nineties   [*Hollyer*

Face page 184

J. L. TOOLE IN WALKER, LONDON

Face page 185

At this dinner also, Israel Zangwill, who was as brilliant and fluent with his tongue as with his pen, made a wittily 'ragging' speech mainly about the author of Auld Licht Idylls, in which he professed his inability to guess at the pronunciation of that title, and wound up by urging the author to tell the company what it meant and how it was spoken, whereupon Barrie quietly stood up and slowly said in his best Kirriemuir manner, 'Gentlemen, it's Auld Licht Idylls,' resuming his seat without another word, much to the amusement but little to the edification of the gathering.

The most arresting thing said at this dinner, however, came from F. W. Robinson when he told the company of brilliant prosemen and poets, all of whom had written of their best for Home Chimes, that he could not trace that an increased sale of a single copy had ever resulted from anything of theirs he had printed! This was merely another way of saying that there was something inherently and congenitally wrong with Home Chimes as a magazine. There was: it lacked ideas and personality, and these must come from the editor, not from his contributors, though it is humiliating to an author to know that his precious contribution proves valueless as a circulation raiser. Why did Barrie's work for The British Weekly add many a copy to the circulation? Simply because its editor had the skill to present it in the right way to the right people. All that the bright brains that wrote for Home Chimes could do was to assist it gravewards. Robinson, I fear, had no genius for editing.

A strange duty fell to Barrie's lot in 1893. The congregation of the Auld Licht Kirk in Bank Street, Kirriemuir, had decided to demolish their ancient barn-like structure and replace it with a new red-sandstone building which I have described elsewhere as a strange blend of the ecclesiastical and the commercial, two retail shops occupying its ground storey. This might have been thought ingratitude to him whose genius had made the old church glamorous throughout the world, but the progressives of the little body were firm for the improvement, and whom, think you, did they ask to open their bazaar to raise the funds for the new building? Him to whom the old one meant so much more than to any of its declining congregation. The strange thing is that he fell in with the proposal, and one who was present tells me that the whole affair was notable for its lack of the usual formalities. ' In quite an impassive way Barrie delivered what in effect might have been an extra chapter for The Little Minister, a chapter so ingenious that I have often wondered if he ever used it anywhere. On that occasion he presented some copies of his books, which were eagerly bought, and the author by main force compelled to autograph them all.' Surely to officiate at the demolition of the most famous of his own literary landmarks is a thing that has seldom fallen to the lot of any celebrated author.

The next event of importance to be chronicled is the production at the Comedy Theatre on August 13th, 1894, of The Professor's Love Story. The theatre is up for the moment in the see-saw that is going on between it and Thrums in the affections of the novelist playwright. Even so, something of Thrums gets carried across the footlights at the Comedy when this new Barrie play takes the stage, for Henders and Pete, though minor characters in the piece, are racy and unconventional. The Professor's Love Story had been produced nearly two months earlier (June 25th) in the United States, where its author's popularity was steadily increasing, and the success of the play there was immediate. It was also well received by the public in London, E. S. Willard being an actor of great distinction who made the most of the somewhat obvious humours of the part of Professor Goodwillie.

In certain details the plot was as wildly improbable as Nicoll had found that of The Little Minister, and the dramatist's inclination at times to turn *farceur*—a besetting sin that may be detected in half-a-dozen of his plays—demanded many other qualities of charm as counter-weight. Fortunately these were present. William Archer's candid opinion of the play, expressed at both the original production and the revival of 1903 (when I first saw it), was severe: 'a calculated disloyalty to art . . . a patchwork of extravagant farce, mawkish sentiment, and irrelevant anecdote.' On the other hand, so good a critic as Edward Morton wrote of it as ' a pretty play,' and went on to say ' it was much more than that, for although it excited no violent emotions, there was a depth of feeling in the story of the Professor's love for Lucy White which touched the soft place in the heart of the audience.'

My own recollection of it is more in tone with Morton's praise than with Archer's denunciation. That it erred occasionally on the side of the farcical, and more often on that of the sentimental, did not seem to minimise the enjoyment of the audience, to whom the cleverly conceived setting of the play, in an atmosphere of sunshine and haycocks, came with a freshness similar to that produced the moment the curtain went up on Walker, London. Its box-office success notwithstanding, the playwright's position in the theatre was not noticeably higher than that to which he had attained with Walker, London.

An English actor named Alexander Woolcott, who in 1923 wrote a book entitled Shouts and Murmurs, told some stories of Barrie and the stage, including a circumstantial account of how the dramatist first took the manuscript of The Professor's Love Story to Henry Irving, 'who was kind and let him read the play aloud.' He was not impressed with it, however, as offering any scope for his own peculiar dramatic powers (one is not surprised at this), but he suggested that it should be brought to the notice of John Hare and wrote a letter of introduction to that fine actor, as eminent in his way as Irving in his. Hare, we are told, was much less sympathetic than Irving, and insisted upon reading the manuscript himself. He seemed uncomfortable in the presence of the author, whom he asked to await his verdict in an ante-room, and proceeded to struggle with the manuscript, which we are told was 'mystical' in the obscurity of its caligraphy. Barrie did not have long to wait: groans and imprecations were soon heard within. The author, fearing something had happened to the actor, opened the door and found him jumping on the script in rage at being unable to decipher it. It was after this bad beginning that, we are asked to believe, the author wrote out a better copy of his manuscript and submitted it to E. S. Willard, who was about to set out on an American tour, with the happy result already stated. The story is given as fact, and there may be a shadow of truth in it, but I am suspicious of the conduct of John Hare, and any manuscript of Barrie's articles about this time that has come under my inspection has appealed to me as being extraordinarily clear and easy to read.

This eventful year, which had seen Barrie almost at death's door, then his convalescence and his marriage, and the production of this stage success, did not pass without its shadow, which left him with a deep sense of personal loss, albeit a sorrow he shared with all the world: Robert Louis Stevenson died suddenly at Vailima, on December 4th. Between Barrie and R. L. S. a very remarkable friendship had developed through the medium of correspondence, and some of the liveliest of Stevenson's letters were inscribed to his younger brother novelist—'we are both Scots besides, and I suspect both rather Scotty Scots,' he wrote. In these letters there is a longing to meet 'little Barrie' and take him by the hand. 'They tell me your health is not strong. Man, come out here and try the Prophet's chamber. . . . Come, it will broaden your mind, and be the making of me.' (Dec. 5th, 1892.) 'We all join in the cry, "Come to Vailima!" My dear Sir, your soul's health is in it—you will never do the great book, you will never cease to work in L., etc., till you come to Vailima.' (Dec. 7th 1893.) 'No, Barrie, 'tis in vain they try to alarm me with their bulletins. No doubt you're ill, and unco ill, I believe, but I have been so often in the same case that I know pleurisy and

BARRIE: THE STORY OF A GENIUS

pneumonia are in vain against Scotsmen who can write. (I once could.) You cannot imagine how near me this common calamity brings you.' (July 29th, 1894.) There are many such evidences as these of the yearning that 'Tusitala' felt to meet in body one with whom he had so often collogued in the realms of fancy, and a few weeks after Barrie got the last of these letters their writer was dead. Barrie's sorrow at the sudden passing of one whom he so profoundly admired found expression in an elegiac poem, Scotland's Lament, which appeared in The Bookman for January, 1895.

Already, as we have seen, he was proving Stevenson to be right in saying that the theatre was the gold mine, but it was still as the author of A Window in Thrums that he was most readily thought of, and it was still with Thrums and the novel that he was most deeply engaged in 1895 despite his profitable venture in the theatre the year before. He was busy with Sentimental Tommy, begun early in 1894, a book in which the author's enjoyment is almost as apparent as that which the reader experiences; yet it was written at a time of much sadness to him.

Mrs. David Barrie, the novelist's mother, died at Strathview on September 3rd, 1895, and three days before that her daughter, Jane Ann, worn with devoted attendance on her mother during her months of illness, had passed away in her sleep, so that mother and daughter were laid to rest together on the 6th of September. How much these two were to each other and to himself their son and brother has told us in a book that he wrote and published within fifteen months of that sad day, a book that will occupy much of our attention in the next chapter.

In the following year the novelist's uncle, the Rev. David Ogilvy, after more than half-a-century of service, retired from his Motherwell charge to Edinburgh, where he was joined by David Barrie, Sara keeping house now for her father as well as for her uncle. In recognition of his long and devoted ministry at Dalziel Free Church his old University of Aberdeen marked his retirement by conferring on David Ogilvy its honorary degree of Doctor of Divinity.

Of great consequence to Barrie's later career was his visit to the United States in the autumn of 1896, undertaken in the company of his devoted friend Robertson Nicoll. They sailed from Liverpool by the Campania on September 26th. It was the heyday of the Kailyard boom, and when the two travellers arrived at New York they were to find everywhere evidences of the astonishing popularity of Ian Maclaren.

About a fortnight before they had left Liverpool the author of Beside the Bonnie Brier Bush had set out from the same port

188

(the Rev. John Watson, D.D., was Minister of Sefton Park Presbyterian Church, Liverpool) on a great lecturing tour through the
United States. He had undertaken no fewer than eighty engagements to lecture, preach and speak, the whole of these to be
covered, together with an immense amount of railway travelling,
within the space of ninety days. Fortunately he was a man of
unusual vigour, as well as of the most attractive personality, so
that he possessed both the means of standing the strain and the
gift of pleasing his audiences. His tour was to be a triumph,
the bookshop windows everywhere had massed displays of The
Brier Bush and portraits of its author, and on the hoardings he
was heralded like a stage 'star.'

Watson was also a man of shrewd common sense, and at no
time had the slightest tendency to inflation as a result of the
excessive popularity which he was lucky enough to win for his
works. He confessed to me, within a year or two of his return
from this American tour, that he was quite convinced his vogue
would be of brief duration, and that it behoved him as a sensible
man to make his hay while the sun shone. He was full of the
sincerest admiration for the work of Barrie, and did not presume to put his own in competition therewith. 'Barrie,' I remember him saying to me, 'is by comparison with the rest of us
Shakespearian.' It no doubt amused Nicoll and his companion
to find themselves confronted with this Ian Maclaren boom on
their unostentatious arrival in the United States, fairly conscious
as each of them must have been of their relativeness to the
favourite of the moment, but no tremor of jealousy would be felt
on either side. Everybody who came in contact with Ian Maclaren was an immediate thrall to the charm of the man, and it is
a curious fact that it fell to Robertson Nicoll during their stay
in New York to introduce Barrie and Watson to each other.

The real reason of Barrie's visit was associated with the increasing importance of his literary and dramatic copyrights in
that country. Several of his earlier books had not been adequately
protected by the very one-sided copyright American regulations
then in force, numerous pirated editions being freely sold; and
The Little Minister, although protected as a book, had attracted
the play pirates. His publishers were so pressed for time that they
had to copyright The Little Minister minus its last chapter. A
copy of the incomplete book was sent by mistake to The Nation for
review and the author was duly chided for its inartistic ending! In
the autumn of 1896, however, Charles Scribner's Sons placed upon
the market the first collected edition of his books, the prematureness
of a 'collected edition' of a living author then only in his thirty-sixth

year being explained by the desire to establish his rights in his works through a special authorised edition issued by by a reputable house. To each of the books in this series he contributed a brief introduction, thus giving an added value to the edition as a whole.

There was another and more important reason for his presence in New York. The circumstances wherein The Professor's Love Story came to be first produced in America have already been detailed. Its success in New York was even more pronounced than in London, where Willard brought it two months later. There is a greater market for the sentimental in America than in any other country, hence the hysterical success of Ian Maclaren; and as Barrie is never again so sentimental in his plays as he was in The Professor's Love Story, the warmth of its American reception was not surprising. Among those who recognized its theatrical qualities was Charles Frohman, just then getting into the full stride of his amazing career as a play-producer. A man of instant decisions, far seeing, courageous in standing to his opinions, he was sufficiently impressed with the stage-craft of The Professor's Love Story first to telegraph and then to write to its author in England and tell him how much he had admired his novel The Little Minister, and how convinced he was that if he would but make a play of it and let him have the honour of producing it he could provide an actress for the part of Lady Babbie who would make its fortune. Here was a big matter indeed to discuss with the man who was even then in a fair way to be America's leading theatrical manager.

Barrie's meeting with Frohman was the beginning of a friendship which speedily developed between these two so different in every characteristic except one: a yearning desire to retain throughout life the illusion of youth. Each had the same strong attachment to his mother, a fact which is probably associated with this attitude of mind. Frohman was a genius in his own particular line, and when one has read the inspiring story of his life so ably told by his brother Daniel and Isaac F. Marcosson in Charles Frohman: Manager and Man, one can see how irresistibly drawn to each other were the producer and the playwright.

He was very dogged (writes Barrie in a foreword to the memoir). I had only one quarrel with him, but it lasted all the sixteen years I knew him. He wanted me to be a playwright and I wanted to be a novelist. All those years I fought him on that. He always won, but not because of his doggedness; only because he was so lovable that one had to do as he wanted. He also threatened, if I stopped, to reproduce the old plays and print my name in large electric letters over the entrance of the theatre.

THRUMS OR THEATRE?

If Frohman is to be accepted as the concrete force that prevailed in determining whether Barrie was to continue his career and establish his fame upon the novel or the drama, he is clearly a very important character in any narrative of the dramatist's life. Colour is lent to Barrie's statement by the fact that we shall very soon be witnessing him taking an affectionate leave of Thrums and ceasing entirely to create new work for the reading public, while he develops a perfect fury of activity as a playwright. Frohman would certainly seem to have prevailed, and perhaps Maude Adams also.

The story of how that brilliant American actress at once became a 'star' and an inspiration to the dramatist who was to provide her with the greatest successes of her wonderful career, is told by Marcosson as follows:

Under Frohman's influence he (Barrie) had begun to consider a dramatisation of The Little Minister, but the real stimulus was lacking because, as he expressed it to Frohman, he did not see any one who could play the part of Babbie.

Now came one of those many unexpected moments that shape lives. On a certain day Barrie dropped into the Empire Theatre (New York) to see Frohman, who was out.

'Why don't you step downstairs and see Rosemary?' said Frohman's secretary.

'All right,' said Barrie.

So he went down into the Empire and took a seat in the last row. An hour afterward he came rushing back to Frohman's office, found his friend in, and said to him, as excitedly as his Scottish nature would permit:

'Frohman, I have found the woman to play Babbie in The Little Minister! I am going to try to dramatise it myself.'

'Who is it?' asked Frohman, with a twinkle in his eye, for he knew without asking.

'It is that little Miss Adams who plays Dorothy.'

'Fine!' said Frohman. 'I hope you will go ahead now and do the play.'

As there might appear to be some reason for believing that Frohman had quietly laid his plans so that Barrie should imagine himself to be the first to discover in Maude Adams the full histrionic possibilities of his heroine, we can appreciate something of the exceptional qualities of generalship possessed by 'this Niagara of a man' whose energy was such that Barrie said 'they could have lit a city with it.' But I must question the accuracy in detail of Marcosson's story, for a reason that will presently be stated.

How little we can rely on the accuracy of our memories is well shown by the confusion of printed evidence concerning Frohman's part in the original production of The Little Minister. I turn now to My Crystal Ball, a book that contains the reminiscences of Miss Elisabeth Marbury, of New York, well-known in the Anglo-American theatre world, who at this time was associated with Addison Bright in London as a dramatic agent, and had numerous business relations with Charles Frohman. The business negotiations relating to The Little Minister were conducted by her in New York and by Bright in London. Her version of Barrie's first important transaction with Frohman ought, therefore, to be of interest. It is. And it completely traverses the statements of 'C. F.'s.' official biographers. Miss Marbury writes:

I had met J. M. Barrie in London, and both Addison Bright and I had advised him to dramatise The Little Minister. To this he agreed, and a contract was then entered into between him and Charles Frohman. Finally the play was finished, and Barrie came to New York, bringing the precious script with him.

He stopped at the Holland House, which was then a popular hotel. He had never at that time met Frohman personally. I had been their intermediary. On Wednesday, the day after Barrie's arrival, I called at the hotel for the play which I was to deliver to Charles Frohman. On the following Saturday the latter was to give his verdict. As this was one of my most important transactions, I naturally felt nervous when I returned early that day to learn how the manuscript had impressed Frohman.

When I entered his office, I was greeted with his usual cordiality. 'The play is all right,' he said. 'There is nothing the matter with it; only it is no good for me.' My heart sank. 'Why, what is the trouble with it?' I asked. 'It is a man's play,' replied C. F., 'whereas I am looking for a play for Maude Adams. I haven't any young actor I want to star as the Little Minister.'

No words can convey the chagrin I felt. My mind was set upon the acceptance and production of this property. I reflected for a few moments, and then said:

'How would you feel about it if Barrie would rewrite it, and make Lady Babbie the leading part?'

'Oh,' answered C. F., 'that would be fine; but I don't believe you can get him to do it.'

'That is up to me,' I said, and off I flew. I found Barrie waiting for me, anxious to learn Frohman's opinion. I repeated our conversation and found the author stubbornly opposed to any reconstruction of his material.

We are now to picture Miss Marbury exercising her woman's wiles upon the Wizard of Thrums. 'I pleaded, I coaxed, I argued.' The last was the right thing to do. The little bit of Scottish granite was softened. 'Barrie consented to make the necessary changes, and Frohman rejoiced at the result of my diplomacy.' Ah, these women, what can they not do when they like! 'Barrie's career as a playwright was established'— and we shall hope he remembers Elisabeth Marbury in his prayers. But, stay, another witness is at hand.

Our best source of information for the events of this American visit is in the letters sent by Robertson Nicoll to Miss Catharine Pollard, who on May 1st, 1897, became his wife. Describing their landing at New York at 8 o'clock on the morning of Saturday, October 3rd, he says:

A number of friends were waiting for us, and a host of interviewers— for Mr. Barrie mainly. Then we had two hours to wait at the Custom House. This was very wearisome indeed. But at last we got away to our hotel, which we reached at ten. We were marched off to lunch at the Aldine Club, and spent the afternoon there very agreeably. We returned at five, rested a little, dined, and then went to the theatre. Mr. Frohman, the manager, put his stage-box at our disposal and we saw Rosemary which was well acted, especially by the heroine, one of the best young actresses I have seen for some time.

Here I am confronted once again with another of those diffi- culties of which the biographer who verifies his facts will discover more in Barrie's life-story than in that of any other celebrity of our time. If Nicoll had not written the letter quoted above with its obviously accurate record of their visit to Rosemary we might have had to choose between the Marcosson and Marbury stories; but as it is impossible to doubt that Barrie saw Maude Adams on the very first day of his arrival in New York and in circumstances totally different from those of either story, we may reasonably attribute as much accident as design to the bringing together of those three striking personalities whose dramatic fortunes were to be so wonderfully intertwined in the coming years. Miss Marbury's name is not mentioned in any of Nicoll's letters, yet Barrie's going to New York with his play in his pocket, and there being induced to alter it to suit Frohman should have suggested some reference to so interesting a matter. More, another credible witness will be called in a later chapter: none else than Cyril Maude, who created the part of the Rev. Gavin Dishart in London. We shall then learn that Barrie first spoke to him about The Little Minister in the summer of 1897, (seven or eight months after the American visit), when he had not yet completed his script of the play, so that it is tolerably clear

Miss Marbury's Crystal Ball has returned some twisted vision of the past to her intent gaze.

Nothing else that happened during the American visit could be compared in importance with the laying of the foundation of the friendship between Frohman and Barrie, which endured without a cloud for the sixteen years that Frohman was to live and in which he carried through so many of the innumerable schemes that originated in his teeming brain: schemes among which the exploitation of Barrie's genius for the theatre was continually in the forefront.

Day by day, the Holland House, at which Barrie and Nicoll were staying, was besieged by interviewers and all sorts of people anxious to meet the author of A Window in Thrums, who contrived to evade most of them. Richard Watson Gilder, the brilliant editor of The Century Magazine, entertained the distinguished visitors at his 'magnificent place' on the Monday after their arrival, and there they met many interesting people, who showed the greatest kindness to both of them, and the sincerest admiration for Barrie. On the Tuesday they had a trip up the Hudson River, which Nicoll thought 'much finer than the Rhine,' and the Sleepy Hollow of Washington Irving was one of the most interesting sights they saw.

The newspapers, of course, were full of flare-headings, and all sorts of extraordinary articles about the celebrated Scottish novelist who was sojourning in their midst. Nicoll had made a great collection of these as curiosities to send home to Miss Pollard, but when he returned from the Hudson trip he found that the chambermaid at the hotel had taken the lot and burned them. After expressing his annoyance at this, he adds: 'Mr. Barrie hates this publicity intensely and will now see no one, so I do not think there will be any more of them.'

For George Washington Cable, the author of Old Creole Days and The Grandissimes, Barrie had long entertained a great admiration (he wrote a study of the latter work in the American Bookman for July 1898), so that a visit to Cable at his home in Northampton, Mass., very agreeably occupied their second week-end on American soil, Barrie in the meantime having been splendidly entertained by his new friend Frohman and shown everything likely to interest him in New York's world of the theatre. Of their visit to Cable, Nicoll writes:

We had a wonderful visit at Northampton, and I despair of telling you about it. Imagine a town of white wooden houses, set well apart, and of about 20,000 inhabitants. It is surrounded by wooded hills.

Apple trees are planted all round, and apples lie strewn on the ground. Mr. Cable's house is most interesting. He has a beautiful wife with white hair, about fifty, tall and dark-eyed. He is himself slender and gentle, with something of the languor of the south. . . . Mr. and Mrs. Cable gave a reception in our honour at which nearly all the town attended. Mr. Barrie is much read there, and I found that I was not unknown—there being several readers of my papers, etc., there.

It is interesting to note that Nicoll puts on record the fact that during one of their evening entertainments at Cable's home, when the American author sang for them some old Creole songs and accompanied himself on the violin, Barrie also took part in the entertainment and ' gave a capital imitation of Irving,' doubtless the same scene of Mathias in The Bells with which fifteen years before he entertained his fellow-students at the meeting of the Dumfries Literary Society in Edinburgh.

At Boston the travellers stayed at the Brunswick, in Copley Square, and were made members during their visit of the St. Botolph Club, Dr. Putnam exerting himself very successfully in their entertainment. It would appear that Nicoll had with him an advance copy of Margaret Ogilvy, as he mentions that at the house of some personal friends, where he visited without Barrie, they made him read two chapters from it to the guests and all seemed greatly to enjoy it.

Their days at Boston must have passed in a whirl of engagements, with visits to Harvard University and the literary landmarks of Concord, and many meetings with the literary notabilities of the time, such as Miss Mary Wilkins, Professor William James, Dr. Charles Eliot Norton and Professor Thayer. At the village of Randolph, some twenty miles from Boston, where they visited Miss Wilkins at her homely farmhouse, they found her ' plump and soft and gentle—just like a duck.' Nicoll adds: ' Mr. Barrie said he was always wondering when she would take to the water. She was very shy with Mr. Barrie, and he with her, but she chatted freely with me.' In the same letter he makes the confession that he did his best at the receptions to be agreeable. Probably Barrie did the same, but his success would not seem to have been so complete, as one of their hostesses was overheard to say in the hall: ' Mr. Barrie is very quiet, but Dr. Nicoll is a most delightful man.'

From Boston they took the long trip south to New Orleans instead of going to Canada, as had been their original intention, and down in that metropolis of the Mississippi swamps they found the steaming heat of the late October too much for them. Both of the travellers were by then anxious to set their faces homeward. Neither of them was cut out for the physical strain of long journeying, which suited Ian Maclaren so well that when they met him in New York Nicoll described him as ' looking very fat and flourishing.' ' Oh, to be home! ' is the burden of one brief letter from New Orleans. ' We have done very well, have got on splendidly together, have met with unbounded kindness, but I am so homesick! ' The journey north was broken at Washington, which they found a most pleasant city after the ' fearfully unhealthy place ' they had left in the far south, and in Washington they were entertained by Nelson Page, the novelist, who, having recently married a very rich widow, was living in great style, and had ' a silver tea-kettle, with balls sticking out, which positively shrieks " How much do you think I cost? " '

Back in New York, where they arrived on Monday, November 2nd, they were again besieged by a stream of callers, and as they were due to sail in five days their brief stay was entirely filled with engagements. There are records of dining with William Dean Howells, the novelist, with Scribner, Barrie's authorised publisher, in whose magazine at that time Sentimental Tommy was running its serial course; with the Aldine Club, at which they were both to make speeches; and with the Century Club, as guests of honour. We are left to suppose that Barrie at least had his moments of nervousness before that dinner of the Aldine Club on the evening of Thursday, November 5th, as Nicoll remarks: ' I do not feel nervous, as I know quite well what I want to say,' but he says nothing about his companion's ante-prandial anxieties. Some 120 representatives of American publishers and men of letters were present on the occasion, and thistles, furze, and heather figured prominently in the table decorations. ' Haggis à la Thrums ' was on the menu, and a piper skirled during the banquet, which was presided over by Hamilton Wright Mabie, then at the height of his popularity as a literary critic and writer on social subjects. In spite of Barrie's confession, when he got up to speak, that this was the only dinner that he had ever allowed to be given to him, and that he felt like getting under the table when called upon to make a speech, the editor of the American Bookman puts on record the fact that ' he won all hearts by his quiet, impressive manner and quaint, playful humour.'

In the course of his remarks he said that he had been asked many questions by the American reporters, but that the commonest one was ' What are the names of your books? ' The next day he would see the titles displayed in the newspapers, and would read with pleasure that he was ' Mr. Barrie, whose books have drawn laughter and tears from all of us.' ' One reporter,' he went on, ' was charmed by my Beside the Bonnie Brier Bush. I said he was very kind to say so, but Dr. Nicoll corrected him. Then he explained that, of course, he meant The Stickit Minister; and when he found that he was again mistaken, declared that what he really meant was that charming serial now running in The Century called Silly Tommy.'

The most interesting question that Barrie had put to him, however, was, ' What do you think of the American girl? ' ' I did not tell them,' he said, ' and I am not going to tell you. I shall tell it to no one except the American girl herself—I think I have already told it to one or two.' This led him to speak of the higher education for women in America. ' The thing that has struck me most of all about your country is your colleges and universities. They are the most splendid things in America. But the ones I liked best of all were the colleges for girls, and the college for girls I liked best of all was Smith College, at North-ampton, Mass., and the Smith girl I liked best—no, I won't tell you! The only speech I ever made in my life I made at Smith College a few weeks ago. I don't know how I got on the platform, but there I was with nine hundred girls in front of me. By and bye I became conscious of someone talking in an eloquent voice, and when I recognised it as my own, I was dumbfounded. I visited other colleges after that, but I made no more speeches. Those Smith girls made me promise not to address any other colleges for girls! '

Sentimental Tommy, which ran its serial course through the pages of Scribner's Magazine from January to November, 1896, where it was charmingly illustrated by William Hatherell, came out in book form in October, while the author was in America. Apart from its intrinsic interest, this novel, together with its sequel, Tommy and Grizel, which appeared four years later, has a further claim to consideration in the fact that it is the first of what may be called the later chronicles of Thrums. In the years immediately succeeding the appearance of The Little Minister it looked as though the author was conscious that Thrums might not prove an inexhaustible mine of character and romance, and that even if the theatre did not triumph in the contest already under way we might expect him to break new ground.

With the appearance of Sentimental Tommy, however, it was clear that Thrums was still to be the background for his play of character in the novel, though it introduced a wider range of scene and society, and started in London. Sentimental Tommy was certainly a score for Thrums against the theatre; the author seemed still bent upon giving his best energies to the novel, however profitably he might from time to time make ex-cursions to the gold mine of the stage.

The reception with which Sentimental Tommy met, so far as my own recollection serves, was scarcely so enthusiastic as that which had greeted The Little Minister. There was no critic of Henley's standing to hail it as 'another book of genius.' And yet there is in its pages as much of the true stuff of genius as may be found in The Little Minister. It was now that the critics began to express the opinion that Barrie, despite the amazing richness of his gifts, was making no substantial progress towards that great novel which he had so long been expected to produce.

Once again his admirers had to recognize certain structural defects in his story, and in his preface to the American edition he himself admits 'This is not in the smallest degree the book I meant it to be. Tommy ran away with the author.' It was the old case of Barrie, pen in hand, playing his imaginative rôle of the everlasting boy. Queen Mary may have been a romantic figure to him all his days and ready to be his heroine in that great novel which he has never written, but first his mother's and next his own youth always made the strongest appeal to his imagination, and Sentimental Tommy is really a break-away from his earlier fiction in so far as it substitutes for the Thrums of Margaret Ogilvy the Kirriemuir of little Jamie Barrie. He is no longer seeing the town and its 'queer fowk' through the eyes of his mother, he is telling us of the days he knew himself, of his own boyhood, his own fantasies.

Many years ago I set down my conviction that Tommy, in his boyhood at least, is essentially an imaginative projection of the author. This Robertson Nicoll declared to be 'from every point of view an error.' After thirty years I persist in my error, and suggest that the reader who has followed my story of Barrie's youth and continues to the end of my chronicle of his later life, and will give himself the pleasure of re-reading Sentimental Tommy, is not unlikely to err with me. Tommy is the playboy of the northern world. The hard realities of life have scarcely any meaning for him; his way lies among its illusions. He lives in a subjective world of his own. He is romance. When the creator of Tommy is in his sixty-eighth year we shall find him on a day at the town of Jedburgh being solemnly presented with the freedom of that borough and responding to this honour in precisely the same spirit as Tommy played at Jacobites in the Den. The fact that he has shown himself a shrewd judge of public taste and more than capable of holding his own in the realm of hard realities, in no wise disproves that a large measure of his existence has been passed in a splendid world of make-believe. He has himself introduced us to that dreamy part of him under the name of McConnachie. What was at the back of Nicoll's mind when he challenged my opinion I have no means of guessing, but I know that an eminent and sympathetic critic of Barrie in writing of

THRUMS OR THEATRE?

Sentimental Tommy expressed the belief that the true object of the book was to present an imaginative study of the boyhood of Robert Burns, and this preposterous suggestion (as it seemed to me) Nicoll allowed to pass unchallenged. I am very willing that the reader should choose between my opinion and this other.

No good purpose would be served here by entering into an exposition of those points in which Sentimental Tommy fails as a novel. If it did not advance its author's reputation as novelist, it unquestionably extended it as the most entertaining writer of his day. You will find in it all his best qualities jostling his worst. Here he is by turn the most delightful of humorists, the most understanding of those who have written about the glorious illusions of youth, a realist who spares his readers nothing, as in that peculiarly unpleasant chapter 'Grizel pays three visits,' which is entirely out of harmony with the spirit of romance, and in this book more than in any of his others sentiment is occasionally allowed to over-step the line that should demark it from sentimentality and the mawkish. His cynicism, which had no place in The Little Minister, and seemed to have been entirely shed, reappears here, which is not surprising since cynic and sentimentalist are so closely akin. But when everything has been said by way of adverse criticism there remains a splendid humanness about the whole book, a true joy of life: despite its patches of realism, it is romance that most informs it. We know well in our hearts that 'End of the Jacobite Rising' is quite improbable and entirely illusory, but it is so much as we should like things to be that we accept it and rejoice in it: in a word, Barrie makes all his readers romancists for the proper enjoyment of his fantasies. The Painted Lady's part in the story aroused much criticism, especially from those who looked upon Barrie in the 'nineties as a writer in those declining days of the 'goody-goody' whose works could be confidently presented to a Sunday-School girl. Yet that pathetic figure is hardly more convincing than a wraith; she is at best a phantom flitting in the dim background of the story.

At the end of the second week in November, when the two travellers returned from America—the only considerable journey that Barrie had so far undertaken,—they were to find the British press vibrant with talk of Sentimental Tommy and of Margaret Ogilvy. Barrie was now the most discussed of all living British authors, and we have to remember that he was in competition for public attention with such commanding figures as those of Meredith, Hardy, Swinburne, Kipling. The astonishing thing, when we look back upon his career, is that the most noteworthy part of it had not yet begun.

CHAPTER IX

A MOTHER OF GENIUS: MARGARET OGILVY

WITH the publication of Margaret Ogilvy, by Her Son, in the autumn of 1896 his mother assumes a new importance to all who find interest in the life and work of J. M. Barrie. Had this book never been written it is unlikely that we should have been more concerned about Margaret Ogilvy than about the mother of any other man of genius, Dickens's, Ruskin's, Stevenson's, whom the biographer has to track through the statements of others as well as in the recollections of her son if he would arrive at some sort of inventory of her character. Isaac Marcosson says in the life of Charles Frohman that Barrie is the only man in the world who has ever written a book about his mother. Like most sweeping assertions this need only be stated to be doubted. There have been many lives of mothers written by their sons —by chance that of Anne Gilchrist lies on my table at this moment—the latest being E. F. Benson's Mother, but it is true that no such book as Margaret Ogilvy was ever written by any other man of letters. And I think it is also true that but for it we should never have appreciated the extent to which the personality of his mother had interpenetrated every manifestation of Barrie's imaginative genius and coloured his whole conception of womanhood.

It is not a biography in any accepted meaning of the word; it is not a 'tribute' or a 'character sketch'; it is not a fiction in the sense that A Window in Thrums is fiction, yet it might as reasonably be catalogued with its author's Thrums stories and sketches as with works of biography, so large is the imaginative element in it. It is a little book, scarcely thirty thousand words in length, made up of ten short chapters in which the author tells us as much, nay, more about himself than about his mother, and yet her presence is felt in every paragraph. I had almost called it an epic of mother-love, when I shuddered at the vision of a Freudian female psycho-analysing it! An 'idealised biography' is another description that has been applied to it, and if we let it go at that we shall not be far wrong.

The book refuses to be classified. It is like none other one

MARGARET OGILVY
A photograph of Mrs. David Barrie taken at Glasgow about 1871.

DAVID BARRIE, THE NOVELIST'S FATHER   [*Major*
Photographed at Kirriemuir after his retirement.

can think of: who touches this book touches a human being. There is an inevitableness about it that is deeply impressive. I mean its need to be written. The reader feels that if ever its author could truly say of any of his books that it was written 'less by me than by an impulse from behind' it is essentially true of this one. Thirty years ago the present writer ventured the opinion that A Window in Thrums and Margaret Ogilvy were Barrie's most valuable additions to our literature. With all the intervening 'surprises' which Robertson Nicoll darkly hinted at now revealed in the light of day there seems no reason to alter that opinion.

Margaret Ogilvy is not to be judged by the common canons of criticism. There were many who cried out against it. Dr. J. H. Millar roundly asserted that Barrie's discriminating admirers would not readily forgive the writing of this book: 'an exercise compared with which the labours of the resurrectionist are praiseworthy, and which many men (I believe) had rather lose their right hand than set themselves to attempt.' There speaks the voice of cultured prejudice: the thing had not been done before, therefore it was wrong. Such a view is narrow and intolerant. What offence to propriety can there be in an author writing a series of sketches whose main theme is derived from his mothers' life and his own part therein? Surely if the writing be sincere and the snare of sentimentality avoided, all the jibes about making copy out of a sacred relationship are futile and pointless.

Margaret Ogilvy is a work of deep sincerity, and has but two or three trivial bits of sentimentality that stand between it and absolute perfection. It is an amazing book: nobody, so far as I have seen, has ever pointed out its humour. In some passages it is definitely comic, and the note is not discordant. For the moment, however, my desire is less to pursue the critical examination of the book than to offer a series of glosses upon it which will help to elucidate what it contains of the strictly factual. That is why I refrained at the outset of my narrative from entering in detail upon the origin and character of the novelist's mother, holding it better to turn to these at this point, where the publication of Margaret Ogilvy introduces her in a manner almost dramatic to the vast audience of readers her son has secured throughout the world; an audience for whom she begins fully to live in the masterly pages of her son only after she has passed from the earthly scene.

The continued use of a woman's maiden name after she had married was, some generations back, common throughout rural Scotland and still persists in Angus (which I read in the papers to-day is to be the official name of Forfarshire in the future, as it was in the remoter past), and Barrie tells us that even her own children would call upstairs to her, 'Are you there, Margaret Ogilvy?' I was informed of an old woman still living in Kirriemuir that the postman on one occasion, when he called at her house in the Roods with a letter addressed to a Mrs. ——, had the letter handed back to him by the woman who answered his knock, as the name was unfamiliar. Seldom in her life had she received a letter, yet this one was for her. From long disuse she had forgotten her own married name! An authentic episode, severely though it taxes belief.

Margaret was the daughter of a stonemason named Alexander (Saunders) Ogilvy whose wife had died in 1827 leaving him with his little daughter of eight and a son of five to bring up. A man of no common mould; a prominent upholder of the Auld Licht kirk, his daily life was ordered by the stern piety enjoined upon its members. A piety, be it noted, that could exist in company with bigotry and prejudice and yet make its exponent beautiful to regard. As the ultimate fountain head of Auld Licht Idylls and of all the stories of Thrums that Barrie has cared to tell was his maternal grandfather—his paternal relatives having no connexion with the Auld Lichts—any glimpse of Ogilvy's character is of value when considering the forces that went to make his grandson the delineator of a community whom he knew chiefly through the stories his mother told him, most of which she had first heard from her father.

Some of the most effective passages in the chapter 'What She had Been' are those that picture the old stone-worker as his grandson sees him through his mother's eyes. He had been dead nine years when Barrie was born.

On the surface (he writes) he is as hard as the stone on which he chiselled, and his face is dyed red by its dust, he is rounded in the shoulders and a 'hoast' hunts him ever; sooner or later that cough must carry him off, but until then it shall not keep him from the quarry, nor shall his chapped hands, as long as they can grasp the mell. It is a night of rain or snow, and my mother, the little girl in a pinafore who is already his housekeeper, has been many times to the door to look for him. At last he draws nigh, hoasting. Or I see him setting off to church, for he was a great 'stoop' of the Auld Licht kirk, and his mouth is very firm now, as if there were a case of discipline to face, but on his way home he is bowed with pity. Perhaps his little daughter who saw him so stern an hour ago does not understand why he wrestles so long in prayer to-night, or why when he rises from his knees he presses her to him with unwonted tenderness.

A MOTHER OF GENIUS

Ogilvy's favourite poem was The Cameronian's Dream, which many a time he repeated dramatically to Margaret as he sat in his chair by the fireside, and he never got through the first line—

> In a dream of the night I was wafted away

without a little scream of delight from her at the re-telling of that old story. Hyslop's gloomy and imitative composition, written when Margaret was a child of two, enjoyed wide popularity as celebrating the heroism of the Covenanters in a later age when religious strife and political revolt were again occupying the thoughts of everybody in Scotland. A few stanzas may be quoted, even though the reader should remember them, as they would appear to have awakened in little James Barrie the same romantic excitement they aroused in his mother, and were not without influence in giving a certain direction to his religious thoughts. The poet dreams he is ' wafted away '

> To the muirland and mist, where the martyrs lay,

the martyrs being Richard Cameron and some sixty armed Covenanters, who were slaughtered at Airds Moss, Ayrshire, in 1680.

> And Wellwood's sweet valley breathed music and gladness—
> The fresh meadow blooms hung in beauty and redness;
> Its daughters were happy to hail the returning,
> And drink the delight of July's sweet morning.
>
> But, oh! there were hearts cherished far other feelings,
> Illumed by the light of prophetic revealings;
> Who drank from the scenery of beauty but sorrow,
> For they knew that their blood would bedew it to-morrow.
>
> Their faces grew pale, and their swords were unsheathed,
> But the vengeance that darkened their brow was unbreathed;
> With eyes turned to heaven in calm resignation
> They sang their last song to the God of salvation.
>
> When the righteous had fallen, and the combat was ended,
> A chariot of fire through the dark cloud descended;
> Its drivers were angels on horses of whiteness,
> And its burning wheels turned upon axles of brightness.
>
> A seraph unfolded its doors bright and shining,
> All dazzling like gold of the seventh refining,
> And the souls that came forth out of great tribulation
> Have mounted the chariots and steeds of salvation.

On the arch of the rainbow the chariot is gliding
Through the path of the thunder the horsemen are riding—
Glide swiftly, bright spirits; the prize is before ye—
A crown never fading, a kingdom of glory!

The Cameronian's Dream is, as you will see, very crude stuff both as poetry and religion. A remarkably feeble imitation of Byron's Hebrew Melodies, it reproduces some actual phrasing, such as:

When in Wellwood's dark valley the standard of Zion,
All bloody and torn, 'mong the heather was lying.

But Byron had set a vogue, and the lilt of his measures was imitated by all the young scribblers of the time, so that a person of simple tastes, like Saunders Ogilvy, might excusably suppose himself to be listening to poetry when it was no more than jingle. As a descriptive piece The Cameronian's Dream is mainly fury and little sense; but even so it reflected the Byronic-romantic, and was effective enough to fire the imagination of her son when Margaret Ogilvy repeated it to him, imitating the solemn tones of her father's declamation.

Ogilvy had the satisfaction of living to see his daughter married with a son and daughter of her own, and to see his son David pass from parish school to Aberdeen University, then to his divinity course at New College, Edinburgh, where Walter C. Smith was a fellow-student, and after charges at Colmonell and Greenock finally settle to his life's work at Dalziel Free Church, Motherwell, where he continued until the year succeeding Margaret's death. His satisfaction in the career of his son may have been modified by the latter's defection from the Auld Licht to the Free Church communion; but to the end of his days Margaret's brother retained an abiding respect for his father's coreligionists, and his whole-hearted approval of the Auld Licht stories of his nephew was the best sort of testimony to their truthfulness.

One makes no comment on the fact that this simple artisan, whose sole income was derived from his work as a hewer of red sandstone at the local quarries, was able to put his son through the universities of Aberdeen and Edinburgh in his determination that he should 'wag his pow in the poopit': it was a commonplace of the time. Had Ogilvy himself enjoyed the advantage of a university education there is no saying what he might not have done to anticipate by two generations the literary fame of the

Ogilvy-Barrie connexion. Witness how 'this stern, self-educated Auld Licht with the chapped hands' could write of 'dear little Lydia,' one of Margaret's children, his own especial favourite, whom death had claimed when she was but two years old:

I cannot well describe my feelings on the occasion. I thought that the fountain-head of my tears had now been dried up, but I have been mistaken, for I must confess that the briny rivulets descended fast on my furrowed cheeks, she was such a winning Child, and had such a regard for me and always came and told me all her little things, and as she was now speaking, some of her lively images of these things intrude themselves more into my mind than they should do, but there is allowance for moderate grief on such occasions. But when I am telling you of my own grief and sorrow, I know not what to say of the bereaved Mother, she hath not met with anything in this world before that hath gone so near the quick with her. She had no handling of the last one as she was not able at the time, for she only had her in her arms, and her affections had not time to be so fairly entwined around her. I am much afraid that she will not soon if ever get over this trial. Although she was weakly before, yet she was pretty well recovered, but this hath not only affected her mind but her body is so much affected that she is not well able to sit so long as her bed is making and hath scarcely tasted meat (*i.e.* food) since Monday night, and till some time is elapsed we cannot say how she may be. There is none that is not a parent themselves that can fully sympathise with one in such a state.

Why the author of Margaret Ogilvy in printing the old and beautiful letter of his grandfather should have chosen to alter the name of the child from Elizabeth to Lydia I cannot explain, but it is, I would suggest, a mere confusion of dates that makes him write: 'The fourth child dies when but a few weeks old and the next at two years.' Elizabeth ('Lydia') was the fourth; the next was Agnes. The old stonemason died 'exactly a week' after writing that remarkable letter, but his daughter, for whose delicate state of health he had so much anxiety, was to live for another forty-four years, and, as her son so finely states it, 'joys of a kind never shared in by him were to come to her so abundantly, so long drawn out, that strange as it would have seemed to him to know it, her fuller life had scarce yet begun.'

Since Barrie himself shows some uncertainty about the births and deaths of his brothers and sisters, and this chapter of our narrative is specially dedicated to Margaret Ogilvy, I give here, at the cost of repeating some dates already noted in Chapter II, a list of her ten children so far as I have been able to compile it from the sources accessible to me.

Alexander Ogilvy, *b.* 26 Mar., 1842; *d.* 16 July, 1914.
Mary Edward, *b.* 26 Jan., 1845; (Mrs. Galloway) dead.
Jane Ann Adamson, *b.* 12 Mar., 1847; *d.* 31 Aug., 1895.
Elizabeth How, *b.* 12 Mar., 1849; *d.* 2 April, 1851.
Agnes Matthew, *b.* 22 Dec., 1850; *d.* Jan., 1851.
David Ogilvy, *b.* 30 Jan., 1853; *d.* 29 Jan., 1867.
Sara Mitchell, *b.* 3 June, 1854; *d.* 25 Aug., 1904.
Isabella Ogilvy, *b.* 4 Jan., 1858; (Mrs. Murray) dead.
James Matthew, *b.* 9 May, 1860. Surviving.
Margaret, *b.* 9 July, 1863; (Mrs. Winter) surviving.

With this list to help them the curious can check in detail
many statements in the story of Margaret Ogilvy as told by her
son, and note how closely or indifferently the author observes
the facts, as these appear on examination. Speaking of the
christening robe which was one of the most precious of his mother's
possessions, he says: 'We had all been christened in it, from the
oldest of the family to the youngest, between whom stood twenty
years,' which is as nearly exact as need be. But in writing of the
great tragedy of her life, the death of her boy David when he was
fourteen to a day, why should he say: 'When I became a man
and he was still a boy of thirteen, I wrote a little paper called
'Dead this Twenty Years' which was about a similar tragedy in
another woman's life'? The twenty years, it will be seen, was
a close approximation to the time, as that chapter first appeared
in The British Weekly of March 1st, 1889. As Barrie has the
romancist's large indifference to precise dates and exact periods
of time, when he does 'condescend upon a date,' as the Scots
law has it, our surprise should be to find him in accord with
ascertainable fact. He tells us that his mother lived twenty-nine
years after the death of her little David, and this is near enough
to the actual time to pass as a simple statement of fact; the
record of the gravestone gives David's death as January 29th,
1867, and the mother's September 9th, 1895.
I have heard it said by those who knew her in Kirriemuir and
Forfar that Margaret Ogilvy was 'naething by ord'nar' grand
to hae a book written aboot her.' We can well believe that she
was no rarer a creature than the good Scotswoman of the cottager
class, whose name is legion. Had she been sharply different from
the class to which she belonged, her life had been a less worthy
theme for a book of genius. The everlasting value of Margaret
Ogilvy resides in its being the intimate life of a woman whose like
might have been found in many thousands of Scottish homes
up till the eve of the War. And that is not the least of Scotland's

glories. The instinct of 'mothering' is strong among Scots-
women. Margaret Ogilvy often said she would have liked fine to
be the mother of this great man or that; never the wife. She even
admitted she would have liked to be the mother of R. L. Stevenson,
while making a fine pretence to think nothing of his works, which
she read with secret joy, as her son tells us in one of his most
delightful chapters. Many a Scotswoman would 'like fine' to
have been the mother of J. M. Barrie.

While in the main typically Scottish, there were some respects
in which Margaret Ogilvy did differ from her class. Her close
comradeship with her children, and especially with her author
son, for example. Comradeship is the right word, I think. She
would seem to have been a chum to all her children. And this is
precisely what the average Scottish mother is not. The English
mother is commonly more intimate with her family; she will
hear their confidences with a sympathy, speak praise of them with
a readiness that is utterly foreign to the Scottish mother. The
Spartan mother is far more common north of the Tweed than
south. As a rule the Scottish mother is undemonstrative about
her children; she 'likes fine' to hear others speak well of them, while
herself denouncing them for feckless bairns of whom she is 'black
affronted'—yet, let anyone else miscall them, and you will note
a sudden change of tune! Although her son tells us that the kissing
of her hand to him as he looked back from the road to the window
where she stood was the only English custom Margaret Ogilvy
ever learned, I would suggest that in the many pretty manifestations of her maternal affection we have something that was more
English than Scottish.

The Scottish mother who will talk about love to her daughters
and discuss sweethearts with them is a rarity; in England, the
love stories of their daughters are the commonest gossip of mothers.
When a northern lad and lassie are in love that is their affair;
they take it too seriously to chatter at large about their feelings;
in their home circles they neither care to speak of it nor to hear
the subject discussed.

I am aware that Barrie can be quoted against me here. 'You
only know the shell of a Scot until you have entered his home
circle,' he says. 'In many ways my mother was as reticent as
myself,' and 'my sister (Jane Ann) was the most reserved of us all;
you might at times see a light through one of my chinks: she was
double-shuttered.' These particular observations are doubtless
just, but when he proceeds to generalise I am ready to doubt:

Now, it seems to be a law of nature that we must show our true
selves at some time, and as the Scot must do it at home, and squeeze

a day into an hour, what follows is that there he is self-revealing in the superlative degree, the feelings so long dammed up overflow, and thus a Scotch family are probably better acquainted with each other, and more ignorant of the life outside their circle, than any other family in the world. And as knowledge is sympathy, the affection existing between them is almost painful in its intensity; they have not more to give than their neighbours, but it is bestowed upon a few instead of being distributed among many; they are reputed niggardly, but for family affection at least they pay in gold.

If this is true of Scots families in general (it is entirely contrary to my own experience) it will surely be difficult for any Englishman, or unrelated Scot for that matter, ever to crack the shell of a Scot, since we are advised that the only way to do so is to 'enter his home circle' which, by this fuller description, would appear to be barred to all outsiders. There are many instances in which the Scots are reticent where the English are communicative; but this contrast is particularly marked in the matter of love.

Does not Barrie himself confess to his embarrassment when confronted with the need to pen a love passage? 'They tell me,' he says, 'that in time I shall be able without a blush to make Albert say "darling," and even gather her (the heroine) up in his arms, but I begin to doubt it. The moment sees me as shy as ever; I still find it advisable to lock the door, and then—no witness save the dog—I "do" it dourly with my teeth clenched, while the dog retreats into the far corner and moans. The bolder Englishman (I am told) will write a love chapter and then go out, quite coolly, to dinner; but such goings on are contrary to the Scotch nature.'

Poor in worldly gear until that fine day when her son's success brought to the modest home wealth undreamed of, had Margaret Ogilvy been born to luxury it can scarce be doubted that she would still have been, in all native goodness of heart, the incarnation of loving-kindness her son presents to us in those precious pages of filial devotion. Yet money meant much to her as she had so long known the lack of it, and there was no mercenary meanness in the picture of her and her daughter counting the lines of James's early articles to figure out how much he had got for them and wondering if the sub-title would mean another sixpence! It was the wonder, the miracle of the thing that possessed her: the magic whereby her laddie could put pen to paper and earn sums beyond her imaginings. The cynical may read with a smile that among her treasures in a little box after her death was found a portrait of James in his childhood tied with a ribbon to the envelopes that had contained his first cheques; but he who relates that had been something of a cynic himself when he wrote the articles that earned those cheques. There was nothing of the cynic left when he wrote about his mother.

We perceive that her early and middle years of narrow means were not her least happy. What joys could riches give that excelled the uncloyed delight that came when she got her six hair-bottomed chairs, for which she had saved up in threepenny bits? To these humble triumphs of the poor the wealthy may not aspire, and many an unknown Scotswoman has lived such golden hours. But not every Scotswoman would have had the playful impulse to make-believe which prompted Margaret to open the parlour door suddenly and take the six chairs by surprise! The altering of worn clothes to fit one member of the family after another, so charmingly described, is another of the many little things in which her life was the counterpart of her neighbours'. Even her incurable dislike to employ servants when the means to maintain them were available was a characteristic of her time. It inspired one of the most delightful chapters of Margaret Ogilvy where the author pictures himself as 'Her Maid of All Work.' Were it not that her daughter Jane Ann was no less set against a servant in the house, it might be argued that the mother in this matter was something to blame for the wearing life of domestic drudgery to which that daughter so cheerfully submitted herself and which was not without its part in giving a tragic ending to their long and lovely domestic comedy. Comedy, yes, for both had a keen sense of humour, and it is not difficult to see whence Barrie the humorist derived his gift. Entirely *sui generis* is her son's story of her in the days of his fame learning scraps of Horace from him that she might in conversation with the scholarly persons who then were frequent visitors at Strathview quote an appropriate tag:

I well remember how she would say to the visitors, ' Ay, ay, it's very true, Doctor, but as you know, " Eheu fugaces, Postume, Postume, labuntur anni ",' or ' Sal, Mr. so and so, my lassie is thriving well, but would it no be more to the point to say " O matre pulchra filia pulchrior? " ' which astounded them very much if she managed to reach the end without being flung, but usually she had a fit of laughing in the middle, and so they found her out.

One can see in this anecdote that Margaret Ogilvy was just as ready to laugh at herself as her son has shown himself a hundred times to poke fun at himself in print. Her laugh was born afresh every morning, he tells us, and in that we know why she received such spilth of devotion from all her family circle during all the days of her life.

BARRIE: THE STORY OF A GENIUS

If Barrie inherited his divine gift of humour from his mother, he also had from her one of his most characteristic literary traits: the personification of things inanimate. To his 'scorned manuscripts', which she would look at sadly at times, she would say (he states) 'You poor cold little crittur shut away in a drawer, are you dead or just sleeping?' She would even pick up from the waste basket a torn page of his own rejected work and kiss it, saying 'Poor thing, and you would have liked so fine to be printed!' In every book he has written, many times do we encounter such apostrophes, and as we may not suspect him of pure invention in 'Margaret Ogilvy' we must attribute this feature of his style, which at times looks suspiciously like a trick, to having been acquired from admiration of his mother's ways of thought and expression.

Apart from what we learn of her in this classic of her son, Margaret Ogilvy has been little written about by others. There are not many anecdotes to relate; but there is a trifling one that I have preserved for thirty years or so. It is a story of her motherly kindness to 'twa lassies, sent to spend a simmer wi' an auld wifie o' Kirriemuir.' It was told by one of them who then remembered of the famous author only that he had wonderful eyes and was 'sae courteous to his sisters,' though shy with 'ither lassies.' The auld wifie gave the visitors not half enough to eat, and bran parritch at that, whereat kind Mrs. Barrie, on being complained to, said, 'Hoots, lassies, throw it in the pig's trough, and come in bye to oor house,' where a good breakfast was supplied the hungry lassies, not that morning only, but for every succeeding one during their holidays.

There is, of course, the letter from R. L. S. in which he says such happy things about the quaint photograph of his mother that Barrie had sent him, showing her seated at a folding table whereon are placed a teapot, cup and saucer, and plate. She is wearing her snow-white 'mutch,' and a loosely knitted shawl, and to judge by her attitude she might be saying grace for viands which are noticeably meagre. This old photograph was afterwards etched and appeared as frontispiece to 'Margaret Ogilvy.' Stevenson's letter from Vailima is dated July 13th, 1894, and here is the passage about Barrie's mother:

In the first place I have had the extreme satisfaction to be shown that photograph of your mother. It bears evident traces of the hand of an amateur. How is it that amateurs invariably take better photographs than professionals? I must qualify invariably. My own negatives have always represented a province of chaos and old night in which you might dimly perceive fleecy spots of twilight, representing nothing; so that, if I am right in supposing the portrait of your mother to be yours, I must salute you as my superior.

Is that your mother's breakfast? Or is it only afternoon tea? If the first, do let me recommend to Mrs. Barrie to add an egg to her ordinary. Which, if you please, I will ask her to eat to the honour of her son, and I am sure she will live much longer for it, to enjoy his fresh successes. I never in my life saw anything more deliciously characteristic. I declare I can hear her speak.

Robertson Nicoll's note at the time of Margaret Ogilvy's death must also find a place here. He wrote it as we see while looking at that same photograph of her which had been the incentive a year before to the gay phrases of R. L. S.:

I am looking at the portrait done by her son not very long ago of the tender mother, and in my mind is a likeness still more vivid. I recall the slow, wise, tender smile. I hear again the gentle voice recalling the past. I understand better than ever the strong, brave faith that coloured every thought and word. Mrs. Barrie was the daughter of Saunders Ogilvy, and to the last in every distress her thoughts went back to him. She was full of memories of him and of others like him—'the strong nails that keep the world together.' To their belief and courage she added more than a woman's tenderness.

Still seeking in 'Margaret Ogilvy' for the biographic rather than the æsthetic, I am constrained to note the strange absence of two figures from the picture: two that we might have expected to see sketchily at least in the background. The father, David Barrie, has a line or two; the eldest brother, whom I have called the good genius of the family, not a mention. There is here some evidence, it might be suggested, of the essential jealousy inherent in all deep love. But I think the explanation is simple: they were both alive when the book was written, and while Barrie could write of himself and his affection for his mother with all propriety, he could not venture freely to introduce these two although they must have meant so much to her. Nay, it has been said that Alexander was not entirely sympathetic to the writing of the book, and if that were so the reason for his conspicuous absence from its pages would be still stronger. In the chapter 'A Panic in the House' there are some amusing passages about servants. When he was eight or nine James was being sent by rail to the home of a relative who kept a servant. He was dressed in black velveteen (his mother made it, I have heard, as a sort of mourning suit after the death of Davy, and it was designed on ample lines to allow for his growth over three or four years) and he had strict instructions as to his behaviour in the train and at the house where the servant was kept: 'Cross your legs when they look at you, and put your thumb in your pocket and leave the top of your handkerchief showing.' 'My relative met me at the station,' he relates, 'a sister greeted me at the door, but I chafed at having to be kissed,' so anxious was he to meet the servant in the kitchen. This may refer to a visit to his uncle's manse at Motherwell, the sister most likely Mary, who taught school there for a time and had been associated with Alexander's school-work at Bothwell until he went to Glasgow in 1867. The distance in age between Alexander then twenty-six, and James, not yet eight, is another reason why the oldest of the family does not figure in the story of the mother: he had so long stood as a father to his younger brother, with whom in the tenderest years of boyhood he had only occasional contacts, that James in his loving admiration for his mother would not have much common ground with Alexander.

Is it the real woman that emerges from the pages of 'Margaret Ogilvy'? That, I feel, is the question that matters most. Is the book a work of art or a human document? So far as I am aware there is no reason why it may not be both, but I venture to say that it is mainly the latter. I am so persuaded of its honesty of purpose that I do not hesitate to accept Margaret Ogilvy at her son's estimate in all essentials, and I find that in my copy of the book, read when it first appeared and many a time again, where the author writes, 'Everything I could do for her in this life I have done since I was a boy; I look back through the years and I cannot see the smallest thing undone,' I have pencilled 'And I believe him!' That sentence of his detached from all context seems almost immodest, yet I have never occupied myself with Margaret's story without being persuaded of its truth, and in truth there is no immodesty. Nowhere has Barrie written a finer page than this, and I do not believe it was written for effect:

My mother lay in bed with the christening robe beside her, and I peeped in many times at the door and then went to the stair and sat on it and sobbed. I know not if it was that first day, or many days afterwards, that there came to me my sister, the daughter my mother loved the best, yes, more I am sure even than she loved me, whose great glory she has been since I was six years old. This sister, who was then passing out of her teens, came to me with a very anxious face and wringing her hands, and she told me to go ben to my mother and say to her that she still had another boy. I went ben excitedly, but the room was dark, and when I heard the door shut and no sound come from the bed I was afraid, and I stood still. I suppose I was breathing hard, or perhaps I was crying, for after a time I heard a listless voice that had never been listless before say, 'Is that you?' I think the tone hurt me, for I made no answer, and then the voice said more anxiously, ' Is that you? ' again. I thought it was the dead boy she was speaking to, and I said in a little lonely voice, ' No, it's no him, it's just me.' Then I heard a cry, and my mother turned in bed, and though it was dark I knew that she was holding out her arms.

Again in the pathos of her question to him 'Am I an auld woman?' when he was fain to think of her as a little girl with a magenta frock tripping through the long parks of Kinnordy, singing to her self and carrying her father's dinner in a flagon, we have the very essence of the magic that has made Peter Pan one of the immortal creations of genius. And what a moving scene is that of her death-bed when she named her children one by one in the order of their coming! 'Only one who should have come third among the ten, did she omit,' the one who lay dead in the next room, Jane Ann to whose memory ' Margaret Ogilvy ' is inscribed. 'After a pause she said her name and repeated it again and again and again, lingering over it as if it were the most exquisite music and this her dying song. And yet it was a very commonplace name.'

In the third page of his book there is a passage which the dictates of art would have placed in the last, and that is but one of many indications that the author's aim was not to score an artistic triumph of literary form but to write the book of his heart as simply and unaffectedly as he could. These are the words I have in mind:

When you looked into my mother's eyes you knew, as if He had told you, why God sent her into the world—it was to open the minds of all who looked to beautiful thoughts. And that is the beginning and end of literature. Those eyes that I cannot see until I was six years old have guided me through life, and I pray God they may remain my only earthly judge to the last. They were never more my guide than when I helped to put her to earth, not whimpering because my mother had been taken away after seventy-six glorious years of life, but exulting in her even at the grave.

There, too, we have a simple statement of his faith, as primitive as that of his mother or her father, from which in nothing that he has written shall we ever find him wavering.

Dr. Alexander Whyte, whose sad duty it was on several occasions to stand by the Barries' hillside grave and read the consolatory service over another of the family to which he was attached by many ties, had, as his biographer reminds us, a very special regard for the mother and father of his close friend Alexander Barrie. 'David Barrie,' he once said, 'had all the clear-headedness of the

Chartists . . . and became one of the saintliest men I ever knew.
. . . Margaret Ogilvy, his wife—I can see her now; a dear
little, sweet, gracious, humorous, tender-hearted soul. I loved
her, and I hoped sometimes she loved me. I once asked Barrie
if his mother read his stories. "No," he replied, "we don't let
her read them: it brings on her hoast" (cough). I can see my old
mother and her drinking their kindly cup of tea together.'

Our interest in the novelist's mother is deepened by his confession that she is the essential heroine of all his books. Something of her finds its way into every character of a good woman,
young or old, that Barrie has created. She is the very heart
and soul of Jess M'Qumpha, she is all that is most precious in
Margaret Dishart, there are some of her qualities in Jean Myles,
and even in Grizel there are touches of her girlhood—a girlhood
which the author says he seems to know as though it were coeval
with his boyhood. 'The reason my books deal with the past
instead of with the life I myself have known,' he writes, 'is simply
this, that I soon grow tired of writing tales unless I can see a little
girl, of whom my mother has told me, wandering confidently
through the pages. Such a grip has her memory of her girlhood
had upon me since I was a boy of six.'

Perhaps the most curious persistence of his mother in his
fictional characters is to be found in the last act of Mary Rose,
where the ghost of Mary is searching for something which she
has long forgotten and cannot be at peace till she finds it. Her
great brawny son brings her that tranquillity when he sits upon
her knee that she may take him in her arms for the last time.
Compare that with this from Margaret Ogilvy's death-bed:

Her desire for that which she could not name came back to her,
and at last they saw that what she wanted was the old christening robe.
It was brought to her, and she unfolded it with trembling, exultant
hands, and when she had made sure that it was still of virgin fairness
her old arms went round it adoringly, and upon her face was the ineff-
able mysterious glow of motherhood.

In Margaret Ogilvy Barrie has raised to the memory of his
mother the most enduring memorial, the most beautiful monument, that ever sprang from filial love. If he had done nothing
more than draw that lovely picture of a good woman's humble,
happy life, he would have deserved well of his generation. It
was a delicate, almost an impossible, task, and only a writer who
was absolutely sincere could have dared to hope for success in it.
That he has succeeded no one who knows Scottish character or
can appreciate the humour and pathos of lowly life is likely to doubt.

CHAPTER X

SUCCESS: THE DRAMATIST ARRIVES

1897–1904

THE American visit of 1896 must be regarded as a pivotal point in Barrie's career. High though his literary reputation was at home, his admirers in the United States, where mass feeling is more pronounced than in purely British communities, were increasing at a still greater ratio; the day was not distant when they were to outnumber those of the home countries. His association with Frohman, so far no more than a professional relationship, was soon to make him as great a favourite with theatre-goers in the United States as he had become with book-lovers there. The staging of The Little Minister was the true foundation of his fortunes in the theatre, and it fell to Frohman to present it to the American public a few weeks before any London audience had the privilege of seeing it. It was produced at the Empire Theatre, New York, on September 27th, 1897. From that memorable night we can date the friendship and artistic association of those three remarkable personalities—Maude Adams, Barrie and Frohman—whose joint influence in the Anglo-American theatre during the next score of years was to be so penetrating.

While the 'feminine interest' in the play as produced on the American stage had been somewhat intensified, so that Frohman in his passion for the making of 'stars 'could present Maude Adams in a part that was the dominant one of the play, there does not seem to have been the same modification of the script so far as the English production was concerned. There certainly was not the same impulse, as Cyril Maude, who had the good fortune to be the creator of the part of the Rev. Gavin Dishart, would have fulfilled even Frohman's requirements as a 'star' actor, and his charming wife, Winifred Emery, was a perfect match for him as a winsome heroine. In the novel the character of the Little Minister is the commanding one: the hero is a personage of greater complexity, and perhaps more worthy of study than the illusively charming Lady Babbie; possibly more convincing.

On the stage the chief attraction of the play lay as much in

the freshness of its setting and the strongly marked character of
the lesser figures as in the strangely eventful love-story of Gavin
and Babbie. In certain details the stage version differed con-
siderably from the novel, wherein was seen the wisdom of the
author who, with the unnumbered failures of novels turned
into plays from the days of Scott and Dickens to warn him, had
taken the main theme of his own successful novel and written a
stage play around it: a play that was not a mere dramatisation
of the novel, but an original creation, a work of dramatic art.
Thus was its success ensured, though a good deal was due to the
perfection of the players' art as exemplified by the carefully
chosen company with which Cyril Maude produced it at the
Haymarket Theatre on November 6th, 1897.

The critics were almost unanimous in their approval. The
voice of the carper was heard, it is true, and there were perfervid Scots who regarded as something approximating to caricature the antics of the elders. I confess that when I saw the
original company perform the play at Birmingham in 1898 I felt
some sympathy with this criticism as the four grotesque figures
arose from behind the wall in that memorable scene of eavesdrop-
ping. But contrasted with the abounding merits and beauties
of the play this approach to the grotesque was of no consequence.
The dramatist had only to be historically accurate in the matter
of costume and demeanour to be well on the way to amusing his
audience, and although, like the novelist, he did not hesitate to
exhibit the Auld Lichts of the past generation in all their natural
grotesquery, he still took care to secure for them a proper measure
of the sympathy of the audience.

In that very genial volume of theatrical reminiscences Behind
the Scenes with Cyril Maude, published in 1927, there are some
notes that should find a place in any outline of Barrie's dramatic
career, and also in the modern history of the London stage.

It was in the summer of 1897 (writes Cyril Maude) that James Barrie
first came into my life. I had at the time played in a piece written
by him and Marriott Watson, called Richard Savage, at the Criterion,
in which I played Sir Richard Steele, and we had become to a certain
extent friends through that, but it was that summer when one day he
told me that he was ready to write a play founded on his delightful
book The Little Minister. He told me this while we were playing
billiards at the Garrick Club. I missed several fine cannons, and,
rushing over to the Haymarket, told Harrison; and sooner than we
could have hoped for, we had the play and put it into rehearsal.
I loved every minute of the work on it. Barrie sat with me on a
little platform we had rigged up in front of the stage and worked and

helped in every minute of the stage management, and we lunched and tea'd together and nursed the lovely thing into the perfection everybody seemed to consider it six weeks later. I got Sir Alexander Mackenzie to write the *chef d'œuvre* ' Little Minister Suite ' of music, which seemed actually to *caress* the play as it moved along. He adored Barrie's writing, and it was a wonderful labour of love for him! He did me the honour of discussing nearly every movement of the music and was delightfully kind and helpful, and most generous, too, for he refused any fees whatever for the music. (Harrison and I gave him a great silver bowl with pictures of The Little Minister engraved on it.) . . .

The cast was *perfect*. Winifred's Babbie was exquisite. Why shouldn't I say so?—everyone said the same! Dear old Mrs. Brooke's Nanny was loved by everyone. Willie Elliot played the old and lordly Father perfectly; and as for the Elders, how superbly they were played by Brandon Thomas, Mark Kinghorne, Holman Clark, and Tyler! And nobody who ever saw that performance is likely to forget Sydney Fairbrother's Micah Dow, the little ragged Scottish urchin. Sir Alexander's own daughter made a perfect little Scottish maid—and among the boys and girls walking on, or rather *running* on, was the lovely Muriel Beaumont, now Lady du Maurier. The scenery, too, was beautiful—painted by Walter Hann and Joseph Harker.

It is easy to see from other references in Maude's very charming and human reminiscences how much The Little Minister (and most of Barrie's subsequent plays) derived from the close personal care of the author during the period of production. The actor describes the playwright as having been 'most wonderfully helpful, even writing in whole scenes when he considered his work needed it.' While engaged on the production of this play an alarming accident happened to its author. That little platform rigged up in front of the stage came near to being a death-trap, for Barrie was inclined to assume odd attitudes in his chair as the rehearsal went forward, and on one occasion, tilting back in his chair against the railing of the platform, which proved a flimsy support, he crashed heels over head into the orchestra, being picked up, as it seemed, lifeless. Carried to a sofa in the manager's room he soon revived, but the abrupt dismissal of rehearsal caused the accident to be talked about, and very soon a newspaper man came hot on the scent. ' I hear that Mr. Barrie has met with an accident,' he said. 'Oh it is nothing,' Mr. Maude replied, cheerily, 'only a severe shock.' 'What!' cried the disappointed reporter, '*No blood?*' This story has frequently been told, and Joseph Harker is one of the latest to re-tell it in his Studio and Stage, where he also adds another and less known anecdote of the playwright. I give it here 'with all reserve':

BARRIE: THE STORY OF A GENIUS

I fancy it was during the early run of this piece that Barrie, anxious to congratulate one actress on the rendering of her part, went round behind, and knocking at the door, shyly asked if he might enter. The lady called out ' come in! ' and as Barrie opened the door she plunged straight into a dissertation on ' Should women propose? ' or some other world-shaking topic of the kind. At last she wound up her peroration, remarking sweetly, as she proceeded to put the finishing touches to her toilet, ' That's all I have to say. Mind you don't misrepresent me, please, and *do* use one of my prettiest photographs with the interview.' She had mistaken Barrie, whom she had never met, for a reporter whose name had been sent in a few minutes before the dramatist arrived!

Without enquiring too closely into the identity of the actress, I would point out that she could hardly have been one of the original cast or she must have seen the dramatist when she attended rehearsals. But there is a Barrie flavour about the story, and we may let it pass, assuming that the lady had joined the company after the play had been running for a time, or that perhaps it was another play altogether!

The old practice of establishing dramatic rights in a new play by having a 'copyright performance' is no longer necessary, I believe, but before the tightening of the copyright laws it was a common thing for a piece to be performed to an audience that technically consisted of the public but actually of a few invited guests, the prices of admission being prohibitive. Such a preliminary performance of The Little Minister took place, a fact that should be recorded, as the author himself assumed one of the minor characters.

The success of the play in Great Britain was such as to satisfy the ambitions of any dramatist, and in America it exceeded all expectations. It ran there on its first production for upwards of three hundred nights, and according to Frohman's biographer it netted gross receipts amounting to no less than 375,000 dollars. Had the playwright never produced another 'winner' his share of this and the British receipts had already made him a man of fortune, and when we think of the many successes that he had still up his sleeve the mind of the ordinary literary worker boggles at estimating the riches that must have come to him when he chose to shake them down.

It must not be supposed, however, that there were no discordant voices in the reception given to the staging of The Little Minister. The Nonconformist conscience was only at the beginning of that enlargement to which it subsequently attained, and which I hold to be in great measure due to Barrie's conquest of the theatre. Many voices were heard throughout the country, and particularly in his native land, protesting against making fun of characters who, though comic in their outward aspect were assumed to be sincerely religious at heart. This delicate matter was boldly put to the test by a Ben Greet touring company on October 28th, 1898, when, greatly daring, they presented The Little Minister to a Kirriemuir audience. The event has not been forgotten by the older generation of Kirriemarians. The audience was composed very largely of farmers and townsfolk, with a sprinkling of the 'quality' from the 'big hooses' in the neighbourhood. The performers were all English, and the astonishing thing is that the local critics considered they came well out of the ordeal of speaking with a Thrums accent. Quite possibly the author had himself seen to this at rehearsals.

An enterprising correspondent of The Glasgow News went to Kirriemuir and interviewed an Auld Licht elder who had been induced to attend the performance, which he had been able to do with a good conscience as it took place in a public hall and not in a theatre, Kirriemuir boasting nothing to which the name could be attached. When the newspaper correspondent met him he was angry, but he was induced to give his opinion, which is thus recorded:

'As a work of art it has great defects—wha ever heard tell sicna woman as Babbie? But it's wi' the releegious aspecks that I fin' fault. The elders can dae nae guid. Jokey buddies, maybe, and fell smart wi' their tongues, but no' becomin' as releegious ofeeshials. Releegion's no' a subject to be jokin' aboot.'

He was then asked what he thought of the piece as a whole, and replied:

'Oh, verra guid, but the releegious aspecks—weel, ye've heard ma views. Fowk tell me Mr. Barrie's din a lot o' good for Thrums, but in view o' this thing, man, A'm dootin' it. A'm dootin' it, A'm sairly dootin' it. In ain o' his books he maks Auld Licht elders sweer. A'm thinkin' if the real Auld Licht elders cud rise frae their graves an' see The Little Minister that wad mak them sweer.'

This local criticism rings true to my ear, and even if we have to allow for some journalistic embellishment it is still *ben trovato*: it represents what a very considerable body of old-fashioned Presbyterians thought at the time. More than likely the performance did something towards broadening the Kirriemuir mind in matters of religion by driving a hearty gust of laughter through the Auld Licht atmosphere.

BARRIE: THE STORY OF A GENIUS

With the successful production of The Little Minister on both sides of the Atlantic a new impetus had been given to public interest in the personality of the author. In the American press his name was now as familiar a subject of gossip as it had been in the preceding ten years at home; many of the legends associated with his name were now originated. There was an intense curiosity as to his next intention: whether it would be a book or a play, and whether he was likely to devote himself in the future to the theatre rather than to the novel. The dramatist had certainly arrived, though he had been slow in attaining the mastery of theatrical technique compared with his ease in ringing the bell both as story-teller and humorist.

While The Little Minister was still running in London and frequent paragraphs in the newspapers told of the enviable fees it was earning for its lucky author Barrie achieved a feat of rapid composition by producing at a sitting a bright little dialogue entitled A Platonic Friendship, which he presented to Winifred Emery and Cyril Maude, who had served him so well as Babbie and Gavin. This piece was produced at the Comedy Theatre at a matinée in aid of the People's Concert Society, and again at Drury Lane, on March 17th, 1908.

Not only was it obvious now that the dramatist had arrived, but that the theatre was in a fair way to demand of him the best he had to give, even though he was known to have some literary emprises still to effect, especially the writing of the later life of Tommy Sandys and his beloved Grizel. The most trifling item of news about J. M. Barrie had become 'good for a par.' He was understood to be contemplating an edition of the Waverley novels with critical introductions, but this he never carried out. Introductions he wrote, however, to Mrs. Oliphant's A Widow's Tale and to George W. Cable's The Grandissimes, both appearing in 1898, and very characteristic of their author are these introductory notes.

His life-long interest in cricket was now at its strongest and he derived much satisfaction from captaining a team of literary cricketers who from time to time tried their strength against other teams, especially the Artists. So early as 1893 his enthusiasm for the game led him to print a private pamphlet for circulation among his friends, in which the Allahakbarries, as his club had come to be known, were the subject of some good-natured japes. His team included Jerome K. Jerome, L. F. Austin, Marriott Watson (who played a masterly innings of two), Charles Whibley and other authors of note. He produced another and more richly illustrated cricket brochure in 1899 called The

SUCCESS: THE DRAMATIST ARRIVES

Allahakbarries Book of Broadway Cricket, which was dedicated to 'our dear enemy Mary de Navarro,' that famous American actress (Miss Mary Anderson) having on her retirement from the stage settled at the charming Worcestershire village of Broadway, where certain of the encounters between Authors and Artists took place. These two pamphlets are the most eagerly sought after of Barrieana and the two or three that have come into the hands of collectors have commanded very high prices.

For many years we shall find Barrie happy in any opportunity that occurs to say something about his favourite game; a game from which, perhaps, he extracted his greatest enjoyment in the imaginative description of what had not happened. If we look forward a matter of five years we shall see him presiding over the Authors' Club on the 30th of May, 1904, when they entertained at dinner P. F. Warner, captain of the M.C.C. team, after his return from a tour in Australia. Barrie was in his most playful mood that night. He made a waggish speech in introducing the guest of the evening, 'I have only twice seen Mr. Warner play cricket,' he said; 'the first time he made one, the second time he was not so successful.' And on the subject of his enthusiasm for England's national game, we may as well take a longer jump forward—to the early summer of 1922, when Earl Haig and Sir James Barrie were entertained at luncheon by the Council of Dundee University College at the opening of the new sports ground for students. One passage from his speech on this occasion I must quote:

Cricket is my game. I do not know whether you observed it or not, but I bowled all the time to the Principal with my left hand. I was put in an awkward position, for I didn't want to put him out. I had a literary team in London for years. I had great knowledge of the game, certainly the actual playing of it. I used to walk about in Surrey with another man and watch the villagers and the way they played, and when these villagers got a bit older we waited one year and challenged them. I set out with a team of well-known people and going down in the train I had to teach them the game. They were full of confidence, and one man always kept saying, ' Intellect succeeds in the end.' They were such a terrible lot that I asked an African traveller, who ran away at the end of each over, what the Moorish for ' Heaven help us ' was. He said ' Allahakba,' and first of all we called ourselves ' The Allahakabas.' Eventually, in compliment to myself, the name was turned into ' The Allahakbarries.'

Again on April 20th, 1926, when the London District of the Institute of Journalists entertained the members of the Australian

221

team to luncheon at the Criterion Restaurant, Barrie was the most interesting of the speakers although he then stood in competition with the Prime Minister, Mr. Stanley Baldwin. He had to propose the toast of Cricket, and a rollicking, ragging speech he made of it, full of amusing personalities about the players which kept the company in a continuous ripple of laughter. The speech was reprinted by Clement Shorter as a twelve-page pamphlet for private circulation, the edition being limited to twenty-five copies. The point of most of his allusions would to-day be obvious only to those skilled in cricket lore, but he concluded in a more serious strain with some remarks that were not only worth making but worth remembering:

Let us pay our opponents this compliment: we are sure that if we had not thought of cricket first, they would have done it, and whether we win or lose, O friendly enemy, you cannot deprive us of our proudest sporting boast, that it was we who invented both cricket and the Australians. And let us not forget, especially at this time, that the great glory of cricket does not lie in Test Matches, nor county championships, nor Sheffield Shields, but rather on village greens, the cradle of cricket. The Tests are but the fevers of the game. As the years roll on they become of small account, something else soon takes their place, the very word may be forgotten; but long, long afterwards, I think, your far-off progeny will still of summer afternoons hear the crack of the bat and the local champion calling for his ale on the same old bumpy wickets. It has been said of the unseen army of the dead, on their everlasting march, that when they are passing a rural cricket ground the Englishman falls out of the ranks for a moment to look over the gate and smile. The Englishman, yes, and the Australian. How terrible if those two had to rejoin their comrades feeling that we were no longer playing the game! I think that is about the last blunder we shall make.

To round off the cricketing recollections of our author I include a story told against him by H. Hillyard Swinstead, the artist, who was a member of the team that used to encounter the Allahakbarries:

Mr. Barrie suggested that, in order to enliven the game, the two worst batsmen on each side should go in first, and be opposed by the two worst bowlers, the bowling not to be changed until a wicket had fallen. Mr. Barrie added that he by no means objected to being considered one of the worst players on the Authors' side.

The Artists readily agreed, but on Mr. Barrie and his fellow ' rabbit ' going to the wicket they made ' complete hay ' of the Artists' bowling, which could not be changed by reason of the agreement, and 50 went up before Mr. Barrie was bowled.

When it came to the Artists' turn to bat it was quite a different story, for the two worst literary bowlers dismissed the Artist ' rabbits ' in a couple of overs; so Mr. Barrie's ingenious plan worked well for his side.

It was at one of the famous Artists *v.* Authors matches that the writing men turned up with ten men in flannels and one famous novelist in a frock coat and cricket cap—an artistic ensemble which tickled the small crowd immensely. This was the day, too, when an envious journalist maliciously reported it, ' Mr. Barrie played superbly for not out O.'

Already I have made some reference to the little inclination which Barrie had always shown towards foreign travel, but mention should be made of the fact that in 1899 he extended his Continental experiences by making a journey in Germany.

In the two closing years of last century the triangular friendship between him, Maude Adams and Frohman was steadily strengthening. Frohman's frequent trips to London (he was called To-and-Frohman) provided the opportunities for personal contact, as the manager was the worst of correspondents, limiting himself to a sentence or two in his letters, but with Miss Adams the dramatist had to keep in touch by letter, and when in the summer of 1899 Frohman, for lack of a new play by Barrie, 'starred' her in Romeo and Juliet she received a whimsical epistle from Barrie asking 'are you going to take Willie Shakespeare by the arm and l'ave me?' By all accounts she did extremely well with Shakespeare, but she was all eagerness to take Jamie Barrie by the arm just as soon as he showed the necessary coming-on disposition, and that, as it happened, was not for another eighteen months.

With the opening of the new century it is the novelist that is again in evidence with his story of Tommy and Grizel, which began its serial publication in Scribner's Magazine (illustrated by Bernard Partridge) in January and appeared in book form in October, 1900. Just before the book had come out, however, he had made another and one of his less successful ventures on the stage with the production of The Wedding Guest at the Garrick Theatre on Thursday, September 27th. Here was the playwright who had made such charming fun of Ibsen nine years before endeavouring to take a leaf from that great master's book by himself attempting a 'problem play.' I fear he was more successful in guying than in imitating him. At all events the play had a short run, and, lacking a part for Maude Adams, it never was put on in America. H. M. Walbrook, who saw the production at the Garrick, considered that its failure was due more to the indifferent acting than to the inherent defects of the play itself. It certainly aroused a good deal of critical discussion, which is usually a box-office asset, and it gave that fervent Ibsenite

William Archer the opportunity of welcoming its author as a serious dramatist. 'Hitherto Mr. Barrie has only trifled with the stage, now we can offer a very sincere welcome to our new dramatist.'

Fortunately the 'new dramatist' was not again tempted to explore the dark possibilities of the problem play, and those who have read The Wedding Guest, the text of which was printed as a supplement to The Fortnightly Review for December, 1900, will have no difficulty in perceiving why the play was not a success. Its Mrs. Ommaney is really the Painted Lady over again, and although her sudden changes are hardly allowable, her madness is most delicately suggested. Most of the characters are shadowy, the episodes almost melodramatic, the sentiment at times tastes sugary. In short it does not have the appeal of a sincere piece of work, but is rather an experiment in a new manner.

The echoes of the controversy over The Wedding Guest had scarcely died away when Tommy and Grizel made its appearance in volume form. I had almost said 'their' appearance, following the author's own lead when he sent a presentation copy of his book to Edmund Gosse with the inscription 'Dear Edmund Gosse,— Tommy and Grizel and I will feel proud if you can find room for us on your self—a shelf for friends' (an inscription which made the volume worth £160 at the sale of Gosse's library in July, 1928).

Tommy and Grizel is usually described as a sequel to Sentimental Tommy, but strictly it is a continuation. Regarded as a sequel, it would have to be placed with the very few works of that category that may be considered successful. No sort of doubt arises as to the success of the novel as an individual work ; its development is obvious. We may, however, question whether the author himself, when he set out to develop the character of Thomas Sandys, had any clear vision of the road he meant to tread. It is permissible to suspect that as the story expanded under his hand what had been planned as a complete novel became no more than 'the story of his boyhood' (such is its sub-title) with a beginning, a middle and an end, and when the novelist pursued his hero's career to a conclusion he found that the dominant character had become the heroine.

The first book is definitely Tommy's, the second no less definitely Grizel's and it enshrines what is perhaps the highest achievement of its author in the splendid presentation of one of the most original and fascinating women in the whole range of British fiction. Quite clearly Tommy got fairly out of hand, though there is nothing in his eccentric behaviour inconsistent with the original conception of his character. In him the artistic temperament is seen at its strongest and at its weakest. While it explains the brilliance of his recorded achievements it detracts largely from his manliness, and at last we are constrained to the opinion that despite his rare gifts of imagination, judged by the standards wherewith we must judge him as a man he is but a 'poor crittur,' the end of him not unmerited. The lack of sincerity in him doomed him from the outset to disaster.

On the other hand, there is in modern fiction hardly any experience more delightful than to watch the growth of Grizel, on whom her creator has lavished all his loving admiration and the resources of his skill. If he is overmuch inclined to remind us how she rocked her arms and too often insists upon that crooked smile of hers, she never appears upon the scene of his story without entertaining the reader, and not for one moment are our sympathies allowed to stray from her. One can say with good assurance that in his Grizel of the crooked smile he had attained to his highest as a creator of character, and this is worth noting, for with the book of Grizel he bade good-bye to Thrums and to all that had meant so much to him as an author.

When he wrote the last page of Tommy and Grizel he had done with the scenes of his mother's youth and with the 'dearest place in the world' to himself. For fifteen years, in most that he had written, he had kept to the same restricted field of life and character, with the portrayal of which he had first found fame, and not again, save here and there in his plays, shall we find him looking back into that closed book of his literary adventure. Tommy and Grizel, enthusiastically received by his immensely increased following, had about it all unknown at that time a sadness of farewell, and it is pleasant to think that at the end of those fifteen years of devotion to one small corner of the countryside which his imagination had peopled with a teeming host of strongly differentiated characters, he concluded on so high a note of achievement as the lovely creation of Grizel.

There was in 1900 a suggestion that Nicoll and Barrie might undertake another journey together. Where they proposed to wander I do not know, but they had doubtless good talk about some alluring projects, as they had most agreeable memories of their American visit of four years before. A letter on the subject is quoted in the life of Nicoll. 'It would be a splendid time undoubtedly,' Barrie writes, 'but outside the holiday of it I question whether I could turn it to much profitable account.' He adds that he would rather go a long holiday with Nicoll than with any other man in the world. Fine testimony to the amiability of both men, as the acid test of friendship is a joint holiday. If the two parties to it are afterwards prepared to journey together again it may be taken that they 'belong.' If Barrie had gone as far afield as Prague this year he would have seen a work entitled Malý Farář in the bookshops there: a Bohemian translation of The Little Minister. Two years later another of his works the title of which he would have more readily recognized Sentimentální Tommy: Povídka O Jeho Dětstvi was also issued in Bohemian.

In his little study at 133 Gloucester Road, just above the entrance porch of that modest home where in those days he resided and in which Porthos, his favourite St. Bernard, 'quite a large dog,' seemed on the big side for the house, Tommy and Grizel had been written and The Wedding Guest also, but he was busy now evolving other fancies and new ventures of the imagination which were to enlarge immeasurably the realm of his popularity and strengthen his hold upon the affections of his admirers on both sides of the Atlantic. He felt that a further domestic move was necessary, and accompanied by Porthos, perhaps the bulkiest factor in deciding upon the new house, many finer residences were being inspected with a view to setting up an establishment more in consonance with his now assured position as dramatist and novelist than the suburban-looking villa in which the first eight years of his married life had been passed. In his drawing-room here, by the way, he had an inscription over the fire-place 'Do not expect too much of your fellow-men,' which was no doubt in frequent use as a conversational opening.

The new home of his choice was a pleasant old Georgian brick-built house named Leinster Corner, Lancaster Gate, to which he removed in 1902, thus changing from the south side to the north of Kensington Gardens, and settling as close as possible to that green patch of London which he was soon to make enchanted ground. Poor Porthos, alas, did not live to grace the ampler rooms of Leinster Corner; always delicate despite his appearance of strength, after seven years of domestic dictatorship he fell hopelessly ill and had to be put to sleep at the Battersea Dogs' Home. Porthos had originally been acquired as a fluffy little pup when Barrie and his bride had been on a trip in Switzerland, early in 1894. There are charming stories of him and his master in Dogs and Men, by Mary Ansell. The one trick in which he excelled was to choose his favourite author from the bookshelves. Asked to do this, he made great show of examining the rows of books and finally selecting one—always the same—'a yellow-backed shocker.' He delighted in undoing parcels, and once was found with a large Christmas package untied, and its contents, a beautiful doll, between his paws. He was devoted to his master. Together they ran races in and out of the rooms, up and down the stairs, out of the front door, in by the back, over and over again. 'A wild whirl of Porthos's tail and over went the hatstand; mats and rugs scattered in every direction.' He used to lie on a sofa in his master's study and watch him at his work, his great eyes benignly following the dramatist as he thought out some 'business' for Babbie or Susan Throssel and suited the action to the word by showing his character how to do it! Once, when his master was staying at Kirriemuir and the family were attending the South Free Church a short distance from Strathview, Porthos followed them and calmly walked down the aisle and up the steps into the pulpit! He looked over the reading desk at the congregation, but fortunately made no attempt to address it, and was ingeniously coaxed from his exalted position by one of Barrie's sisters before the scandal had gone too far. At home in London it was rarely that he and his master missed their airing in Kensington Gardens or their visit to 'a certain toy shop' where Barrie often bought a new toy ostensibly for some mythical child but actually for none other than Porthos, whose taste in toys was both wide and discriminating, as faithfully related in The Little White Bird. It is to Porthos that we should attribute something of the credit of tugging his master back into boyhood at a time when he might have been in danger of 'settling down,' and his too early end must have left the novelist very sad at heart.

With the publication of Tommy and Grizel, not only had the creator of Thrums said his definite good-bye to the Kailyard, but it was the swan song of that school. Just as Auld Licht Idylls and A Window in Thrums had originated the new vogue of the story of Scottish life and character, so Tommy and Grizel shut the door and turned the key upon it. Of course some of the lesser writers continued at work in the same field, but the pith had gone out of the movement, and oddly enough it was in October of 1901 that the first, and indeed the only effort at a counter-blast, was made in the publication of George Douglas Brown's gloomy and unpleasant story, The House with the Green Shutters: a book that enjoyed a brief but considerable success.

The critics of the Kailyard, and perhaps also those envious fictionists who had to contemplate the success of a vogue in which they were unable to share, had long represented the writers of the school which grew up around Barrie as giving a one-sided picture of Scottish life by exhibiting the peasantry and the common folk of the country town through a veil of filmy sentiment. There was a measure of truth in this, although these critics ignored the fact that the Kailyarders were essentially romantics, none of whose business it was to attempt the realistic. Any blockhead knew that a Scottish Zola would present a picture of Kirriemuir very different from that which a Barrie chose to paint, but perhaps he would not know that the two pictures could be equally truthful.

In the controversy which arose with the appearance of The House with the Green Shutters there was much confusion of argument. One critic, who was intimate with the author and his aim, contended that 'it was not written because he hated the Kailyard school, though all cheap pathos was most distasteful to him; not because he had a distorted view of humanity, not because his outlook on life was gloomy.' It was written, we were assured, because the author 'considered the ordinary cut-and-dried style of fiction wrong, that a book should be a living thing, not a mechanism, stiffly moving and hampered by the garments of convention; he wrote the end first, and became enamoured of his figures—and, alas! he knew that in some lives there is an inevitableness of disaster.' The author's own apology reads: 'I wrote it so cruelly, because I hate the cruel scandal that misinterprets poor human beings. I had rather have the sinner at all times than the man who mocks at his infirmity.' And again the appreciative critic takes up the apologia: 'The book hurts but is alive—vibrant, gruesome, cruel—but clever, the characters written from inside; therefore it is more than mere talent.'

All very fine and noble, but I, for one, have never ceased to believe that the book was written with no impulse other than a fury of indignation at the more saccharine products of the Kailyarders, for which his imitators, and at no time Barrie himself, were responsible. So fine and frank a critic as Professor Raleigh, himself a Scot of sorts, hailed the novel in these words: 'I love the book for just this, it sticks the Kailyarders like pigs.' In that ferocious sentence you will find the truth about The House with the Green Shutters, a novel which, in its over-stressing of all that is mean, sordid and disagreeable, falls into the same error its author had resented in the over-wrought sentimentality of Ian Maclaren, S. R. Crockett and others of less renown. Barrie would doubtless be content that the verdict of the reading public as between his Thrums and Brown's Barbie should stand.

I notice that in the autumn of 1928 one of the popular weeklies reprinted The House with the Green Shutters, but I cannot believe that this was done more to give pleasure to its readers than to acquaint a new generation with a piece of grim realism which thirty years before had enjoyed a brief success of ire; unless, indeed, the common readiness to be entertained by the miserable and the gruesome, which makes the chronicles of our police courts the favourite Sunday reading of the British masses, may also be shared by book-readers of a higher stamp. What is certain, however, is that the assault of George Douglas Brown upon the Kailyard school was a blow struck in the air, as the energies of that school had expended themselves before his attack.

So far as the author of A Window in Thrums was now concerned, his mind was exploring an entirely new realm of the imagination. In that little study of his at Gloucester Road, from which he was so soon to 'flit,' he had already effected a tremendous imaginative flitting. He had written a new play—none other than Quality Street, and this we must regard as the bridge whereby he crossed from Thrums to that new wonderland of make-believe in which he was to wander with so much joy to himself and delight to his audiences for many years to come. In this entirely charming play, where his absolute mastery of stage technique is placed beyond all cavil, we find ourselves in the realm of pure romance, and he takes us there trailing fragrant clouds of Thrums: the Misses Susan and Phœbe Throssel, their Blue-and-white Room and their little school at Quality Street in the days of the Napoleonic Wars, are none other than our friends, Ailie and Kitty, of the Dove Cot, magically 'translated.'

To Miss Maude Adams fell the distinction of being the first to interpret to the world the charming character of Phœbe Throssel. This took place at the town of Toledo, in Ohio, early in the autumn season of 1901, and when the play was brought to New York on November 11th, at the Knickerbocker Theatre, the actress scored another of her historic successes and the dramatist had taken one more step towards his eventual ascendancy in the Anglo-American theatre. It was not until September 17th of the following year that an English audience had the opportunity of seeing this lovely dramatic work, when it was given at the Vaudeville Theatre with Miss Ellaline Terriss as Phœbe, Miss Marion Terry as Susan, and Seymour Hicks as Valentine Brown. To what a changed tune the fastidious William Archer was now writing of Barrie's efforts in the theatre! 'The play is sure to become a stage classic,' was his verdict on Quality Street, and at the subsequent revivals of the play it has won the hearts of theatre audiences afresh. In my own opinion the dramatist has never been better served in the interpretation of any of his creations than with the revival of Quality

Street in August, 1921, when Miss Fay Compton appeared as
Phœbe, Miss Mary Jerrold as Susan, and Leon Quartermaine gave
a superb impersonation of the dashing Valentine Brown.

Although he was soon to become a multiple playwright in the
sense of having several of his works performed in London theatres
at the same time, while touring companies in the provinces and
throughout the United States were presenting them to curiously
different audiences, this year of 1902 was the first that saw two
important plays of his running concurrently in London. Quality
Street, with its brilliant record in America behind it, was sure of
success from the moment the curtain rose on it in London, and it
should be noted that this was the beginning of the Barrie-
Frohman productions on the London stage. But in November
of the same year a new and more intriguing work from the same
pen was presented at the Duke of York's Theatre, London, with
H. B. Irving in the title rôle and Miss Irene Vanbrugh as the
leading lady.

This new play, The Admirable Crichton, is by common consent one of the most important of Barrie's contributions to the
stage, although a similar motive had been used six years earlier
in a German work, Robinsons Eiland, by Ludwig Fulda. It is
a problem play, in the sense that it propounds a serious and
engrossing proposition. It asks us, in effect, what would happen
if the artificial repressions imposed upon human character by
the social conditions of life were removed. In Caste T. W. Robertson sought no more than to represent the humorous and pathetic
results that followed the mixture of persons of different social
status in a society whose conventions were beginning to break up
long before the Great War and which the War itself almost swept
away. But in The Admirable Crichton the dramatist had a
philosophic point of view to the exposition of which his play was
directed.

He conceived a large and a legitimate dramatic idea when he
made Bill Crichton the very model of a butler in the home of a
superficially democratic peer, and then landed the whole of his
personages on a Robinson Crusoe island to work out their social
salvation as a primitive group. The moral ascendancy of the
butler and the toadying admiration of the peer are splendidly
realized in the unfolding of the plot, and it is difficult to think,
as William Archer seemed to think, that the dramatist was himself
unconscious of the gravity of his attack upon the constituted
social order. To my mind there is little doubt that it was precisely his consciousness of this that gave such perfect point to the
contrasts in character as these were evolved in the primeval con-

ditions of the island. Dramatically considered, no moment in modern comedy provides so fine a thrill as that when the boom of the gun from the rescue ship is heard by the marooned men and women with whom the dramatist has been working out his problem. The social order conquers, the wheels go round again as before, the butler bows his head and his hands assume their old pose of deference, the peer issues his orders with a confidence that is the social growth of ages, yet we have been shown that, given the right soil, free from social growth character alone will tell—and society will begin! The trouble is that there is so little of the right soil available in closely settled communities.

A well-known novelist has related that, meeting Barrie a day or two after the production of The Admirable Crichton, he up-braided him upon the ending of the play, urging that as he had set himself a problem in psychology he should not have evaded a solution that involved the definite ascendancy of the stronger mind. Crichton, this novelist argued, was entitled by all the laws of fair play to 'come out on top.' The dramatist is said to have half-agreed with his critic, but added 'the stalls wouldn't stand it.' If the story is true, we can assume that Barrie was merely pulling the leg of his brother-novelist in making this apology. While it is not to be gainsaid that the element of farce enters too largely into the second half of the play, it is difficult to see how any other solution than that at which the dramatist arrived was reasonable.

The Admirable Crichton is essentially a thoughtful work, stimulating and original, and no better third act than The Happy Home has ever been written in a four-act comedy. But my suspicion is that when the idea first occurred to the dramatist, many years before it reached the stage, it presented itself to his imagination as a serious problem requiring serious treatment. We know that he began as a writer bent upon making his readers laugh, and on the stage he had succeeded thus far by allowing full play to his own particular imp of humour. His most noteworthy failure had been an effort to be wholly serious. 'To get the laugh,' as he puts it in Pantaloon, was the surest way to theatrical popu-larity unless one were a genius of the Ibsen type, who could present the clash of human passions with the intensity that lifts a play to tragic heights. Barrie must now have concluded that the serious drama of large and desolating passions lay beyond the periphery of his art, and wisely he decided upon the comic treat-ment of his theme. Even so, in certain details of The Admirable Crichton he had done better had he held his hand more firmly when he felt twitchings of the farcical coming down his right arm (it was many years later that he took to writing with his left hand and eerie stuff came down that arm!), as the laugh is got at times by devices that savour of the pantomimic. (I have in mind Crichton admonishing the others with his automatic notices 'Let dogs delight to bark and bite', and similar puerilities.) Nevertheless the play was a worthy addition to the Barrie theatre, and as a comic criticism upon the society of the time it showed the dramatist as something more than one whose sole aim was entertainment. For many months The Admirable Crichton and Quality Street at their respective theatres in London simultaneously 'played to capacity', as theatrical folk are fond of saying.

During the extraordinary post-war vogue of the cinema The Admirable Crichton was filmed in 1921 under the flamboyant directorship of Cecil de Mille and shown as Male and Female, a stupid change of title adopted by the producer perhaps to drag in that sex interest with which he had appealed in such leeringly suggestive film-titles ('all the dirt in the title' as Edgar Wallace put it) as For Wives Only and Bachelor Brides.

Even more significant than either of these two plays, and the fact of Barrie's advancing popularity in the theatre, was the publication in November, 1902, of what we might regard as his last literary work, The Little White Bird. For some months rumour had been busy with the announcement that the author of Tommy and Grizel was deeply engaged upon 'a novel of London life,' in which he was expected to strike a new and productive vein. When the 'novel' did appear, it bore no resemblance to that literary form, and the London life that it sought to portray was such as few Londoners had ever experienced. Yet The Little White Bird is probably, after A Window in Thrums, the most important of his works, considered strictly in its historical relationship to his career as author and dramatist. Just as his early Thrums stories introduce us to the first phase of his achievement, so does The Little White Bird introduce us to the second and perhaps the more important: his sovereignty of that indeterminate realm of fancy whence have issued in later years such things of beauty as Peter Pan, A Kiss for Cinderella, The Old Lady Shows Her Medals, Dear Brutus, and Mary Rose.

The critics were frankly puzzled by The Little White Bird. It is no more a continuous narrative than A Window in Thrums, indeed more than one of its chapters had been independently published years before and afterwards incorporated into the book and bound to the other chapters with the thinnest possible thread of narrative. It is not a novel, but it contains several perfect short stories, and one of the finest fairy tales ever written for young or old. It is just a collection of writings in which the author has enjoyed himself vastly by letting his fancy play with the day dreams of a sentimental bachelor. 'Ik Marvel,' a generation earlier, in his Reveries of a Bachelor, had done something similarly inspired but far less distinguished. Captain W. of The Little White Bird gives at the end a quite satisfactory explanation of his elaborate plans to filch the affections of little David from his mother: he has 'stored within him a great fund of affection, with nobody to give it to.' There was a woman he wanted to marry—but that was twenty years ago. The sentimental possibilities are obvious, and as boys and girls were once little white birds flying about in Kensington Gardens, still more obvious; but numerous amusing touches of cynicism skilfully introduced supply the necessary corrective that restrains the sentimentalism, and the whole thing issues as the most delicious of whimsies. If I were to describe it as 'the quintessence of Barrieism,' I feel that none of the admirers of his genius would demur to such a label, and to them no description is necessary since they have all read the book.

In The Little White Bird, there is probably as much of the innermost Barrie as in any book he has ever written. His humour is here at its finest, his sentiment at its purest. It matters not a fig that in its general outline it conforms to no literary convention with which one is familiar. It was described on its appearance by the Times reviewer in these very understanding phrases:

The fact is that, since he tells the story, he is bound to be the vehicle for all Mr. Barrie's thoughts; and for so much beauty and so much truth, so many hearty laughs and so many insidious tears as lie between the pages of this book we are content to barter all the matter-of-fact probabilities and all the dull laws of construction in the world. To speak in sober earnest, this is one of the best things that Mr. Barrie has written. From beginning to end it is a fantasy, of fairies, birds, old bachelors with old love stories, pretty young wives and their children —but especially their children. If a book exists which contains more knowledge and more love of children, we do not know it.

This says all that need to be said by way of appreciation. I would only add that there are probably fewer openings for fault finding in The Little White Bird than in any other of his books. One would have preferred, for instance, that Peter had not been first brought down by Captain W. with a blunt arrow, as something of the same kind had happened seven years before in Wells's Wonderful Visit; nor when we read that the old bachelor took David and hailed a hansom saying to the cabbie 'Drive back six years and stop at the Junior Old Fogeys' Club,' can we help remembering that Wells also wrote The Time Machine in 1895. But the humour of even its inconsequential passages is irresistible: 'I simply wave my stick at Cecco Hewlett's tree, that memorable spot where the boy called Cecco lost his penny, and looking for it found twopence. There has been a good deal of excavation going on there since.' Or when we are told of Porthos that his master has forgotten how he became possessed of him and thinks he 'cut him out of an old number of Punch.' The sentence that follows: 'He costs me as much as an eight-roomed cottage in the country,' is a statement possibly approximating to the truth.

Out of The Little White Bird there grew the greatest of all its author's triumphs in the drama of fantasy: Peter Pan. A vital part of the play is to be found in Chapter 14, which bears its name, and we have the story of the little house in Kensington Gardens, which is 'the only house in the whole world that fairies have built for humans,' and through the whole book we have the haunting form of Porthos, though the dog that bore this name in the story book was not a bit like the one that supplied the actual model for Nana in the play. Thus early, too, we find adumbrated the motive of Mary Rose. It occurs in the short chapter entitled 'A Night Piece':

The only ghosts, I believe, who creep into this world, are dead young mothers, returned to see how their children fare. There is no other inducement great enough to bring the departed back. . . . What is saddest about ghosts is that they may not know their child. They expect him to be just as he was when they left him, and they are easily bewildered, and search for him from room to room, and hate the unknown boy he has become. Poor passionate souls, they may even do him an injury. These are the ghosts that go wailing about old houses, and foolish wild stories are invented to explain what is all so pathetic and simple.

Among the many odd things to be discovered in this perfect treasury of the fantastic is a piece of thinly veiled autobiography which, though it runs to no more than twenty lines of type, forms almost half of the chapter strangely headed Sporting Reflections, the rest being but a few paragraphs to suggest why Captain W. dropped the letter that was to have so great an influence on his own life and on that of David's parents. In these twenty lines Captain W. is made to refer to 'a passage in the life of a sweet lady, a friend of mine' (none other than Margaret Ogilvy can be intended) 'whose daughter was on the eve of marriage when suddenly her lover died.'

SUCCESS: THE DRAMATIST ARRIVES

And here we have the story of the author's sister, Margaret, who some years after that sudden tragedy married the brother of her dead sweetheart. The union was a very happy one, and Margaret Barrie became Mrs. Winter after all. Her husband, like his brother, was a man of exceptional character and widely respected, so that Margaret Ogilvy, to whom everything associated with marriage was peculiarly sanctified, could look upon the proposal and encourage the match with a good conscience, and yet so strong a hold had the Rev. James Winter on her affection that she could not entirely conquer her unreadiness to acknowledge his brother as the suitor of her daughter, though his own merits made her 'take him to her heart and boast of him.' Captain W. tells us that this sweet lady friend of his 'dressed her pale daughter in her bridal gown, and with many smiles upon her face cast rice after the departing carriage,' but he chanced upon her in her room soon after the bridal couple had gone away and she was on her knees in tears 'before the spirit of the dead lover,' asking his pardon on the plea that she was old 'and life is grey to friend-less girls.' 'The pardon she wanted was for pretending to her daughter that women should act thus.'

This curious passage, which seems somewhat out of place with its direct pathos amid so much that is whimsical, fantastic and unreal, may be considered a little over-charged, but my readers will appreciate its documentation, which offers us a further insight into the fineness of feeling that was characteristic of the author's mother in her attitude to all the solemnities of life.

Perhaps one of the most delightful of the many sequelæ to the publication of The Little White Bird was the charming action of the old Duke of Cambridge within a year or two of his death. Whether the idea originated with him as Park Ranger, or was merely a suggestion put to him by a third party, is of no importance compared with the fact of its fulfilment. He wrote to the novelist a charming letter expressing his personal delight in the book and enclosing a key to the Lancaster Gate of Kensington Gardens, opposite which stood the author's new residence. He rightly considered that no gift could be more fitting for the author of such a delightful book. In later years Barrie was to have the freedom of more than one town conferred upon him, but to be made a freeman of Kensington Gardens was surely a unique distinction, and it was moreover a privilege that he was able to make use of on many a summer evening when the crowds had withdrawn and he could wander with his dog in this enchanted realm which his imagination had peopled with so many fairy figures.

BARRIE: THE STORY OF A GENIUS

About the time of the appearance of The Little White Bird a new anecdote of its author came into circulation: an anecdote which seems to come from the right mint. 'It is all very well to be able to write books,' Barrie is reported to have said to H. G. Wells, 'but can you wag your ears?' This charming accomplishment had been denied to his brilliant contemporary, but it had been one of Barrie's distinctions as a boy and he straightway gave evidence that he could still boast what the evolutionists, hold to be one of the many signs of our simian origin.

Early in May of this year (1902) David Barrie, the novelist's father, who, as we are aware, had been residing in Edinburgh with his brother-in-law, the Rev. Dr. Ogilvy, and his daughter Sara, returned to Kirriemuir for the purpose of superintending some alterations at Strathview during the summer months, as it was the intention of Dr. Ogilvy, the owner of that property, to come back to his native town and settle there with his brother-in-law for the remainder of his days. David Barrie, now in his eighty-eighth year, was still noted for his physical fitness, and thought nothing of a walk of eight miles at that age. But soon after he had come to Kirriemuir he was knocked down, while crossing the High Street, by a vehicle whose distance he had unfortunately miscalculated, and although the injuries he received did not seem to be severe, the shock to his system proved very serious, and instead of being occupied as he had hoped in the pleasant task of carrying out some improvements at Strathview he lay there an invalid for nearly two months before he passed away on Thursday, June 26th.

So vanished from the scene one of whom more would doubtless have been written had not the matriolatry of his son so firmly focussed our attention upon his wife. He was in many ways a man of the most remarkable character, and until the day of his death took a lively and intelligent interest in all public affairs. The great hero of his life had been William Ewart Gladstone. In an age when hero-worship was much more common than it is to-day such a statement as that was also an index to the character of the worshipper, for Gladstone had already a legendary quality about him which isolated him from the contagion of politics and united his admirers in a sort of ideal brotherhood that cleaved to the worthier things in public life. Dr. Whyte's admiration for David Barrie has been mentioned more than once, and when Whyte was Moderator of the Free Church Assembly he induced his old friend to deliver a short address at one of the Assembly breakfasts, in the course of which David Barrie gave some very racy reminiscences that were afterwards frequently quoted.

SUCCESS: THE DRAMATIST ARRIVES

In the days when the legend was developing about the excessive shyness not only of Barrie himself but of all his family, Mr. James Greig, now the art critic of The Morning Post, and formerly a popular draughtsman, was sent to Kirriemuir to make some sketches of the Barrie landmarks there for a magazine, and while engaged in drawing the exterior of the Strathview house—he had not had the nerve to ask for admission—the genial form of the novelist's father appeared at the door and the artist was greeted in the pleasantest possible manner by David Barrie, who examined Mr. Greig's sketch and while complimenting him on the accuracy of it, suggested that he might put in another window here and move the door there in order to make a still more effective picture, as he felt that the house would be improved by these alterations. ' When you have finished your drawing maybe you would like to come in and have a look at Jamie's study,' the father suggested; a proposal which fitted nicely with the wishes of the artist, who had the satisfaction of noting among the numerous pictorial souvenirs decorating the walls one of his own original sketches of a scene in which Barrie had a particular interest. The back window of the study looked directly across the road to the House on the Brae, and by it stood the high desk at which the author did his writing and his proof correcting when on his visits to Strathview. Such an incident as this just related goes ill with the numerous stories that used to be current concerning the inaccessibility and the taciturnity of the Barries.

A sadness is gathering around Strathview, for although Dr. Ogilvy and his adopted daughter had .come to reside there soon after the death of David Barrie, Sara did not long survive the return to her native town, and her death on November 1st, 1903, left her uncle desolate. She passed away very suddenly. On the Saturday she had complained of a cold, but attended the service preparatory to the Communion and went to bed apparently in her usual health. Early on Sunday morning she was found dead. Only a day or two before she had written a letter to her brother, a letter that was full of life and spirit, as Sara Barrie was a woman of very striking intellectual gifts associated with high qualities of character. She is still remembered by those who knew her as brilliant and vivacious in conversation and the very soul of frankness. Her devotion to her uncle during the many years she kept house for him at Motherwell was complete, and in every way she helped him in his ministry, endearing herself to his congregation as his wife had done in her day.

Robertson Nicoll, in writing of her at the time of her death, said: ' It was beautiful to see the devotion she gave and received.

Everything seemed to hang on her. She filled the house with brightness. Between her distinguished brother and Miss Barrie there was a very strong sympathy, and she was often to be found along with her uncle at his London home, where she entered with unaffected zest into the enjoyment of the new surroundings. She carried with her the happiness which is never denied to spirits so unworldy and so unselfish as hers was.' It had been a great pleasure to her and her father and uncle during the years they were together in Edinburgh to ' sit under ' their old and tried friend Dr. Whyte at Free St. George's, and she had no sooner returned to Kirriemuir than she had busied herself again in those religious and charitable services she was so fitted to perform. Her uncle did not long survive the loss of her care and companionship, as on August 25th in the following year, 1904, he was laid beside her in the cemetery on the hill. With these three deaths following so soon one upon the other, Strathview became for the novelist more a grey house of memories than the bright centre of his living affections.

Though the shadow of domestic sorrow was lengthening, his artistic energy knew no abatement, and all was brightness wherever the adventures of his pen chanced to lead. The procedure observed in respect to both The Little Minister and Quality Street, which were produced in America, and were received there with great favour before they were seen in London, was reversed in the case of The Admirable Crichton, which Frohman did not put on in New York until November 16th, 1903, when it was presented at the Lyceum with that very able American actor William Gillette in the part which H. B. Irving had created in London a year before with so much distinction. It was this same play that first introduced Barrie to a French audience. On Monday, June 8th, 1903, it was given in English at the Renaissance Theatre, Paris. But at the same theatre in the autumn of that year a French translation by Octave Uzanne was successfully presented and favourably received.

Barrie's growing popularity as one of our leading dramatists had been seen in two of his plays running at different West End theatres with equal success month after month, and the production of any dramatic work he now chose to offer had become an event of first importance. He had also been honoured by the King and Queen commanding a performance of Quality Street. But the new play with which in the autumn of 1903 he rightly calculated to fill Wyndham's Theatre for some months scarcely ranks among his more noteworthy successes. Produced on September 17th, it added a new phrase to our colloquial speech, and created considerable discussion. It was, moreover, a very good play and entirely characteristic of its author, but it is a significant fact that it has never been revived.

Little Mary was an elaborate gastronomic joke, and the mere mention of the name is sufficient to remind the reader how quickly it was absorbed into our slang. One might have thought—indeed the bulk of the first-night audience did so think—that when the plot of this very diverting comedy was explained in cold print by the critics on the following morning, the hilarious laughter with which the curtain fell at the end of the last act was not likely to be heard again. To have foreknowledge of the joke which the author was playing upon his audience was supposed to rub the edge off its enjoyment, but this did not prove to be the case, and crowded audiences went for months to see how Lord Carlton's great discovery that the British aristocracy eat too much was arrived at. The play was stuffed with such a liberal supply of Barrieisms that the thinness of the plot did not interfere with its enjoyment. It was also, though that need scarcely be mentioned, most admirably acted by a brilliant cast, which included John Hare, Gerald du Maurier, Eric Lewis, Clarence Blakiston and Miss Nina Boucicault.

The Admirable Crichton had ended a very prosperous run only a week or so before the curtain rose on Little Mary, but Quality Street at the Vaudeville, which had started six weeks before The Admirable Crichton, was still going strong, so that at the end of 1903 Barrie was still in the then uncommon position of having two highly successful plays running in London.

An oft-repeated anecdote of the author's intimate relations with the Llewellyn Davies family, of which we shall hear a good deal in our chapter on Peter Pan, relates to the production of Little Mary. The mother of little Thomas Davies (a sister of Gerald du Maurier) warning him against eating too many from the large packet of sweets which his devoted friend and playmate, J. M. Barrie, had brought for him, said: 'If you eat all these you will be sick in the morning,' to which the little chap promptly replied: 'Not in the morning, mummy—to-night.' The dramatist was so delighted with the humour of the retort that he asked leave to introduce it into the new play he was about to bring out, and agreed to pay his collaborator a royalty of a halfpenny for each performance. A contract was drawn up with all the usual legal phraseology, 'indeed, I believe,' says the dramatist in his dedication to the book of Peter Pan published in 1928, 'there still exists a legal document, full of the aforesaid and Hence Forward to be called Part Author,' in which he was tied down 'to pay Number

239

2 (the said Tommy) one halfpenny daily throughout the run of the piece.' The line was spoken every night while Little Mary was played and never failed to raise a laugh.

Despite the growing legend of Barrie's aversion from all public appearances and dislike of speaking before an audience, he made at least two very successful efforts in the course of 1904, first when he was the guest of the evening at the twentieth annual dinner of the Playgoers' Club on March 6th, and again when he presided over the dinner of the Royal Literary Fund two months later.

At the first of these functions the famous dramatist probably felt himself a little more free to let his fancy play around the subject of his speech, which was the reply to the toast of the Drama, tersely proposed by A. B. Walkley, the brilliant critic of The Times. Walkley had said that while we had the theatres, the organization, the managers and the actors, there were (at that time) no plays of any value being offered and that if the British drama did not quickly escape from the close atmosphere of drawing-room intrigue, club scandal and restaurant orgies into places of 'country-featured truth and honesty' he was afraid it would die. Barrie joined with Walkley in deploring the state of the drama but pointed out that it had its bright patches. 'What would the English stage have been like for a good few years if there had been no Pinero?' he asked. He also spoke with admiration of the work of Henry Arthur Jones, and said that in his opinion the best comic play of the last twenty years had been The Importance of Being Earnest. His allusions to 'the miserable way' in which the stage found itself were particularly happy. He had once been in the room of a dying man in Scotland, when a discussion took place as to which local carpenter should make the coffin, and the dying man joined in the discussion (this, by the way, is a statement of fact). It sometimes struck him that almost the only question concerning the drama at that time was who was to get the coffin? He said he would like to see a fine repertory theatre started in London, and he even went so far as to add that if one existed he would send every play he wrote to it before submitting it anywhere else.

His speech, which, according to one who was present, was spoken 'in a spasmodic but curiously effective manner,' entertained his critical audience immensely, and was in every way a success, but in a report of it before me I find that he said: 'This is the first time in my life that I have been the guest of the evening anywhere,' a statement that was not strictly true. It was surely Barrie who was the guest of the evening at the Aldine Club in New York eight years before, although his friend and companion,

SUCCESS: THE DRAMATIST ARRIVES

Robertson Nicoll, was naturally associated with him in the honour, and when in January, 1894, he had taken the chair at the Greenock Burns Club the distinction between occupying the chair and being the guest of the evening was a very thin one. But these little gestures of inexperience, surprise and hesitation, which used to be accepted as authentic, have really long been employed by Barrie with all the finesse of an accomplished actor. Those who knew him with any intimacy a quarter of a century ago were well aware of the fact that there were few more effective after-dinner speakers in competition with him when he cared to do his best.

At the dinner of the Playgoers' Club he gave his idea of what a serious play should be—an idea I need hardly say that was born of whimsicality. He described the entrance of the leading lady who said to her husband 'How pale you are!' and, imitating the husband, he soliloquized aside 'Ah, if she but knew.' The husband and wife are then supposed to go out and return. 'The lady takes off her hat because she looks better without it.' Her name depended on the theatre at which the performance would take place, but he would call her Eleanor.

'Have you discovered my guilty secret?' she asks her husband.
'Have you discovered mine?' is his response. 'When we met in Oxford Street I thought you had a past.'
'I thought as everyone had a past I'd have one,' replies the heroine. 'What's to be done?'
'What's to be done with the child?' he demands.
'There is no child.'
'I forgot.'
'Bring in a child—any child!'
And the curtain descends as he places his hand on its head. But not before the husband says, 'I cannot leave you. Why should you be left and not me?'

The foregoing amusing extract from a very brilliant speech will serve to show the reader how long and how thoroughly Barrie's stage effects are prepared and considered, as we have here the germ idea of A Slice of Life, which was not written till six years later.

If Barrie had been the supersensitive, thin-skinned and awkward little genius of the popular conception, his appearance in so conspicuous a position as chairman of the Royal Literary Fund dinner would have been an ordeal from which he might well have fled in panic. He did not; but carried it off with complete aplomb. For one hundred and fourteen years that annual event had been under the patronage of the great ones of the State, its chair was one of the seats of the mighty, and it is an indication of the general acceptance of Barrie as the leading personality in the new generation of literature and the drama that he should have been chosen to break down a long established tradition. Singularly appropriate that the occasion of his presiding should have been the first when ladies were admitted to this distinguished assembly. Robertson Nicoll was present, and wrote a very lively account of the proceedings which he headed 'Mr. Barrie in the Chair,' following the Chairman's own lead in his National Observer article, to which, by the way, Nicoll openly referred, thus anticipating by at least twenty-four years the 'revelation' made by an ill-informed journalist late in 1928.

According to Nicoll 'the chairman was completely at his ease, quite deliberate, even slow, and with the exception of the close of some sentences, I should think every word was heard by those present.' He also 'gave away' Barrie's method as a public speaker, which is evidently based upon his early experiences as an amateur actor and reciter. 'Mr. Barrie I believe,' Nicoll wrote, 'does not write his speeches, but composes them in his mind, and is able without difficulty to produce them as prepared.' A very sound procedure, for anyone who was reared in the atmosphere of Scottish Presbyterianism knows the horror with which a ' paper minister ' (that is one who read his discourse) was regarded; at the same time the minister, or any speaker, who showed lack of preparation was also the subject of disapproval. 'I am one,' said a speaker on a Scottish platform in the presence of a minister whom he was urging to make a speech, which the latter could hardly be expected to have prepared, 'who would not give twopence for a minister that couldn't shake a sermon down his sleeve at a moment's notice.' 'And I am one,' said the minister in question when he got up to say what he might, 'that would not give twopence for the sermon that was shaken down.' Nicoll has here let us into the real secret of Barrie's numerous brilliant appearances in subsequent years: his laborious preparation, his nicely calculated effects of humour and sentiment. His speeches are just as much works of art as his writings, and it is only one in whom the dramatic instinct is supreme that could give the appearance of spontaneity and accidental effect to what has been carefully prepared at the study table. Certainly nothing could have been happier than the speech he delivered at the Royal Literary Fund dinner; it gave great pleasure and satisfaction to all who had the opportunity of hearing it.

No one, Barrie thought, outside the committee could know how many authors there were for whom, as it had been said, the stage was darkened before the curtain fell. In the history of the Society, he said, there had been at least four cases of immortals whose stage had darkened prematurely. The Society had relit that stage and kept the curtain up, and all the world was richer by that. No doubt, he went on to say, there were others who might have winged their way to immortality had it not been that the darkness was never lifted for them. This led him to philosophise upon the triviality of literary distinction, and he chose the brilliant meeting over which he was presiding as an illustration. As such things went, it was a great meeting, but what was it, after all, more than a very little street in London? We pretend that that street is the world, with its newspaper organs, its dinners, its speeches, and no one paying any attention except ourselves! There were those, however, who had not even had their hour in that street. They deserved better things, they had given faithful service, and there must surely have been some days of inspiration, one pretty thought. This point he elaborated so:

The linnet we know has only one pretty thought, but then, he is such a stylist; and everyone who has had one pretty thought in literature has soared once to the vaults of heaven, and breathed for one moment the air the immortals breathe. Perhaps their faces are not turned from him as he waltzes by with the evening star on his arm. The evening star has most wet in her eyes for those novelists who fail most hopelessly. Perhaps she cannot abide the geniuses, though she has to go with them. But whether they are in the sky or here at dinner, or perhaps hungry outside, we of the pen, the loathly lovely pen, have a great amount of good fortune and bad fortune parcelled out between us.

Robertson Nicoll, in The British Weekly of May 12th, 1904, testifies to the unqualified success of Barrie's chairmanship, and the close attention and enthusiastic approval with which his ingenious and sympathetic speech was listened to, and there were other speakers noted for their brilliant oratorical gifts, including John Oliver Hobbes (Mrs. Craigie), that woman of genius whose untimely death took place just two years later, and Mrs. Flora Annie Steel, who, although already an elderly lady, had still a quarter of a century to live. Lord Tennyson proposed the health of the chairman in very happy terms, and spoke of Barrie's great popularity in Australia, from which he had just returned after his term as Governor-General. For Margaret Ogilvy he reserved a particularly warm eulogy, no doubt very pleasant hearing to its author, who in replying said that he coveted 'nothing more than the respect and good will, and if it might be, something of the affection of his brothers and sisters in literature.'

CHAPTER XI

ALL enduring things of life and art are of gradual growth. A book or a play that will be more than the success of a season is never produced by the simple process of ' taking thought.' There have been many, and there are still a few, competent craftsmen in the theatre who, by applying a well-tried formula, could be almost certain of producing a play that would ' give the public what it wants.' The plays that endure are not so produced. Their authors may not even guess how good they are until they have been translated to the stage. It was so with Peter Pan, or The Boy Who Would Not Grow Up. There is nothing more certain in its strange, eventful history than that its author was the last person who at Christmas of 1904 foresaw this most characteristic creation of his genius playing to well-filled houses a quarter of a century later, with all the appearance of going on for many years more.

I somehow think that had it been produced with the title which it bore in the original script, The Great White Father, its history might have been different. There is much in a title: it provides a rallying point for the mind of the artist, giving a certain direction to his thoughts which, with a different title, they might have missed. When Charles Frohman said that he loved the play but would prefer another title he did the author an inestimable service. Apart from all else that his undying enthusiasm for Peter Pan achieved, the little American genius of the theatre became thereby a joint artificer with his playwright.

The origins of Peter Pan were extraordinarily complex and little under the conscious control, in their earlier stages at least, of him who was to give tangibility to this thing of dreams. There is something of it to be found in so many other things its author had written and done in his earlier years. In his own child's play in the little wash-house at the Tenements, and in the umbrageous recesses of the Den, we have natural ' sets ' for Wendy's house and the Neverland; in Moat Brae garden at

244

Dumfries are the veritable trees still standing down whose ample boles Peter was to hollow those passages to admit the Lost Boys to their home underground: in their upper branches that most alluring of elevated dwellings, Wendy's airy seat, Tree Tops, was first built; away in the sunny south at Black Lake, near Farnham, are the Mermaids' Lagoon and Marooners' Rock, and also, I fancy, the woods where Pirates and Redskins met in deadly conflict, the Pirates most considerately warning you of their approach by their incurable habit of chanting as they marched:

> Avast, belay, the English brig
> We took and quickly sank,
> And for a warning to the Crew
> We made them walk the plank!

And beyond all these there are Kensington Gardens, the Round Pond, and the little white birds that fly about there. Chiefly Peter Pan would seem to have grown out of The Little White Bird and the removal of the author's home to Leinster Corner overlooking the Round Pond, and that area of Kensington Gardens in which years before had originated one of the most charming associations of Barrie's London life. The true story is told in detail, but together with so much that is purely fanciful, in his dedication to the text of Peter Pan (for which the reading public had to wait just twenty-four years), that we have to verify our references as we read.

' The Five,' to whom is addressed the most delicious dedication ever written, were the children, all of them boys, of Sylvia and Arthur Llewellyn Davies, daughter and son-in-law of George du Maurier, the celebrated Punch artist and author of Trilby. These five in order of years are George, born in 1893, who was No. 1, and who was killed in the War; Jack, one year younger; Peter, the No. 3, who is supposed to be the recorder of the terrible adventures of The Boy Castaways (being then something over four), and is now a London publisher; Michael, who was drowned while bathing when he was up at Oxford; and Nicholas, who dates from the first year of the play. Time goes on: the last named and Jack are married now. How Barrie first came to know these children whose lives were to be so closely interwoven with his own has been told by ' One who Knows ' and is repeated in Mr. Thomas Moult's little book Barrie: A Critical Estimate. But as his story makes the dramatist ('a small gentleman with a black moustache ') start by encountering all five boys at play during one of his walks in Kensington Gardens, I am afraid that ' One who Knows ' may not be trusted. I also take leave to doubt Mr. Moult's statement that The Little White Bird was written at Leinster Corner.

The fact is that Barrie's earlier house in Gloucester Road was only a short walk from Kensington Gardens, and his sauntering there was an old habit of his long before his removal to the northern boundary of the Gardens. The Davies children had been first encountered there on a day when Barrie was still living in Gloucester Road, but not more than three of them had taken human form, the other two were still flying about as little white birds. This is made plain by the mention in his dedication of initiating No. 4 into their secret society ' when he was six weeks old, and three of you grudged letting him in so young.' The ceremony, we are informed, took place in a garden at Burpham. The Little White Bird being published in 1902 and Barrie still residing at Gloucester Road in 1901, we may conclude that the Peter Pan chapters were the first fruit of this romantic friendship which had happened so casually: the stories were first read to the children for their exclusive entertainment. So much for ' One who Knows.'

Meanwhile, there had been much make-believe and children's play going on between Barrie and the Davies boys, the little man with the black moustache still as much a child as any of them. In those days the dramatist had his country home at Black Lake Cottage, near Farnham, and many joyous hours were passed there when the Davies children could be spared by their parents to play at pirates on the lake with its alluring island or to track Red Indians on the trails through the neighbouring woods. There is impeccable documentary evidence for the time and place of these doings in the shape of the rarest of all Barrie's printed works, The Boy Castaways of Black Lake Island. Two copies only were printed, and one of them got lost in a railway carriage; what a prize was here had the finder but known! Certain extracts from the unique copy in the possession of the author are embodied in the Peter Pan dedication. This booklet purports to be 'a record of the terrible adventures of three brothers in the summer of 1901 faithfully set forth by No. 3.' Its title-page has the imprint ' London: Published by J. M. Barrie in the Gloucester Road 1901.' All this is of a piece with children's play for many generations; Barrie was amusing himself with these delightful boys, in a more boyish fashion perhaps but in a way very reminiscent of Stevenson's play with his step-son, Lloyd Osborne, which produced so many and delightful burlesques in the pirate-story manner. As The Boy Castaways bears the date of the year preceding The Little White Bird and on the admission of the author himself the figure of

Captain Hook (first called Captain Swarthy) has already made his appearance in the tale, we must give first place to this among the incunabula of Peter Pan.

It is not permissible to doubt the originals in the child's play whence Peter Pan was evolved. Their creator is precise as to how he developed the wonder boy from them. He rubbed the five of them together, after the manner of savages producing fire with two sticks, an operation that has never ceased to fascinate the boyish mind of Barrie himself. 'That is all he (Peter) is, the spark I got from you.' It has been stated (on the authority of The Daily Mail's social chronicler) that 'the original inspiration' for Peter Pan was none other than the Hon. Sylvia Brett, daughter of Viscount Esher and now Ranee of Sarawak. I mention this merely that the statement may be tabled alongside the author's own quite definite explanation.

The outstanding thing about Peter Pan is that its author did not make a resolve that he would write a fairy play and sit down in cold blood to fill the bill. It was a thing of slow growth. It was mainly to please his dreamy self, McConnachie, and when the practical J. M. Barrie had completed the play he felt that in letting McConnachie have his head the result was something that might not attract the theatrical manager. Nay, so diffident was he of offering this rarest flower of his genius, that being under promise to provide Frohman with a new play he actually gave him Peter Pan and another at the same time. His reason was that this eerie, fairy thing, which was really the play of his heart, would probably have no commercial value in the theatre, and, in order that the manager might be recompensed for any loss in producing it—the setting of Peter Pan being immensely more costly than that of any three-act comedy—he had written another play which his theatre experience told him would be a financial success, and would more than recoup Frohman for the quixotic enterprise of presenting the fairy play.

This other piece, as we know, was Alice Sit-by-the-Fire, and although by no means an indifferent success from the box-office point of view, in that respect it fell far short of several other plays from the same hand. How little are even our geniuses the masters of their fate! The airy nothings to which in Peter Pan the dramatist had given a local habitation and a name turned out to be a gold mine whence several fortunes were extracted by author, producer, and certain famous players.

Although his blind faith in the genius of Barrie made Frohman promise to produce both plays before he had read a line of either, his first reading of Peter Pan was the most thrilling pleasure of

BARRIE: THE STORY OF A GENIUS

his life. So great was his enthusiasm for the play before he had even started to cast the parts that 'he would stop his friends in the street and act out the scenes.' It is easy for the critic and the playgoer to arrive at a comfortable verdict as to the merits of a play which has been offered to them with all the illusion of the stage and through the living personalities of the actors, but it requires vision and a very uncommon intelligence to see the whole thing staged and acted when naught but the written words are available. Frohman possessed this rare faculty of visualising what was in the dramatist's mind, and from his remarkable sense of the theatre could quickly detect possibilities of improved effects in the presentation of a play. When he said in later years that he should like to be remembered as the man who gave Peter Pan to the world there was no tincture of arrogance in this: next to the genius who wrote the play Frohman deserves to be remembered for having brought to the young and old of the English-speaking world the finest contribution to their pleasure in our era. His biographers say with good reason that 'It required the most stupendous courage and confidence to put on a play that, from the manuscript, sounded like a combination of circus and extravaganza: a play in which children flew in and out of rooms, crocodiles swallowed alarm clocks, a man exchanged places with a dog in its kennel, and various other seemingly absurd and ridiculous things happened.'

The play was first produced at the Duke of York's Theatre, on December 27th, 1904, and the great expense to which Frohman had gone to make it complete down to the littlest detail was triumphantly justified in the enthusiasm of the audience on that historic first night. Away at his country home at White Plains, in Westchester County, New York, Frohman was sitting with his friend Paul Potter feverishly awaiting the cabled news of the play's reception, and when the brief message was telephoned from New York, 'Peter Pan all right looks like a success,' he registered one of the happiest moments of his life. One has only to look back at the critical columns for the last four days of December, 1904, to see that not only had this wonder play captivated its first audiences, but that it had fused all the forces of criticism into one instrument of Barrie worship. Hardly a dubious note was heard and before long Peter Pan had become a cult which only the bolder spirits among the critics dared to attack.

Miss Nina Boucicault was the first actress who had the distinction of playing the part of Peter Pan, and I doubt if she has been rivalled by more than one of the other twelve actresses who in the annual London revivals of the play during twenty-four

248

SIR JAMES BARRIE   [*Lizzie Caswall Smith*

Face page 248

PETER PAN'S STATUE IN KENSINGTON GARDENS, LONDON   [McLeish

Face page 249

years have undertaken the part. One or two of the impersonations I cannot conceive as having been other than ill-judged,
knowing the limitations of the performers, but I can imagine
that the latest of the long line of talented actresses who have
played the Boy Who Would Not Grow Up, Miss Jean Forbes-
Robertson, must have brought new touches of elfin eeriness
to the part, her personality being more suited to one's conception
of the immortal Peter than that of any other who has essayed to
present him to the material eye. A whole chapter, indeed a
considerable volume, could be written about the actors and
actresses whose names have been associated with the play; some
day possibly, a theatre critic may attempt a complete chronicle
of the play and its players, and a fascinating book should be the
result. Certainly no single play of modern times has a theatrical
history remotely to be compared with it.

In the United States all the earlier Barrie successes paled before
that of Peter Pan. To Maude Adams the character and the
whole strangely various interests of its five crowded acts made
as swift an appeal as they had to Frohman. In Peter she saw
' the idealization of everything that was wonderful and wistful
in childhood.' Marcosson gives details of her methods of preparing for her interpretation of the immortal boy, which methods
he says were characteristic of her attitude to all her work:

She took the manuscript with her up to the Catskills. She isolated
herself for a month; she walked, rode, communed with nature, but
all the while she was studying and absorbing the character which was
to mean so much to her career. In the great friendly open spaces in
which little Peter himself delighted and where he was king she found
her inspiration for interpretation of the wondrous boy.

The production was ' tried out ' at Washington before being
brought to New York, and the first-night audience there seemed
to be somewhat mystified, not quite certain what to think about
it. But in New York, where it was produced on November 6th,
1905, it caught the fancy of the patrons of the Empire Theatre
from the very start and, according to Marcosson, ' on this night
developed the remarkable and thrilling feature which made the
adorable dream child the best beloved of all American children.
It came when Peter rushed forward to the footlights in the frantic
attempt to save the life of his devoted little Tinker Bell, and asked
" Do you believe in fairies? " It registered a whole new and
intimate relation between actress and audience, and had the play
possessed no other distinctive feature, this alone would have at
once lifted it to a success that was all its own.'

BARRIE: THE STORY OF A GENIUS

It would seem that this, perhaps the most meretricious gesture in the play, caught the fancy of the American public more than some of its finer features. I find in a recent American work, Our Times, a reference to this point. ' Maude Adams, in a suit of boyish buckskins, playing Peter Pan, asked " Do you believe in fairies?" There were not many children there (said John Corbin). It was an audience of grown-ups, a typical New York first-night audience, but under the spell of the sweet Barrie fantasy, the impish Barrie laughter, the half-mocking Barrie melodramatics, it had become just so many little children; at the sound of Peter's plea it rose and shouted, Yes!' Myself, although I saw the play in its first year and for several succeeding years, I cannot state with confidence whether this incident was a later interpolation, but Mr. Walbrook, if I read him correctly, does not suggest that Peter's frantic appeal was ever omitted or that it was an afterthought.

Hard though it is to justify on artistic grounds, and 'cheap' as it seems to me, there is little doubt that this episode contributed immensely to the success of the play in America. The essential vanity of parents in their offspring and the American passion for doing as one's neighbours do induced thousands of mothers and fathers throughout the United States to promise their children a visit to Peter Pan and the thrill of taking part in this episode. The fact that on one occasion a child rose in a box at the New York Empire a full quarter-of-an-hour before Miss Adams was due to make her appeal on behalf of Tinker Bell and said out loudly to an astonished house, 'I believe in fairies,' will show how astutely human nature had been gauged in the conception of this particular moment of the play.

Writing from the purely American point of view, Marcosson remarks that Peter Pan did more than give Miss Adams her most popular part:

It became a nation-wide vogue. Children were named after the fascinating little lad Who Never Would Grow Up; articles of wearing-apparel were labelled with his now familiar title; the whole country talked and loved the unforgettable little character who now became not merely a stage figure, but a real personal friend of the American theatre-going people.

On the whole, the British are less given to popular crazes than their Transatlantic friends, so that while there never have been such perfervid expressions of public enthusiasm for Peter Pan among the author's own countrymen the idea of the boy who would not grow up had so firmly taken possession of the public fancy

250

that probably no intelligent person, young or old, in the British Isles is not now familiar with the idea which the name connotes. In innumerable places every week 'Peter Pan' is used to suggest a condition of enduring youth. Only the other day a long article on Albania in a leading newspaper was headed 'A Peter Pan Nation'; another journal had some notes upon certain parliamentary personages with the caption 'Peter Pan Politicians.' A far-fetched application of Peter Pan to an article of common use is that of a firm in Kirriemuir who will supply you with packets of Peter Pan Scotch oats with the picture of the familiar statue on the outside! To associate porridge with Peter is surely a triumph of the inapposite. In England, just as in America, the name of Peter had a new vogue, and if a census of the girls who bear the name of Wendy could be taken we should be astonished to find how many thousands have been so christened. That name is said to have had its origin in the effort of W. E. Henley's little daughter, Margaret, to describe her father's friend Barrie, who was an occasional visitor during her short life, as 'friendly.' The best her childish tongue could make of it was 'wendy,' and thus, like the once celebrated name of Ouida, a child's effort to pronounce Louisa, that of the little mother of the Lost Boys had a similar origin.

Perhaps the visualising of Peter in the form of an animated and dainty statue, sculptured by Sir George Frampton and set up in May, 1912, at the very centre of those scenes in Kensington Gardens which Barrie's magic has made for ever a part of elfinland, may have helped in some degree to confirm Peter's place in the popular imagination. This statue is probably as familiar to the British public as the Albert Memorial, and is infinitely more esteemed, although I confess it has always appeared to me a somewhat weak piece of sculpture. When I reconsider the whole of Barrie's work I am impressed with what I might call its sexlessness. In all that he has written, despite his continuous harping upon the idea of motherhood and mothering, there is probably less of what we know as 'sex appeal' than in any other novelist or dramatist. Peter Pan, it might be urged, is only a boy by name in which certain well defined traits of universal boyhood are ingeniously illustrated, but the fact that he has never been represented on the stage except by girls and women does seem to suggest a lack of virility, and in Frampton's very graceful but not very boyish figure, with his 'horn of elfland faintly blowing,' this same lack is probably due to the absence of any sense of sex.

I suspect that this is also the reason why some good critics have found the whole conception of the statue intolerable. On the other hand, it is as surely the reason why its appeal to the children has been so immediate and enduring. The joy of coming to the actual scene of Peter's adventures and being able to look upon his lively effigy has delighted almost as many thousands of young folk as the play itself. It was a significant fact that when Frampton died on May 21st, 1928, most of the obituary notices were headed 'Death of the Sculptor of Peter Pan.'

As the erection of the Peter Pan statue must be regarded as a notable event in the history of the dramatist the facts may be stated here. In 1910 the Board of Works, having some time before put up a children's shelter on the west side of Kensington Gardens, had the happy idea of fixing a number of panels in that structure to illustrate the adventures of Peter Pan. Consulting with the dramatist about this proposal the First Commissioner of Works (Lewis, later Viscount, Harcourt), who happened to be a great admirer of Barrie's play, gladly accepted the suggestion that the creator of Peter Pan should himself provide a statue of his most famous creation to be placed where all the children coming into the gardens could see him and play round about him in the open air. Kensington Gardens being Crown property the proposal had to go before King Edward, who welcomed it and took a keen interest in the progress of the statue. From the first it was intended that the sculpture should suggest nothing of the monument type, but that the children who came to look upon it and play around the carven tree trunk which serves as a pedestal, with its interlacing branches where sprites and fays, squirrels, rabbits, and other 'wee sleekit, cowrin, tim'rous beasties' lurk and peep, should look upon it as some delicate, graceful thing that belonged to them. It is from this point of view that it should be judged, and not from that of the conventional statue or decorative monument.

The secret of Peter Pan, what is it? There is a vast body of literature on the subject; no other modern play has been subjected so often or so variously to critical analyses. Of one thing I am persuaded, the secret is not to be found in the central idea of the play: the idea that was so old a one with the author that in Tommy and Grizel he tells of a new work by Thomas Sandys which was 'a reverie about a little boy who was lost.' 'His parents find him in a wood singing joyfully to himself because he thinks he can now be a boy for ever; and he fears that if they catch him they will compel him to grow into a man, so he runs farther from them into the wood and is running still, singing to himself because he is always to be a boy.' Childhood has many illusions, but seldom or never is the hope or desire to remain for ever young one of these. No one who has watched children at play need be told that the consuming desire of childhood as it is of youth is to move onward in age, to play at being grown-up. The universal urge to develop, to grow, is implicit in every human thing, and only when the shock of the shortness of life comes upon one, round about the fifties, does the wish arise to mark time or to put back the clock.

This notion of boys or girls never growing up originates in the adult mind, as when the mother looking sentimentally on one of her darlings may have said, 'Ah, if you could only stay as you are for ever!' The May week debate at the Cambridge Union in 1927, revolved about this very question. The motion before the house was 'That this House envies Peter Pan,' and Major Ian Hay Beith and Mr. Mitchell Banks, K.C., M.P., were the principal speakers. Both of them strongly attacked the idea that to be always young was an enviable condition. Said Mr. Banks: 'The reason why older people are happier than young people is because they are more conscious of happiness. It is in memory that thorough pleasure lies. The wish to be always a child, always a youth, is a coward's wish. It is not the wish of a man.' This appealed to me as the truest thing said in the report of the debate that came under my notice. There is no real happiness that is divorced from memory. Youth has nothing to do with the number of years: it is a quality of the mind.

I submit, therefore, that the secret of Peter Pan is not to be found in the idea conveyed by the sub-title of the play. Nor is it in the purely fairy element of the play that anything of its secret abides. No sort of literary wares would a young author find more difficult in getting a publisher to print to-day than a book of fairy stories. The bottom has simply fallen out of what was once a very popular market. Despite the fact that Sir Arthur Conan Doyle has publicly come forward on the side of the fairies and seriously offered himself as a believer in their actual existence—what a score for Peter Pan if the creator of Sherlock Holmes would stand up in the stalls and personally avow his faith in fairies when Tinker Bell is *in extremis!*—the average boy and girl from six to eight years of age to-day has no use for them. Let us see to what Frohman himself attributed the success of Peter Pan. To Harper's Weekly in April, 1906, he furnished an article on the subject, and from this I make the following extracts:

Life in the big cities where huge buildings shut off from the child all contemplation of the open sky, and where dull grey streets have replaced green fields, where the lesson of the day is ' getting on in the

253

world ' rather than being a child and enjoying the dream-while of pirates, fairies, and Indians—all these are pointed out as tendencies towards early self-consciousness and the stagnation of the imagination. We are reminded that the whistling boy and the little girl singing her own improvised airs—those mirthful little Peter Pans and Wendys of yester-day—are no longer with us. To-day they are bent rather upon aping their elders. And it is asserted that with their disappearance will go that imaginative impulse which creates for a nation its great songs and lyrics.

As against these facts we know that men, women, and children have sincerely appreciated Peter Pan—a play which appeals to them because they come of a people possessed of a healthy imagination. At every performance old hearts and old brains live over again the thrills and sensations of romantic youth. Its appeal is universal.

There is joy in it for all classes and all ages. It is simply a matter of light attracting light. The pleasure taken by the audiences at Peter Pan has come, I think, from the fact that whatever is human and health-ful in thought or feeling in them has been touched by Barrie's humanity. Everybody who has been gripped by the charm of Peter Pan has only to thank himself that he has within him that to which the author has successfully appealed. Neither the skill of Miss Adams nor the power and genius of Barrie could have availed but for the responsive hearts and sympathetic feeling of the audiences. It has fallen to Barrie to evolve, what in all my experience, the American stage has only now accorded—namely, an entertainment creative of pure fancy in the city-bred child, and quickening to the imagination of the little people whose natural Fairyland we grown-ups have possessed—an illusion of a night during which the mother or father and child find abundant delights in common and realize new joys in being complete chums.

This I think is a very shrewd estimate not only of the secret of Peter Pan but generally of the charm of Barrie's plays. It has very little to do with old-fashioned notions of fairyland or belief in fairies, though something of that most ancient of beliefs lingers in us all. Primitive man believed in fairies just as sincerely as in daemons and demons, and wisps of these ancient beliefs float about in the dim background of all our minds.

Myself, after a recent re-reading of the text, I would incline to attribute the hold the play has taken upon old and young alike to the amazing skill with which a group of the most universal of human experiences is assembled and presented to the material eye with a naturalness that implies both faith and knowledge. Consider for a moment some of these. All children, doubtless little Zulus as well as little Scotsmen, want to 'fly.' It is a natural impulse which has often led to broken noses; it is the commonest of dreams, and possibly in another million years human beings may have developed the necessary physical equip-

ment for flying and such a scene as that of the opening act of
Peter Pan may be as common as walking downstairs to-day.
Then, when Peter remarks to the children that there are pirates
in the Neverland, John, grabbing his tall Sunday hat, exclaims:
'Pirates! Let us go at once!' What more natural? Lives there
a boy since the days of Mayne Reid or W. H. G. Kingston who
would not have responded with equal alacrity? Redskins, too,
make their appearance very soon, wolves also, and Peter had
shown the Lost Boys how to frighten the wolves away by looking
at them through his legs, a bit of wood lore every boy inherits
with that which enables him to catch birds by putting salt on
their tails. Then Mermaids are there. Wendy was 'awfully
anxious to see a mermaid,' like every other child that has been
born for many generations back. The building of Wendy's
house by the Lost Boys, what is it but the most natural of all
the make-believe games of childhood? The lagoon, the kite, and
the walking of the plank and a dozen other elemental memories
of our childhood's days; the stories told to us, the stories we read
ourselves; these are the things that make the whole entrancing
entertainment the loveliest experience for grown-ups and by a
perfect wizardry of presentation make it equally alive for the
children whose memories have not yet begun to lay by the
precious things which in years to come they will delight to take
out and fondle again. What Barrie really does in Peter Pan
is to 'flipe' the mind of his own boyhood, as a Scotsman might
say: to turn it inside out, as he used to do with his jacket in
some of his games at Kirriemuir. The result is an imaginative
epitome of all boyhood, with which is interwoven just the right
amount of 'feminine interest,' but no sex consciousness. In
the ordinary way nothing would more readily repel a healthy boy
than any suggestion of the feminine, but he is caught in the
motherly coils of Wendy before he knows where he is, or it may
be that his own masculine interests are so predominant throughout the play that he is never conscious of this feminine element
which has done its work by capturing at the outset both mothers
and fathers and the whole range of girlhood.

We have to picture Peter as a changeless creature, to whom
time and space mean nothing, but the play about him has been
the subject of continual change. Hardly two years in succession
has it been the same in every detail, nor is it easy to account for
the frequent alterations which the author has made in his text.
Some must be attributed to the whim of the moment when
revising the script. In one or two of the earlier representations
I listened with delight to the soliloquy of Captain Hook in which

he was tormented by the dread thought that, perhaps, after all he had not been a bad man. What if, with all his anxious striving to be bad, he had failed, and was somehow good! A delicious piece of irony this, which would seem to have been cut out in later years and does not appear in the final text. Why? On the other hand, I was aghast at this most unwarranted interpolation:

> PETER—You mustn't touch me.
> WENDY—Why?
> PETER—No one must ever touch me.
> WENDY—Why?
> PETER—I don't know.
> (*He is never touched by anyone in the play*)

I must see the next production of the play, to observe how this belated discovery of its author concerning the untouchableness of Peter works out in action. So far as I recollect any of the half-dozen representations I have seen, it would simply ruin the whole scheme of things; more, it weakens the conception of Peter as having anything of the boy about him. We cannot have the same sympathy for a changeless and deathless thing that may not be touched by mortal hands that we had for a Peter who used to be half mortal and half immortal. The immense sense of loneliness which 'the tragic boy' left upon us came from the mortal part of him. Cut out his humanness entirely and we lose touch with him—how could Wendy ever again let her hands play in the hair of him?—we can hardly believe he ever gripped his dagger and cried 'Hook or me this time!' In this particular instance at least, in my judgement, the author should have left well alone.

These changes began very early in the history of the play. A discussion arose over the first production concerning the mothering of the Lost Boys; Wendy was not the only mother that went to the Neverland. Some critics urged that the mothers should be abolished, and others would have them retained. When E. V. Lucas wrote about its first revival in 1905 he mentioned that the mothers had been swept away, 'even the author, it seems, has gone over to the enemy.' There were no mothers any more to offend the hypercritical, and never again would Liza 'throw an antimacassar over her head and call herself "the mother of twelve, and wishes there were twenty."' But 'the melancholy sea' appears to have been introduced this year for the first time, only in later years to be swept away, mermaids and all! The mermaids and the sea reappeared with great satisfaction to the audience in 1928 after nine years' absence!

PETER PAN'S FIRST TWENTY-FIVE YEARS

What purpose may be served by these arbitrary variations I cannot suggest. But there was an historic innovation on the last night of the 1907–8 season, which, being specially designed 'for one night only,' calls for mention in this record. It is as futile as it is natural to speculate about the after-life of characters that have fascinated us in book or play; nothing so bootless perhaps as to wonder what becomes of Wendy and John and the others who, unlike Peter, can't help growing up. And yet the desire to know abides. The author himself when he turned the play into a story and wrote Peter and Wendy (1911) felt the tug of this curiosity, and carried his fantasy a stage beyond the last curtain of the play:

All the boys are grown up and done for. . . . You may see the Twins and Nibs and Curly any day going to an office, each carrying a little bag and an umbrella. Michael is an engine-driver. Slightly married a lady of title, and so he became a lord. You see that judge in the wig going out at the iron door? That used to be Tootles. The bearded man who does not know any story to tell his children was once John.

Wendy is grown up and has a daughter Jane, to whom she tells the most wonderful stories of Peter. And one night Peter comes back to ask Wendy to come away to the Neverland as he is needing a mother just for a week; it is spring-cleaning time. But she has long forgotten how to fly. Peter, quite without feeling, suggests that Jane should come as Wendy had done when she knew how to fly, and off goes Jane. Each spring-time for a while Peter comes for her and she flies to the Neverland to tell him stories about himself which are quite new to him. Jane grows up and has a little daughter Margaret who becomes Peter's mother in turn and so on for ever and ever.

There is something dangerously like an anticlimax here. But it was no sudden thought of the author's, as we find it both in the new scene presented on the occasion above referred to, and expounded in the last chapter of Peter and Wendy. On the stage, one of the characters appeared before the curtain and explained that the dramatist had told them what happened to Wendy when she grew up, and so they were able to present this new scene showing her married, with a daughter of her own, whom she was sending to sleep by telling her of Peter Pan and her own childhood days. In the silence, as the child slept, Peter appeared, and told how Tinker Bell was dead, and how much he needed Wendy. After Wendy's daughter flew away with Peter, just for one week, the story reverted to the original version.

257

This interlude, which was interpolated between the Nursery and the Tree Tops scenes, was never repeated, but Miss Hilda Trevelyan is the lucky owner of the manuscript entitled Afterthought: Or What Happened to Wendy, and inscribed 'To Hilda Trevelyan, my incomparable Wendy, from J. M. B., March 1908.' On this particular occasion, the wind-up of Peter Pan's fourth London season, there was an extraordinary demonstration of enthusiasm from every part of the Duke of York's Theatre, and after about a quarter-of-an-hour Barrie showed himself sitting at the door of the house in the tree tops, between his two young leading ladies, waving a handkerchief in each hand.

The repeated success of the play year after year had even attracted the notice of those perversely vigilant persons who look after the gathering of our taxes and are the least likely members of the community to believe in fairies. When the fifth season was running, Miss Jane Wren, whose name has figured in the play-bill of Peter Pan at every revival since 1904, her only rival in this respect being Mr. George Shelton, whose impersonation of Smee, the nonconformist pirate, has earned him a place of distinction among Barrie players, received an assessment form with the usual peremptory demand to make a return of her income. One more instance, this, of the many in which Barrie's fun has so often been taken seriously with comic consequence. 'Jane Wren,' as all who have seen the play will know, is merely the author's jocular way of including the mechanical fairy 'Tinker Bell' in the cast. Presumably the whole of the company whose names appear in the programme had received similar missives, and as these are sent out in a dull mechanical way it was appropriate, perhaps, that one should reach the mechanical fairy.

Not content with the bounteous popularity of Peter Pan in Great Britain and America, nothing would satisfy Frohman but that the Anglo-American community in Paris, and the Parisians who knew English, should have the opportunity of seeing the play there, and at immense expense in the summer of 1908 and again in 1909 he transported the entire London production to the Paris Vaudeville for a five weeks' season. The company was one of the best that have ever graced the play, Pauline Chase, A. E. Matthews, George Shelton, A. W. Bascomb and Faith Celli, and a very fine time they had during their visits, the author on one occasion going over to see the show. On his initiative a cricket match between the men and women of the company was arranged at St. Cloud, where the teams lunched under the trees, with Barrie himself sitting at the head of the long trestle table. In the match, he is credited with having made the largest score—ten—for his team, and is said to have been very pleased about it.

On neither occasion was the Paris enterprise financially successful, Frohman being very heavily out of pocket but delighted at having introduced his beloved play to continental audiences. The French temperament has no place for a Peter Pan, and the critics of Paris showed little comprehension of the fantasy, although the native children were not unresponsive to its humours. There is a French translation of Peter and Wendy, and later on the film of the play was favourably received in France as well as in other foreign countries. But it would seem that Peter Pan has been performed in Italian, as a correspondent of The Times (April 16th, 1929) states that a travelling company produced it at Turin in 1911, and a friend of his played Nana (a part that presented no language difficulty) during the run of the play there.

I have referred above to Mr. George Shelton's long association with the play. His interpretation of Smee, although only a secondary character, will take its place among modern stage traditions: a tribute alike to player and playwright. The part is rich in humour and character out of all proportion to the space it occupies in the text, and the unctuous manner in which this actor has discharged the rôle at every performance in London since the historic first night in 1904 has left no possibility unexplored. In his little book entitled It's Smee, Mr. Shelton makes several contributions to the stage history of Peter Pan. He tells us that his fellow-actors have often chaffed him upon his long association with the play, and he has often replied that his Smee will be remembered when many Hamlets are forgotten, a very reasonable and proper retort, as it has been given to few actors indeed to appear before so many countless thousands of young people at their most impressionable age. In the affections of several generations of children, after Peter and Wendy, the nonconformist pirate probably comes next, although the mock badness of Captain Hook has endeared even that ferocious personality to many of them. Mr. Shelton writes:

That first visit to the theatre is never forgotten, for as a rule it makes an impression so great as to stand by itself. This is where Smee, as well as each of the other characters in Peter Pan, comes in. Each part, whether it be Peter, Wendy, the Crocodile, Captain Hook, Tootles, or any other, is perfectly fresh in the mind of every child who sees the play as his or her first adventure into the magic world of the stage. Here is an illustration of what I mean. When I was playing in Passers By at Wyndham's Theatre, one of my own Peter Pan admirers, a youngster, of course, wrote to me saying: 'Dear Smee. I see you are now playing a cabman. What a come-down for a pirate!'

Another of Mr. Shelton's recollections concerns one of the occasions on which the play with its London company was presented away from its spiritual home. Ireland was being favoured with a visit, and performances were given in both Dublin and Belfast:

The piece was as great a success in Belfast as it had been in Dublin. Now the date had been given to the Belfast management upon condition that they guaranteed the arrival of the company in Manchester by seven o'clock on the Sunday evening immediately following the last performance in Belfast on the Saturday night. This is how the promise was kept—to the exact minute. After the performance on Saturday, we were all hurried on board a ship which had been used, many years before, as a passenger boat, but which had now descended in the social scale and had become devoted to the carriage of cargo. Never had it such queer cargo as it carried upon that voyage, I'll be bound! We set out from Belfast at midnight, flying the Peter Pan flag at the mast-head, and the rest, as far as the Peter Pan Company was concerned, was silence—for a few hours. But when daylight came, we all took possession of the ship, and had the merriest of voyages across the Irish Sea. In the Mersey our ship caused a sensation, as the Peter Pan flag was observed and as Peter Pan itself was known and loved in Liverpool; and finally we reached the most interesting part of the voyage—the slow journey up the Manchester Ship Canal. Should we arrive in time? We did, after a splendid voyage, the first of its kind, and in all probability the last, ever undertaken by a touring theatrical company; and we opened at Manchester upon the Monday night.

I have said that, next to Peter himself, perhaps Smee is the most popular of the characters appearing in the play, but I was forgetting Nana the dog. If a plebiscite of the young folk who have seen the play could be taken there would be an enormous number ready to plump for Nana, so that she might emerge, if not as the favourite, at least high on the list. Elsewhere I have indicated that the real original of Nana was the noble St. Bernard who for seven years had been the devoted companion of his master, and who figures under his own name of Porthos in The Little White Bird. When Peter Pan was being written poor Porthos had ceased to be, and before long another big dog came, not quite to take his place, but to bring back to his master some of the delights of doggie companionship which had ended with his too early death. This new dog was a fine Newfoundland named Luath, and as Peter Pan was written in the splendid early years

of Luath's youth, although it was Porthos and the dear memories
of him that inspired the dramatist with the idea of the canine
nurse, the outward shape of the important rôle of Nana (the sex
having been changed to conform with the convention of children's
nurses) was studied from the curly coat and general bearing of
Luath. The actor who had to impersonate the dog came to the
dramatist's home at Leinster Corner and made a careful study
of Luath's little ways: his habit of beating on the floor with his
forefeet when expressing delight, his own peculiar way of wagging
his tail, and so on. It was a sketch of Luath that was taken to
the theatrical wig-maker, who had to furnish a make-up for the
actor with some resemblance to the living dog.

After the play had been produced and Nana was already established as the favourite of innumerable nurseries, Luath was taken
to the theatre at a matinée to see the performance, and at the end
of the nursery scene he went on when the principals were taking
the curtain. Some moments elapsed before the audience realized
that they were looking at a real dog and not the theatrical counter-
feit, and when they expressed their enthusiasm in the usual way
Luath did not hesitate to return his thanks in a loud and very
real bark. There are many stories told of this fine Newfoundland,
who has long since gone to join Porthos in the land of shades,
one of the best being related by his mistress: she once saw him in
Kensington Gardens take an unoffered bun out of the hand of
a baby in a perambulator and eat it. He was tremendously interested in all the babies there; he would snatch their toys and
pretend to run away with them. 'He walked about the Gardens
as though they belonged to him,' which is not surprising as he
must have guessed how much more interesting and valuable they
had become since his beloved master and his fairies had taken possession of them. Servants in the neighbourhood used to borrow
Luath to have the honour of being photographed with him.

Perhaps the most extraordinary performance of the play was
that which, early in its history, took place in the sickroom of the
boy who is best entitled to be named the original of Peter (if
in truth Peter had any 'original'). The episode is thus related
in Frohman's biography:

No one will be surprised to know that in connection with Peter
Pan is one of the most sweetly gracious acts in Frohman's life. The
original of Peter was sick in bed at his home when the play was produced in London. The little lad was heartsick because he could not
see it. When Frohman came to London Barrie told him about it.
' If the boy can't come to the play, we will take the play to the boy,'
he said.

Frohman sent his company out to the boy's home with as many 'props' as could be jammed into the sick room. While the delighted and excited child sat propped up in bed the wonders of the fairy play were unfolded before him. It is probably the only instance where a play was done before a child in his home.

Of the many actresses identified with the play probably none has left more pleasant memories of a charming personality than Miss Pauline Chase, who came over from America as a lovely young fair-haired girl to appear as one of the Twins in 1905 and soon graduated as Peter Pan himself, continuing for eight successive seasons to be a universal favourite in the title rôle. Both Frohman and Barrie took a personal interest in this fascinating girl, who won the hearts of all with whom she became associated. Indeed, in March of 1906 the author of Peter Pan became her godfather, and Ellen Terry her godmother, when, possibly out of regard for her adopted country, she was baptized into the Church of England at St. Martin-in-the-Fields, a stone's throw from the Duke of York's theatre where she was performing. Ellen Terry, Barrie, and Miss Chase's mother, Mrs. Bliss, were among the little group of six who attended the ceremony, Miss Chase being baptized as Ellen Pauline Matthew, the first name after her godmother and the last after her godfather. The clergyman who prepared Miss Chase for her baptism and performed the ceremony had himself been an actor before taking Holy Orders. This ceremony was followed in due course by another when the actress was confirmed at the parish church at Great Marlow, Frohman being present on that occasion.

The story of how Pauline Chase came to take so prominent a place in the life of Frohman and in that of Barrie at this time is told by Frohman's biographers, and must be re-told here. She had filled a small part in a musical play with Edna May at one of his New York theatres without attracting any particular attention, but when she appeared as the Pink Pyjama Girl in Liberty Belles at the Madison Square Theatre the discerning eye of Frohman saw her possibilities as a vivacious young actress, and he sent her to London to play one of the Twins in Peter Pan and to understudy Miss Cecilia Loftus, who had succeeded Nina Boucicault in the name part. Miss Loftus fell ill in 1906 when the play was showing at Liverpool and Miss Chase had to assume the part. Both Frohman and Barrie went down to see her perform, the manager sending her this message: 'Barrie and I are coming down to see you act. If we like you well enough to play Peter, I will send you a sheet of paper with a cross mark on it after the play.' By the end of the first act the anxious young girl had the much-desired piece of paper sent to her in her dressing-room with the significant mark upon it, and she was told that the manager and the playwright could not wait to the end as they were catching an earlier train back to London. They had seen enough of her talent to know that they had a perfectly charming interpreter of the part; one, moreover, whose youth would enable her to carry on for many seasons. It was thus that from 1906 to 1913 there was no change in the name part of Peter Pan and Pauline Chase had become another of the many 'stars' made to twinkle in Frohman's firmament. There was a curious fitness in her being invited to Liverpool twenty-two years later to take part in the ceremony of uncovering the replica of the Frampton statue of Peter set up in Sefton Park there, the event being marked by a Peter Pan pageant.

When Pauline Chase was in the heyday of her Peter Pan fame she received so many letters from the admiring juveniles who came to see her that at the Christmas of 1908 she made a book of these, Peter Pan's Postbag, published by Heinemann, and from her introduction to this the following delightful story, which has the true ring of childhood, will I am sure be welcomed by my readers:

I know of one little girl whose mother expected to have to comfort her in the agony scene when Hook puts his head in at the door and glares at Peter asleep. This is the moment that curdles their blood most, but she was not dismayed. ' I do love that man,' she called out so that we all heard her. No, you never can tell how they will take it. Hook has a soliloquy on the pirate ship, ' No little children love me,' and stern voices in front have been heard calling out in reply, ' Serves you right! ' but all are not so hard-hearted. I remember two mites being brought round behind the scenes because they had something they wanted to say to Captain Hook, but awe fell upon them when he shook their hands (with his hook), and they could only stare at him, and say not a word. When he had gone, however, they looked very woeful, and kept repeating, ' We wanted to tell him, we wanted to tell him,' and they explained to me that what they wanted to tell him was that they loved him.

The year 1928 was in many ways noteworthy in the history of Peter Pan, and of his statue. In March a writer in The Morning Post told of his alarm at the news that 'Peter Pan is falling down' and how he hastened to the scene to find workmen busy at the base of the statue. A policeman reassured him. 'It's some fancy of Sir George Frampton's,' he stated, 'for purely ornamental reasons.' (Sounds like Cinderella's romantical Policeman to me.) The flagstones were being partially removed, and red and grey tiles, geometrically arranged, were taking their places.

'Does Sir James Barrie come here often?' the Post man inquired. 'He used to when he lived at Peter Pan House over there. I last saw him in mowing time, when the notice, "Keep off the grass" was removed and left lying against the statue. "Why is that thing there?" he demanded. "The children must not be prevented from approaching the statue and fondling the fairies and animals. It is here for that purpose."' 'Look,' he added, 'the edges of that rabbit are worn bright by the children's fingers,' and concluded, 'yes, Sir James is always genial, he's a very nice chap.'

Shortly after this the sculptor died; in June the replica presented to Liverpool by Mr. George Audley was set up in Sefton Park there; in August, as related presently, a mysterious affair happened in Kensington Gardens; in October the text of the play was first published, and in December Peter had to prepare for his annual re-appearance with no Barrie to watch his rehearsals, his first absence for many years, as the playwright was confined to his rooms with a cold. Truly an eventful year for Peter.

The pageant elaborately arranged and successfully carried out by the Liverpool enthusiasts, their Lord Mayor (a lady, by the way, Miss Margaret Beavan) taking a spirited part in it, was evidence of the firm hold which the Peter Pan legend has taken upon the public mind. It will not be surprising if this is not the last of these public glorifications of the spirit of youth. Miss Pauline Chase had a real enough adventure in the course of the celebration by falling into the lake from the raft on which she was escaping from the pirates! The dramatist himself did not attend, but his niece, Miss L. K. Barrie, formerly headmistress of the Girls' High School at Wallasey across the Mersey, represented him, and was delighted with the whole unique celebration, at the beginning of which the following telegram from the master of magic had been received: 'Peter Pan, Sefton Park, Liverpool— Behave to-day if only for the time. Take care the Lord Mayor does not find you out. For heaven's sake don't grow when they remove your swathing sheet—Barrie.' No doubt the statue of Peter is as living to the lively imagination of the genius that created the original as it would appear to any of the thousands of children who crowded Sefton Park to have a first look at him when he was uncovered. There is a delightful inconsistency, which could be guessed at by nobody until some months later when Barrie gave us his final text for the play, in Peter Pan's reply. That was as follows:

A GROUP AT STRATHVIEW
Dr. Ogilvy, David Barrie and Sara Barrie, the uncle, father and
sister of J. M. Barrie, in 1902.

MR. AND MRS. ALEXANDER BARRIE IN 1909
Photographed at Strathview.

SIR JAMES BARRIE AT A COFFEE STALL ON THE EMBANKMENT, LONDON

Sir James Barrie, Adelphi Terrace, London—Thank you, Mr. Author. Thank you very, very much. Wendy loves her new home in Sefton Park. We wish you were here. We have put Jimmy Hook in the lake where the crocodile is. Our love and kisses. PETER PAN.

If no person in the play may now touch Peter, of what value are his kisses?

It may have been in some way a reaction from this Liverpool fêting of Peter Pan that tempted some ill-conditioned persons to commit a stupid outrage on the night of Tuesday, August 21st, when the statue in Kensington Gardens was smothered with tar and feathers, the latter evidently shaken out of an old cushion. No clue to this folly was discovered, and after a day or two in which the children bemoaned the temporary eclipse of their hero, Peter reappeared as clean as ever. It is difficult to conceive the type of mind that could find satisfaction in such an act. This had its significance, however. To some, perhaps to many, the statue is distasteful; some of the adverse criticisms it has elicited appeal to me as reasonable, but the state of London's statuary, if all of us who disapproved of public monuments expressed our dislike in similar fashion, would call for shiploads of tar and feathers beyond the resources of the bird kingdom. Those who tarred and feathered Peter Pan were probably some obscure students from Chelsea whose notions of art would attach them more to Epstein's Rima in the neighbouring park: the birds with Rima are certainly more like 'Never birds' than any with Peter. No one could admire both works of art, and as both are dedicated to the nature spirit and attempt to visualise it, it would be instructive if the two sculptures could be placed side by side for a week and the little ones asked to choose between them. The verdict would be no bad indication of the power of the artist to awaken sympathy in unsophisticated minds. We can, I think, see the children turning with horror from the grotesque Rima, with her bestial brow and loathly paps, to the graceful Peter: a proof of the appeal of naturalness in art.

We had a further piece of Barrie make-believe when the final text of Peter Pan appeared in October. With a fine pretence at seriousness in the dedication he alleges that he has quite forgotten the writing of the play, and gravely examines such evidence as he can bring forward to establish its authorship. In the early productions of Peter Pan little Liza used to appear before the curtain and make her bow as the 'Author of the Play,' so his vagueness is of long standing. There might well be some truth in the failure of his memory on this point: he has so often rewritten it in the succeeding twenty-four years that the original script would now be quite unfamiliar to him. Plays of his dating many years earlier stay clear in his mind in all details of their writing, but he cannot recall the actual composition of Peter Pan. Having hit upon an idea so whimsical, no difficulty is presented to his agile mind in making good fun out of it, and in no late piece of writing have we the everlasting Barrie better employed at his old game of make-believe.

An unpublished anecdote relating to Barrie and his children's classic demands a place in this chronicle. It was told to me by Mrs. Rowell, the accomplished lady who is custodian of Dr. Johnson's house in Gough Square and whose extensive and peculiar knowledge of Johnsoniana has been put at the service of so many famous visitors from all parts of the world. Barrie had been shown over the house by her and one day she met him in his usual walk along the Strand. He hesitated and seemed to recognize her. Mrs. Rowell had also stopped before she quite knew why; but with a woman's wit quickly recalled their previous meeting and asked if she might put a question to him about Peter Pan. Barrie consented readily. The question was about the closing of the window to keep Peter out. She said she was always unable to read out that part of the story because her daughter Betty would cry; she thought Mrs. Darling such a cruel mother.

'Tell her,' said Barrie, 'it was not Mrs. Darling's fault. I wanted Peter back in Kensington Gardens. I told her it was dangerous to leave the window open. If she didn't shut it she might be ill; then she wouldn't be able to look after Peter. Night came, and Peter, finding he could not get in through the window, went to Kensington Gardens.'

Barrie added that Betty should not try to fly from the mantelpiece. The fairy seeds were getting scarcer and scarcer and might not work.

'May I ask another question?' Mrs. Rowell enquired.

'Certainly.'

'It is about the " crow " on the statue—is it really a crow?'

'Well, it is a crow and not a crow—a great, great (I don't know how great) grandfather of the crow who looked after Peter on the Island.'

Could one imagine a more delightful episode than this: the world-famous author standing on the bustling pavement of the Strand, amid all the sights and sounds of our material progress, so gravely concerned about the world that never was?

A complete bibliography of the books about Peter Pan and

the numerous ideas and adaptations of the story in its earliest form, Peter Pan in Kensington Garden, extracted from The Little White Bird, would run to well over a score of items, while essays, criticisms and other newspaper and magazine articles concerning this, the most celebrated, and most certain of immortality, among all Barrie's creations, would have to be numbered by the hundred. A Peter Pan trifle, with all the old knack of making boys behave in print in the most utterly boyish manner, is The Blot on Peter Pan, printed in The Treasure Ship, a children's annual issued by Partridges, in 1926. The blot on Peter we discover by the end of this very charming story, which runs to fully six thousand words, is 'cockiness.' Neil and Tintinabalum printed in The Flying Carpet, a similar collection, issued in the preceding year by the same publishers (both were edited by Barrie's friend Lady Cynthia Asquith), first introduces us to the delightful Neil, another of the many dream children to whom the creator of Peter has acted as 'god-father.' There are French, Spanish and Italian editions of Peter and Wendy and also of Peter Pan in Kensington Gardens, but even here, as in his other books and plays, Barrie has been less translated than any other writer of our tongue who has attained to anything like his popularity. Yet English dramatic literature contains hardly anything more un-English in conception than Peter Pan.

In April, 1929, it was announced that Sir James Barrie had made over to the Great Ormond Street Hospital for Sick Children, London, the future annual income in perpetuity of the copyrights, literary and dramatic, in Peter Pan: a noble celebration of Peter's twenty-five years of unbroken success.

CHAPTER XII

THE TRIUMPH OF THE THEATRE

1905–1920

By 1905 Barrie is a writer whose talent is now and henceforth devoted exclusively to things of the theatre. That contest between his own alleged inclination to be a novelist and Frohman's determination that he should be a dramatist is now finally settled. The theatre has won. And in the theatre the dramatist goes from success to success with only occasional and unimportant regressions.

What an abundance of dramatic invention the record of these next sixteen years reveals! In sheer quantity it does not exceed nor even approach that of some of the old theatrical craftsmen whose work never rose above the level of the merely competent. (I have in mind such as Boucicault, Sims and Pettit, Buchanan and Grundy.) T. W. Robertson, who died at forty-two, might have been more productive had he lived; at his best he was certainly comparable with Barrie. But to have written nearly thirty plays in sixteen years and among them such masterpieces as Peter Pan, Dear Brutus and Mary Rose in those of the full length, and The Twelve-Pound Look and The Old Lady Shows Her Medals in the one-act category, is an achievement surely unique in our age.

In the present chapter I propose briefly to chronicle the more noteworthy facts about the production of each of those plays, and to make such critical observations concerning them as may seem to me in point. First in date comes Pantaloon, produced at the Duke of York's Theatre as a front piece to Alice Sit-by-the-Fire on April 5th, 1905. A typical Barrie trifle, this little piece is informed with the true spirit of fantasy, and all who saw it on the stage, though they may remember no more of it than 'You'll never be rubbed by a clown again, Mr. Joseph,' will still retain a lingering impression of its wistfulness and tender humour which none but Barrie has been able to create and to project across the footlights. In no other of his minor pieces

268

is the effect of this magic more immediate on the sensitive auditor. So much of the tiny play was 'business' that in the printed version of it nearly half of the text goes to the elaboration of the stage directions.

The whimsical element is also strong in Alice Sit-by-the-Fire which had as sub-title A Page from a Daughter's Diary, omitted in subsequent printings of the text. Neither comedy, drama, nor farce, it is one of his plays that gravelled the critics for a descriptive tag, and they had to content themselves by cataloguing it as 'Barrie.' No contemporary playwright would have tackled a situation so untrue to life, none but Barrie could have made his group of impossible personages so lifelike and appealing that the sympathy of the audience was instantly secured for each of them, their most unlikely actions and sentiments accepted without demur. The play had the great advantage of having its heroine impersonated by the most gifted and charming actress the British stage has possessed in the life-time of the dramatist: Ellen Terry. One of the critics, I seem to remember, headed his review of the play 'Ellen Terry Sits by the Fire.' Though Barrie had travelled many long leagues from the Scottish atmosphere of his earlier stage work, he was still, as we shall find him to the end of the chapter, actuated by that concept of eternal motherhood which, in serious drama, in farce, or burlesque, remains his most powerful impulse. The daring yet tender picture of a mother and her yearning love for the children she has been prevented from knowing until their individual characters have been developed and set, is as much in harmony with the original inspirations of his fiction as Margaret Dishart or Grizel herself.

It was stated at the time and, I think, with good enough authority, that Alice Sit-by-the-Fire had been specially written for Ellen Terry. The dramatist had thus not only the satisfaction of maintaining his now established and high reputation with this entirely charming piece, but also the pleasure of providing the most winsome of English actresses with a character which, in her later life when no longer equal to the strain of her great Shakespearean parts, enabled her for some years to give the deepest pleasure to the immense public that loved to see her on the stage. Barrie, from early years, had himself been one of her devoted admirers, and it was a happy coincidence that when he became Rector of St. Andrews University Ellen Terry was one of the distinguished group representative of literature and drama who in 1922 received honorary degrees on the day he delivered his rectorial address. She was fortunately able to be present in person. It gave him an opportunity, when he spoke of the drama, to describe her as 'the loveliest of all young actresses, the dearest of all old ones,' and to add that it seemed 'only yesterday that all the men of imagination proposed to their beloved in such frenzied words as these: "As I can't get Miss Terry, may I have you?"'

In New York this year Frohman had produced Peter Pan at the Empire, on November 6th, and Maude Adams had added to her already pre-eminent reputation as a star, and as the favourite interpreter of Barrie parts by her impersonation of Peter, which had no likeness to any of her earlier rôles. Another of those wonderful actresses whom it was Frohman's delight to discover and to turn into 'stars' had the good fortune to fall in for a charming Barrie part in Alice Sit-by-the-Fire, staged at the Criterion, New York, on Christmas Day. This was Ethel Barrymore. A very delightful account of how she became one of the bright galaxy of famous actresses who have impersonated Barrie heroines is given in Charles Frohman: Manager and Man. It is as follows:

Charles now secured the manuscript of Alice Sit-by-the-Fire. He was immensely taken with this play, not only because it was by his friend Barrie, but because he saw in it large possibilities. Miss Barrymore was with him in London at this time. Frohman told her the story of the play in his rooms at the Savoy, acting it out as he always did with his plays. There were two important women characters: the mother, played in London by Ellen Terry, who philosophically accepts the verdict of the years, and the daughter, played by the popular leading woman, Irene Vanbrugh, who steps into her place.

'Would you like to play in "Alice?"' asked Frohman.

'Yes,' said Miss Barrymore.

'Which part?'

'I would rather have you say,' said Miss Barrymore.

Just then the telephone bell rang. Barrie had called up Frohman to find out if he had cast the play.

'I was just talking it over with Miss Barrymore,' he replied.

Then there was a pause. Suddenly Frohman turned from the telephone and said:

'Barrie wants you to play the mother.'

'Fine!' said Miss Barrymore. 'That is just the part I wanted to do.'

In Alice-Sit-by-the-Fire Miss Barrymore did a very daring thing. Here was an exquisite young woman who was perfectly willing to play the part of the mother of a boy of eighteen rather than the younger rôle, and she did it with such artistic distinction that Barrie afterwards said of her:

'I knew I was right when I wanted her to play the mother. I felt that she would understand the part.'

The following year was a lean one judged by his contributions to the theatre. Possibly the two short pieces which he was responsible for, and which were produced at the Comedy exactly twelve months after Alice Sit-by-the-Fire, on April 5th, 1906, have been long forgotten by all but Barrie enthusiasts. Neither Josephine nor Punch, as they were respectively entitled, has been thought worthy of inclusion in the 1928 edition of The Plays. The first named was described by its author as a 'revue in three scenes,' but like a later and more ambitious effort to adapt himself to the French medium of political and social satire Josephine had to be written down a failure. It was not unjustly described by E. A. Baughan as 'a damp political squib,' and the thinly-veiled political celebrities who figured in it can hardly have felt a prick from any of the arrows aimed at them. Its author lacked adequate knowledge of the true inwardness of British politics to make his satire really illuminating, and the impression left on most of those who saw this so-called revue was that of a strangely ineffective skit directed against persons rather than the tendencies for which they stood. It gave the critics an opportunity to point out the limitations of Barrie, who, it must be conceded, was in some danger of becoming intolerably successful in every dramatic form that he attempted.

Punch, a briefer and hardly more successful effort than Josephine, was also classed as a dramatic skit. Such interest as it possessed was derived from the notion of presenting Bernard Shaw in a top hat and frock coat as the rival to Punch and Judy. Not without some of the Barrie touches which made such a trifle as Pantaloon memorable, it used over again, as the careful student of Barrie will so often find in other instances, part of the idea from which that charming trifle was evolved.

A blank year in both London and New York intervenes before we arrive at another of his outstanding successes: What Every Woman Knows, at the Duke of York's, September 3rd, 1908. In this four-act comedy the dramatist had gone back for the last time to his native countryside for his characters and the opening scene: every bit of the ground he trod was long familiar. Although he has written better plays, there are a sureness of touch and a niceness of effect in its dialogue and movement which are representative of him at his best. This play has never been one of my favourites; personally I always boggle at Maggie's share in John Shand's speeches, and especially at the hoary jape worked into the fateful oration with which we are asked to believe she succeeded in rehabilitating her humourless husband as a politician. But the play abounds in fresh and delightful comedy, and the contrasts of the cruder sides of Scottish life with brilliantly conceived scenes in the higher world of social England are undeniably effective.

Playgoers on both sides of the Atlantic were enthusiastic about What Every Woman Knows, and coming as it did after a year or two of minor productions, and followed as it was by eight years of one-act pieces before the dramatist again engaged himself successfully upon a full-length play, it seems to call for a position of importance in the Barrie theatre which is perhaps beyond its intrinsic merit. At all events there was no question about its popularity with the public, although we need not believe a statement in a leading daily of September 5th, 1908, that it caused a noticeable increase in the number of Scottish visitors to the metropolis. These visitors were alleged to besiege the box-office at night, expecting to gain admittance by their readiness to pay cash, but they were astounded to find that the seats were all booked up and their ready money availed them nothing. They were supposed to wonder why their national dramatist had not secured the Coliseum or the Albert Hall for the production of his play and so avoided the deplorable necessity of turning away good money at the Duke of York's. This newspaper article may have been inspired by one of those paid propagandists euphemistically known as Press Agents, but it cannot have been other than distasteful to Barrie himself, who has never stood in need of the despicable methods of 'boosting' which, especially since the creation of 'cinema stars,' has disfigured our journalism and made a laughing-stock of truth.

A more pleasing and an authentic anecdote of the production of What Every Woman Knows relates to the success of Miss Hilda Trevelyan as Maggie. The play had been produced in London under the Frohman management, and after seeing how splendidly the heroine acquitted herself on the first night the author cabled to his friend and manager in New York in terms of the highest praise of Miss Trevelyan's acting. On coming down to breakfast next day that charming little actress had the gratification to receive a cablegram from Frohman doubling her salary. That was his practical way of responding to the dramatist's compliment.

Before the curtain went up on the first representation of the paid at the Empire, New York, on December 23rd, with Maude Adams as Maggie, so great was the demand for seats that Frohman was said to be in the extraordinary position of having in hand the large amount of £19,000 paid in advance by the ticket agencies and the general public. The subsequent receipts in America are stated to have averaged £360 a night, while as much as £3,800 was taken in a single week.

According to Frohman's biographers What Every Woman Knows was written expressly for Maude Adams. 'It was a drama- tisation of the roguish humour and exquisite womanliness that are her peculiar gifts.' The author himself has justified this statement by saying that he wrote the play because 'there was a Maude Adams in the world,' adding, 'I could see her dancing through every page of my manuscript.'

Concerning the association of the famous American actress with this play Frohman's biographers go on to say:

Curiously enough, in What Every Woman Knows Miss Adams has a speech in which she unconsciously denies the one peculiar and elusive gift which gives her such rare distinction. In the play she is supposed to be the girl 'who has no charm.' In reality she is all charm. But in discussing this quality with her brothers she makes this statement: 'Charm is the bloom upon a woman. If you have it you don't have to have anything else. If you haven't it, all else won't do you any good.'

What Every Woman Knows was an enormous success, in which Richard Bennett, who played John Shand, shared honours with the star. Miss Adam's achievement in this play emphasised the rare affinity between her and Barrie's delightful art. They formed a unique and lovable combination, irresistible in its appeal to the public. Commenting on this, Barrie himself has said: 'Miss Adams knows my characters and understands them. She really needs no directions. I love to write for her and to see her in my work.'

Nor could there be any more delightful comment on Miss Adams' appreciation of all that Barrie has meant to her than to quote a remark she made not so very long ago when she said: 'Wherever I act, I always feel that there is one unseen spectator, James M. Barrie.'

Among some of the older generation in Kirriemuir there is an idea that the dramatist might have had in mind a certain local family increating the quaint group comprising Maggie and her three humourless brothers. The last of this family died some years ago. Many stories of them are still current throughout the district, but one of the best was told to me by a Scotsman in an English industrial centre, where the merchandise in which the brothers dealt had an important market. My in- formant, engaged in the same business, had some fifteen years before 'opened an account,' as merchants say, with a trader in this English town, and the opening of this account had meant the closing of one with the Kirriemuir brothers. Some years ago the then surviving brother was visiting this English town on business, a few weeks after his brother's death; my friend met him and sympathised with him on his loss. 'Aye, he suffered sair juist aboot the end, but I maun tell ye that he was michty comforted in his last days to hear that after fifteen years we had got back Mr. Blank's accoont.' Here is an index to a certain type of Scotch mentality: that a man worth many thousands of pounds should take comfort on his death-bed from his firm having recovered a small amount of annual business, so paltry, my informant assured me, that it made the difference of only a few pounds on his annual commissions! It is not suggested that What Every Woman Knows has any sort of basis in fact, but I am ready to believe that in developing his characters it is not improbable that the dramatist may have incorporated certain characteristics of these local worthies in his Wylie family, whose family name might even have had some punning significance.

One more story about this play. The three-hundredth night of its run was celebrated by a supper given by the dramatist at the Duke of York's Theatre to a very distinguished company. The last 'set' of the play, as those who saw it will remember, is the very bright drawing-room of the Comtesse de la Brière (I note that the author describes it as a 'pretty comic drawing-room'), gay with chintzes and knick-knacks, and in this scene, after the play was over, supper was served to upwards of sixty guests seated at flower-laden tables. Among them was Ellen Terry and also M. Bernstein, who was being lionised in London that season. Barrie is reported to have made a very telling speech, but the hit of the evening was contributed by Mrs. (later Lady) Tree, who recited this *jeu d'esprit* of her own composition in honour of the host of the evening:

> Had I the tongue as I've the heart
> To tell the praise of Barrie's art,
> My speech would be a lyric poem.
> And yet my thoughts, too nice for prose,
> Are just what every woman knows,
> And so he's almost sure to know 'em.

At the beginning of 1909 an anonymous play at Wyndham's Theatre was arousing a very remarkable interest. Entitled An Englishman's Home, it was almost prophetic of actual events that had to be envisaged a few years later. Everywhere An Englishman's Home was discussed and accepted as a call to action. I remember one well-known journalist, who had before and has since given much of his energy to advocating pacificism, being so impressed by a performance of this virile dramatisation of the danger then threatening England that he advocated the immediate organizing of a number of companies to perform it in all parts of the country, believing that its representation would do more for the cause of national service than all the speeches ever made. The name of the author was not at first revealed, and the fact that Barrie had attended two or three of the rehearsals, 'merely as a great admirer of the play and thankful that we had a management with the courage to produce it,' gave rise to an impression that he was either its author or in some way connected with its authorship. This impression was strong enough to induce him to send a disclaimer to The Daily Mail, in which he said: 'The piece is entirely the work of one man and no other person whatever has had any sort of hand in it.' But there was another reason for his interest in the play as well as that given. Gerald du Maurier was concerned in its production, under Frank Curzon's management, and he explained in the Press that the author was 'a soldier, a clever writer, and not a bad actor.' Being abroad at the time he had no idea of the furore his play had produced. The author was Major Guy du Maurier, brother of the celebrated actor and uncle of 'The Five' to whom in later years Barrie was to dedicate the text of Peter Pan, as it was from their child-play that the most famous of all his theatrical successes originated. Here was a very good reason for his attending the rehearsals, and not unlikely the production derived something from his advice.

At the beginning of 1910 Charles Frohman was induced by the editor of The Saturday Evening Post (Philadelphia) to contribute an article on the dramatic methods of Sir Arthur Pinero, and in this he made certain inevitable comparisons between Barrie and his older contemporary. Coming from so fine a connoisseur of drama and one so sympathetic to both playwrights whose work he had been proud to present to Anglo-American audiences for many years, these views command our respect. I extract the following paragraphs:

It is with the utmost precision and only after a solid year or two of reflection that Pinero will take up a pen to lay the foundation of a play. Then the work proceeds with all the deliberation and deftness of a superb architect laying the ground-work of a building that, once sketched out in the flat, must inevitably rise in but one way. Pinero's plays are like perfectly woven tapestries—except that, unlike tapestries, they read brilliantly whichever side is looked at. Or they are like perfectly proportioned mosaics, each word precisely placed in each sentence, each speech deftly thought out, exquisitely chiselled and always contributing to the whole; each act a combination of cumulative scenes, and the whole moving, like the inevitable march of Fate, to a conclusion that is about as easy to deny as the total sum of a correctly added column of figures.

Barrie, on the other hand, is just as apt to start writing a play by beginning at the third act. Then, when by writing through the third and fourth acts he has reached the fifth and is nearly ready to commence the first, he thinks it great fun to decide suddenly that the third act shall be the first. That is the difference between the two men. They are like two architects—the one first sees his building as a drawing in the flat, which when finished in all the multiplicity of its details will rise inevitably as it was originally planned; the other first sees his building as a completed structure, and then works inwardly from that picture to the gradual arrangement of details.

Our dramatist is next heard from in the theatre on March 1st, 1910, when, in lieu of a new three-act comedy, he added two new one-act plays to his growing list of short pieces. Both of these he thinks sufficiently well of to include in his volume of collected plays, but the merit and popularity of one so outshine those of the other that there must be many thousands of playgoers to whom The Twelve-Pound Look is as familiar as Old Friends is forgotten or unknown. Both were produced at the Duke of York's, forming, with The Sentimentalists, a dialogue rather than a dramatic piece by George Meredith, a very remarkable ' triple bill.'

There probably never was and never will be a better one-act play than The Twelve-Pound Look; a masterpiece of stage technique and sympathetic understanding, it contains in its brief space as much of humour and sentiment as have served many a competent dramatist for a full length comedy. With Edmund Gwenn as Sir Harry Sim, Irene Vanbrugh as Kate, his former wife, and Miss Mary Barton as his second wife, the appeal of that dramatic gem was instant. Whenever it has been revived, particularly as an item in a variety bill, as often at the London Coliseum, it has been the feature of the evening. It leaves an impression entirely distinct from that of the ordinary music-hall sketch, no matter how clever, and not less satisfying than a well-balanced three-act comedy.

The Twelve-Pound Look was not given in America until February 13th of the following year, when Miss Ethel Barrymore created the part of Kate at the Empire. The play was one of Frohman's favourites, indeed he placed it second only to Peter Pan, for which, as we know, his enthusiasm was boundless. When it was in rehearsal he was never absent, and wherever it was being played he went to see it if there was any possibility of fitting that in with his time. His biographers very properly observe that ' like most others, he realized that in this one act of intense life was crowded all the human drama, all the human tragedy.' Ethel Barrymore had great delight in the part of Kate, and it served to exhibit her to the American public as the most versatile and gifted of the younger actresses of that day.

This very interesting story of the way in which The Twelve-Pound Look came to be produced is told by Frohman's biographers.

When the repertory for the theatre was being discussed one day by Barrie and Granville Barker at the former's flat in Adelphi Terrace House, Barker said:

'Haven't you got a one-act play that we could do?'

Barrie thought a moment, scratched his head, and said:

'I think I wrote one about six months ago when I was recovering from malaria. You might find it somewhere in that desk.' He pointed toward the flat-top table affair on which he had written The Little Minister and Peter Pan.

Barker rummaged around through the drawers and finally found a manuscript written in Barrie's hieroglyphic hand. It was The Twelve-Pound Look.

I cannot agree with H. M. Walbrook that Old Friends is ' a ghastly story told with tragic power.' He also describes it as ' a concentrated tragedy by a master craftsman.' For my part, I am surprised that its author has printed it; to me it reads like the merest melodramatic sketch, and nowhere shows a trace of the master hand that wrote it. This tiny piece seems to me so artificial that it is worth examining as an illustration of how a master of dramatic art may fall short not only of his own best, but of a very common standard of merit. Conceive a man of sixty, a despicable secret drinker until he was fifty-seven when he loses taste for the vice, though imagining that he has conquered it. He has a daughter of twenty, engaged a few hours since to be married, and a sad wife who has not only known the shameful secret of his own life but has hidden another which, in the true spirit of melodrama, is revealed to him this night. The daughter has inherited his craving; she, too, is a dipsomaniac, though father, sweetheart and everybody else, except her mother, have never suspected the truth. Brief though the sketch is, it is unpleasant in conception and strained in presentation. In common with all Barrie's dramatic work, even this slight piece would appear to have been heavily revised, unless Mr. Walbrook in his J. M. Barrie and the Theatre is trusting entirely to memory in his summary of it. According to him, when he saw the piece performed, the period of the father's abstinence was understood to be twelve years and the dialogue at the tensest moment ran thus:

BARRIE: THE STORY OF A GENIUS

'But I broke myself of the habit!' cried the wretched father. 'Never!' is the wife's bitter reply. 'Never! The habit *left you*. It had worn you out. You could entertain it no more, and it left you. Our vices *leave us*—we don't drive them away. Their consequences remain—shadows that speak—old sins that have become Old Friends.'

Here is how this passage reads in the author's own text:

Stephen. Haven't I given it up?
Mrs. Brand. Not as I have thought the thing out, Stephen. I don't think you gave it up—it gave you up. I was looking on; I saw. It wearied of you, and left you. But it has come back now—for her. Easy enough to find a way back to the house—for such an old friend of yours.

The reader may think I have made a needless fuss about a negligible trifle in lingering for a paragraph or two upon Old Friends, but there are spots on our sun and in my judgement here is one. In its particular way Old Friends is just as definitely a failure as The Twelve-Pound Look is a success, and it is rather comforting than otherwise to find that our master craftsman is at times human enough to have a shaky hand.

A third dramatic sketch was produced this year as a surprise item at a Duke of York's matinée on June 7th. It was A Slice of Life, a real Barrie conception; that of a newly married couple who have both pretended to somewhat hectic pasts though both have led the most innocent and humdrum lives until they meet. When they have each to confess again that their pasts will bear the closest inspection, the comic possibilities of the situation are obvious.

This little piece was afterwards produced in New York, on January 29th, 1912, with Ethel and John Barrymore in the cast, and it would appear to have been more popular in America than in England, although at its first production, with Gerald du Maurier, Irene Vanbrugh and Cecilia Loftus, it is said the audience positively 'ate it '—' and choked over it.'

When it was rehearsing in New York Frohman was lying ill at the Knickerbocker Hotel, and, being very much interested in the little play, he had the rehearsals held in his rooms there. Whenever his pain was particularly severe he would send a message across to the Empire Theatre, 'Send Ethel over to rehearse, I want to forget my pain,' and with her brother John, and Hattie Williams, who took the third part, they would come to the hotel and Frohman would soon be conquering pain with laughter.

Frohman, whose usual correspondence was conducted with telegraphic brevity, wrote to Barrie in February of 1912 the longest letter printed in his biography: it concerns this little play, and as it touches the important question of the actor's co-operation with the author it demands a place in this record:

I haven't written you because lately I have been having a lot of pain. I sent you papers which will tell you how wonderfully your fine play—A Slice of Life—has been received. It has caused a tremendous lot of talk; but I just want to tell you that there is absolutely no comparison, in performance, as the play is given here and the way it was given in London. Fine actors although the London cast had, my people here seem to have a better grasp of what you wanted. They have brought it out with a sincerity and intelligence of stroke that is quite remarkable. Ethel Barrymore never did better work. Her emotional breakdown, tears, her humiliation—when she confesses to her husband that she had been a good woman even before she met him all this is managed in a keener fashion, and with even a finer display of stage pathos than she showed in her fine performance in Mid-Channel. As the husband, Jack Barrymore is every inch a John Drew. He feels, and makes the audience feel, the humiliation of his position. When he confesses, it is a terrible confession. Hattie Williams, in her odd manner, imitated Nazimova—as Nazimova would play a butler. So these artists step out in the light—before a houseful of great laughter; one feels that they have struck the true note of what you meant your play should have. I think the impossible seriousness of triangle scenes in modern plays has been swept off the stage here— and A Slice of Life has done it. . . . The effect of A Slice of Life is even greater and more general than The Twelve-Pound Look. All agree that each year you have given our stage the real novelty of its theatrical season. And the fine thing about it is that you have given me the opportunity of putting these before the public.

Rosalind, another one-act play, and one that vies in its finished perfection with even The Twelve-Pound Look, was produced at the Duke of York's on October 14th, 1912, although two years were to pass before Maude Adams appeared in it in America. There is nothing new in the root idea of the piece, which is essentially that of Charles Reade's Nance Oldfield, the most popular of Ellen Terry's impersonations in her middle career. Youth falls in love with what he imagines to be the most bewitching of young actresses and finds her in private life a woman of mature years. With Miss Irene Vanbrugh in the title part the brilliant material provided by the dramatist was put to the best use and Rosalind took its place forthwith among Barrie's masterpieces of the short length.

BARRIE: THE STORY OF A GENIUS

The autumn of the following year witnessed renewed activity in the theatre, and no fewer than three original pieces by Barrie were staged in the month of September. The Will, and The Adored One, the first named a one-act play and the second a three-act comedy, were both produced on the evening of September 4th, 1913, at the Duke of York's. Mr. Walbrook, who was present, records the fact that ' for the first time, the final fall of the curtain on a Barrie play evoked nearly as much hissing as cheering, and the audience came away bewildered and depressed.' He adds that he left the theatre in company with Sir Douglas Straight, Editor of The Pall Mall Gazette, who remarked to him, ' A melancholy evening! a very melancholy evening! '

There could have been nothing but applause and sincere appreciation for The Will, which ranks among Barrie's best achievements in the short play, wherein success is no less difficult to attain and more rarely attained than in plays of three or four acts. The Adored One was the cause of the disappointment, and from its description it sounds a melancholy joke indeed. A charming lady (Leonora) travelling with her little daughter, who has a cold, pushes a gentleman out of a railway carriage, and so kills him, because he would not have the window closed. In the subsequent trial she wins the hearts of the judge and jury and all the officers of the law, and is triumphantly acquitted. Here was an idea that could have been turned to excellent use by the author of the Bab Ballads (whose Trial by Jury may have inspired the second and third acts), but it would seem that here again Barrie had reached beyond the limits of his persuasive art, and his first three-act play for five years was as flat a failure as What Every Woman Knows had been a success. The critics left him in no doubt about the fate of the play, so he courageously set to and entirely re-wrote it, making out Leonora's story of the murder to be a figment of her own vivid imagination, presenting the burlesque scenes of the trial as a dream episode, and adding a new act in which the heroine and he who adored her came to happy agreement at the end. In three weeks from the production of the first version this new play was staged, but not even Mrs. Patrick Campbell's fascinating personality saved it from the initial failure. That great actress in her reminiscences blesses Barrie for intervening when the ' producer ' of the play was directing her to do something in a way that did not appeal to her rendering of the part. ' Out of the stalls on to the stage, with his pipe in his mouth and his hat on the back of his head, came the author, and with that Scotch accent that leaves you calm and cool, said: " I think perhaps she

280

SIR JAMES BARRIE, ON HIS ELECTION AS RECTOR OF ST. ANDREW'S
UNIVERSITY, WITH EARL HAIG

SIR JAMES BARRIE AND DAME ELLEN TERRY
At St. Andrew's on the occasion of delivering his Rectorial address.

will do better if you leave her alone." ' She describes the play as a thing of ' magical tenderness, fun, and beauty.' After the first performance, late at night, Mrs. Campbell, accompanied by the Countess of Lytton and Viscountess Gladstone, went to seek the playwright at his Adelphi flat, but all was silence there and opposite at Bernard Shaw's darkness also prevailed. After supper at the Savoy the three ladies at a most unconventional hour returned to the hermit's retreat and found him in. ' With what gentleness and dearness he received us—and how proud we were to talk with him at that time of night! '

The Adored One does not appear in his collected edition, only the memory of a Barrie failure lingers among English playgoers. But in America, where it was produced as The Legend of Leonora, on January 5th, 1914, with Maude Adams in the name part, it had an entirely different reception from critics and playgoers alike. The former overwhelmed the play with such epithets as ' delightfully extravagant,' ' deliciously whimsical,' ' charmingly humorous,' and accused the London public of a lack of humour in having given it so unsympathetic a reception. They were reasoning from false premises, for The Legend of Leonora was a vastly different play from The Adored One, and if the re-written version had been the first to be seen on the London stage it might have received a different verdict. It is notorious that no re-writing of an initial failure, however skilfully done, can recover the ground lost on the first night. The real explanation of the American success and the English failure is possibly revealed in the message of the New York correspondent of The Times, who wrote as below:

Miss Maude Adams, who appears in the title rôle, forms a complete contrast in figure, voice, manner and personality with Mrs. Patrick Campbell, who undertook the part in London. She is exquisitely tender, appealing, roguish, and laughter-provoking throughout, ' a very woman.' In fact, as one critic observes, ' Sir James Barrie has again fulfilled his mission as a playwright, so far as America is concerned, by fitting Miss Adams, its most popular actress, perfectly. Without Miss Adams, the critics confess, the play would have been unintelligible to a New York audience.'

In connexion with the production of The Legend of Leonora an interesting fact has to be recorded. It was in this character that Barrie for the first time saw the actress, whose name will always be pre-eminently associated with his plays and the Frohman management, interpret one of those characters he had created for her more than for any other of the many gifted women whose names are identified with his long roll of heroines. Maude Adams since 1897 had been playing Babbie, Phœbe Throssel, Maggie Wylie, Peter Pan, and in not one of these had the dramatist seen her act. But at the close of 1913 he took another trip to America and saw her get the elusive character of Leonora across the footlights in the first week of 1914. He would naturally have her in mind for the American production, and it must have been peculiarly gratifying personally to witness the American success of his work after its rejection at home. It is said that the only instructions he attached to the manuscript of the play concerning Miss Adam's part was: ' Leonora is an unspeakable darling, and this is all the guidance that can be given to the lady playing her.'

Touching the historic association of these three famous people, dramatist, manager and actress, I turn again to the lively pages of Frohman's biography for the following summing up:

> On her last starring tour under the personal direction of Charles Frohman, Miss Adams combined with a revival of Quality Street a clever skit by Barrie called The Ladies' Shakespeare, the sub-title being ' One Woman's Reading of The Taming of the Shrew '. With an occasional appearance in Barrie's Rosalind, it rounded out her stellar career under him.
>
> Miss Adams's career as a star unfolds a panorama of artistic and practical achievement unequalled in the life of any American star. It likewise reveals a paradox all its own. While millions of people have seen and admired her, only a handful of people know her. The aloofness of the woman in her personal attitude toward the public represents Charles Frohman's own ideal of what stage artistry and conduct should be.
>
> By tremendous reading, solitary thinking, and extraordinary personal application she rose to her great eminence. With her it has always been a creed of career first. Like Charles Frohman, she has hidden behind her activities and they form a worthy rampart. The history of the stage records no more interesting parallel than the one afforded by these two people—each a recluse, yet each known to the multitude.

Barrie's other short play in 1913, Half an Hour,* was equally popular in London and New York. A cleverly written little melodrama, it was presented at the London Hippodrome on September 29th, and at the New York Lyceum on the same date. Soon after its production Frohman wrote to say that it was ' Going splendidly and had a fine reception the first night.' He was then looking forward to the revision of The Adored One as ' a

---

* This little play was made the basis of a 'talk film' by W. G. de Mille, entitled The Doctor's Secret, first publicly shown at the Plaza, London, on April 15th, 1929.

splendid programme for Miss Adams.' He added in this letter to Barrie: 'All the Americans coming home have seen your play and are delighted with it in every way,' which indicates that there is a point where American and British tastes cease to have much in common.

A dramatic trifle written by Barrie in 1913 was the little sketch entitled The Dramatists Get What They Want dealing in an amusingly satirical way with the question of stage censorship which at that time was having one of its periodical airings in the newspapers. This was incorporated in Hullo Ragtime! a revue then running at the London Hippodrome, and it was produced at the Globe Theatre, New York on the same day (October 12th). Its satire did not succeed with a New York audience, as it was directed against an institution with which they were not familiar. Mr. Albert de Courville, the London producer, so lately as 1928 made what he describes as the first disclosure of ' Barrie's secret play,' the revue sketch in question, the author having stipulated that his name should not appear on the programme. Mr. de Courville was evidently not aware that the authorship of the sketch had been ' disclosed ' in the Frohman memoir twelve years before.

As the next date in my chronicle of the Barrie theatrical productions is December 21st, 1914, I have roughly passed ten years in review since the production of Pantaloon, and it cannot be said that these ten years represent one of the most fruitful decades in his career, though there are dramatists of note who would have been proud to have scored so many successes in that space of time: Alice Sit-by-the-Fire and What Every Woman Knows are two fine feathers in the cap of any writer for the stage, and when we add to them The Twelve-Pound Look, Rosalind, and The Will there is about enough to make the fortune of any ambitious playwright, but it was really a period in which our master of the theatre was not doing full justice to his own peculiar talent. He was now in the mid-fifties, with a reputation almost unrivalled, but some of his best work, and certainly his best of all, was still to be written. The Great War had broken out, and as it dragged its slow length along his natural desire was to devote something of his dramatic talent to comforting the Allies, and here his unequalled facility in the short play gave birth during those years of stress to a number of pieces in which his stage technique is seen at its best. Pursuing my chronological method, each of these will come up in turn for consideration, together with his later works of larger importance and also his occasional lapses due to an adventurous impulse to experiment in dramatic forms which he was not fitted to use so effectively as other playwrights of inferior merit. Less than another decade of theatrical activity remains to be recorded, but it contains the two masterpieces of his maturest powers.

Among the critics there was a disposition to regard the finely conceived and admirably written one-act play of purely serious import Der Tag as a mere piece of propaganda. This was due to a faithful attachment to the ancient dogma that, the end of art being to please, where we have a conscious purpose, such as the advocacy of some specific deed or thing, there must be a lowered measure of artistic achievement. But exceptions to this rule are so numerous that there is no more foolish cry, when these come up for judgement, than ' Back to Aristotle!' Der Tag, as I remember it when produced at the Coliseum (December 21st, 1914) with Norman McKinnel and Irene Vanbrugh in the principal parts, lost little if anything of artistic value from being, as it was intended to be, an impressive and beautiful presentment of the cause of the Allies in their stand against Teutonic aggression. It was really a page of history written with great spirit, yet dispassionately, and containing many noble lines. Propaganda was never so divorced from fustian and misrepresentation. Der Tag certainly showed its author to be an absolute master of stage situation and effective dialogue. In the whole series of his war plays we shall seldom find the dramatist working at any level below his best.

In this same December Hodder & Stoughton brought out the first published volume of Barrie's plays under the title of Half Hours. This contained Rosalind, Pantaloon, The Will, and The Twelve-Pound Look and was the beginning of what eventually must have proved a very profitable enterprise, though not yet had the public taste for the reading of plays been developed. That was to be one of the many changes in literary taste that followed the period of the War. Saving only the acting versions used mainly by amateurs, the demand for plays in book form was still so small that not even the most successful works of such able dramatists as Pinero and Henry Arthur Jones commanded any considerable sale with the general public. Nowadays the book of every successful play is quickly published and runs into numerous editions. Half Hours was a success, although four years passed before Barrie offered another collection of his shorter plays to the book-buying public: Echoes of the War, which contained The Old Lady Shows Her Medals, The New Word, Barbara's Wedding and A Well Remembered Voice, appearing as a five-shilling volume in November, 1918. The reception of this was such as to encourage the publishers to continue, and the Uniform Edition of his plays began to appear. Within the next ten years ten volumes in all had been published, including the two mentioned, which were reprinted in the Uniform Edition as The Twelve-Pound Look and Other Plays, and The Old Lady Shows Her Medals and Other Plays. In 1928 we had the splendid collected edition in one volume containing all that had appeared in the Uniform Edition and four extra one-act pieces: Half-an-Hour, Seven Women, Old Friends, and Shall We Join the Ladies?

The second year of the War witnessed another of our dramatist's mistakes, and provided one more instance of his limitation. The failure of Josephine had not convinced him that the revue form was either unworthy of his dramatic powers and better left to lesser playwrights, or was one for which his particular gifts were not adapted. Possibly on the theory that the greater includes the less he felt that there was nothing in stagecraft beyond the reach of the author of The Admirable Crichton. With a strange obsession of taste he chose one of the most poorly endowed of 'artistes' for whom to attempt another revue. Mlle. Gaby Deslys had numerous admirers, but her talents were of the thinnest, her successes being chiefly derived from the wearing of monstrous hats and innumerable changes of costume. She was the star of Rosy Rapture, or The Pride of the Beauty Chorus, one of the most mirthless and boring entertainments at which I have ever assisted, as the French say. It was produced at the Duke of York's on March 22nd, 1915. From the moment when the curtain was raised in darkness (someone thumping a log of wood on the stage as the signal) until it mercifully fell upon Gaby Deslys bowing amidst a wagon-load of flowers, which had been handed up in basketfuls from supposed admirers, I can recall nothing that was worth remembering. Mr. Jack Norworthy, an American music-hall comedian of some talent, did his best to give some life to the show, and I think I remember him singing a song of the telephone with the refrain 'Which switch is the switch for Ipswich?' But I have forgotten what Mr. Walbrook recalls: a burlesque of David Copperfield, then being superbly played by Beerbohm Tree and Sidney Fairbrother at His Majesty's. This he says 'had its humours.' And having said so much we shall let the curtain stay down on Rosy Rapture. It was the last of the long and unrivalled series of Barrie plays produced by Frohman, whose death on the Lusitania took place six weeks later. Everybody would have liked to see that historic dramatic partnership end on a note of triumph.

285

BARRIE: THE STORY OF A GENIUS

There was one bright spot on the evening of Rosy Rapture, as another and entirely charming little Barrie piece preceded it. The New Word must have touched the hearts of thousands who saw it afterwards on various repetitions at the Coliseum and elsewhere. The new word was ' 2nd Lieutenant,' and the deftly written sketch showed any British father in the intensely emotional atmosphere of the night preceding his son's departure for the fields of France. The ' fourth wall ' was a fire place, the kerb and fireirons occupying the centre of the stage immediately before the footlights: a ' set ' which only the inventiveness of Barrie could have contrived. The text of The New Word appears in the collected edition of the plays and one can recapture something of the emotions of war-time from it.

On November 19th of the same year another and less noteworthy dramatic sketch, The Fatal Typist, was given at the matinée at His Majesty's in aid of the Australian wounded. It is described by Mr. Walbrook as ' one of the author's practical jokes.' I should be inclined to include The Real Thing at Last, first given at the London Coliseum on February 7th, 1916, in the same category. It was a freakish idea: a burlesque version of Macbeth for which a number of our more celebrated actors were accommodating enough to enter into the fun of the thing and have themselves filmed in the Shakespeare characters. The film was shown with a comic pianoforte accompaniment, and suitable burlesques of the American idea of ' titling,' a good example of which was: ' Dear Macbeth, The King has gotten old and silly. Slay him. Yours sincerely, Lady M.' A further touch of the ridiculous was added by Edmund Gwenn, distinctly overdressed and smoking a large cigar, acting as showman to the film, and maintaining in an exaggerated American accent a running commentary on the scenes as they unfolded.

After this somewhat ineffectual trifling, it was a relief to ardent playgoers to be able to welcome another and more adequate expression of Barrie's dramatic genius in A Kiss for Cinderella, at Wyndham's Theatre, on March 3rd, 1916. Though falling short of his very best this pleasing three-act comedy is a very passable example of Barrie's genius for the theatre. Throughout it there is a delicate play of fancy and a wonderful weaving together of the real and the unreal. It is joyous all through, and there was no better effort in the theatre to lessen the gloom of 1916. Of the pleasantest are one's recollections of Gerald du Maurier as the ' romantical ' policeman and Hilda Trevelyan as Miss Thing (once again issuing from the old font of eternal motherhood), and the hark-back to an old Thrums scene with the little

286

children in their boxes nailed to the wall. Though our thoughts in the second act may have strayed back to Alice in Wonderland, the whole thing was carried off in the essential spirit of Barrie fantasy. New York first saw the play at the Empire on Christmas night, after a week's trial at the Academy, Baltimore.

Shakespeare's Legacy, a dramatic trifle given at Drury Lane on April 13th, 1916, was a contribution to a matinée organized for the purpose of raising funds to help the war work of the Y.W.C.A. I have no note of the exact nature of this sketch, but it is not to be identified with The Ladies' Shakespeare written for Miss Maude Adams in 1914, and first given by her at Hamilton, Ontario, on October 26th of that year. This would appear to have been worked over again as the substance of Barrie's speech to the Stationers' Company on July 3rd, 1925.

The dramatist had apparently got into his stride once more with A Kiss for Cinderella, after three years in which his most notable production had been The Will. For 1917 is another fruitful year, with two absolute masterpieces to his credit and a third short piece that is no unworthy example of his talent. On April 7th, at the New Theatre, The Old Lady Shows Her Medals was given for the first time, with that very talented Scottish actress Miss Jean Cadell as Mrs. Dowey, the charwoman who ' does her bit ' by contriving to ' adopt ' a hefty private of the Black Watch as her son. This little piece is perfect in its masterly blending of humour and sentiment, and although directly inspired by war-time conditions it is difficult to imagine that it can at any time lose its charm, the emotions upon which it plays requiring no temporary circumstances to touch them. In the same bill at the New Theatre was another short piece entitled Seven Women, a brilliant study of feminine character, all seven women being comprised in one, and that one the Leonora who had failed to awaken the sympathy of a London audience in The Adored One. On May 14th, The New Word, Old Friends and The Old Lady Shows Her Medals were all produced at the New York Empire in a special bill for the Stage Women's War Relief.

But the real triumph of the year took place on October 17th when Dear Brutus was first produced at Wyndham's Theatre. There is nothing in our dramatist's theatre more exquisitely perfect than this. There is a deeper depth of meaning in Dear Brutus than in anything else he has written for the stage: the humour is entirely unforced, the sentiment has philosophic war-ranty, and against a background of the most charming but credible fantasy we see evolving something that we can definitely recognize as the inherent destiny of character. Unlike even some of his finest plays it has not a single jarring note, and the interest moves at a crescendo to the curtain of the last act. For artistry in stage effect surely his wonderful first act, with the coming of the magic wood at the end of it, has never been bettered. Gerald Du Maurier had one of his finest parts as Mr. Dearth, the painter, round whom and his wife, and their dream child, the latter so wistfully impersonated by Miss Faith Celli, the tensest moments of dramatic interest revolve. Dear Brutus has been revived several times since its original production, and I remember a very fine performance of Mr. Dearth by H. V. Esmond. In America it was first produced at the Apollo, Atlantic City, December 12th, and moved to the Empire, New York, on the 23rd of the same month.

After so lovely and enduring a gift to the British theatre the dramatist could afford to rest a little before his next high effort, and more than two years went by with nothing but another short piece, A Well-Remembered Voice, which, produced at Wyndham's on June 28th, 1918, and at Parson's, Hartford, U.S.A., on December 30th, concluded his series of one-act war plays. Once again I cannot share the enthusiasm of a critic who describes this as ' enthralling,' but I agree that the acting of Sir Johnston Forbes-Robertson as the father, to whom the spirit of his son lost in the War reveals itself, rather than to his mother or his sweetheart who were using crude spiritualistic devices to ' get through,' left an ' ineffaceable impression.' The piece still reads well in the printed text, but I can find no under-frame of philosophy in its presentation of a very grave subject and the sentimentality of the pass-word in the spirit world whence Dick had that night escaped, ' Love bade me welcome ', not to say the implication that the midnight rule was still rigid there, reacts on the whole with a sense of triviality. The Truth About the Russian Dancers, put on at the Coliseum on March 15th, 1920, need only be mentioned as the hors d'œuvre of the year's banquet—Mary Rose.

The last (we may reasonably hope it is not the final) of Barrie's stage masterpieces was the theatrical event of two continents in 1920. Mary Rose was produced at the Haymarket Theatre on April 22nd, 1920, and the curtain fell on the first night amid scenes of enthusiasm such as had not been witnessed in a London theatre since the beginning of the War. For more than a year this delicately beautiful piece of dramatic invention was superbly played to crowded audiences at the Haymarket by as fine a company of actors as ever came together on the English stage. There was much discussion as to the meaning of the last act of the play in which the ghost of Mary Rose wanders disconsolately about her old home until her actual son, now grown into a burly Australian soldier, sits upon her knee, and lets her take him in her arms for the last time. I have pointed out in another chapter that we shall find the germ of this situation in The Little White Bird, and it is hardly necessary to add that the major idea of the play, the disappearance of Mary Rose on the mysterious island of the Hebrides and her return twenty-five years later unaltered in appearance and in mind, is as old as the hills of dream. It is the theme of James Hogg's Kilmeny and has attracted many another poet. But there could be no greater triumph of dramatic genius than to take these eerie fancies and mingle them in the most convincing manner with living scenes of everyday life. No person of any imagination who witnessed a performance of Mary Rose could fail to be thrilled and impressed by its romantic beauty or to realize that the much discussed ending of the play could tolerate no discussion but merely required a simple surrender to its imaginative beauty. A well-known journalist asked Miss Fay Compton, whose performance of the title rôle has become a tradition of our stage, what she considered was the inner meaning of the part she had played so perfectly. 'I don't know that it has any inner meaning,' she said, or words to that effect, adding ' I just go on and say my words as they appeal to me.' A fine tribute this to the power of the dramatist. Mary Rose was first performed in America at the New York Empire on December 22nd.

Early in 1929 a dramatic recital of Mary Rose was given to the convicts of Parkhurst Prison by Joseph Clark, and one of the convicts, in proposing a vote of thanks to him, said: ' I feel a free man. There will be no prison walls round me to-night; my thoughts will be full of this beautiful play!' Mr. Clark felt deeply touched, and still more so a few days later when the prison governor told him that this man, who was new to prison, had slept soundly that night for the first time since his conviction. Whatever its inner meaning may be, here is remarkable evidence of its emotional appeal.

American audiences enjoyed a Barrie novelty in 1921 which British playgoers have not had the opportunity of sharing: Quality Street turned into a musical comedy. The play certainly lends itself to a musical setting, and it would appear to have had some success in that form. The book was adapted by Ed. Delaney Dunn, the music was composed by Walter Kello, and Phœbe of Quality Street as a title served to distinguish it from the ' straight ' comedy. It was ' tried out ' at Wood's Theatre, Atlantic City, on April 24th, and opened at Schubert's, New York, on May 9th.

Two more first nights remain to be noted, the production of Shall We Join the Ladies? at the opening of the theatre of the Royal Academy of Dramatic Art in Gower Street on May 27th, 1921, and the performance of Barbara's Wedding, a one-act play written in 1915 but remaining unacted until produced by Robert Loraine at the Savoy, on August 23rd, 1927. I make some reference to the latter in a succeeding chapter; it was an event of no importance in the story of the Barrie theatre. Regarding the first-named of these two pieces, we have been asked to believe that it was intended as the first act of a play, the remaining three acts of which had still to be written. This I shall take leave to doubt, because it seems to me improbable that even the genius of a Barrie could have maintained the interest awakened by the first act with any dramatic fitness throughout three more. Rather does it belong to the order of stories that leave their hearers entirely in the air, and have no dénouement because the original proposition would be destroyed in any attempt to carry it to a logical conclusion. There certainly never was a finer first act of any play than Shall We Join the Ladies? but we must remember that it is within the power of many very ordinary dramatists to produce a good first act: the real trouble comes with the third or fourth. Not until January 13th, 1925, was Shall We Join the Ladies? produced in America, where it was first put on at the Empire, New York.

Our chief interest in Shall We Join the Ladies? is the unique-ness of the cast that performed it on its first production. In printing the text of the play in the collected edition the author himself describes it as ' the first act of an unfinished play,' and adds that the circumstance of its original production ' accounts for the brilliancy of the cast, and the brilliancy of the cast excuses the proud author for giving it in full.' Those who saw it after it was put into the evening bill at St. Martin's Theatre, on March 8th, 1922, when Leslie Faber gave an unforgettable interpretation of the character of the monomaniac Sam Smith, the host of the party, will remember that the entire company is discovered seated round a dinner table, and the whole breathless action of the play takes place in the medium of their conversation. The original cast was as follows:

Sam Smith (the host)	.	.	Mr. Dion Boucicault
Lady Jane Raye	.	.	Miss Fay Compton
Mr. Preen	.	.	Mr. Charles Hawtrey
Lady Wrathie	.	.	Miss Sybil Thorndike
Sir Joseph Wrathie .	.	.	Mr. Cyril Maude

THE TRIUMPH OF THE THEATRE

Mrs. Preen	.	.	.	.	Lady Tree
Captain Jennings	.	.	.		Mr. Leon Quartermaine
Mrs. Castro	.	.	.		Miss Lillah McCarthy
Mr. Vaile	.	.	.		Mr. Nelson Keys
Mrs. Bland	.	.	.		Miss Madge Titheradge
Mr. Gourlay	.	.	.		Sir J. Forbes-Robertson
Miss Isit	.	.	.		Miss Irene Vanbrugh
Miss Vaile	.	.	.		Miss Marie Löhr
An Officer	.	.	.		Mr. Norman Forbes
Lucy (a maid)	.	.	.		Miss Hilda Trevelyan
Dolphin (a butler)	.	.	.		Mr. Gerald Du Maurier

In this brief review of sixteen years of Barrie's maturity we have seen his work as dramatist attaining to its highest reach of beauty and falling more than once to a level of mediocrity to which we are almost pained to think he could ever descend, but on reflection we may be inclined to regard this as the saving grace of imperfection that retains him among our human kind and makes us like him all the more that, with his amazing talent for success, he has also shown some redeeming capacity for failure. But what is obvious throughout this chronicle (from which is excluded all reference to a multitude of personal matters that shall engage us presently) is the fact that, in the period under review, the theatre and nothing but the theatre concerned him as an artist. One book only was written by him between 1905 and 1920, Peter and Wendy, published in October, 1911, which was just a re-telling of the Peter Pan story as a gift book for the multitudinous children to whom the seeing of Peter Pan is one of the outstanding landmarks in their lives. Peter and Wendy reads as though Barrie enjoyed writing it as much as anyone will enjoy reading it. More obviously than the play itself Peter and Wendy shows us that its inspiration is just the same as that of Tommy and Grizel: it is a fantasy of motherhood, and I even find the author making Peter say to Wendy when 'he was tingling with life and also top-heavy with conceit,' 'Am I not a wonder, oh, I am a wonder!' The same words were used by Tommy many a year before Peter emerged from the head of his creator, and possibly so long ago as the days of the wash-house drama in Kirriemuir the thought they convey might have occurred to little Jamie Barrie when he felt he was 'getting across' to his juvenile audience. One of his earliest articles in the Edinburgh Dispatch put the question 'Am I a genius?' I do not know the terms in which he answered himself, but who with the record of his achievement in front of him will object to the question being answered with an emphatic 'Yes'?

CHAPTER XIII

THE HERMIT OF THE ADELPHI

1905–1923

HAVING in the preceding chapter outlined the course of Barrie's dramatic work from 1905 until 1920, I now propose to take my reader back again to the beginning of that period and lightly to sketch the events of these years that had no immediate reference to the activities of the dramatist. It may be objected that I have somewhat anticipated events in the title of the present chapter, as several years had to pass before our hermit had established his retreat in the antique quarter of the Adelphi; but before we have gone more than a paragraph or two we shall have his own admission that by 1905 he had 'grown into a hermit,' and for most of the period covered Adelphi Terrace House has been his London home as it is to-day. There he has written several of his best known plays, including such masterpieces as Dear Brutus and Mary Rose, there in his top-floor flat, with its wide windows commanding the most romantic and moving river scene in all the world, he has dreamed some of his loveliest dreams, and at his lonely desk, where the strident noises of the Strand sound faint and far off from that garish theatreland nearby where his own name and the names of his plays are so often seen in gleaming lights to guide his admirers to the theatres of their desire, his magic pen has woven for us so many nights of enchantment. The erstwhile wizard of Thrums has long been the hermit magician of the old Adelphi.

In the Memoirs of Lord Pentland, published in the autumn of 1928, there is a definite statement concerning Barrie and politics which must be held to dispose of what had been at one time a vague rumour, though often subsequently cited as a fact. Towards the end of 1905 it was reported that he was likely to stand as Parliamentary candidate for the Universities of Edinburgh and St. Andrews. The suggestion was that Barrie himself had thoughts of entering Parliament, and had that been true there could have been no seat more suitable for him. His literary admirers did not receive the news of his proposed candidature with elation, feeling that in the almost certain event of his being elected his political duties would go ill with the far more important work to which he was so brilliantly devoting his genius.

At that time it was something of a fashion among prominent men of letters to take up Parliamentary service. Hilaire Belloc was the Liberal candidate for South Salford, to which he was elected in 1906; A. E. W. Mason (perhaps the most intimate of all Barrie's literary friends) at the same election was returned for Coventry; Sir Gilbert Parker had already represented Gravesend for several years, and Barrie's old friend, Sir Arthur Conan Doyle, had unsuccessfully contested Central Edinburgh as Unionist in 1900, and at the 1906 election was rejected by Hawick Burghs as a Tariff Reform candidate. There were other instances of literary men hankering after the dusty arena of politics, but these will serve to show that if Barrie had been similarly inclined he would have been 'in the movement.' It would appear, however, that the initiative in the matter did not come from him, but from one of the many admirers of his work, who happened to be in a position to advance his candidature had the novelist been willing to stand. Lord Pentland (then Captain Sinclair) was a personage of influence with the Liberal leaders, one of the party whips, his wife a daughter of the Marquess of Aberdeen, and he it was who made the proposal to Barrie, as related in the memoir already mentioned. After reflection Barrie wrote to him in December, 1905:

The Universities would have been an ideal seat if I had been able to stand at all, but I am convinced it is wiser I should not. Public life would be too much out of my line. I have grown into a hermit. Politics is a great and a fine calling, but it is not for me. . . . Thank you very heartily. . . . I am with you heart and spirit in the Liberal cause.

This brief note shows that the proposal was none of Barrie's seeking. To a man of his sensitive and conscientious nature it might have been a disaster had he listened to the voice of the charmer and allowed himself to be put forward as a candidate. In striving to perform faithfully his political duties his work as a dramatist would almost certainly have suffered, or in maintaining the latter he would have had to neglect his constituency. Two of the men of letters already named had this experience and voluntarily gave up their political careers rather than endanger their literary work. However well meant the suggestion, it was a thoroughly bad one, and it is reassuring to know that Barrie himself had not seriously entertained it.

He speaks of having become a hermit, but we have seen that in the preceding year he had twice come out of his cell to the great pleasure of discriminating audiences, and although it is true that for a year or two we shall rarely hear of him facing the public, the hermit was no more than a passing phase. In my next chapter we shall witness him so far from his hermitage that he has become as public a character as a member of the Treasury bench.

When he was prevailed upon to unveil the memorial to Mrs. Oliphant, the famous authoress for whom he had always shown so great a regard and who had reciprocated his admiration by writing very charmingly of him at the outset of his career, he was discharging a duty from which he felt he could not shrink. The memorial, which consists of a bronze medallion bust in a green marble setting fixed to the wall of the Albany aisle in St. Giles' Cathedral, Edinburgh, was unveiled on Thursday, July 17th, 1908, and Barrie on the occasion delivered a beautiful speech, entirely worthy of the devoted woman who was being commemorated and of his own literary ideals. The concluding words were especially happy: 'A national monument in this historic pile means that to another of her children Scotland has said "Well done." By your wish—and it is a solemn thought—Mrs. Oliphant joins the great shades who take care of Edinburgh and patrol the city inaudible.' An ironic fate had ruled that the work of collecting the contributions and superintending the provision of the memorial should fall largely upon Dr. J. Hepburn Millar, the brilliant University lecturer whose onslaught upon Barrie and the Kail-yarders has already attracted our attention.

Barrie was back in Edinburgh again in the spring of the following year to attend the graduation ceremony at the University when his alma mater conferred upon him the honorary degree of LL.D. Sir Ludovic Grant was the orator on the occasion, and his eulogy was singularly well phrased. He said:

To speak of the charm of Mr. Barrie's creations is to speak of what every woman knows, of what every man knows, and of what every well-bred child knows. No need for me to enumerate by name the volumes which have flowed with almost annual regularity from the fertile pen of Gavin Ogilvy. May we not hold them as read and re-read? The author has revealed himself as the *vates sacer* of Scottish homely life, the reverent interpreter, whose magic portraiture is potent to invest the lowliest scenes with universal interest. The *Alma Mater* of Scott and of Stevenson delights to reflect that she is also the *Alma Mater* of Barrie, and in proud appreciation of his literary and dramatic work offers her highest honour to her illustrious *alumnus*.

What an effective antidote this, from the spokesman of his old University, to the slashing criticism which one of its lecturers (now its Professor of Constitutional Law) had chosen to print six years before in his Literary History of Scotland!

Soon after receiving this honour from Edinburgh University it was stated that he had been offered a knighthood on the occasion of the Birthday honours, which this year included the names of another famous dramatist, Arthur W. Pinero, and Beerbohm Tree the actor, but that Barrie had expressed his unwillingness to accept it. There was perhaps a sad reason for this decision, as will presently be apparent to the reader without any need for me to point it out.

Meanwhile another of the heroes of his admiration had departed with the death of George Meredith on May 26th, 1909. Barrie had early developed an enthusiasm for Meredith as a novelist —it was from him we may suspect that he acquired the trick of talking about his characters and exhibiting them in the phrases of his admiration rather than allowing them to develop in their own actions and speech—and soon after settling in London he had sought the acquaintance of one whom he looked upon as a master. Meredith, on his part, was no less interested in the personality of the shy young Scotsman, and when increasing infirmity chained the author of The Egoist to his cottage at Box Hill Barrie was a welcome guest there on many occasions. He was one of the privileged few who dined with Meredith on his eightieth birthday. He is credited with a quaint story of his first sight of Meredith, for some details of which he would probably decline to be put on oath. Hoping to catch a glimpse of the sage of Box Hill, the young Scotsman is said to have gone down there, taken up a seat outside the house, and waited. 'Presently,' so the story goes, 'the fine face appeared at the window. Barrie trembled. A few moments and the door was opened. Meredith himself appeared and walked to the garden gate. Consternation seized his admirer and in panic he fled—back to London.'

By the hazard of the alphabet, of the thirty men and women, distinguished chiefly in literature, who signed the congratulatory address to Meredith on his eightieth birthday, the name of Barrie stands first. He had written much concerning the art of Meredith in the days when he still gave some of his energies to literary criticism, but best of all he wrote a profoundly moving and inspiring article on his funeral, beginning with these words: 'All the morning there had been a little gathering of people outside the gate. It was the day on which Mr. Meredith was to be, as they say, buried. He had been, as they say, cremated. The funeral coach came, a very small thing was placed in it and covered with flowers. One plant of the wallflower in the garden would have covered it.' This lovely tribute, which was dated 'Box Hill, May 22,' appeared in The Westminster Gazette of May

BARRIE: THE STORY OF A GENIUS

26th, headed 'Neither Dorking nor the Abbey,' and was afterwards printed as a brochure by Constable & Co., with the title
'George Meredith, 1909, by J. M. Barrie.' It is now one of the
items of Barrieana sought after by collectors on both sides of
the Atlantic.

This year was indeed one of sadness for J. M. Barrie. Few
authors in any age and none in our own have so endeared themselves to their readers. Literary success does not always, nor
often, imply that those who enjoy it find a straight and easy path
to the hearts of their readers, but perhaps the most unusual
feature of Barrie's extraordinarily successful career has been
the way in which the personality of the man has drawn forth
the affection of his literary admirers. It is not too much, therefore, to say that when, on October 13th, 1909, he had to sustain
the ordeal, terrible to one of his extreme sensitiveness, of bearing witness in a case before the President of the Divorce Division,
which resulted in the dissolution of his marriage, he was the
subject of universal sympathy. No good purpose would be served
by dwelling upon this most regrettable but entirely creditable
episode in his life, beyond the simple statement I have made;
but this I would venture to add, that in the later development
of the circumstances which led to so unhappy an ending, the
attitude of the lady, whose highest honour it had been to share
his life for fourteen years, was not altogether unworthy of respect.

In later years that lady, under her maiden name of Mary
Ansell, wrote a little book entitled Dogs and Men, which appeals
to me as a work of haunting charm. It shows high gifts of the
mind, and to all who read it with understanding, in the studied
simplicity of its narrative it sends some other figures to join
the throng of those already haunting the region of the Round
Pond through the creative genius of J. M. Barrie: they come
a little timorously perhaps and wistfully desiring to mingle with
those we have loved so long. Dogs and Men is certainly worthy
of a place among the little books of the heart that we call 'human
documents.'

My tale is still one of loss and severance. An intimate friend
of Barrie's had been Addison Bright, to whom reference has
already been made as the business associate of Miss Elisabeth
Marbury, the dramatic agent. Bright, who at one time had acted
as dramatic critic of The Daily Mail, was no mere agent per-
functorily negotiating the sale of dramatic copyrights; but himself a man of the theatre, competent to advise and to contribute
from his experience to the successful production of the works
of his clients. For years he had been not only the trusted agent

296

WITH HIS OLD MATHEMATICAL MASTER, JOHN NEILSON, AT DUMFRIES,
DECEMBER, 1924

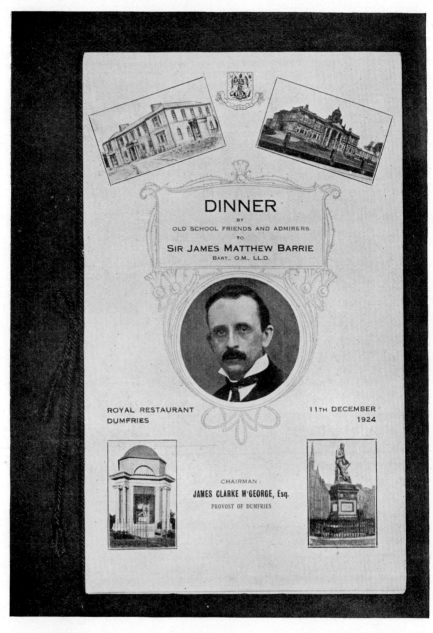

DINNER

BY

OLD SCHOOL FRIENDS AND ADMIRERS

TO

SIR JAMES MATTHEW BARRIE

BART., O.M., LL.D.

ROYAL RESTAURANT
DUMFRIES

11TH DECEMBER
1924

CHAIRMAN :

JAMES CLARKE McGEORGE, Esq.

PROVOST OF DUMFRIES

MENU OF THE BARRIE DINNER AT DUMFRIES, DECEMBER 11TH, 1924

Face page 297

but the friend of J. M. Barrie. And I well remember reading, in The Daily Mail I think, a short note of tribute and farewell written by Barrie himself on the premature death of Addison Bright. It was found soon after his death that the affairs of his dramatic agency, in which Mr. Arthur F. Hardy had joined him as partner a short time before his death, were in a somewhat involved condition, and an extraordinary action relating to this partnership came up for decision in the Chancery Division on February 2nd, 1910. It appeared that £28,000, collected by Addison Bright's agency in his lifetime had not been received by the authors on whose behalf he had acted. Of this sum no less than £16,000 was due to Barrie, £8,000 to Conan Doyle and lesser amounts to E. W. Hornung and Anstey Guthrie (F. Anstey). The whole of these sums was duly paid over by Bright's executors to the playwrights whose works had earned them. It is not suggested, of course, that there might have been any deliberate intention on the part of the dramatic agent to withhold from his friends and clients their full royalties, but that Addison Bright's ill health some time before his death tended to a lowering of his business perception, and made him slack and irresponsible where before he had been competent and reliable.

I have mentioned this remarkable case mainly to show how greatly the dramatist was succeeding in working the gold mine of the theatre. When Barrie gave his evidence before the Chancery judge he said that he knew nothing about the irregularities until the executors asked him to look into his accounts, when he found there was £16,000 odd due to him. 'I am not a business man,' he said, 'and I put the matter into the hands of solicitors, who made a claim for the £16,000, and the executors paid it.' When a writer has attained to such a financial position that the non-payment of £16,000 of the royalties due to him could pass unquestioned, one may infer that the sums he was receiving were immense.

But money was now of small consequence to the most popular dramatist of his time. Success followed success with almost mechanical precision: the worlds of literature and the drama were now completely conquered by him who had once engaged in the rude pantomimics of boyhood in a tiny wash-house, honours of many kinds which in his earlier years looked hopeless of attainment were beginning to heap upon him, he was advancing to a position of fame and fortune almost unexampled in the history of letters. Yet withal a great loneliness was upon him. More than ever he clung to the romantic friendship he had formed with the young members of the Davies family, 'The Five' to whom in after years when only three of them remained alive, he dedicated his final text of Peter Pan. They entered deeply into his life, and helped to keep it sweet and happy with their juvenile enthusiasms.

His old admiration for men of action, especially for those who ventured into strange lands with no motive other than to add to our knowledge of the uncharted places, had drawn him to Captain Robert Falcon Scott, with whom and his gifted wife a warm friendship had been established. On the birth of a son to the Scotts there was no name but Peter for him. Had they been blessed with a daughter she would surely have been called Wendy. When Scott sailed in 1910 on his last ill-fated expedition to the Antarctic he knew that whatever fate had in store for him his little son had a wonderful friend and guardian in him who had given a new charm to the name of Peter. Thus, when early in 1912 the tragic end of Captain Scott stirred the sympathy of the whole world, it meant another old tie of friendship broken and a poignant new sorrow for his friend Barrie, though it brought to him the solace of his duty as guardian to the explorer's son. Two years later, when Charles Turley compiled from Scott's own works a popular account of his life and achievements under the title of The Voyages of Captain Scott, Barrie took advantage of an appropriate occasion to put on record his admiration for the hero who had been his friend, by contributing an introduction to the book.

Among the papers found in Scott's tent where he and his companions so manfully met their cruel fate was a letter addressed to Barrie, which eventually reached his hands, and ten years later in delivering his Rectorial address on Courage to the students of St. Andrews, he took the actual letter with him that his audience might have an opportunity of seeing ' the little filmy sheets.' He said of it:

The writing is in pencil, still quite clear, though toward the end some of the words trail away as into the great silence that was waiting for them. It begins ' We are pegging out in a very comfortless spot— Hoping this letter may be found and sent to you, I write you a word of farewell. I want you to think well of me and my end.' After some private instructions too intimate to read he goes on: ' Good-bye—I am not at all afraid of the end, but sad to miss many a simple pleasure which I had planned for the future in our long marches. . . . We are in a desperate state, feet frozen, etc., no fuel, and a long way from food, but it would do your heart good to be in our tent, to hear our songs and our cheery conversation. . . . Later '—it is here that the words become difficult—' We are very near the end. . . . We did intend to finish ourselves when things proved like this, but we have decided to die naturally without.'

I think it may uplift you all to stand for a moment by that tent and listen, as he says, to their songs and cheery conversation. When I think of Scott, I remember the strange Alpine story of the youth who fell down a glacier and was lost, and of how a scientific companion, one of several who accompanied him, all young, computed that the body would again appear at a certain date and place many years afterwards. When that time came round some of the survivors returned to the glacier to see if the prediction would be fulfilled—all old men now; and the body reappeared, as young as on the day he left them.* So Scott and his comrades emerge out of the white immensities, always young.

So recently as 1928 the house at 174 Buckingham Palace Road which Captain Scott had occupied during his service at the Admiralty, and from which he set out on his last expedition, fell before the 'improver,' making way for a new building. With it went a scene of many happy memories to the guardian of Peter Scott, Barrie having been a constant visitor here by virtue of his interest in the upbringing of the explorer's son, with whom, as indeed with all children, he could play divinely. One of the most exciting games which he invented consisted of flicking up to the ceiling a moistened postage stamp, laid upon a penny, in the hope of getting it to stick there. Barrie held the record of getting three to adhere permanently! These quaint souvenirs of unquenched youth were there when the house-breakers arrived to obliterate all the memories of the place. The London County Council had just arranged to affix a commemorative plaque on the front of the house when they heard that it was coming down.

Lady Scott (a posthumous K.C.B. having been conferred upon the explorer) had in 1922 become the wife of Sir E. Hilton Young, and when they had to move from the old house in Buckingham Palace Road it was a happy arrangement that enabled them to take over in 1927 Barrie's former residence, Leinster Corner, Lancaster Gate. What used to be the dramatist's study there, a lightly-built detached apartment at the other side of the garden, became Lady Hilton Young's studio, so that it is still dedicated to one of the Arts. She is an accomplished sculptor, and a vigorous statue of her former husband which stands in Waterloo Place, facing the Athenæum and not many yards away from the opening scenes of The Little White Bird, is a good example of her work.

What a day June 14th, 1913, would have been for Margaret Ogilvy had she been spared! On that day Barrie's eminence as

* This is the theme of several tales, notably Paul Hervieu's The Secret of the Lower Glacier, and Frederic Jesup Stimson's Mrs. Knollys.

author and dramatist was recognized by the conferring upon him of a baronetcy, so that once again, after many years, Scotland's foremost man of letters was of the same social rank as the great Sir Walter. It is sad to think that all whom he had held ost dear, his mother, his father, his sisters Jane Ann and Sara, his Uncle David, were gone. Only his brother and his family and his youngest sister, Mrs. Winter, remained to rejoice in the honour which the King had conferred upon their family name. The arms which the new literary baronet chose to bear should be noted. Described in the jargon of heraldry these are:

Arms—Barry of six argent and gules, in chief a lion passant guardant counterchanged, and issuant from the base reeds proper.
Crest—An open book amid reeds all proper.
Motto—Amour de la bonté.

An explanation of the above in ordinary language might run thus: A shield divided across into six equal spaces or bars, coloured silver and red alternately, a heraldic lion (not ' rampant ' as might have been expected) occupying the two topmost spaces, being coloured red in the silver and silver in the red space, and rising from the base of the shield a bunch of reeds in their proper colour (green). The crest consists of an open book supported among reeds; the motto ' Love of Goodness.' Obviously the arms come within the punning category in the use of the ' barry ' and the reeds might also conceal another pun, but more probably suggest the source of paper or even the ancient use of reeds for pens. The new baronet himself must have read the heraldic description of his crest with amusement: ' an open book amid reeds *all proper!* '

Some of his more intimate friends took the occasion of his baronetcy to entertain him at an informal club dinner. There was little speaking and no report of the affair was ever made public, but fortunately that genial humorist Pett Ridge has preserved for us what must have been the *bon mot* of the evening as related in his book of reminiscences A Story Teller. 'When I began writing novels,' Barrie remarked, 'people said they were not real novels. When I began writing plays, folk said they were not real plays. I expect men are going about now saying I am not a real baronet!'

Although the pen of the novelist—real or otherwise—had by this time been laid aside and no more books were to come from a literary workshop given over entirely to things of the theatre, there was no lowering of public interest in his published works,

which continued to sell freely and to be almost as widely discussed as the books of the younger men who were coming to the
front. It was seventeen years since Barrie had, somewhat prematurely, attained to the distinction of a 'collected edition,' which
eventually ran to twelve volumes, and now another complete
set of his works was published in a limited impression. The
Thistle Edition of 1896 had been essentially an American enterprise of which Scribners were the moving spirit, the type set up,
the volumes printed and bound in the U.S.A., only a certain
number of copies being issued by Hodder & Stoughton for British
book-buyers.

That edition, it will be remembered, appeared in the year after
the death of the novelist's mother, and it had been the original
desire of the author that it should be known as the Margaret
Ogilvy Edition, but in the end Scotland's floral emblem was
chosen for its title and used as the decorative *motif* in its binding.
The 1913 edition honoured his native town by being called 'the
Kirriemuir.' It was published on both sides of the Atlantic by
his principal British publishers, Hodder & Stoughton, who
now had thriving branches in New York and Toronto; the text
was set up by T. & A. Constable and printed at their Edinburgh
University Press. It consisted of ten volumes, the impression
being limited to one thousand copies, and each set was numbered
and signed by the author. The Kirriemuir Edition includes all
his published works, except his plays, from Better Dead in 1887
to Peter and Wendy in 1911. I note that the copyright of Better
Dead, originally owned by Sonnenschein & Co., had now passed
to George Allen & Co., by arrangement with whom it was included in the Kirriemuir.

The course of my narrative takes me back again to the Barrie
home at Strathview, Kirriemuir. On July 16th, 1914, Death,
who a few years before had become a too familiar visitor there,
knocked at this door again. This time it was the novelist's eldest
brother, Alexander Ogilvy Barrie, who was summoned hence.
Together with his wife and the younger members of his family
he had been living there for some years since his retirement from
his long and honourable service as one of H.M. Inspectors of
Schools. In earlier chapters I have already had occasion to
speak of this remarkable man, and there is not a great deal that
need be added here, though space must be found for some further
personalia relating to him. By all accounts, he bore no close
resemblance to his famous brother: sturdy and well set up, he
belonged to the bearded generation of men. He is everywhere
remembered for his genial demeanour, his bright and ready

conversation. Leaving Dumfries in 1899, he was transferred to the Edinburgh district and was responsible for the schools in the burgh of Leith, a large part of the county of Midlothian and the whole of the county of Haddingtonshire. He continued his onerous duties until 1907, when he retired from the service under the age limit, having held office for fully 36 years. The report for that year of the senior chief inspector for Scotland, from which some of these facts have been gleaned, has this reference to Alexander's work: 'During this long period Mr. Barrie had proved himself an able and efficient officer—sound in judgement, loyal to the department, fair and considerate in his treatment of managers and teachers.' Some time after his retirement he had given up his home at Correnie Gardens, Edinburgh, and removed to Strathview, that house, as I have earlier explained, having become his property after the death of his uncle, Dr. Ogilvy.

If a man may be known by his friends, Alexander Barrie's friendship with Dr. Alexander Whyte was as fine a memorial of his character as any need wish. When Whyte was made Principal of New College, Edinburgh, in 1909 he wrote to Mrs. Alexander Barrie:

I wish your husband had been in the Assembly last week. There is no man I would like to share all this with me more than ' Barrie '. Assure him that his name is written among the deepest in my heart, and indelibly.—God bless you both, and all yours.

Alexander Barrie was laid in the cemetery on the Hill, in the 'lair' alongside that in which his father and mother and several of their children were already at rest, but as became the head of a family a separate memorial stone in the form of a Celtic cross was reared above his grave and for many years no other name but his appeared upon its plinth. It may be accounted to him for happiness that he reached the allotted span and left our world of old beauty just as the clouds of war were about to envelop it. Sorrows were to come to his own family, such as he had never feared, and he was not to be there helping his devoted wife to bear them. From what we know of him, he would willingly have been spared to shoulder that burden had the fates so decreed.

He had a family of six children: two sons and four daughters. Lilian, the eldest, was that Miss Barrie of whom we shall hear more when her famous uncle is induced by her to quit his hermit's cell and go down to Wallasey, to tell the scholars of her school there some charming things about life and character, and incidentally about his talented niece. The elder of the sons and second of the family was Charles David Ogilvy Barrie, born at Dumfries, May 19th, 1881. The career of his uncle was probably the incentive that took Charles into journalism, and although he does not appear to have shared noticeably in his uncle's literary gifts, he was at least a competent newspaper man on the editorial side, making good progress in his profession, and the father of a family, when he answered his country's call by joining the ranks of the 14th London Regiment. The first day of the Battle of the Somme was his day of fate, and the name of Corporal Barrie appeared in the list of those who fell on July 1st, 1916. The third of the family, and the younger son, was William Cowan Ogilvy Barrie (the maternal name was Cowan), born at Dumfries, September 25th, 1882. As a lieutenant in the 1/5 Black Watch he fell fighting at Thiepval, three months after his brother, on October 14th, 1916.

Mrs. Barrie, a woman of strong character, bravely bore these quickly succeeding bereavements. She had the solace that the war, which had robbed her of her sons, at least left her daughters unscathed. Ethel Margaret was the fourth of the family, and became the wife of Canon Philip of the Episcopal Church at Kirriemuir ('We called the episcopal the chapel when I was a boy and I always held my breath as I hurried past it,' Sir James told the London Scots on St. Andrew's Day, 1928), so that she continues the old connexion of her father and his parents with Kirriemuir. The married name of another sister, Dorothy, is Smart, and Mary Cowan, the youngest of the family, is now the mistress of Strathview, where she keeps the hearth warm for those rare days when her uncle the novelist may care to revisit that house of many memories to which he is attached by the strongest ties of family affection and literary travail.

Through the long agony of the war Barrie was always ready to do his bit with his pen or to take active part in the various enterprises set afoot by authors and journalists to help the men in the trenches. At Red Cross sales some of his manuscripts fetched considerable sums when put up for auction. Several of the plays which he wrote in war time may be regarded as contributions to the momentous task of keeping up the national spirit: Der Tag, The New Word and, above all, The Old Lady Shows her Medals occur to the mind. But it required the ingenuity of the author himself to discover that Dear Brutus was a play with a purpose designed to promote Anglo-American friendship and co-operation. The fact that he made this discovery after he had written the play and only when it came to be produced before an American audience makes it the more interesting: it may have been that he builded better than he knew. The disclosure was made by William Gillette, on its production at the Empire Theatre, New York, in this letter from the dramatist which the actor read to the audience:

Dear Brutus is an allegory about a gentleman called John Bull, who, years and years ago, missed the opportunity of his life. The Mr. Dearth of the play is really John Bull. The play shows how on the fields of France father and daughter get a second opportunity. Are now the two to make it up permanently, or for ever drift apart? A second chance comes to few. As for a third chance, who ever heard of it? It's now or never. If it is now, something will have to be accomplished greater than war itself. Future mankinds are listening for our decision. If we cannot rise to this second chance ours will be the blame, but the sorrow will be posterity's.

Mr. A. C. R. Carter, of The Daily Telegraph, made an entertaining addition to Barrieana in that journal of October 13th, 1928, under the heading '"Shakespeare" MS. by Barrie,' which related to an event of ten years earlier. According to this, Christie's, the famous firm of auctioneers, possess a unique souvenir of the Red Cross sales conducted by them during the war to raise funds for helping the wounded. The fourth of these sales took place in 1918 and a copy of the catalogue autographed by the donors of the items enumerated in it, the signatures of the King and Queen heading the list, was presented to the auctioneers. Barrie, who had been one of the most zealous workers in securing gifts of books and original papers from eminent writers, added immensely to the value of this memento by writing in it memoranda of the gifts which the committee for various reasons had declined. Among proffered items were two letters from Queen Elizabeth to the Governor of Fotheringay Castle about the execution of Mary Queen of Scots, one, for publication, 'begging him not to do it,' the other 'marked "strictly private—burn this!" saying that if he does not do it he will be hanged, drawn and quartered.' Then there were four letters from Shakespeare to Lady Bacon. The note on this 'nice clean lot' runs thus:

These letters prove conclusively that Lady Bacon was the real author of the so-called Shakespeare plays. She was ashamed to admit it, and William Shakespeare agreed to father them for £5 apiece. He evidently thought little of them, and in one of the letters he asks Lady Bacon to make it clearer whether Hamlet was really mad. A nice clean little lot.

304

Other gifts refused by the committee were a Receipt to the Publishers for the sum paid for Paradise Lost : £5; the Tub of Diogenes; Canute's chair, from which he rebuked the waves; the identical set of bowls Drake was playing with when the Armada was sighted, 'one chipped'; and, surely hardest of all to reject, a Great Pearl Necklace, 'presented by the babies of Great Britain, each of whom has agreed, in the noblest spirit of patriotism, to present the finest of all pearls—his or her first tooth. This will completely knock out the other pearl necklaces.' The other necklaces were more substantial items strung together from gems which ladies generously gave from their own necklaces, £100,000 being raised from this source alone at the sale.

The war, which had taken away two of his own near kinsmen, also robbed him of one of his most devoted friends, Charles Frohman. So frequent were Frohman's voyages across the Atlantic in the furtherance of his numerous theatrical ventures in New York and London that he had come to be known as 'To-and-Frohman.' On one of these trips he met his death, in company with twelve hundred other innocent souls. 'C. F.' was a fine type of American, a true humanitarian to whom from its start the war was the most horrible thing that had ever happened, cutting athwart all the peaceful ways of life which he loved so well. Like all good showmen, he derived his chief joy from the satisfaction of making thousands of people happy. To diffuse pleasure among the theatre-goers of two continents was his mission, and he pursued it apart from all considerations of fortune, though always striving to make his productions financial successes. His successes greatly outnumbered his failures. His deep faith in the cause of the Allies led him, against the advice of his colleagues, to produce in New York on April 19th, 1915, a war play, The Hyphen, because he felt that the play hit hard at one of the reasons for America's attitude as the aloof spectator of Europe's agony. He smiled at the storm the play provoked. He smiled again twelve days later at those who warned him not to sail for England in the Lusitania. There was still a smile in his heart when that great vessel, six days afterwards, was sinking off the Head of Kinsale and he said to those around him as she slowly heeled over, 'Why fear death? It is the most beautiful adventure of life.' His last brave words were suggested by his beloved Peter Pan, who says 'Death would be an awfully big adventure.' With him went down the brilliant American novelist and playwright who had written The Hyphen, Justus Miles Forman. He was accompanying Frohman as his guest on this fateful voyage for the express purpose of being introduced to Barrie and some of his other English friends.

BARRIE: THE STORY OF A GENIUS

Nobody who reads Marcosson's memoir of Frohman will lay
that volume down before a strong affection has been awakened
for this amazing man who was as fine in his attitude to death as
in all the actions of his life. Here, indeed, Barrie was fortunate
in friendship. ' The men became great pals,' says the biographer.
' They would wander about London, Barrie smoking a short
black pipe, Frohman swinging his stick. On many of these
strolls they walked for hours without saying a word to each other.
Each had the great gift of silence—the rare sense of understanding.'
It is said that Frohman's faith in Barrie was so complete that if
the latter had asked him to produce a dramatisation of The
Telephone Directory he would have smiled and answered with
enthusiasm, ' Fine! Whom shall we have in the cast?' His biographer is probably wrong in saying that Frohman was responsible
for Barrie's first visit to Paris, as we have seen that the dramatist
had visited the Continent and toured in Switzerland years before
he met Frohman, but the spirited account of a visit which Barrie
paid to the French capital is no doubt close to the facts (if we
allow for trimmings) and merits quoting in this place:

Frohman was aglow with anticipation. He wanted to give Barrie
the time of his life. ' What would a literary man like to do in Paris?'
was the question he asked himself. In his usual generous way he
planned the first night, for Barrie was to arrive in the afternoon. He
was then living at the Hotel Meurice, in the Rue Royale, so he engaged
a magnificent suite for his guest. He ordered a sumptuous dinner at
the Café de Paris, bought a box at the Théâtre Français, and engaged
a smart Victoria for the evening.

Barrie was dazed at the splendour of the Meurice suite, but he survived it. When Frohman spoke of the Café de Paris dinner he said
he would rather dine quietly at the hotel, so the elaborate meal was given
up.

' Now what would you like to do this evening?' asked his host.

' Are there any of those country fairs around here, where they have
side shows and you can throw balls at things?' asked Barrie.

Frohman, who had box seats for the most classic of all Continental
theatres in his pocket, said:

' Yes, there is one in Neuilly.'

' All right,' said Barrie, ' let's go there.'

' We'll drive out in a Victoria,' meekly suggested Frohman.

' No,' said Barrie, ' I think it would be more fun to go on a ' bus.'

With the unused tickets for the Théâtre Français in his waistcoat,
and the smart little Victoria still waiting in front of the Meurice (for
Frohman forgot to order the man home), the two friends started for
the country fair, where they spent the whole evening throwing balls
at what the French call ' Aunt Sally '. It is much like the old-fashioned

side-show at an American country fair. A negro pokes his head through a hole in the canvas, and every time the thrower hits the head he gets a knife. When Frohman and Barrie returned to the Meurice that night they had fifty knives between them. The next night they repeated this performance until they had knives enough to start a hardware store. This was the simple and childlike way that these two men, each a genius in his own way, disported themselves on a holiday.

At Barrie's flat in the Adelphi, Frohman was a constant visitor during his stays in London. Here he would ' sit curled up in the corner on the settee, smoking a fat black cigar and looking out on the historic Thames. Here he knew he would not have to talk. It was the place of Silence and Understanding.' When friends come to mean so much to each other as Frohman and Barrie did there is hardly any relationship of blood that can mean more, and with Frohman there went down into the depths something of Barrie's own heart that had been shared by them alone. The beautiful tribute to ' The man who never broke his word,' which Barrie wrote in The Daily Mail, May 10th, 1915, was reprinted at the front of Charles Frohman: Manager and Man, by Isaac F. Marcosson and Daniel Frohman, 1916.

The war was still dragging its woeful course when in May, 1918, Hodder & Stoughton published a set of books that provided a fine example of the mutual friendliness occasionally shown between artists of the pen and more rarely between followers of the other arts. Leonard Merrick is a novelist whom most of his fellow authors had long considered a writer of true distinction, worthy to stand in the front rank of his contemporaries, but whom the general public seemed to pass by in its indiscriminating preferences. A group of his famous admirers agreed to write introductions to what might be called a testimonial edition of his novels, and that to which Barrie stood sponsor was Conrad in Quest of his Youth, one of Merrick's best works. Barrie also contributed about this time to Reveille, a publication edited by his friend and former neighbour in the Adelphi, John Galsworthy. Devoted to the disabled sailors and soldiers, only three parts were published, the end of the war, which came as suddenly as the beginning, also ending the need for such charitable publications. Then again, it was characteristic of Barrie that when Newman Flower in February, 1919, wrote a popular account of Barnardo's Homes to help that most admirable institution, under the title of The Boy Who Did Grow Up, the author of Peter Pan readily contributed an introductory note which no doubt served to widen the appeal of the book. In May of the same year he assisted materially, by writing a preface, to make a success of Miss Daisy Ashford's The Young Visiters, the whole of which some readers were prepared to believe he had written as a literary diversion, but which there is every reason for regarding as a genuine piece of precocity, therein unlike several literary fakes that have been successfully foisted on the public in recent years. A foreword to David Donald's Conversations of Padan Aram (1921) showed that he was still as ready to help in this way as he had been thirty-two years before when he wrote his introduction to Leaves from Logiedale, and he also contributed an introduction to the Comedies of Harold Chapin, that promising young American actor-dramatist who died for England at Loos on September 26th, 1915. Chapin had played in What Every Woman Knows in 1909.

One more tie with the old days of Kirriemuir, Glasgow and Edinburgh was severed, and another of the men whose influence on Barrie's life in the crucial years had been profound passed from the scene on the morning of January 6th, 1921, when Dr. Alexander Whyte died at Hampstead within seven days of his eighty-fifth birthday. Barrie had dined and spent an evening with his old hero at his Hampstead retreat, in Church Row, on his eighty-fourth birthday, and six months later the veteran preacher was amused by the receipt of the following characteristic note concerning one of Whyte's own books which he had sent to his famous townsman .

Many thanks for your book. I have been reading it with much happiness and often, too, with thoughts of the old days when I sat in St. George's. I hope all is well with you and the household despite the rain. To-day I had to mend my umbrella with tin-tacks—a masterly performance. (The fishing will be good in the Prosen this week-end.)

Darlow in his life of Robertson Nicoll prints an interesting letter from the author of An Edinburgh Eleven in connexion with the death of Dr. Whyte. I quote a few lines:

When I read that Dr. Whyte was dead I unearthed, with some difficulty, a copy of that volume [An Edinburgh Eleven] to read what I had written of him so long ago, and to my bewilderment I find that he was not one of the eleven, though his name occurs. How that came about I do not know—he might so well have been their captain, he or Masson, for those were certainly to me the two great names in Edinburgh at that time.

It had always seemed to me an odd thing that Whyte was omitted from An Edinburgh Eleven, especially as he was the subject of Gavin Ogilvy's first contribution to The British Weekly. To keep his team number he would have had to omit one of his professors if Whyte went in, or perhaps to sacrifice Joseph Thomson, the explorer, and the last named being a newcomer in his gallery of heroes possibly he could not bring himself to eject him even for Dr. Whyte. More likely it was some quite temporary reason that led to the omission, or it may have been that the author was unable to satisfy himself that The British Weekly sketch was sufficiently worthy of its subject to bear reprinting. Whatever the reason, the fact is curious.

When he was writing those sketches over the name of Gavin Ogilvy, he could little have expected to see himself one day at the apogee of his literary career admitted a member of the most exclusive company of distinguished Britons. The Order of Merit was not instituted until 1902, but by reason of its being limited to twenty-four members, though taking no precedence over any of the other Orders, it had immediately acquired distinction, and the insignia which George Meredith had been proud to wear, and John Morley and Thomas Hardy, was the right of James Barrie from January 2nd, 1922, when he was admitted to the Order. The conferring of this honour upon him gave general public satisfaction, and to the dramatist himself it must have been a source of proper pride that he had been thought worthy to share this distinction with the two men of letters whom above all he had loved and admired.

We are now well into what one might call his gathering years, in the double sense that while he is advancing into his sixties the years are also bringing high honour and increase of public affection. No man of the pen in our time has had richer harvest of his own sowing. That lucky star I wrote of in my earlier chapters may have once for a little been occluded but it is shining still with no lessening ray.

Comes yet another of his great days in this same year: it is May 3rd, 1922, and he is giving the customary address at St. Andrews University, of which he had been elected Rector. The occasion was one of great distinction, as with Sir James Barrie a number of others very eminent in their several ways were being honoured by the University. Ellen Terry was there to receive the honorary degree of LL.D., and Earl Haig as Chancellor, but on the Rector's friends Thomas Hardy and Robertson Nicoll the degree had to be conferred in absence. The last named wrote to Barrie to say that he had set his heart upon being among his audience on this occasion, which he felt sure would be historical. He added ' this is the only function I ever regretted being absent from.'

BARRIE: THE STORY OF A GENIUS

None of Barrie's public speeches has been more frequently quoted from than this Rectorial address. It was a great and brilliantly successful effort. The theme was Courage, and that is the title under which it was afterwards printed in booklet form by Hodder & Stoughton and dedicated 'To the Red Gowns of St. Andrews.' Especially was it noteworthy for introducing us to the real Barrie. Until it had been delivered we were all under the impression that Barrie was just a remarkable man of genius. But we then learned that he was really a dual personality and, most remarkable of all, the Barrie part of him was the hard-headed man of the world, the genius who wrote those eerie plays and was for ever playing hide and seek with the angels was McConnachie. All this goes ill with Barrie's confession ' I am not a business man,' and had he told us that the practical part of him was McConnachie we had found belief the easier: indeed, at least two of his literary admirers have read the St. Andrews speech to so little purpose that they have written of McConnachie in these very words!

It would have been no proper Barrie speech had it not been shot through with delicate strands of humour. ' A good subject for a Rectorial address would be the mess the Rector himself has made of life.' Who before has ventured such a phrase on so grave an occasion? It belauded Youth and deplored the burden which Age had put upon Youth in the Great War. ' We told Youth, who had to get us out of it, tall tales of what it really was and the clover beds it would lead to.' There were many fresh aphorisms in the speech and many an old truth restated in an arresting way. ' Never ascribe to an opponent motives meaner than your own ' is a good one.

Here is a penetrating comment on the elder statesmen who had the fate of Youth in their hands too long during the years of war:

Another sure way to fame is to know what you mean. It is a solemn thought that almost no one—if he is truly eminent—knows what he means. Look at the great ones of the earth, the politicians. We don't discuss what they say, but what they may have meant when they said it. In 1922 we are all wondering, and so are they, what they meant in 1914 and afterwards. They are publishing books trying to find out, the men of action as well as the men of words.

He was doubtful if we had learnt the lessons of the war, and feared that we were struggling back into the old grooves—a fear to which he might have given even more emphatic expression a few years later.

310

From the life of Burns he had some apt illustrations to warn and encourage youth. ' The greatest Scotsman that ever lived wrote himself down a failure,' he said. And he cheered the young Red Gowns by telling them that when they reached the evening of their days they would realize that we are all failures, at least all the best of us.

If you want to avoid being like Burns there are several possible ways. Thus you might copy *us*, as we shine forth in our published memoirs, practically without a flaw. No one so obscure nowadays but that he can have a book about him. Happy the land that can produce such subjects for the pen.

But don't put your photograph at all ages into your autobiography. That is a tragic mistake. My Life; and What I Have Done with It. That is the sort of title, but it is the photographs that give away what you have done with it. Grim things these portraits; if you could read the language of them you would often find it unnecessary to read the book.

Henley and Stevenson he offered as examples of Courage; Meredith and Hardy also. ' The pomp and circumstance of War will pass away,' he said, ' and all authors now alive may fade from the scene, but I think the quiet figure of Hardy will live on.'

But the richness of this great speech is such that no quotation short of reproducing the whole can represent it and there can hardly be any admirer of Barrie who has not long ago familiarised himself with it. If there be any such, he had better make good this omission forthwith.

How little we should accept any of Barrie's statements about himself as bearing strict relationship to fact is seen in his announcement at the end of his Rectorial address that it was his ' first and last public appearance.' Had McConnachie said so we should have had to take him at his airy word, but his practical little partner could not get away with it so easily. We all knew it was not his first appearance; that it was no trembling tyro in public speech who faced the Red Gowns of St. Andrews; and so far from being his last it was but the beginning of a new chapter in his life, during which he was to appear time and again in public and never without delighting and edifying his audiences.

It was in May that the Rectorial address was published as a booklet, and one of the first things its author did was to send a copy to Robertson Nicoll inscribed ' To W. R. Nicoll from his affectionate friend J. M. Barrie,' which brought a grateful letter of thanks from the recipient. ' What a long journey we have had together! And if the end for me is approaching yet I look back on the past with great thankfulness, and one of the most thank-worthy things is my association with you, which has always been a source of much happiness and pride to me, and which is now crowned by your gift.'

The sweet of the year had just been tasted in 1923 when for Barrie and many another friend of his it was dashed with the bitter of Nicoll's death. That extraordinary man, one of the frailest creatures physically who ever achieved an immense body of literary and journalistic work, had reached his seventy-second year, and only for a little over a year before the end had he ceased to maintain his old high average of weekly writing: an average which for freshness, force and felicity has never been matched by any other journalist. To me the surprising and happy thing was that Nicoll's poor health had served him well enough to carry him beyond the allotted span, him who in his early manhood and through most of his life seemed fated to go down before the first blast of winter. Fourteen or fifteen years before his death he used to talk to me about his intention of retiring. 'When I am well enough off to stay here (at Bay Tree Lodge) and live in my present state of comfort without the need to earn any more money, I shall retire,' he said; but I knew he was only amusing himself with the prospect, and that he would be found at his task so long as he was able to sit at his desk in that fireside corner of his great study at the top of his house, where even in the height of summer he kept a blazing fire and his visitors had to stay as distant as possible from his end of the apartment to escape its heat. 'I am just a salamander,' he would say as you moved your chair still further away. Having already written so much about Nicoll in these pages, I need add but little more about the man and his friendship with Barrie, but in the tribute which the latter wrote in The British Weekly at the time of Nicoll's death, and from which I have already quoted, there is a phrase that tells more about him than a whole column might reveal: ' He was so fond of books that I am sure he never saw a lonely one without wanting to pat it and give it sixpence.' Nicoll would have chuckled could he have read that.

Barrie's last letter to his old friend was written on April 5th when Nicoll lay critically ill on the bed of sickness from which he never rose again, his death taking place exactly a month later. It was a letter of tenderest sympathy, beautifully phrased. 'One thing that certainly has not changed in me, nor, I am sure, in you, is our old affection.' The writer contemplates in his mind's eye the two of them embarking once more aboard their lugger

SIR JAMES BARRIE AS D.C.L. AT OXFORD UNIVERSITY   [*Photopress*

Nov 4 1927

Dear Mr Walsh,

Please let the fellow within tell you
that he has been having some very happy
hours over "The Key above the Door". Indeed
I could put it more strongly, for I can
almost assume invalid rather thrilled that
such a fine yarn should have come out of
the heather. I felt like a discoverer too,
as I alighted on it by accident and without
any anticipation of the treat that was in store.
I am enamoured of your work and slip to
give you these thanks.

Yours sincerely

J.M. Barrie

Specimen of Barrie's Left-hand Writing
His letter to Mr. Walsh, the author of The Key above the Door,
referred to in page 320.

for the U.S.A. 'Again I see us driven from place to place as your room became uninhabitable through the size of the Sunday editions in it.' The dying man must have been greatly cheered in his last days by this final avowal of feelings of personal affection unaltered after two score years, though there never was a moment in that long span of time when a cloud of misunderstanding came between them.

In his later years Nicoll made some odd friends, evincing a desire to get outside his own world of books and religion in these acquaintances. Mr. Harry Preston we know as the friend of princes and pugilists, but less as the friend of religious authors. Nicoll was a frequent visitor at one of the two hotels managed by Mr. Preston in Brighton, and to my own knowledge he was very appreciative of the comfort and attention he received there, where he always went when he felt the need for the treatment of 'Dr. Brighton.' In his Memories, published in 1928, Mr Preston had some notes on both of these friends, Nicoll, I should suspect, having first introduced him to Barrie. Of Nicoll he says that he was one of the hardest workers he had ever met. 'I enjoyed his friendship for twenty years. He was a great talker. When he came down to stay with me he always brought his secretary, and spent most of the time dictating articles: he called this "coming down for a rest." He was devoted to Sir James Barrie and enjoyed talking about him. He thought that Barrie spoke as well as he wrote.' Concerning the dramatist, Mr. Preston has this to tell us:

Sir James Barrie invited me to dine at Brooks's Club one night. It was an enchanting little dinner. Candles gleamed on the celebrated silver plate. Afterwards, we went upstairs to smoke, and together we looked through some of the old Club Chronicles.

We all went back in a cab afterwards to Sir James's apartment overlooking the river on Adelphi Terrace. He took us from room to room, switching the electric light on as we entered and off as we passed out. There was one room like a ship's cabin, from the windows of which we looked out on the nocturnal river. We wound up a very happy evening, I remember, playing billiards, and talking mightily of men and things.

Barrie as a member of the exclusive Brooks's, that ancient haunt of Whigs, seems something out of place, but he has been a member of many clubs and coteries in his time in addition to the Athenæum, and is still on the list of the Reform Club, though few can remember when he was last seen there. Least of all do we associate the hermit habit with membership of Brooks's. But the long years in which he had clung to it are ending; in our next chapter we shall see the hermit boldly quitting his Adelphi cell and showing himself in his walks abroad to all sorts of people, breaking his vows of silence, and letting his voice be heard above the din and confusion of the many that clamour for attention in our time. For when he is minded to do so all the world is willing to listen.

Mr Barrie in the Chair

BARRIE'S CALIGRAPHY: RIGHT-HAND SPECIMEN

Facsimile, on slightly reduced scale, of opening lines of article by Barrie in National Observer, February 3rd, 1894, reproduced from The Evening Times, Glasgow. See illustration facing page 313 for specimen of his left-hand writing.

CHAPTER XIV

THE HERMIT WALKS ABROAD

1924 and after

ALTHOUGH we shall now see our hermit making frequent sallies from his retreat and find him often where the 'spot light' shines, there is still something cloistral about him; he is less to be looked upon as having overcome his old reticence and come out at long last into the rough-and-tumble of social London, than as clinging still to his lonely and contemplative habit of life, but in these later, mellow years displaying at times a new readiness to mingle with his fellows, to be jostled in the crowd. The Hermit walks abroad!

The passing of Robertson Nicoll must have been as poignant a sorrow as any that Barrie had to bear: the sense of personal loss as keen as in the case of Frohman's death, though the tragic circumstance was absent. On the day he heard of Nicoll's death he could not fail to take a journey back into memory's domain. A still farther journey into his own past he had to make in the following year. On the night of February 27th, 1924, he spoke to the girls of Wallasey (Cheshire) High School, where his niece, Miss Lilian K. Barrie, was then headmistress, and again towards the close of the same year when Dumfries honoured itself by honouring him with the freedom of that ancient town, where his happiest schooldays were passed.

At Wallasey he said some pointed things about English education in a jesting way, and his speech must have been as great a success with Miss Barrie's scholars as it was with the newspapers, which could not have made more out of it had it been an important pronouncement by the Prime Minister; indeed, Barrie by now had come to rank with those public speakers of whom the daily Press of London and the provinces gives full reports in the first person instead of short summaries in the third. I can call to mind no man of letters in our time, or indeed at any time since the daily Press became a national institution, to whose public utterance this consideration has been shown. Whenever Barrie chose, within the last ten years, to speak in public on any subject the reporters had instructions to take him down verbatim, and the Press agencies telegraphed full accounts of his remarks to their subscribing journals. No wonder, for most of these speeches have been practically 'free copy' from a master humorist and inspired commentator on the spirit of the age.

There was much that was pure Barrie in this address at Wallasey, especially his sly digs at the famous public schools of England. A Something is acquired by the scholars in these schools ('not scholarship—pooh'!) which nobody seems able to define or to show how it is acquired. If it is so well worth having that persons everywhere are seeking it for their sons, he thought that some slabs of this Something ought to be made available for the boys outside, who have meanwhile to get along with the Something Else. But he addressed himself particularly to the girls, and spoke with enthusiasm of the usefulness of such schools as that over which Miss Barrie was presiding in securing opportunities for them. The new sense of independence which the higher education is bringing to the young women of our country 'ought soon to give them a more serene look.' He then went on to say:

I remember being in Paris on the night of the Armistice, and I think the most wonderful sight I have seen in this world was the changed appearance of the women as they realized that the black years had come to an end. No Cinderella ever looked more different after she was dressed by her god-mother. 'It's over,' was the universal cry— nothing boastful, just a shining thankfulness.

Such schools as yours are a bursting of light through the gloom of the past. Never again will it be impossible for a girl, poor or rich, to adorn herself in the fair garments of learning. 'It's over, the dark days are over,' you can cry at last.

Well, that is going too far, but you can at least say 'It has begun to be over.' It will largely depend on you and myriads like you—the young women of tomorrow—when it is to be completely over.

I should like to give you a motto, something to strive for. I should like to see it blazoned over the entrance to your school, the words, 'That Every Child born into the British Empire should get an Equal Chance.' That will need some doing.

But the most fruitful excursion into his own past was made by Barrie when he went back to what he used to call his 'jumping-off place for England,' to receive the freedom of Dumfries. This was presented to him on the afternoon of December 11th, 1924, and his burgess ticket stated that it was given 'in token of the admiration and gratitude of the citizens for the great gift of literature and drama which, by his genius, he has given to the world, and of their pride that here he spent the best of his youth, and that his old school, the Academy of Dumfries, is honoured in her son.'

I have already made such inroads upon this speech to enrich my earlier chapters that hardly anything remains in it to be quoted here. Of all the speeches he has made in public this, from the biographer's point of view, has the most plums in it. Next to his great address on Courage it ranks as the best of his achievements in oratory. There is, however, one more passage that I must filch from it concerning Burns. I quote from The Times report:

I thank you humbly for the great honour given me by inscribing my name in an illustrious roll, in some cases so illustrious that it is almost strange to think that they have all to take the kerb to make way for an exciseman. Among them belted earls and a' that, such as he liked when the wind was in the east to pour a molten fire upon, but every one of them now, we may be sure, glorying chiefly in being burgesses of Dumfries, because he was one also. One-half of Burns we can all fathom, for he was so Scotch that he was, and is, our blood relation, the one who lived more vividly than the rest. He was so frank about himself that we know that flame of life as we don't know even Dr. Johnson. All the miseries of him, his misdeeds, his follies, we understand, as we know some loved and erring son with whom we have sat up all night in the fields. That is the mortal part of him, which is ours. There is also the immortal part, to which we don't belong, the part that is now a walnut tree for all the world. The errors and woes of Burns are, perhaps, too much harped upon. In his life even he, too, had his walnuts, and by all the gods, he could crack them. To know how best to crack your walnuts! There have been many definitions of genius; I offer you that as another one.

The references to walnuts and the walnut tree arose from the happy use of an old Spanish proverb, 'God gives us walnuts when we have no teeth to crack them,' on which the speaker played most effectively throughout his address. And it should be added that at this time the old story about Barrie writing a play on Burns was revived. He may have entertained the idea at some time or other, but I doubt if he ever made a beginning upon it. Like his great novel about Mary Queen of Scots, it remains one of his 'enchanted cigarettes.'

His visit to Dumfries enabled him to renew many old associations, especially that with Mr. John Neilson, his mathematical master at the Academy, who was happily still alive at the age of 87 to take his place on the platform beside his one-time pupil, and that with a companion of his Edinburgh college days, Mr. James Geddes, solicitor, one of the most highly respected of

Dumfriesians, who took active part in the organization of the dinner given to the new burgess by his 'Old School Friends and Admirers,' on the evening of December 11th. The toast of 'Sir James M. Barrie' was proposed by that veteran of medicine Sir James Crichton Browne, then in his eighty-fourth year, who twenty years before Barrie had also been a Dumfries academical and an alumnus of Edinburgh University. 'I shall probably ask you to say a few words—something bright and sparkling,' was the tag from The Admirable Crichton printed under the entry of this particular item in the toast list, and Barrie in his reply did not disappoint his audience.

Altogether this was one of the red letter days of his life, yet not without its undertone of sadness, to which he made reference at the outset of his speech, when he remarked that the burgess ticket certainly did not make him feel young. 'Too many loved ones who walked Dumfries in my time will not pass this way again,' he said, 'among them the brother who was far more fitted than I for the noble compliment you have paid me.'

After these two brilliantly successful appearances of 1924, Barrie had again to wrap his hermit's cloak around him and keep out of sight of the numerous institutions, social and philanthropic, that would have had him as the star attraction of their annual gatherings. It had long been evident to those who had followed his career that his disinclination to speak in public arose from no lack of confidence in his own ability as an after-dinner orator, but as he would never trust himself to the 'inspiration of the moment' (which Lewes said was like trusting to a shipwreck for your first lesson in swimming), and took immense pains to make each speech a finished composition, he wisely shrank from accepting any engagement that did not give him an opportunity of saying something he particularly wanted to say to the world at large or advancing some cause with which he was in sympathy. So, for a time, many applicants for his presence at their gatherings had to be content with a polite negative. Indeed, he gave it out that he was to speak no more in public. He kept his word—for about two years, emerging again in 1926 when the claims of the Printers' Pension Corporation could not be resisted, but before then he had made, on July 3rd, 1925, a semi-public appearance, when he was elected an Honorary Freeman and Honorary Liveryman of the Stationers' Company along with the Earl of Balfour and Rudyard Kipling. All three of them had to make brief speeches at the luncheon at the Stationers' Hall and the corporation thought the occasion so noteworthy that they issued in 1926 a finely printed booklet entitled An Historical Event at the

Stationers' Hall, containing a record of the proceedings and the speeches of the distinguished liverymen.

His speech at the Printers' Pension dinner, on November 16th, 1926, added greatly to the gaiety and the success of that gathering. Major J. J. Astor, M.P., chief proprietor of The Times, presided and there was a very distinguished company of speakers and guests. Barrie's was the speech of the evening. He had to reply for Literature and the Press, a toast that had been proposed by the Rt. Hon. Winston Churchill. This was, I think, the first occasion on which he also had to face the microphone. His remarks were largely of his 'let's pretend' variety. He started by pretending to be an 'interesting octogenarian,' but soon found himself, as Shaw might have said, back to Methuselah, recalling comic encounters with Napoleon to the entire satisfaction of his audience, as The Times report of his speech is peppered with 'laughter' and 'loud laughter.' His closing reference to the profession of letters was amusingly phrased but obviously sincere:

All, I think, is very well with Literature, especially with the young authors, from whose looms comes much brave literature, devised by cunning hands, women's equally with men's. There is no question whether a woman is worthy of a place in our Cabinet. Those young authors! All hail to them! Happy they! Multitudinous seas incarnadine boil in their veins. They hear the thousand nightingales which we once thought we heard. They have a short way with the old hands, but in our pride in them we forgive them for that. Perhaps they sometimes go a little to excess, treating even God as if He were, shall we say, the greatest of the Victorians.

Major Astor had also to preside this same year over the annual festival dinner of the Newsvendors' Benevolent and Provident Institution at the Hotel Victoria, London, on November 8th, 1926, and had the satisfaction of announcing that Barrie had presented the complete holograph manuscript of his war play The Old Lady Shows Her Medals to be auctioned for the benefit of the institution. The letter with which he accompanied the gift Barrie suggested should be presented to the purchaser of the manuscript, who was announced as Mr. Walter T. Spencer, of 27, New Oxford Street, and the price paid 325 guineas. The letter, which was read out to the gathering, was as follows:

Dear Major Astor,

If the enclosed suits your purpose for the Newsvendors' Benevolent and Provident Institution, you are very welcome to it. To help in the smallest way the charity that was a favourite child of Charles Dickens —that is very pleasant to any author.

BARRIE: THE STORY OF A GENIUS

Should this manuscript find a purchaser, please break the information to him that soon after The Old Lady Shows Her Medals was written my right hand (probably horrified at the sight of my caligraphy) gave out, and I have ever since had to write with my left, to the joy of my correspondents. Indeed, you had better present this note to him, to show him that in one way I write better now that I write worse.

He will wish that my right hand had given out sooner.

Yours sincerely,
J. M. BARRIE.

In the following year, on June 7th, Major J. H. Beith ('Ian Hay') told the Cambridge Union Debating Society that Barrie had confessed to him he had written that 'eerie, drearie bit, Mary Rose' with his left hand, and that 'there are things that come down your left arm that never come down your right.' He had always been ambidextrous, but the odd thing was that when he was attacked by neuritis in the right arm he wrote a neater and more legible script with his left hand than he had ever written with his right. A good example of his left hand caligraphy was widely circulated this same year in the form of a letter which he had sent to the young Scottish author Maurice Walsh, whose novel The Key Above the Door, published by W. & R. Chambers, Barrie had just been reading. This letter is worth putting on record as being typical of many written by him to encourage young authors such as he had spoken of with so much sympathy at the Printers' Pension dinner. From his earliest days of literary fame he was always ready to help the newcomers. No other author of established reputation has shown himself more eager to recognize the merits of his contemporaries both before and after they have made their way. The letter ran thus:

Dear Mr. Walsh,

Please let a fellow author tell you that he has been having some very happy hours over The Key Above the Door! Indeed, I could put it more strongly, for I lay a-bed a semi-invalid, rather thrilled that such a fine yarn should have come out of the heather. I felt like a discoverer too, as I alighted on it by accident and without any anticipation of the treat that was in store. I am enamoured of your book and stop to give you three cheers.

Yours sincerely,
J. M. BARRIE.

Another little act of graciousness was recorded of him about the same time. On a night of June, 1927, he was dining in the restaurant of the Berkeley Hotel, in the room long noted for its

320

famous silver frieze, which was designed in the 'fifties and shows in high relief, modelled with spirit, a succession of sporting scenes, such as pig-sticking, ferreting, hare-netting and wild duck-driving, against a background of trees. The manager mentioned to him that this frieze was doomed by the impending extension of the room and a new scheme of decoration. The dramatist urged that it should not be broken up, ' one can't be ruffled or out of patience when one can look on a picture like that,' he said. As a consequence it was decided not only to save this piece of old Victorian decoration, but to reproduce a continuation of the design in the new part of the restaurant.

There would be no difficulty in giving many other instances of the very practical expression of his sympathy with deserving persons and things inanimate, the latter being to him, from his old habit of thought, instinct with personality. I am sure that he would just as readily have patted that silver frieze, if he could have reached it, as he said Robertson Nicoll would have patted any lonely book. But hardly anything would be more distasteful to him than to find any of his good deeds emerging into the light. I feel, however, that I may venture to mention an incident of which I was informed by one who overheard the words that mattered. At a select dinner to a certain literary dignitary, not long since dead, Barrie was a guest, and my informant was speaking to him when a gentleman unknown to either was seen anxiously waiting for an opportunity to have a word with Barrie. This my friend made possible by stepping aside. The gentleman introduced himself and spoke with great earnestness and appreciation of what Barrie had done to start some young man, to whom the stranger was related, on the road to success. The benefactor was ill at ease as he listened, and all that he could say was ' Oh, I liked the laddie.'

On the eve of 'Lord's,' July 7th, of this year, Barrie addressed the First Hundred at Eton, as the outcome of 'a sort of challenge' made to him in a speech by the Provost at luncheon there on June 5th. He had been challenged to disprove that 'James Hook, the pirate captain, was a great Etonian but not a good one.' He began a lengthy and carefully prepared discourse on this intriguing topic with: 'Now in my opinion Hook was a good Etonian though not a great one, and it is my more or less passionate desire to persuade you of this—to have Hook, so to speak, sent up for good—that brings me here this afternoon in spite of my better judgement.' The whole fantasy was carried out mainly in a solemn imitation of a biographical study with hilarious passages of exaggeration. The complete text of the address is given in

The Times under the heading 'Captain Hook at Eton,' with no hint as to how it was received.

Although he was now giving no new works to the stage, 1927 was to prove one of the most interesting of his later years in the number of theatrical events associated with his name. In January of the preceding year The Admirable Crichton had been performed by a cast composed of the children of famous players on behalf of the Cheyne Hospital for Children, and on January 11th, 1927, a similar matinée was given at the Savoy, the play chosen on this occasion being Quality Street. The performance was described as 'a delicious miniature of the original masterpiece, and the admirable elocution and extraordinary sense of all that constitutes "finished" acting by the young players was a joy to behold and hear.' These matinées were charming tributes to the esteem in which the theatrical world held the dramatist, to appear in one of whose plays had long been regarded as an honour by most of our leading actors and actresses. Here the young folk, to whose everlasting joy he has devoted one of his finest achievements, had an opportunity of showing him what children could do as interpreters of his mature art, and many of those juvenile performers will no doubt make names for themselves on the stage within the next decade.

In August London playgoers had the now rare privilege of seeing a new Barrie piece. Since Mary Rose had come, on April 22nd, 1920, as the crowning triumph of the dramatist, there had been nothing new from him excepting only the slight piece Shall We Join the Ladies? in the summer of 1921. The new Barrie play of 1927 was really an old piece of dramatic work written in 1915 and familiar to all who had read his plays in the volume Echoes of the War, published in 1918. Barbara's Wedding was produced at the Savoy Theatre by Robert Loraine on August 23rd, as a front piece to Strindberg's tragedy The Father. The fame of its author was responsible for the numerous lengthy criticisms of the playlet, which, had it been the work of an unknown dramatist, would have been dismissed in many cases with a short paragraph where a column of critical analysis was given to it. It was described by one competent critic, James Agate, as a 'lugubrious trifle,' and the truth is that Barbara's Wedding is the least satisfactory of Barrie's war-time plays, wherein that nice balance of sentiment, invention and actuality, which had characterised nearly every dramatic composition of its author since he had overcome the weaknesses of The Professor's Love Story, was temporarily lost. It reflected something of the excess of sentimentality which the circumstances of 1915 produced.

322

No doubt the little piece had long attracted so fine an emotional actor as Robert Loraine because of the possibilities which he thought he saw in the character of the old Colonel, who fought in the Crimea and whose tottering mind in the days of the Great War makes him live again in a dream world of the past; but good though his performance would appear to have been it was, in the judgement of the critic above mentioned, 'something marred by the fact that the old gentleman had the full round voice of a sergeant-major on parade.' There seems no doubt, however, that the little play did give satisfaction to the Savoy audiences, who were indifferent to the opinion of the critics that its effects of sentiment were achieved by methods too direct.

If there was a lingering doubt as to the wisdom of putting this war-time trifle on the stage, there was nothing but enthusiasm for the production in French of The Old Lady Shows Her Medals, which took place at the Comédie Française on October 19th of the same year. This was a signal honour, Barrie being the first British dramatist to have had a play produced at the classic theatre of France during his life-time. There was a further circumstance about the production peculiarly French. M. Fernand Nozières, the French playwright, had suffered a rebuff at the hands of the British censor, who refused permission for the London production of his play La Riposte, so he took an 'exquisite revenge' by translating the little Barrie piece, which was presented under the title of La Vieille Maman. Professor Lyon Phelps, of Yale, who saw the representation at the Comédie, described it as a 'stunning performance.' He wrote:

The old women were perfect; and their conversation delighted the audience. The big Highland soldier was clad in the appropriate Highland costume, and you soon forgot he was speaking French, because his acting was so absolutely convincing. Although it was midnight when the curtain fell, because a long French play had preceded the one by Barrie, nobody seemed to leave the auditorium. The audience stood up and, with tears on their faces, shouted and cheered as the actors were recalled again and again.

Mr. John Pollock, the Paris correspondent of The Morning Post, attended the fourth performance of La Vieille Maman, and his description of the event is so enthusiastic that I must add it to that of Professor Phelps. The audience had 'coughed steadily' through both of the native French plays which preceded Barrie's, but—

From the moment the curtain went up on La Vielle Maman to its fall, there was not one cough in the whole packed house, and at its

323

fall there was scarcely one dry eye. The intensity of silence during the last scene, where the Old Lady, without one word, lays out the uniform of her son in the spirit, fallen in *her* war, was something rarely to be experienced, and the storm of enthusiasm at the end rarely to be heard. Such is the effect of Sir James Barrie's genius, the only playwright of our day who can draw true tragedy out of everyday life, on the most traditionally French of French audiences. It is one of which all lovers of English drama should be proud. The Old Lady is destined to show her medals long and gloriously at the Comédie Française.

Here indeed was a dazzling triumph for the laddie of Thrums, who first started his theatricals in that lowly wash-house at the Tenements: to take his place in the foremost theatre of the world, on the classic stage of Molière! But it was by no means his first appearance as a dramatist before a Paris audience, The Admirable Crichton, translated by M. Alfred Athis, having been produced at the Antoine some years before by Gémier, who played the butler; nor was it the first time the Old Lady had shown her medals in France, as Signora Emma Grammatica, the celebrated Italian actress, had taken the part of Mrs. Dowey at a representation of the play in Italian at the Théâtre Edouard VII in 1927. And, as we have already heard, Peter Pan (in English) had also been produced in Paris as far back as 1908, and proved a costly failure for Frohman.

Unlike the plays of his friend Bernard Shaw, with their metallic brilliance and their appeal to the intellect rather than to the heart, those of Barrie have never captured the Germans, among whom Shaw has long been one of the most popular dramatists. But in December, 1927, a German translation of What Every Woman Knows under the title of Maggie was staged at the Vienna Comedy Theatre and met with a very favourable reception, the occasion being an important social event, attended by the Austrian President and the British Minister.

And what shall we say now of those resolutions to make no more public speeches when we come to the year 1928? 'They all went whistling down the wind,' as the resolutionist might have said, and behold him almost the favourite orator of the year! Certainly no man of affairs in 1928 could vie with Barrie in the attention he received from the Press on his various public appearances. In one week alone many hundreds of columns of our daily newspapers were devoted to full length reports of two speeches which he delivered with a night of silence intervening. The laconic Barrie of the 'nineties had become almost garrulous. The hermit of past days, the shy playwright who would never face the footlights in response to the shouts of 'Author!' could now stand before large audiences and microphones without betraying a quiver of nervousness. Of the two quickly following speeches just mentioned there were none who heard them that would not have been glad to listen to the speaker again just as soon as they could get the chance. They were to be his two last public efforts in oratory, although he did not say so in either of them save by implication: his 'Hail and Farewell.' We shall still indulge the hope that he may yet be tempted to regale us further with his fancy and philosophy as a speaker—for in these mellowing years there has been a very perceptible increase of serious intent in his utterances—since he has slowed down as a teller of tales and a writer of plays.

But before we follow our hero in these honorific tasks which shall largely engage him this year there are more losses to be chronicled; the gathering years must also be the losing years. The first was the death of Thomas Hardy, which took place on January 11th, 1928, and meant that the last of the older generation of literary men to whom Barrie was peculiarly attached by bonds of friendship and artistic sympathy had passed away. The interest of Hardy in his younger contemporary was very sincere. Barrie treasured his friendship as one of the most precious things he had been privileged to enjoy. Hardy was the rarest of visitors to London in his later years, and the home and personality of the Scottish son of genius had become its main attractions for him. At Adelphi Terrace he was also revisiting the scenes of his own remote youth, as there in a room at No. 8, which is now the library of the British Drama League, the future author of The Dynasts sat at a window as a young draughtsman in the office of Sir Arthur Blomfield, the famous architect. Barrie was actively solicitous in all the difficult arrangements for the final bestowal of the remains of the great novelist and poet, and none was better fitted than he to bear the little casket of Hardy's ashes from Dorchester to Westminster Abbey.

The next loss occurred in February, when his sister-in-law, Mrs. Alexander Barrie, died suddenly at Strathview, Kirriemuir. The daughter of an Edinburgh jeweller named Cowan, Mrs. Barrie was a woman of strong character and great ability. For some years her brother-in-law had not revisited his native town. It was the sad duty of standing by the grave wherein his brother lay and helping to lower there the mortal remains of her who had been that brother's devoted companion that brought Barrie back to the old places of his heart. After the purpose of his visit had been fulfilled, he remained for a day or two to renew many of his former acquaintances, Kirriemuir being in a state of pardonable

excitement at the return of its famous son after so long an absence.
All his friends of old days were looked up, and to the joy of those
who had known him before his rise to fame and had got but furtive glances of him in the intervening years, when he seemed to
be shy and elusive, he had become the very soul of geniality;
in contact with the younger folk his interest in them was declared
charming to behold.

What a surge of emotion must the author of A Window in Thrums
have battled with as the funeral party left his old home at Strathview, whence he had seen his mother and father, his sisters Jane
Ann and Sara, and his uncle, all taken to their graves on that
hillside across the little valley: past the House on the Brae, and
T'nowhead, through the Square ('in which I seem to see all your
characters revolve,' wrote R.L.S. to him), along Bank Street,
where had stood the Auld Licht Kirk and the Hanky School,
by the Tenements and the old whitewashed Manse to the stiff
little brae that leads to the cemetery gates: what an emotional
journey! Surely they are few who have been privileged in their
younger years to discover their native town a commonplace
cluster of houses and by the exercise of their art to make it glamorous throughout the world and still be permitted by a kindly fate to
walk its streets again conscious of the marvel wrought by the power
of genius. 'God grant you find one face there you knew when
all was young'—Barrie had the felicity to find many, and having
preserved youth in his own heart he was able to find it in others.

These few days spent amid the old scenes and in contact with
old familiar folk, whose very speech was an everlasting bond with
him, must have been among the profoundly moving experiences of
his life. A local journalist describing Barrie's movements about
Kirriemuir—he was pursued by press photographers and reporters,
but had seemingly lost his sensitiveness as he endured the ordeal
smilingly—has an interesting note on his re-visiting the house of
his birth after nearly sixty years, during which he had not again
crossed its threshold:

On leaving the cemetery Sir James took his nephew—who was
returning to England that afternoon—towards the Tenements, and
stopped at the door of the dwelling in which he was born. After
knocking genially he greeted Mrs. David Thomson, who, with her
husband and family, have occupied the house for several years. Mrs.
Thomson was somewhat taken aback when she realized who her visitor
was, but on entering Sir James, by his homely manner, soon put her
at ease.

It was apparent that he wished his nephew to see the interior of the
first home of the Barries. Sir James was quite familiar with the apart-

ments, and quickly noted any changes that had been effected. He led the way to the little room upstairs, which he informed his nephew was where he had been brought into the world. He also entered the room ' ben the hoose,' which seemed to conjure up a wealth of bairnhood memories, which he gleefully imparted to his relative.

' I remember well when that window was put in, and the wonder with which I saw the scaffolding.' ' In this room I used to play underneath a table just like that one over there.' ' There used to be a closed-in bed here.'

And so the details were filled in, much to the evident interest of his nephew—and Mrs. Thomson.

On taking his departure, Sir James remarked he had never been in this house since he left it on the top of a cart when the family flitted to Forfar.

He had returned to his flat in Adelphi Terrace House only a few days when the papers were again lively with columns on Barrie. In these later years a strong friendship had grown up between him and the Rt. Hon. Stanley Baldwin who, as becomes a cousin of Rudyard Kipling, is an ardent lover of books, and perhaps the most widely read of our latter-day statesmen. On various occasions Barrie was among the week-end guests at Chequers, when Mr. Baldwin was Prime Minister. One outcome of this friendship was his appearance as a speaker at the second annual banquet of the Worcester Association, held at the Hotel Victoria on February 29th, when Mr. Baldwin presided and the Prince of Wales was the principal speaker, delivering, by the way, a brilliantly witty and happy speech. In spite of such formidable competition as that offered by the Prince and the Premier, it was Sir James's speech that monopolised the headings in the daily Press next morning; even so, it was not one of his best efforts.

Three or four days after the Worcester banquet it was announced that Barrie had accepted the invitation of the Incorporated Society of Authors to become their president in succession to Thomas Hardy. The invitation was one that involved acceptance, as it was the final hall-mark upon his reputation, not only with the world at large but with his own craft of letters. He had been a member of the Society since 1891 and now became its fourth president since its formation in 1884. The first was Lord Tennyson, the second George Meredith. Especially gratifying it must have been to him to succeed to the seat of honour which had been occupied by the two giants of Victorian literature whom he most admired as artists and valued most as friends: Meredith and Hardy. He had the further distinction later in the year of being the first President of the Society of Authors to be present and deliver an address at its annual dinner.

This took place at Hyde Park Hotel on November 28th, and although there are other matters of note that should appear in our chronicle before we reach that date, the remarks of the President on his friendship with his two predecessors make it desirable to introduce them here. There is also his explanation of the reason for his being elected:

In Scotland (he said) at social functions the great problem of a hostess is which of the clergymen present she should ask to say grace. There must be some apparently good reason or the feelings of the others will be lacerated. I have heard her ask without a quiver, ' Will you say grace, Mr. So-and-So, as you are the nearest the door? ' Ladies and gentlemen, I see now why you elected me your president: it was because I was nearest the door. Quite a nice reason, but nothing grand about it. Is there no inspired playwright present who can give me a better entrance? Yes, there is. Suddenly every one in the room, including myself, realizes that I shall be famous in the hereafter as the last male president of the Society of Authors.

The grim jest about being 'the nearest the door' did not seem to be fully appreciated by the gathering of brainy folk whom the Society of Authors comprises. To those of us who had grown up within hail of Barrie's beginning days it came as a reminder of the flight of time. The President was elected in his sixty-eighth year, yet many of us remember his earliest successes as things of yesterday. He is now the veteran of our eminent men of letters, but coming as he does of a long-lived race we may reasonably hope that he will show no greater hurry in reaching that Door than did Meredith or Hardy: the one was in his eighty-second, the other in his eighty-eighth year when it closed upon him. The presidency of the Authors' Society, like the occupancy of the Papal Chair, seems to be associated with length of years.

Already I have made some reference to the story of Barrie's first sight of George Meredith. He re-told that story to his brethren of the pen in a more condensed form but with several circumstances that give authenticity to the main part of it as I have earlier set it down. Of his long and noble tribute to Hardy, in which humour (Hardy himself would have desired it so) was most perfectly blended with grave and tender admiration, I feel that I must include this fine paragraph:

Hardy could easily be hurt by not ill-intended pens. He had things to do, and without meaning to they got in the way of his doing them, but he never desired his fame. If it could have been separated from

BARRIE REVISITS KIRRIEMUIR, FEBRUARY, 1928
Coming up the Brae with a friend.

Face page 328

BARRIE'S HOUSE IN THE ADELPHI   [*McLeish*

The photograph shows Adelphi Terrace House, at the corner of Robert Street and Adelphi Terrace. The top flat is that occupied by Sir James Barrie.

his poesy he would have given it to any beggar at the door. When he published Tess I warned him that he was heading straight for glory—and he winced. When The Dynasts came out I said, 'Now you've gone and done it,' and I expect he said, 'We won't have that man at Max Gate any more.' Whatever angel guards the portals of Elysium, he must have had to push Thomas Hardy in. Most of them there are too dashing for that quietest figure in literature, with their Olympian revels and their boisterous talk about everything—no, not about everything—not about style. He was not quite as others are. Every one knows that he had an intimacy with trees surpassing even that of Giles Winterbourne; but there was an eerier element in it than that. The trees had a similar knowledge of him, and when he passed through their wood they could tell him from all other men. Perhaps that was the price he paid.

He pictured Hardy in the Elysian Fields eager, first of all, to discover 'which is Shelley'; but the odd thing to be noted of Barrie's literary friendships is that, excepting Robertson Nicoll, his greatest friends have been non-Christian. Frohman, like most Jews who have turned from their ancient faith, had the vaguest sort of belief in an after life; both Meredith and Hardy were splendid Pagans: remote in their habit of thought from the pietistic atmosphere of Barrie's earlier life.

Of the stories which he told in the course of his speech concerning his entry into journalism and the publication of his first book I will say only this, that in both cases I prefer the original versions as they appear in my chapters on The Courting of the Grisette and The Making of a Humorist. He alleged that the old newspapers he pulled down the chimney to begin studying leader-writing were there because it was summer time; but summer does not start in January either in Dumfries or Kirriemuir, and the elaboration of detail about the girl who perused Better Dead in Denny's book box in old Holywell Street tends to throw doubt on what was entirely credible more briefly told in 1896.

At Oxford on June 20th, Barrie was principal speaker at the annual dinner to the Rhodes Trustees, and in proposing the toast of the Rhodes Scholars he addressed himself especially to those who were about to return to their homes in Britain over-seas, making his remarks the more vivid by directing them to one 'William K. Brown' who was supposed to typify them all. He said:

Now that the stage direction is, alas, 'Exit, William K. Brown'—that fascinating fellow, yourself (your interest in whom passes the love of woman)—what is to happen to you next?
'Chapter One—I Depart from Oxford, Determined to Make Public Duty My Highest Aim.' Bravo. But how? 'Chapter the Last—

The Result in My Case.' Namely? Ah, Mr. Brown, how we wish we could guide you through the paper hoop; but we know as little as yourselves what is being spun for you. Yet the beginning of all you are to be already lies inside you—a little speck that is to grow while you sleep, while you are awake, and that in the fullness of time, according to whether you control it or it controls you, is to be the making of you, or to destroy you.

You will know a great deal more about that speck when you come back here, years hence—not perhaps so bright as you are to-day, but, I am sure, all very able.

Education is a noble word in Mr. Rhodes's conception of it, fellowship. I can just remember days in a little Scottish town, the only place I know that beats Oxford—I don't mean in games—where weavers of all ages trudged on their shanks to distant St. Andrews or Aberdeen in quest of college bursaries. If they returned victorious they reappeared by day, but if they failed they hung about the outskirts till nightfall, and then stole to their homes. Early next morning you heard them at their looms again, teeth set, waiting for next year. Dour times—dogged students—no Cecil Rhodes, but that speck under control.

In this strain of gay wisdom, he went on to give most excellent counsel to the young scholars, telling W. K. Brown that it would be wiser, if it did not incommode him too much, to stop short of greatness. ' "Chapter 18—I Reach the Summit," another and they sometimes fall off. To be very able is safer. One place where the immortals are never seen is the top table.' In so short a speech he has seldom excelled this effort at Oxford for witty philosophising on the problems of life. It was reported in full throughout the Press of the Empire, and William K. Brown may be heard of again.

The next public event with which Barrie was identified this year was when Jedburgh followed the lead of Dumfries and presented him with the freedom of that royal borough, 'in recognition of his pre-eminent place as a prose writer and dramatist and of the distinction he has thereby brought to his native land.' This took place on October 15th with due ceremony and the now inevitable speech, 'broadcast' throughout Scotland on this occasion. The conferring of the burgess ticket upon him was presumably a quite serious affair. It was conceived and carried out by the grave and reverend councillors of the town in connexion with his visit to open a bazaar for raising funds to acquire and restore the house of Mary Queen of Scots, one of the historical attractions of the town. A friend of his college days, Mr. Frederick Scott Oliver of Edgerston, near Jedburgh, had been responsible for this scheme, having offered to provide the price of the historic house on condition that the money necessary to put it and the garden in order was raised before the end of the year. Barrie stayed at Edgerston as the guest of the Olivers, and he certainly discharged his undertaking handsomely.

He opened the bazaar on Thursday the 11th with an address on Mary Queen of Scots, which as a masterpiece of whimsy he might with but little extension have turned into a contribution and sold for as much as the bazaar aimed at raising, and handing over the money to Jedburgh he could have achieved the object of the bazaar without more ado. Those who had the privilege of hearing him deliver his charming composition were thankful he had not chosen so practical a short cut to the desired end. Barrie might have favoured it, but doubtless McConnachie was all for going through with the playboy part of it:

Before I begin, may I ask you to make sure that all the doors are locked? We want no Government spies in here.

However innocent our intention, there is no denying that this meeting for the preservation of the house of Mary Queen of Scots has many of the marks of a Stuart rising, positively the last leaf on the tree.

Though great efforts have been made to keep this assemblage secret, we cannot be certain that something has not leaked out. Quite possibly tomorrow's news sheets may bear startling head-lines:

EXTRAORDINARY JACOBITE GATHERING AT JEDBURGH

THE TOWN COUNCIL INVOLVED

J. M. BARRIE ESCAPES TO FRANCE

F. S. OLIVER ARRESTED AT EDGERSTON

How strange if Mr. Oliver, who has done such manful deeds for Queen Mary's house—Ah, don't cheer him, it may be remembered against you at the trials—how strange if, as the result of this meeting, he were to end his days confined in a dungeon in that very house.

That was how he began his speech, which was really no speech at all but an entrancing fantasy presented by the speaker with appropriate gravity and dramatic intensity. He might have been Stroke back again in the Jacobites' lair, and I dare say that when he was delivering this fantastic discourse the years between the Den and Jedburgh were as they had never been. He had been adventuring in the realms of old romance, and among his encounters was one with Queen Mary at Loch Leven. He had gone

331

upon his knee to her and called her 'My Liege.' 'It may mean
caves for me, but it was worth it.' He intrigued her with news
of the bazaar at Jedburgh:

> She said she must see the bazaar—you know how—how hasty she
> was—and putting her hands in mine in that confiding way which is
> either the best or the worst thing in woman—she was dressed in black
> velvet with a white ruff about her neck and a white veil flying—and so
> we came here—by the longest route.
> When she saw the lovely stalls she fingered the display, calling them
> by old lavender names, and some of them she tried on, and she clapped
> her hands and exclaimed, ' Whosoever buys at my bazaar I will always
> have a leaning to him.'
> ' Him ' she said, though I had told her that most of the work was
> done by ladies . . .
> Then I did a foolish thing. I asked her whether she would like to
> buy some little article herself, and at that she began to fade away—
> a sure proof that she was no Frenchwoman but Scotch to the core.

Can one be surprised that the newspapers of the country and
throughout the whole English speaking world 'featured' this
Queen Mary fantasy in their next issues? Seldom do they get
such delicious copy free of cost. The Daily Mail, with characteristic acumen, displayed it splendidly with portraits of Queen
Mary, Queen Elizabeth, Barrie himself and a view of the house
at Jedburgh, using as its headlines the very phrases which, with
his unerring journalistic insight, the author had himself suggested.
On the following Monday came the ceremony of conferring
the freedom, which I have said was no doubt conceived in seriousness though the recipient of the honour, whatever his true feelings
may have been, was still in the mood of the Queen Mary fantasy,
and his reply to the Provost who handed him the pear-wood casket
containing the grant of the freedom was in the main supplementary
to his speech at the bazaar. No doubt Barrie was influenced
to some extent in agreeing to accept the freedom of Jedburgh
because Burns was among its burgesses. In the poet's diary
of his Border tour there is an entry under Jedburgh, 'Was waited
upon by the magistrates and presented with the freedom,' but
unfortunately Burns's name was not inscribed upon the burgess
roll, though the ticket presented to him was traced in after years
to the time when it was inadvertently destroyed with other papers.
Neither Dumfries nor Jedburgh has been lavish in the conferring
of its freedom, and as Burns was a burgess of both towns, it must
have been pleasing to Barrie to be singled out by them for similar
honour.

THE HERMIT WALKS ABROAD

Perhaps it may be well, when I am chronicling this extraordinary year of speechifying, to be done with that side of it before turning to other points that call for note. There were two more, and both of them important orations; but one of them has fortunately been disposed of earlier in this chapter, that given at the annual dinner of the Society of Authors on November 28th. Two nights later he was again facing a very large audience, this time of 'brither Scots,' when he presided over the 264th St. Andrew's day festival of the Royal Scottish Corporation at the Holborn Restaurant. It was a great occasion in the history of that Corporation, and greatly did the president honour it in proposing the toast of 'The Royal Scottish Corporation.' This was one of his happiest addresses, full of new and quaint fancies, and carrying also some salutary criticism of Scottish characteristics framed in amusing phrases.

He spoke of the lean year the Scots were passing through, having only one Scotsman among two Archbishops of England, when they had so long been accustomed to have both. 'Mind you I am not defending Archbishops. We have none in my Church, and that settles the matter. That is one of our faults—arrogance!' He had been to a shop in Geyanqueer Lane (his own countrymen will best relish the allusion) to pick up some bright items for his speech (that about the Archbishops cost him seven and sixpence) but he was disappointed that they could not supply him with stories that put the Scots in a bad light and showed up their faults, as he felt it was about time someone took that course. 'In my native place,' he went on, 'which is superior to your native place—there is another of our faults!' How much of truth is conveyed in these sly asides with which his speech abounded! All his laughter-provoking allusions were steadily leading up to a final and very effective appeal on behalf of the funds of the Corporation as typified by the Scots Box, the ancient receptacle, dating back to 1611, in which Scotsmen who came to London after the accession of James I put their contributions for the relief of their poorer brethren. The identical box that was the humble beginning of this great charity stood on the table in front of the chairman, who never before had made a more gratifying, or a more successful appearance in the presence of so large and distinguished an assembly of his fellow-countrymen. In reply to the toast of his health he said:

Lord Balfour of Burleigh has wondered how some of my Scottish phrases translated in other languages. He mentioned The Little Minister. When this was going to be produced in America I said

333

to the American manager, ' What will the Scotch be like? ' He replied, ' Don't you worry about the Scotch. You would not know it was Scotch, but the American public will know.'

A pleasing fact about this gathering which can have been known to few only of those present, was the presence of Mr. Wellwood Anderson among the guests, that 'Wedd' of Barrie's academical days at Dumfries, who directed the amateur theatricals in which the future author of Peter Pan took part and who was, indeed, Barrie's first stage manager. When the chairman saw the name of his boyhood's friend in the list of those assembled to hear him speak he would be back again ranging the bookshelves of the old shop kept by Mr. Anderson's father where Wellwood's playfellow had the freedom of the shelves; a privilege of which he made such fruitful use.

I am confident that none who heard Barrie delivering any of this series of remarkable addresses in 1928 would have missed a chance to hear him again. At the Authors' Society and again at the Scottish Corporation I had the good luck to hear him give two speeches within three nights, but, as a faithful chronicler, I am glad that his oratory for the year had finished or I know not to what lengths this chapter might have extended. That we have heard the last of him as a public speaker I am unwilling to believe: it would not be fair to his generation to impose a self-denying ordinance upon himself as it was rumoured he had decided to do.*

A writer in The Daily Mail had some interesting information to convey concerning Barrie's methods in preparing for and discharging these 'star turns' at important public functions and as his information confirms and adds to what Robertson Nicoll had written in 1896 I reprint it here:

Sir James Barrie speaks far too seldom in public, but when he does it is only after careful preparation and with the art that conceals art. That he took so much trouble was indeed a very great compliment to his audience. Those who heard him open the bazaar at Jedburgh with that charming and whimsical speech thought he was delivering it *extempore*—evolving the delicate and humorous phrases as he went on. But he was not. It had been written days before, and most of the reporters sat checking his speech with proofs of it in their hands and marvelling at his accuracy. For he used no notes whatever.

* First at the Annual Dinner of the Newspaper Press Fund, April 23rd, when the manuscript of The Twelve Pound Look fetched 2,300 guineas at auction for the benefit of the Fund, and again on July 29th, when Edinburgh presented him with her burgess ticket, he added to his list of public speeches in 1929. At Edinburgh he told his audience that one of the landladies of his university days, a Mrs. Edwards, had been the original of his Mrs. Dowey in The Old Lady Shows her Medals.

He rose and went behind his chair and stood there looking mostly into space or up towards the ceiling. His face was grave, his air that of a man rather ill at ease, while he spoke for nearly half-an-hour in his strong, low, and slightly hoarse voice. And he was almost word perfect; he knows how important that is.

That speech was written as his plays are written; there was laughter in it, there was sentiment, there was even ' business,' calculated and deeply thought out, as when he took out of his buttonhole the sprig of white heather he said that Mary Queen of Scots had given him.

Whether he enjoyed delivering the speech it is impossible to say. He bore all the signs before it began of being extraordinarily nervous, and during it he betrayed no evidence of satisfaction at the laughter and applause it occasioned.

'Sir James speaks far too seldom!' If in his earlier years he had spoken as often as he did in 1928 he would have outshone Mark Twain as a humorous orator and collections of his speeches would have been selling in the bookshops as freely as his stories or the uniform edition of his plays.

The autumn season was noteworthy for the publication of the final text of Peter Pan in that edition, and also for the production of The Plays of J. M. Barrie in one comprehensive volume at the price of a guinea. There is an air of finality about this volume, which suggests that we have heard the last of Barrie the dramatist: a suggestion that few will be ready unreservedly to accept. The exclusions from the volume in question are significant: Walker, London, The Professor's Love Story, The Wedding Guest, Little Mary, none of these finds a place, and several of the one-act plays are also absent. This fine volume is adorned with one of the most pleasing portraits of the dramatist ever published—one of those amateur snapshots which R. L. S. was right in thinking so often excel the efforts of professional photographers—and under this new portrait are printed some lines by Thomas Hardy written at a rehearsal of Mary Rose to which the dramatist took him on one of his rare visits to London.

In the summer of the year Barrie had been staying at Stanway Hall, near Moreton-in-the-Marsh, the Earl of Wemyss's fine old mansion in the Cotswolds, within easy reach of Stratford-on-Avon and Broadway, the scene of the Allahakbarries' encounters with the Artists in the years that have gone. This he had rented as a summer place where he could pass a month or two as a change from the top floor of Adelphi Terrace House, and where he could entertain his friends in a lovely countryside. Augustine Birrell and other celebrities of the world of letters and affairs were to be met there; but all signs of the prosperity which the vulgar mind associates with the wealthiest of British authors and dramatists were noticeable by their absence. No Rolls to meet you, nor for your host to run you about among the historic villages which abound in the district: an old car hired from a local contractor sufficed for the simple wants of the celebrated tenant of Stanway Hall and served his guests not too badly.

Some years earlier he had rented for the shooting season Killiecrankie Cottage, in the neighbourhood of Pitlochry, and there had acted host to a few and carefully chosen friends whose company he valued. At both places, by the way, he was coming into contact with a vanished celebrity of quasi-literary fame: Miss Marie Corelli, who also used to rent Killiecrankie Cottage, and who, as we all know, went down in her later years and took possession of the territory of Shakespeare which borders upon the corner of Gloucestershire that contains Stanway Hall. In the autumn Barrie was 'half-expected' to re-visit Kirriemuir. He is one of the godfathers to the Earl of Airlie's second son, whose christening took place then at Cortachy Castle, but he was unable to be present. Margaret Ogilvy would have 'liked fine' to have seen her son acting as godfather to the child of the nobleman who is overlord of immense domains in the neighbourhood of Kirriemuir.

Barrie's old friend Mr. James Robb had visited him in June and stayed at Adelphi Terrace House. There is some evidence of this recent contact with him in the newly-written dedication to Peter Pan, which appeared in October. On Mr. Robb's return to Kirriemuir he carried with him from his life-long friend a letter whose contents were to be communicated to the council of his native town. This brief epistle is of considerable interest from several points of view. It is as follows:

Dear Mr. Robb,—When you get back to Kirrie I should be beholden to you if you would place before the Town Council a wish on my part, if they approve, to present the town with a cricket and football pavilion on the Hill in Kirriemuir in memory of happy days and of friendships formed there, the chief of which was with yourself. I need not go into details here, as our talks on the subject, both in Kirrie and London (you see which one I place first), will enable you to explain my views to the Town Council and the matter can be more formally arranged later. Your old friend,   J. M. BARRIE.

The announcement of the gift to Kirriemuir gave the utmost satisfaction there, and it was generally regarded as an ideal offering to his native place on the part of its most famous son. But it was not the first pavilion presented by the same donor for the enjoyment of cricketers and the devotees of other sports, as some

time before this his interest in the villagers of Stanway had led
him to provide them with a shelter which was designed after
the style of Wendy's hut, having a real thatched roof, and on the
grass in front of it mammoth mushroom stools carved in stone.

It was soon after the announcement of this gift to his native town
that the fact of his birthplace having been purchased by Major R. D.
Lauder so that it should be preserved for the nation was made
public. General satisfaction was expressed at this public-spirited
action of Barrie's fellow countrymen.

The hero of all this and of all these wonderful years is in person the most unassuming little man you would meet in a day's
walk. Many years ago he was described as 'a little man who
walks about London looking as though he hadn't a friend in
the world,' and save that this might be said of many a thousand
others it is quite a true description. Often have I seen him strolling along the Strand, his head a little bent, his hands loosely
clasped behind him, and holding a rough walking stick, his clothes,
hat, and general appearance so ordinary that no passers-by gave
him a second look. On one occasion in particular, he was at the
corner of Arundel Street when a wagon-load of Americans were
having Australia House or St. Clement Danes pointed out to them
by a guide who, had he but known, might have shown them in
this little man, whose hat no more than cleared the pillar box,
something they would all have turned from half-a-dozen Australia
Houses to have seen. Again, in walking westward to the Savage
Club with a fellow member we noticed ahead of us the figure
of Barrie, and from Chancery Lane to the Adelphi he kept steadily
on his way, looking neither to right nor left, save once when for
a moment he paused to read the contents bill of an evening paper.
Not once in the journey did one of the many hundreds who
passed show any recognition of him. A writer in The Daily
Mail, of October 29th, 1928, had some reflections on Barrie in
his walks about town, and as these confirm my own observations
I reprint them here:

Sir James Barrie is probably the most contemplative pedestrian in
London; whenever one sees him out walking he always appears to be
so deep in thought that one positively fears for his safety. Yesterday
when I saw him strolling in the Strand, puffing at a big pipe and swinging
a walking-stick with both hands behind his back, he seemed to be looking
at a vision instead of where he was going. I fully believe he was unaware
that half a dozen persons stepped aside just in time to avoid colliding
with him, and that a taxicab providentially pulled up within an inch
or two of him when he stepped off the kerb!

BARRIE: THE STORY OF A GENIUS

But it would be wrong and misleading to leave the impression that, however ordinary in height and mien our genius may appear to a casual observer, he is so when one has the opportunity to see him at leisure. The face is one of real and rare distinction; the eyes especially reveal an intensity of feeling, alive with intelligence and comprehension. The brow is high and pale, the still abundant hair shows little sign of silvering and remains almost as black as in his early manhood; only the greying of the moustache and the inevitable lines which time must write upon the face remind us that 'youth's a stuff will not endure.' Sir George Douglas, in a little thumbnail sketch of Barrie written more than thirty years ago, remarked 'to me the face bears a certain resemblance to portraits of Edgar Allan Poe,' which is a very just comparison. Above all, the one thing that even a leisured look at Barrie does not suggest is any affinity with the typical Scot. With his finely modelled features and sensitive nose, he has always seemed to suggest a southern type, more akin to the swarthy French Celt than to the homelier lowland folk of Scotland. But we have his own assurance that he is 'as Scotch as peat' (one might also be as Irish as peat), and assuredly in most things of the mind and the heart he is the essential Scot, and in our time the finest embodiment of Scotland's national genius. That, and something even rarer, for the fantastic element in Barrie is neither Scottish nor English; if it belongs anywhere it is to the Celtic twilight.

INDEX

Adams, the Misses, of the Hanky school, 16

Adams, Maude, friendship with Barrie, 215, 223; as Babbie, in The Little Minister, 191; as Phœbe Throssel, in Quality Street, 229; as Peter Pan, 249; as Maggie, in What Every Woman Knows, 272; in The Legend of Leonora, 281; Barrie first sees her act, 282

Adelphi Terrace House, Barrie at, 292.

Admirable Crichton, The, produced, 230; in New York, 238; in Paris, 238; French translation, 324

Adored One, The, produced, 280; as The Legend of Leonora in America, 281

Alice Sit-by-the-Fire, 247; produced, 269

Allahakbarries Cricket Club, pamphlets by Barrie, 220

America, Barrie's visit with W. Robertson Nicoll, 188; success of The Little Minister, 215; Peter Pan produced in, 249; Barrie's second visit, 282

Anderson, David Elder, companion of Barrie at Forfar Academy, 34

Anderson, Wellwood, with Barrie at Dumfries Academy, 49; editor of The Clown, 42; Dumfries theatricals, 47, 334

Ansell, Mary, marriage, 181; Dogs and Men, by, 226; divorce, 296

'Arcadia' mixture, in My Lady Nicotine, 157

Archer, William, criticism of Quality Street, 229

Ashford, Daisy, Barrie and The Young Visiters, 308

Auld Licht Idylls, publication and appreciation of, 25, 132

Auld Licht Kirk, 12

Authors' Society, Barrie elected president, 327

Baldwin, Stanley, friendship with, 327

Ballantyne, R. M., 45

Bandelero the Bandit, 47

Barbara's Wedding, 290, 322

Baring Gould, S., Barrie's criticism of, 152

Baron, Bernhard, 158

Baronetcy, and coat of arms, 299, 300

Barrie, Alexander Ogilvy (eldest brother) 10, 11; friendship with Alexander Whyte, 18; master at Glasgow Academy, 28; Inspector of Schools at Dumfries, 32, 38; at Aberdeen University, 72; death, 301

Barrie, Charles David Ogilvy (nephew), death at the Somme, 303

Barrie, David (father), at Kirriemuir, 9; his character and personal appearance, 11 sq.; influence on Barrie's career, 23; at Forfar, 30; return to Kirriemuir, 37; in Edinburgh with David Ogilvy, 188; death, 236

Barrie, David Ogilvy (brother), 10; tragic death, 22

Barrie, Isabella Ogilvy (sister). See Murray

Barrie, J. M., boyhood, 14 sq.; 24, 35; boyhood's books, 44-45; eternal boyishness, 25; his brothers and sisters, 10, 206; visits to America, 188, 282; Dumfries, 38 sq., 47 sq.; Edinburgh University, 54, 61; at Forfar, 32 sq.; at Glasgow, 27 sq.; various legends concerning, 94, 113, 182; and the Kailyard School, 179 sq.; in London press 104; marriage, 181; and Sir W. Robertson Nicoll, 122 sq.; at Nottingham, 97; his shyness, 11; 78; see also Speeches and Addresses

Barrie, Jane Ann (sister), 'Leeby,' 10; death, 188

Barrie, Lilian (niece), 302; Wallasey High School, 315

Barrie, Margaret (sister), at Miss Oliver's school, Edinburgh, 77; death of fiancé, 172; see also Winter

Barrie, Margaret (mother). See Ogilvy, Margaret.

Barrie, Mary Edward (sister). See Galloway, M. E.

INDEX

INDEX

Fatal Typist, The, produced, 286
Fishing, early interest in, 13, 16
Forbes-Robertson, Jean, as Peter Pan, 249
Ford, Ernest, composer of Jane Annie, 175
Forfar, Barrie family at, 30-32
Forfar Academy, Barrie entered, 32; his time at, 34
Fortnightly Review, The, humorous article Pro Bono Publico, 129; The Wedding Guest appears in, 224
Frampton, Sir George, 251
Fraser, Campbell, Professor, 66
Frohman, Charles, friendship with Barrie, 190, 215, 223, 306; and Pauline Chase, 262; comparison of Pinero and Barrie, 275; produces Peter Pan, 248; reasons for success of Peter Pan, 253; produces Alice Sit-by-the-Fire in New York, 270; on A Slice of Life, 279; death, 305
Fyfe, James Hamilton, joint founder of Pall Mall Gazette, 57
Fyfe, John R., first of Kirriemuir journalists, 57

Galloway, Mary Edward, 10, 84
Galloway, Robert, on Barrie at Edinburgh University, 74
Galt, John, Annals of the Parish, etc., 135, 147
Garland, Herbert, Bibliography of Barrie, 121 sq., 148
Gillette, William, in The Admirable Crichton, New York, 238
Gilmour, T. Lennox, on Nottingham Journal with Barrie, 86
Glasgow Academy, Barrie at, 27 sq.
Gloucester Road, 133, Barrie's house, 226, 246
Good Words, contributions to, 160; A Tillyloss Scandal, 152; The Little Minister, published in, 159
Gordon, Harold and Stuart, boyhood friends at Dumfries, 46
Great Ormond Street Hospital, Peter Pan copyright given to, 267
Great Windmill Street, Bloomsbury, Barrie's lodgings, 113
Greenwood, Frederick, 107

Half-an-Hour, produced, 282
Half-Hours, first collection of Barrie's shorter plays, 284
Hanky School, Kirriemuir, 16
Hardy, Thomas, Barrie's study in Contemporary Review, 152; friendship, 325; tribute to, 328

Hare, John, in Little Mary, 239
Henley, W. E., 139, 163
Heraldic arms, of Sir James Barrie, 300
Hibbert, H. J., 86, 96
Hicks, Seymour, in Quality Street, 229
Hilton-Young, Lady, at Leinster Corner house, 299
'Hippomenes,' pen-name of Barrie, 89
Hole, William, illustrator, 66
Home Chimes, edited by F. W. Robinson, 108; Barrie's contributions to, 104, 109; early Auld Licht articles in, 117; ceases publication, 184
'Hook, Captain James,' his career at Eton, 322
House with the Green Shutters, The, 227

Ibsen's Ghost, 169
Illustrated London News, Contributions to, 162
Irving, H. B., in The Admirable Crichton, 230

Jane Annie, words by Barrie and Conan Doyle, 174
Jedburgh, freedom of, 330
Jerome, Jerome K., reminiscences of Barrie, 113
Jerrold, Mary, in revival of Quality Street, 230
Josephine, produced, 271

Kailyard School, The, 143, 177 sq.; decline of, 227
Kensington Gardens, Barrie and his dog in, 226; key to, 235; in Peter Pan, 245 sq.; Peter Pan's statue, 252
Kipling, Rudyard, and Barrie in 1889, 140; Barrie on, 154
Kirriemuir, Barrie's birthplace, 8; his boyhood here, 12-27; change to Forfar, 30; its schools, 18; return from Forfar, 37 sq; Auld Licht articles, 117, 134, 142; Auld Licht Kirk rebuilt, 185; Thrums sketches in The Speaker, 155; in The Little Minister 166; The Little Minister performed at, 219; in Tommy and Grizel, 223; later chronicles of Thrums, 197; return of the Barries to, 236; the Ogilvy family and Thrums, 202; funeral of Mrs. Alexander Barrie, 1928, 326; presentation of Cricket Pavilion, 336; later days, 301
Kirriemuir Edition (1913), of Barrie's works, 301

341

INDEX

Kirriemuir Observer, 20
Kiss for Cinderella, A, produced, 286

Laing, Charles, and Barrie at Forfar, 35; at Edinburgh University, 73
Lauder, R. D., purchase of Barrie's birthplace, 21, 336
Legend of Leonora, The, American version of The Adored One, 281
Leinster Corner, Barrie's house, 226; Lady Hilton-Young (Scott) at, 299
Literary Calling, The, 125 sq.
Little Mary, 239
Little Minister, The, publication in Good Words, 160 sq.; reviewed by Henley, 163; dramatisation of, 191 sq; produced in New York, 215
Little White Bird, The, 232
Loftus, Cecilia, in Peter Pan, 262; in A Slice of Life, 278
Loraine, Robert, in Barbara's Wedding, 323
Lunan, Bell, 13

'McConnachie,' 115, 198, 247, 310
Mackenzie, Sir Alexander, music for The Little Minister, 217
McKinnel, Norman, in Der Tag, 284
Maclaren, Ian, 164, 177, 189
MacMillan, James, at Dumfries Academy with Barrie, 40
'Maggie,' German version of What Every Woman Knows, 324
Marbury, Elisabeth, and The Little Minister, 192
Margaret Ogilvy, publication (1896), 200
Mary Rose, 214, 234, 288
Masson, Professor David, 58
Maude, Cyril, story of The Little Minister, 193; as Gavin Dishart, 215
Maurier, George du, and the Llewellyn Davies boys, 245
Maurier, Gerald du, in Little Mary, 239; in A Kiss for Cinderella, 286; in Dear Brutus, 288; in A Slice of Life, 278
Meredith, George, Barrie's study of, 152; tribute to, 295
Merit, Order of, see Order of Merit
Merrick, Leonard, 307
Millar, J. H., the Kailyard School, 143, 178, on Margaret Ogilvy, 201
Moult, Thomas, his Barrie: A Critical Estimate, 117; on use of Scots vernacular, 143 sq.
Murray, Isabella Ogilvy, 10, 78

My Lady Nicotine, in St. James's Gazette, 113; publication of, 155

'Nana,' in Peter Pan, 260
National Observer, Barrie's contributions to, 160, 183; see also Scots Observer.
Neilson, John, Barrie's master at Dumfries, 50
New Amphion, The, contribution to, 65
New Word, The, produced, 286
Nicol, John, sonnet on, 161
Nicoll, Sir William Robertson, The British Weekly and Barrie, 122; on Barrie's genius, 148, 159; visit with Barrie to America, 188 sq; on The Little Minister, 193; death, 312
Nottingham Journal, The, Barrie on staff (1883), 85 sq.; in When A Man's Single, 101

Ogilvy, Alexander (maternal grandfather) 202
Ogilvy, D.D., Rev, David, at Strathview, 37; death, 238
Ogilvy, Gavin, pen-name, 116, 123 sq.
Ogilvy, Margaret (mother), her children, 10; death of her son David, 22; her memories of Kirriemuir, 25; her idealised biography, 200 sq.; death, 188
Old Friends, short play, 276
Old Lady Shows Her Medals, The, produced, 287; MS. auctioned, 319; in French, 323; original of, 334
Oliphant, Mrs., 220, 294
Oliver, Miss, school at Edinburgh, 77
Order of Merit, conferred on Barrie, 309

Pall Mall Gazette, The, Barrie's contributions to, 108
Pantaloon, produced, 268
Paris, visit with Frohman, 306
Parliament, suggested candidature for, 292
'Penny,' foreman compositor, 102 sq.
Peter and Wendy, published, 257
Peter Pan, the play, original of Wendy's house, 21; origins of, 234, 244 sq; London production, 248; New York production, 249; success of, 253 sq.; variations and changes in, 256 sq.
Peter Pan Statue, 251; malicious damage to, 265; replica in Liverpool, 263-4

INDEX

Pinero, Sir Arthur, 275
Platonic Friendship, duologue, 220
'Porthos,' favourite dog, 226; in The Little White Bird, 234; original of 'Nana,' 260
Preston, Harry, memories of Barrie, 313
Printers' Pension Dinner, speech at, 319
Prior, James, a forgotten novelist, 100
Professor's Love Story, The, production, 186; in America, 190
Punch (playlet), produced, 271

Quality Street, produced, 229; revival, 230; as musical comedy, 289
Quartermaine, Leon, in Quality Street, 230
Quiller-Couch, Sir A. T., 150, 155, 167

Raleigh, Sir Walter, on the Kailyard School, 228
Real Thing at Last, The, 286
Reveille, contributions to, 307
Rhodes Trustees, speech at Oxford, 329 sq.
Riach, Alexander, editor, Edinburgh Evening Dispatch, 115
Richard Savage, play by Barrie and Marriott Watson, 168
Robb, James, early friendship, 13; visit at Adelphi Terrace, 336
Robinson, F. W. 108, 184
Rosalind, 279
Rosy Rapture, 285
Royal Literary Fund Dinner, Barrie in chair, 241
Royal Scottish Corporation, St. Andrew's Day Speech, 333

St. Andrews University Rectorial Address, 115, 298, 309
St. James's Gazette, contributions to, 106, 110, 120, 127, 131, 156; My Lady Nicotine series, 113
Savage Club, The, Barrie joins, 126; as 'The Wigwam,' 137
Scots Observer, The, Henley's 'Young Men,' 139; contributions to, 151; See also National Observer
Scots Vernacular, in Auld Licht Idylls, 133; in A Window in Thrums, 143 sq.
Scott, Lady. See Hilton-Young, Lady
Scott, Robert Falcon, friendship with, 298
Scribner's Magazine, 197, 223
Sefton Park, Liverpool, replica of Peter Pan statue, 263-4

Sentimental Tommy, in Scribner's Magazine, 197 sq; autobiographical, 16, 25
Seven Women, short play, 287
Shakespeare's Legacy, 287
'Shakespeare' MS., a Barrie jest, 304
Shall We Join The Ladies? 290
Shelton, George, in Walker, London, 171; in Peter Pan, 258 sq.
Shorter, Clement, and Illustrated London News, 162
Slice of Life, A, produced, 278; speech to Playgoers' Club, 241
Smith, Rev. Walter C., Edinburgh, 67
'Smuggle the Geeg' (Smuggleerie), a childhood game, 14
Speaker, The, Barrie's contributions to, 155
Speeches and Addresses, at Dumfries Academy, 46, 48; Stevenson Memorial, 55; Printers' Pension Dinner, 69, 319; St. Andrews Rectorial Address, 115, 298, 309; Aldine Club Dinner, New York, 196; on Cricket, 221; Playgoers' Club, 240; Royal Literary Fund dinner, 241; Mrs. Oliphant memorial, 294; on Education, Wallasey High School, 315; at Dumfries, 316 sq; at Eton College, 321; Worcester Association, 327; Society of Authors, 327; Rhodes Trustees dinner, 329; freedom of Jedburgh, 330; Royal Scottish Corporation, 333; Barrie's method of preparation, 334
Stationers' Company, Freeman of, 318
Stevenson, R. L., friendship with, 187; memorial speech, 55; imaginary meeting, 69; on A Window in Thrums, 149; Barrie's mother, 210
Stickit Minister, The, by S. R. Crockett, 177
Strange Case of Sir G. Trevelyan and Mr. Otto, The, 127
Superfluous Man, A, serial story, 142

Terriss, Ellaline, in Quality Street, 229
Terry, Ellen, in Alice Sit-by-the-Fire, 269; godmother of Pauline Chase, 262
Terry, Marion, in Quality Street, 229
Theatre, Barrie's toy theatre, 20; the Dumfries Amateur Dramatic Society, 47 sq; early days as dramatic critic, 80 sq., 121; The Complete Playgoer, 89; success in America, 215; speech, (1904), 240; last phase, 268 sq.

INDEX

DATE DUE
REMINDER

OCT 1 3 2002

Please do not remove
this date due slip.